The
TREASURY *of*
ENGLISH
POETRY

The
TREASURY *of*
ENGLISH
POETRY

Edited and with an Introduction by

Mark Caldwell and
Walter Kendrick

Doubleday & Company, Inc.
Garden City, New York

Library of Congress Cataloging in Publication Data

Main entry under title:

The Treasury of English poetry.

Includes index.

1. English poetry.   I. Caldwell, Mark.   II. Kendrick, Walter M.

PR1174.T73   1984   821'.008

Library of Congress Catalog Card Number 82–46028

ISBN: 0-385-18533-2

COPYRIGHT ACKNOWLEDGMENTS

Grateful acknowledgment is made to the following for permission to reprint their copyrighted material.

Every reasonable effort has been made to trace the ownership of all copyrighted poems included in this volume. Any errors which may have occurred are inadvertent and will be corrected in subsequent editions, provided notification is sent to the publisher.

"Poem and Message" and "Watching a Cloud" from *Collected Poems* by Dannie Abse. Copyright © 1977 by Dannie Abse. Reprinted by permission of the University of Pittsburgh Press and Anthony Sheil Associates Ltd.

"The Soldier Loves His Rifle," "Lay Your Sleeping Head, My Love," and "Musée des Beaux Arts" from *The English Auden: Poems, Essays and Dramatic Writing* by W. H. Auden, edited by Edward Mendelson. Copyright 1936, 1940, renewed © 1968 by W. H. Auden. Reprinted by permission of Random House, Inc., and Faber and Faber, Ltd.

For Gary W. Delius
and
Robert J. McCandless, Jr.

ACKNOWLEDGMENTS

For their helpful suggestions and comments, we would like to thank Daniel Applebaum, Louise Bishop, Anna dalPino, James Earl, Constance Hassett, Gerard Reedy, S.J., and James Richardson.

For their invaluable help in preparing the manuscript and seeing it through the press, we would like to thank Florence Eichin, Nell Hanson, and Mary Sherwin.

CONTENTS

BEN JONSON, 1572–1637

ROBERT HERRICK, 1591–1674

xxvi

INTRODUCTION

English possesses the richest poetic tradition of any Western language. For more than a dozen centuries, an unbroken succession of poets both great and minor has steadily contributed to what Algernon Charles Swinburne called "the best creative literature, the rarest intellectual inheritance, of the world." This very richness, splendid though it is, presents a special problem: there is simply too much good English poetry to fit between the covers of any reasonably sized anthology. Rigorous selection is necessary, yet rigor must always be guided by concern for both the vast historical range of the tradition and its amazing, inexhaustible variety. In the *Treasury*, we have tried to strike a rewarding compromise between virtually unlimited possibilities and limited space. Our selections, we believe, are ample enough to portray the unique qualities of the more than a hundred English, Irish, Scottish, and Welsh poets we include, and also representative enough to offer a concise overview of the continuous tradition to which all these poets belong.

Though it is continuous, the tradition can be conveniently divided into eight periods or phases, each of which has its own distinctive character. The first of these, commonly called the Old English period (ca. 500–1100), contains the first known poetry written in anything resembling English. The language is Anglo-Saxon, and to a modern reader it looks utterly foreign. Here, for example, is the first line of our first selection, "Caedmon's Hymn," in its original Northumbrian form:

Nu scylun hergan   hefaenricaes uard

We have translated "Caedmon's Hymn" and our other Old English selections into idiomatic modern English, rendering them intelligible to the modern reader without losing, we hope, the strange, stark beauty that belongs to them in the original.

The Anglo-Saxon world portrayed in these poems is simple to the point of deprivation, full of violence, mystery, and terror. Even poets are warriors, living among a small group of soldiers, all of whom owe fealty to a lord. In return for their loyalty, the lord gives them food, shelter, and such treasure as he is able to win in the wars they fight for him. The community we glimpse through these great Anglo-Saxon poems is small, close, fierce and fiercely proud, hemmed in all around by a dark universe whose mystery and ultimate hostility are not dispelled by the poets' sincere and deeply held Christianity. At times this world seems utterly remote from our own, and yet certain primal passions—pride, envy, loneliness—ring as true to us today as they can have done when these poems were first written, more than a thousand years ago.

The second great phase of English poetry, the Middle English period (1100–1500), can be seen as a direct result of the Norman invasion of England under William the Conqueror in 1066. The Conquest produced, over the years, a fundamental transformation of the language, the culture, and the daily life of Britain. The island was now in easy touch with the vibrant intellectual life of continental Europe; towns and cities grew, with their intricate social and commercial networks. Middle English literature, culminating with Chaucer in the late fourteenth century, is more richly decorated, more copious, and more consciously worked than Anglo-Saxon poetry. The world of this new poetry is sunnier, as if the darkness had been pushed back; new emotions appear, like love, joy, and most of all, humor. Through the influence of French, English acquired a new richness of vocabulary and range of expression, moving a step closer to the language we speak today. Here is the first line of the Prologue to Chaucer's *Canterbury Tales*, in its original Middle English:

Whan that Aprill with his shoures soote

A modern reader can decipher Chaucer without great trouble, but for the sake of accessibility we have chosen a fine modern verse translation of our selections, which captures both the elegance and the bawdy humor of the original.

Middle English poetry is in every way more elaborately structured, more lavish in specific observation, and more philosophically sophisticated than anything that went before it. These developments continued and accelerated in the next phase of English poetry, the Renaissance (1500–1660). Now the language is recognizably our own, and we have been able to stick very close to the original versions of our selections, in most cases modernizing only the spelling and punctuation. A new spirit of critical inquiry is visible everywhere in Renaissance poetry: the relative unanimity of opinion that characterized the medieval world has begun to disintegrate in a crossfire of conflicting theories and competing creeds. Early in the sixteenth century, the Church was split asunder by the Reformation; the ancient belief that the earth was the center of the universe began to give way to the disturbing theories of Galileo and Copernicus. The New World opened up fresh opportunities for wealth and discovery, but also for piracy and war. Renaissance poetry reflects the cultural ferment of its time: it is by turns rich and spare, complicated and simple, detached and deeply emotional, sophisticated and crude, skeptical and naïvely credulous. It ranges brilliantly from the tantalizing ambiguities and sensuous textures of Spenser and Shakespeare to the hirsute intellectuality of Donne and the cultivated simplicity of Herrick. It cannot be categorized, but in all its forms it is dazzling.

The most decisive event in seventeenth-century England was the deposition and execution of the king, Charles I, in 1649. From then until 1660, England was a so-called Commonwealth, ruled for most of that time by Oliver Cromwell—the first break in the continuity of the English monarchy since 1066, and the only one it has ever known. English literature also pauses during these years: Charles II took the remnants of the court and many of the literati with him into exile in France, where they absorbed the epicurean delights of French neoclassical culture. When, in 1660, Charles returned in triumph to England, he brought with him a retinue imbued with a taste for the refined, the elegant, and the urbane. This transformation ushered in the fourth major phase of English poetry, commonly referred to as the Restoration and Eighteenth Century (1660–1800).

The sometimes crude vigor of the Renaissance now gives way to the finely tuned ironies and the polish of Dryden, Pope, and Prior. The city becomes the central focus of the literary imagination, and satire is the genre that best reflects society's preoccupation with its own cultivation and good sense. Refinement and finish become the sought-after values in all forms of literature; the expression of emotion takes second place to smoothness of technique and delicacy of style. The epitome of the era is found in Pope's matchlessly turned heroic couplets, which, in their author's words, seek praise not for novelty or passion but for conveying "what oft was thought, but ne'er so well expressed."

Underneath the orderly surface of the eighteenth century, however, unruly forces were at work, preparing the way for the shortest and most tumultuous phase of English poetry, the Romantic period (1800–30). All during the century, life was becoming steadily more complex and compartmentalized, as England's ancient agricultural economy succumbed to the onslaught of the Industrial Revolution. As the forces of economic specialization worked to make life urban, uniform, and organized, strong resistance grew in favor of individual freedom and emotional expression, its imaginative center in the country instead of the city. Such feelings remained more or less latent, however, until the publication of Wordsworth and Coleridge's *Lyrical Ballads* in 1798. The newly proclaimed Romantic commitment to freedom, the dignity of the individual, and the quest for personal knowledge led to the most extraordinary efflorescence of poetic genius that English literature had ever known. In the space of a single generation more great poetry was written than any whole century had seen before: Blake, Wordsworth, Coleridge, Byron, Keats, Shelley, Hunt, Southey, Landor—the names speak for themselves.

But the Romantics, self-doomed, died young; or else, like Wordsworth, they burned themselves out early. The sixth great phase of English poetry, the Victorian-Edwardian period (1830–1914), took as its emblem the rigid domestic pieties embodied in Queen Victoria and her beloved consort Albert, the furthest possible remove from the flamboyant excesses of Byron or Shelley. This rigidity, though obviously sincere, was in part a reaction to increasing doubt. England had amassed the vastest empire in human history, but it was beset from within by forces of social unrest. Old beliefs were under attack from new scientific theories like Darwin's; faith and security seemed everywhere under assault. Victorian-Edwardian poetry reflects this restlessness and uncertainty. Without renouncing the values of their Romantic predecessors, the major poets of the time like Browning, Tennyson, Taylor, and Dobson, show an uneasiness and skepticism which would have been unimaginable for Shelley or Blake. These poets turn from sweeping philosophical issues to minute investigations of human psychology, from bold forays into the unknown to disconsolate musings on the vagaries of fate and character.

With the outbreak of World War I, English poetry entered on its seventh and penultimate phase, the Modern period (1914–50). The last vestiges of traditional thought were blasted away in a carnage that destroyed not only human lives by the millions, but also the very terrain on which, for centuries, human lives had been led. Modern poetry is haunted by the vast destruction of the Great War, by visions of endless trenches, dug for no clear purpose, leading nowhere. Exhaustion and despair haunt many of the poems written in the wake of the first war and amid the currents that drew England inexorably toward the second. Increasingly, poets give vent to a conviction of present or impending doom, or turn away altogether from such speculations to the comforts of close, value-free observation of nature or the textures of daily life.

World War II produced another decisive break with the past. The even more cataclysmic devastation of this war had the effect, by justifying despair and toppling the few remaining pillars of certitude, of purging the possibly fruitless agonies characteristic of much Modern verse. The fact that the present phase of English poetry has no more distinctive title than the Post-Modern period is suggestive of the relative aimlessness, sometimes even the willful triviality, that marks much contemporary poetry. Post-Modern poetry is characterized by a wide variety of themes and techniques, but there is a certain listlessness about much of it; it is rich in talent and promise, but it seems to be seeking a new direction, new sources of strength and vigor.

The distinctive flavor of each of these periods should be plain enough in the poems themselves; we have organized our poets chronologically, but we have not grouped them according to period, since such tidy labels can often be misleading. Literary periods are not airtight compartments: the careers of many great poets, like Hardy and Yeats, have spanned more than one period, and some—Blake and Hopkins, for example—have hardly anything in common with their historical contemporaries. We have presented English poetry as a single unbroken development, emphasizing thereby both the continuity of the tradition and the special genius of each individual poet.

We have also refrained from the elaborate apparatus of explanatory footnotes that clutters the pages of many modern anthologies. Not only do such editorial indulgences look ugly—giving such books the dreary appearance of technical manuals—but they also interfere with what is, after all, the primary aim of any poetry collection, to put the reader in contact with poems. In most cases, the reader will find that obscurities of vocabulary and reference are minor and superficial. The Oxford English Dictionary is an especially useful aid for archaic words and phrases, but any good-sized dictionary will solve the vast majority of problems. Minute topical allusions are rare, and when they do occur they are generally of such slight importance that their elucidation would hardly enhance the reader's enjoyment of the poem. The best poetry is concerned with the ebb and flow of fundamental human emotions, which have not changed over the centuries. We have only gone so far as to bring spelling, punctuation, and capitalization into accordance with contemporary British usage.

All the most famous and best-loved English poems are here, in their entirety when space has permitted. In the case of very long poems like Chaucer's *Canterbury Tales* and Milton's *Paradise Lost,* we have chosen extensive excerpts which will give the reader a good sense of the quality and scope of the full poems. Not all our selections, however, are well-known. The greatest English poets are often remembered for a mere handful of poems, though their output was large and its overall quality very high. We have included the most familiar of the great poets' works, but we have also added a few that are every bit as moving as the famous ones but that have been unjustifiably neglected and seldom anthologized. Among these are Lord Byron's splendid satire "The Vision of Judgment," Robert Browning's wryly humorous "Sibrandus Schafnaburgensis," and Matthew Arnold's tender tribute "Geist's Grave."

Great poems, too, are not always written by great poets. There are some poets who, in a lifetime of mostly forgettable work, produce one or two poems which deserve to be ranked with the very best. We have included a large selection of these, such as Thomas Hood's rousing "Song of the Shirt," Leigh Hunt's touching "Rondeau," and Ernest Dowson's hauntingly melancholy "Non Sum Qualis Eram." These poets were second-rate, perhaps, but only by comparison with the greatest poets of all time; and at their best they could sometimes do work that even the greatest might envy. It is also true, however, that some poets won extravagant praise from their contemporaries, only to fall into utter obscurity once they had died. We have made a special effort to include in the *Treasury* a few selections from poets whom posterity has, perhaps deservedly, forgotten, though they were fabulously popular in their own time. Thomas Moore, for example, is still remembered for his sentimental songs—"Believe Me, If All Those Endearing Young Charms" is the most famous of them, and we include it—but who now reads his book-length Oriental romance, *Lalla Rookh?* Our excerpt from this poem, "The Light of the Harem," might not exactly suit a modern reader's taste, but it is a charming period-piece, a sample of what our great-grandparents kept by their bedsides a century ago.

The range of English poetry is so vast and various that its qualities defy easy generalizations. Every possible mood and emotion is portrayed in it, from the gentlest to the most violent; every conceivable rhythm and style is employed by it, from the delicate notes of a love sonnet to the thunderous chords of the epic. The *Treasury* has been designed to offer a generous sampling of this rich variety, to give the reader as clear a picture as possible of this splendid poetic tradition. Pleasure, as Horace said two thousand years ago, is the aim and purpose of all poetry, and if any single attribute links all these poems together, it is their brilliant success in achieving that goal, each in its own unique way.

Mark Caldwell
Walter Kendrick

ANONYMOUS
OLD ENGLISH POEMS
(500–1100)

CAEDMON'S HYMN

Now let us praise heaven's Emperor,
Master of Fate, universal Father,
Eternal King, by Whose shaping hand
All these wonders came to be.
Holy Creator, He first devised
Heaven's roof for the sons of men;
Ruler of mankind, He next prepared
This earth where now we praise Him,
Eternal King, almighty Lord.
                    —*translated by Walter Kendrick*

THE WANDERER

"Long may the lonely one wait for comfort,
The comfort of God, though, heart-heavy,
In long labor a weary time
He plunge his hands in the snow-cold sea,
On the paths of exile, fulfilling his fate."
—So spoke the Wanderer, mindful of hardships;
Of fierce slaughters; of the death of his kin.
   "Alone in the silence of the hour before dawn
I speak my sorrow. For now of the living
None is left, none to learn,
To know of things hidden in my soul's heart.
   It is a noble thing in a weary man
To lock his spirit; to keep his secret
Held in his breast, think what he will.
For his fate assails him, tired in soul,

And, hunted yet fierce, his mind cannot help.
So, hiding dark thoughts in a locked heart,
He strives for glory, the darkness kept secret.
So it was with me: my secret heart
Often steeped in sorrow, driven from home,
Far from kin, bound in chains,
My generous lord long before
Laid in the earth. And so I left,
Laden with winter-care over the waves,
Longing for a hall and a giver of treasure,
Seeking a home far or near,
Where love might greet me, the friendless one;
Kindness might comfort me in the high mead-hall
With beautiful things.
                              He learns who lives it
The cruelty of sorrow. A friend to others
Who has himself few friends to name,
He knows exile, not hammered gold;
A frozen heart, and nothing of warmth.
He remembers the hall-friends, the giving of gifts;
Remembers how once a generous lord
Gave him good feast, a thing now gone.
He learns who must long to forego
The good counsel of a loved lord.
And when sorrow and sleep, wound together,
Lie upon the lonely one like twisted chains,
He dreams in his soul of holding and kissing
His lost lord, hand and head
Upon his knee, as he did long ago,
In the dim past when the lord kept the throne.
But then he awakes, the friendless man,
Sees, stretching before him, the yellow-green waves,
Where the sea-birds plunge, then spread their wings;
Where the frost and snow fall with the hail
And with what is heavier, hurts in the soul,
Sore for a loved one. The sorrow comes back
When the memory of kinsmen floods the soul:
Searching with his eyes, he eagerly meets
Companies of men, yet rarely finds
Familiar words. So again in soul
He crosses the sea. The sorrow comes back
To him who must drive again and again

A burdened heart across the waves.
And I cannot think, knowing this world,
Why my burdened heart might not grow dark
As the lives of men pass through my thought.
So quickly they leave the warmth of the hall,
The noble warriors; so quickly this world
Day by day decays and falls.
   And a man is not wise before he has passed
His share of winters. He must learn to wait:
Not to act rashly, nor speak too soon;
Neither slow to decide, nor driven by haste,
By fear or by joy, or by excess of greed,
Or hunger for glory before his time.
He must learn to wait; to withhold a vow
Until he is certain, knowing clearly
The hidden drift of the thoughts of men.
And a wise man must know how desolate it is,
The world's wealth, lying deserted,
As now it does throughout the earth—
How the walls stand beaten by the wind,
Covered by the snow, open to the storms;
How the wine-halls crumble, their king lying dead,
Senseless to joy, his men long fallen,
Proud by the wall. War carried some
Into the darkness. The bird took one
Out to the sea. The wolf took one
And gave him to death. A man took one
And hid him in a grave, grief upon his face.
And so the God of men destroyed this place,
Making it empty of mirth and of men,
And the great halls stood desolate.
   He who considers the fallen walls;
He who considers this dark life,
Wise in his soul often remembers
Many deaths, and speaks these words:
Where did the horse go? The youth and his lord?
Where did the halls go, and the feasts that filled them?
Alas, bright cup! Alas, warrior,
And prince's glory! How the time flew,
And the day grew dark as if it never were!
Where once men dwelt is an empty place,
A solitary wall carved with snakes.

3

The men are gone, with their strong spears,
Hungry for slaughter: so fate ordained.
And storms besiege the stone walls
And the snow falls, locking the earth,
And the winter comes, and the darkness comes,
With the shadow of night; from the cold north
The hail comes, a scourge to men.
All is hardship in the realm of the world;
Under the skies fate rules all.
For here goods pass; a friend passes;
A kinsman passes; man himself passes;
And the frame of earth grows empty soon."
　　—So spoke the wise one in his heart as he sat alone in thought.
The good man keeps his faith, holding the force of his grief;
Keeping silence in his breast, unless in his heart he knows
The answer to his sorrow. And indeed there is mercy to him,
Solace from his Father in heaven, where all stability stands.

—translated by Mark Caldwell

DEOR

Weland, that dauntless man, well learned to bear
The heavy weight of hardship, winter's woe.
For comrades he had only care and pain,
Relentless longing that each dawn renewed.
The greed of Nithhad laid him in those bonds,
Hamstrung by one not half so great as he.
　　That passed in time; this, too, shall pass.

Fair Beaduhilde mourned her brothers' deaths,
But her own sorrow stabbed her deeper still.
She knew it when she felt that in her womb
The child of him who murdered them had stirred.
She gazed upon her fate unflinchingly,
And saw that she was helpless in its hands.
　　That passed in time; this, too, shall pass.

They tell the tale of Maethhild's tragic love
For her lord, Geat: lamentation grew
Unbounded, till it robbed her of all sleep.
　　That passed in time; this, too, shall pass.

4

For thirty winters Theodoric held
The Maerings' city: many know this tale.
   That passed in time; this, too, shall pass.

We also know of cruel Ermanaric,
Who held the Gothic kingdom in his grasp
And ruled it as a wolf might rule a flock.
So many brave men sat in sorrow's chains,
Foreseeing only sorrow, wishing for
The time when that foul tyranny would fall!
   That passed in time; this, too, shall pass.

Obsessed by cares, bereft of any joy,
A man may feel the darkness fill his mind
And think that endless sorrow is his lot.
Let him remember that, all round this world,
The wisdom of the Lord works changefully.
To many he shows favour, certain bliss;
To some of us he grants a share of woe.

And I would add one thing about myself:
For years I graced the Hedenings with my song,
And my dear master; Deor was my name.
For winter after winter I served well,
My noble Lord, but now Heorrenda,
That crafty singing-man, owns my estate
And all the bounty you once granted me.
   That passed in time; this, too, shall pass.
                    —*translated by Walter Kendrick*

ANONYMOUS
MIDDLE ENGLISH LYRICS
(1100–1400)

Western wind, when wilt thou blow?
The small rain down can rain.
Christ, that my love were in my arms
And I in my bed again!

*

Summer is icumen in;
Loude sing cuckoo!
Groweth seed and bloweth meed,
And springth the woode now.
Sing cuckoo!

Ewe bleateth after lamb,
Loweth after calfe cow;
Bullock starteth; bucke farteth;
Merry sing cuckoo!
Cuckoo, cuckoo.
Well singest thou, cuckoo.
Ne swik thou never now!

GEOFFREY CHAUCER
(ca. 1340–1400)

from *THE CANTERBURY TALES*

from THE PROLOGUE

When in April the sweet showers fall
And pierce the drought of March to the root, and all
The veins are bathed in liquor of such power
As brings about the engendering of the flower,
When also Zephyrus with his sweet breath
Exhales an air in every grove and heath
Upon the tender shoots, and the young sun
His half-course in the sign of the *Ram* has run,
And the small fowl are making melody
That sleep away the night with open eye
(So nature pricks them and their heart engages)
Then people long to go on pilgrimages
And palmers long to seek the stranger strands
Of far-off saints, hallowed in sundry lands,
And specially, from every shire's end
Of England, down to Canterbury they wend
To seek the holy blissful martyr, quick
To give his help to them when they were sick.
    It happened in that season that one day
In Southwark, at *The Tabard*, as I lay
Ready to go on pilgrimage and start
For Canterbury, most devout at heart,
At night there came into that hostelry
Some nine and twenty in a company
Of sundry folk happening then to fall
In fellowship, and they were pilgrims all
That towards Canterbury meant to ride.
The rooms and stables of the inn were wide;
They made us easy, all was of the best.
And, briefly, when the sun had gone to rest,

I'd spoken to them all upon the trip
And was soon one with them in fellowship,
Pledged to rise early and to take the way
To Canterbury, as you heard me say. . . .

THE MILLER'S TALE

Some time ago there was a rich old codger
Who lived in Oxford and who took a lodger.
The fellow was a carpenter by trade,
His lodger a poor student who had made
Some studies in the arts, but all his fancy
Turned to astrology and geomancy,
And he could deal with certain propositions
And make a forecast under some conditions
About the likelihood of drought or showers
For those who asked at favourable hours,
Or put a question how their luck would fall
In this or that, I can't describe them all.
 This lad was known as Nicholas the Gallant,
And making love in secret was his talent,
For he was very close and sly, and took
Advantage of his meek and girlish look.
He rented a small chamber in the kip
All by himself without companionship.
He decked it charmingly with herbs and fruit
And he himself was sweeter than the root
Of liquorice, or any fragrant herb.
His astronomic text-books were superb,
He had an astrolabe to match his art
And calculating counters laid apart
On handy shelves that stood above his bed.
His press was curtained coarsely and in red;
Above there lay a gallant harp in sight
On which he played melodiously at night
With such a touch that all the chamber rang;
It was *The Virgin's Angelus* he sang,
And after that he sang *King William's Note*,
And people often blessed his merry throat.

And that was how this charming scholar spent
His time and money, which his friends had sent.

    This carpenter had married a new wife
Not long before, and loved her more than life.
She was a girl of eighteen years of age.
Jealous he was and kept her in the cage,
For he was old and she was wild and young;
He thought himself quite likely to be stung.

    He might have known, were Cato on his shelf,
A man should marry someone like himself;
A man should pick an equal for his mate.
Youth and old age are often in debate.
However, he had fallen in the snare,
And had to bear his cross as others bear.

    She was a fair young wife, her body as slender
As any weasel's, and as soft and tender;
She used to wear a girdle of striped silk;
Her apron was as white as morning milk
Over her loins, all gusseted and pleated.
White was her smock; embroidery repeated
Its pattern on the collar, front and back,
Inside and out; it was of silk, and black.
The tapes and ribbons of her milky mutch
Were made to match her collar to a touch;
She wore a broad silk fillet, rather high,
And certainly she had a lecherous eye.
And she had plucked her eyebrows into bows,
Slenderly arched they were, and black as sloes;
And a more truly blissful sight to see
She was than blossom on a cherry-tree,
And softer than the wool upon a wether;
And by her girdle hung a purse of leather,
Tasselled with silk and silver droplets, pearled;
If you went seeking up and down the world,
The wisest man you met would have to wrench
His fancy to imagine such a wench;
And her complexion had a brighter tint
Than a new florin from the Royal Mint.
As to her song, it was as loud and quick
As any swallow's chirping on a rick;
And she would skip or play some game or other
Like any kid or calf behind its mother.

9

Her mouth was sweet as mead or honey—say
A hoard of apples lying in the hay.
Skittish she was, and jolly as a colt,
Tall as a mast and upright as a bolt
Out of a bow. Her collaret revealed
A brooch as big as boss upon a shield.
High shoes she wore, and laced them to the top.
She was a daisy, O a lollypop
For any nobleman to take to bed
Or some good man of yeoman stock to wed.

   Now, gentlemen, this Gallant Nicholas
One day began to romp and make a pass
At this young woman, in a mood of play,
Her husband being out, down Osney way.
Students are sly, and giving way to whim,
He made a grab and caught her by the quim
And said, 'Unless I have my will of you
I'll die of secret love—O, darling, do!'
Then held her haunches hard and gave a cry
'O love-me-all-at-once or I shall die!'
She gave a spring, just like a skittish colt
Boxed in a frame for shoeing, and with a jolt
Managed in time to wrench her head away,
And said, 'Give over, Nicholas, I say!
No, I won't kiss you! Stop it! Let me go
Or I shall scream! I'll let the neighbours know!
Where are your manners? Take away your paws!'

   Then Nicholas began to plead his cause
And spoke so fair in proffering what he could
That in the end she promised him she would,
Swearing she'd love him, with a solemn promise
To be at his disposal, by St Thomas,
When she could spy an opportunity.
'My husband is so full of jealousy,
Unless you watch your step and hold your breath
I know for certain it will be my death,'
She said, 'So keep it well under your hat.'
'Oh, never mind about a thing like that.'
Said he; 'A scholar doesn't have to stir
His wits so much to trick a carpenter.'

   And so they both agreed to it, and swore
To watch their chance, as I have said before.

When things were settled thus as they thought fit,
And Nicholas had stroked her loins a bit
And kissed her sweetly, he took down his harp
And played away, a merry tune and sharp.

It happened later she went off to church,
This worthy wife, one holiday, to search
Her conscience and to do the works of Christ.
She put her work aside and she enticed
The colour to her face to make her mark;
Her forehead shone. There was a parish clerk
Serving the church, whose name was Absalon.
His hair was all in golden curls and shone;
Just like a fan it strutted outwards, starting
To left and right from an accomplished parting.
Ruddy his face, his eyes as grey as goose,
His shoes cut out in tracery, as in use
In old St Paul's. The hose upon his feet
Showed scarlet through, and all his clothes were neat
And proper. In a jacket of light blue,
Flounced at the waist and tagged with laces, too,
He went, and wore a surplice just as gay
And white as any blossom on the spray.
God bless my soul, he was a merry knave!
He knew how to let blood, cut hair and shave,
And draw up legal deeds; at other whiles
He used to dance in twenty different styles
(After the current school at Oxford though,
Casting his legs about him to and fro).
He played a two-stringed fiddle, did it proud,
And sang a high falsetto, rather loud;
And he was just as good on the guitar.
There was no public-house in town, or bar,
He didn't visit with his merry face
If there were saucy barmaids round the place.
He was a little squeamish in the matter
Of farting, and satirical in chatter.
This Absalon, so jolly in his ways,
Would bear the censer round on holy days
And cense the parish women. He would cast
Many a love-lorn look before he passed,
Especially at this carpenter's young wife;
Looking at her would make a happy life

11

She was so neat, so sweet, so lecherous!
And I dare say if she had been a mouse
And he a cat, she'd have been pounced upon.
  In taking the collection Absalon
Would find his heart was set in such a whirl
Of love, he would take nothing from a girl,
For courtesy, he said, it wasn't right.
  That evening, when the moon was shining bright
He ups with his guitar and off he tours
On the look-out for any paramours.
Larky and amorous, away he strode
Until he reached the carpenter's abode
A little after cock-crow, took his stand
Beside the casement window close at hand
(It was set low upon the cottage-face)
And started singing softly and with grace,
  'Now dearest lady, if thy pleasure be
  In thoughts of love, think tenderly of me!'
On his guitar he plucked a tuneful string.
  This carpenter awoke and heard him sing
And turning to his wife said, 'Alison!
Wife! Do you hear him? There goes Absalon
Chanting away under our chamber wall.'
And she, 'Yes, John, God knows I hear it all.'
If she thought more of it she didn't tell.
  So things went on. What's better than 'All's well'?
From day to day this jolly Absalon,
Wooing away, became quite woe-begone;
He lay awake all night, and all the day,
Combed his thick locks and tried to pass for gay,
Wooed her by go-between and wooed by proxy,
Swore to be page and servant to his doxy,
Trilled and rouladed like a nightingale,
Sent her sweet wine and mead and spicy ale,
And wafers piping hot and jars of honey,
And, as she lived in town, he offered money.
For there are some a money-bag provokes
And some are won by kindness, some by strokes.
  Once, in the hope his talent might engage,
He played the part of Herod on the stage.
What was the good? Were he as bold as brass,
She was in love with gallant Nicholas;

12

However Absalon might blow his horn
His labour won him nothing but her scorn.
She looked upon him as her private ape
And held his earnest wooing all a jape.
There is a proverb, true, as you may find,
That *Out-of-Sight* is also *Out-of-Mind.*
For Nigh-and-Sly has the advantage there;
And, much as Absalon might tear his hair,
And rage at being seldom in her sight,
Nicholas, nigh and sly, stood in his light.
Now, show your paces, Nicholas you spark!
And leave lamenting to the parish clerk.

    And so it happened that one Saturday,
When the old carpenter was safe away
At Osney, Nicholas and Alison
Agreed at last in what was to be done.
Nicholas was to exercise his wits
On her suspicious husband's foolish fits,
And, if so be the trick worked out all right,
She then would sleep with Nicholas all night,
For such was his desire and hers as well;
And even quicker than it takes to tell,
Young Nicholas, who simply couldn't wait,
Went to his room on tip-toe with a plate
Of food and drink, enough to last a day
Or two, and Alison was told to say,
In case her husband asked for Nicholas,
That she had no idea where he was,
And that she hadn't set eyes on him all day
And thought he must be ill, she couldn't say;
And more than once the maid had given a call
And shouted but no answer came at all.

    So it continued, all that Saturday
Without a sound from Nicholas, who lay
Upstairs, and ate or slept as pleased him best
Till Sunday when the sun went down to rest.

    This foolish carpenter was lost in wonder
At Nicholas; what could have got him under?
He said, 'I can't help thinking, by the Mass,
Things can't be going right with Nicholas.
What if he took and died? God guard his ways!
A ticklish place the world is, nowadays.

I saw a corpse this morning borne to kirk
That only Monday last I saw at work.
Run up,' he told the serving-lad, 'be quick,
Shout at his door, or knock it with a brick.
Take a good look and tell me how he fares.'

   The serving-boy went sturdily upstairs,
Stopped at the door and, standing there, the lad
Shouted away and, hammering like mad,
Cried, 'Ho! What's up? Hi! Master Nicholay!
How can you lie up there asleep all day?'

   But all for nought, he didn't hear a soul.
He found a broken panel with a hole
Right at the bottom, useful to the cat
For creeping in by: so he looked through that,
And, in the end, he saw him through the crack.
This Nicholas lay gaping on his back
As if he'd caught a glimpse of the new moon.
Down went the boy and told his master soon
About the state in which he found the man.

   On hearing this the carpenter began
To cross himself and said, 'St Frideswide bless us!
We little know what's coming to distress us.
The man has fallen, with this here 'astromy',
Into a fit, or lunacy maybe.
I always thought that was how it would go.
God has some secrets that we shouldn't know.
How blessed are the simple, aye, indeed,
That only know enough to say their creed!
Happened just so with such another student
Of astromy and he was so imprudent
As to stare upwards while he crossed a field,
Busy foreseeing what the stars revealed;
And what should happen but he fell down flat
Into a marl-pit. He didn't foresee that!
But by the Saints we've reached a sorry pass;
I can't help worrying for Nicholas.
He shall be scolded for his studying
If I know how to scold, by Christ the King!
Get me a staff to prise against the floor.
Robin, you put your shoulder to the door.
We'll shake the study out of him, I guess!'

   The pair of them began to heave and press

14

Against the door. Happened the lad was strong
And so it didn't take them very long
To heave it off its hinges; down it came.
Still as a stone lay Nicholas, with the same
Expression, gaping upwards into air.
The carpenter supposed it was despair
And caught him by the shoulders mightily,
Shook him and shouted with asperity:
'What, Nicholas! Hey! Look down! Is that a fashion
To act? Wake up and think upon Christ's passion.
I sign you with the cross from elves and sprites!'
And he began the spell for use at nights
In all four corners of the room and out
Across the threshold too and round about:
    Jesu Christ and Benedict Sainted
    Bless this house from creature tainted,
    Drive away night-hags, white Pater-noster,
    Where did you go, St Peter's soster?
    And in the end the dandy Nicholas
Began to sigh, 'And must it come to pass?'
He said, 'Must all the world be cast away?'
The carpenter replied, 'What's that you say?
Put trust in God as we do, working men.'
Nicholas answered, 'Fetch some liquor then,
And afterwards, in strictest secrecy,
I'll speak of something touching you and me,
But not another soul must know, that's plain.'

    This carpenter went down and came again
Bringing some powerful ale—a largish quart.
When each had had his share of this support
Young Nicholas got up and shut the door
And, sitting down beside him on the floor,
Said to the carpenter, 'Now, John, my dear,
My excellent host, swear on your honour here
Not to repeat a syllable I say,
For here are Christ's intentions, to betray
Which to a soul puts you among the lost,
And vengeance for it at a bitter cost
Shall fall upon you. You'll be driven mad!'
'Christ and His holy blood forbid it, lad!'
The silly fellow answered. 'I'm no blab,
Though I should say it. I'm not given to gab.

Say what you like, for I shall never tell
Man, woman or child by Him that harrowed Hell!'
    'Now, John,' said Nicholas, 'believe you me,
I have found out by my astrology,
And looking at the moon when it was bright,
That Monday next, a quarter way through night,
Rain is to fall in torrents, such a scud
It will be twice as bad as Noah's Flood.
'This world,' he said, 'in just about an hour,
Shall all be drowned, it's such a hideous shower,
And all mankind, with total loss of life.'
    The carpenter exclaimed, 'Alas, my wife!
My little Alison! Is she to drown?'
And in his grief he very near fell down.
'Is there no remedy,' he said, 'for this?'
'Thanks be to God,' said Nicholas, 'there is,
If you will do exactly what I say
And don't start thinking up some other way.
In wise old Solomon you'll find the verse
"Who takes advice shall never fare the worse,"
And so if good advice is to prevail
I undertake with neither mast nor sail
To save her yet, and save myself and you.
Haven't you heard how Noah was saved too
When God forewarned him and his sons and daughters
That all the world should sink beneath the waters?'
'Yes,' said the carpenter, 'a long time back.'
'Haven't you heard,' said Nicholas, 'what a black
Business it was, when Noah tried to whip
His wife (who wouldn't come) on board the ship?
He'd have been better pleased, I'll undertake,
With all that weather just about to break,
If she had had a vessel of her own.
Now, what are we to do? We can't postpone
The thing; it's coming soon, as I was saying,
It calls for haste, not preaching or delaying.
    'I want you, now, at once, to hurry off
And fetch a shallow tub or kneading-trough
For each of us, but see that they are large
And such as we can float in, like a barge.
And have them loaded with sufficient victual
To last a day—we only need a little.

16

The waters will abate and flow away
Round nine o'clock upon the following day.
Robin the lad mayn't know of this, poor knave,
Nor Jill the maid, those two I cannot save.
Don't ask me why; and even if you do
I can't disclose God's secret thoughts to you.
You should be satisfied, unless you're mad,
To find as great a grace as Noah had.
And I shall save your wife, you needn't doubt it,
Now off you go, and hurry up about it.

   'And when the tubs have been collected, three,
That's one for her and for yourself and me,
Then hang them in the roof below the thatching
That no one may discover what we're hatching.
When you have finished doing what I said
And stowed the victuals in them overhead,
Also an axe to hack the ropes apart,
So, when the water rises, we can start,
And, lastly, when you've broken out the gable,
The garden one that's just above the stable,
So that we may cast free without delay
After the mighty shower has gone away,
You'll float as merrily, I undertake,
As any lily-white duck behind her drake.
And I'll call out, "Hey, Alison! Hey, John!
Cheer yourselves up! The flood will soon be gone."
And you'll shout back, "Hail, Master Nicholay!
Good morning! I can see you well. It's day!"
We shall be lords for all the rest of life
Of all the world, like Noah and his wife.

   'One thing I warn you of; it's only right.
We must be very careful on the night,
Once we have safely managed to embark,
To hold our tongues, to utter no remark,
No cry or call, for we must fall to prayer.
This is the Lord's dear will, so have a care.

   'Your wife and you must hang some way apart,
For there must be no sin before we start,
No more in longing looks than in the deed.
Those are your orders. Off with you! God speed!
To-morrow night when everyone's asleep
We'll all go quietly upstairs and creep

17

Into our tubs, awaiting Heaven's grace.
And now be off. No time to put the case
At greater length, no time to sermonize;
The proverb says, 'Say nothing, send the wise.'
You're wise enough, I do not have to teach you.
Go, save our lives for us, as I beseech you.'
    This silly carpenter then went his way
Muttering to himself, 'Alas the day!'
And told his wife in strictest secrecy.
She was aware, far more indeed than he,
What this quaint strategem might have in sight,
But she pretended to be dead with fright.
'Alas!' she said. 'Whatever it may cost,
Hurry and help, or we shall all be lost.
I am your honest, true and wedded wife,
Go, dearest husband, help to save my life!'
    How fancy throws us into perturbation!
People can die of mere imagination,
So deep is the impression one can take.
This silly carpenter began to quake,
Before his eyes there verily seemed to be
The floods of Noah, wallowing like the sea
And drowning Alison his honey-pet.
He wept and wailed, his features were all set
In grief, he sighed with many a doleful grunt.
He went and got a tub, began to hunt
For kneading-troughs, found two, and had them sent
Home to his house in secret; then he went
And, unbeknownst, he hung them from a rafter.
With his own hands he made three ladders after,
Uprights and rungs, to help them in their scheme
Of climbing where they hung upon the beam.
He victualled tub and trough, and made all snug
With bread and cheese, and ale in a large jug,
Enough for three of them to last the day,
And, just before completing this array,
Packed off the maid and his apprentice too
To London on a job they had to do.
And on the Monday when it drew to night
He shut his door and dowsed the candle-light
And made quite sure all was as it should be.
And shortly, up they clambered, all the three,

18

Silent and separate. They began to pray
And *'Pater Noster* mum', said Nicholay,
And 'mum' said John, and 'mum' said Alison.
The carpenter's devotions being done,
He sat quite still, then fell to prayer again
With one ear cocked, however, for the rain.

The carpenter, with all the work he'd seen,
Fell dead asleep—round curfew, must have been,
Maybe a little later on the whole.
He groaned in sleep for travail of his soul
And snored because his head was turned awry.

Down by their ladders, stalking from on high
Came Nicholas and Alison, and sped
Softly downstairs, without a word, to bed,
And where this carpenter was wont to be
The revels started and the melody.
And thus lay Nicholas and Alison
Busy in solace and the quest of fun,
Until the bell for lauds had started ringing
And in the chancel friars began their singing.

This parish clerk, this amorous Absalon,
Love-stricken still and very woe-begone,
Upon the Monday was in company
At Osney with his friends for jollity,
And chanced to ask a resident cloisterer
What had become of John the carpenter.
The fellow drew him out of church to say,
'Don't know; not been at work since Saturday.
I can't say where he is; I think he went
To fetch the Abbot timber. He is sent
Often enough for timber, has to go
Out to the Grange and stop a day or so;
If not, he's certainly at home to-day,
But where he is I can't exactly say.'

Absalon was a jolly lad and light
Of heart; he thought, 'I'll stay awake to-night;
I'm certain that I haven't seen him stirring
About his door since dawn; it's safe inferring
That he's away. As I'm alive I'll go
And tap his window softly at the crow
Of cock—the sill is low-set on the wall.
I shall see Alison and tell her all

My love-longing, and I can hardly miss
Some favour from her, at the least a kiss.
I'll get some satisfaction anyway;
There's been an itching in my mouth all day
And that's a sign of kissing at the least.
And all last night I dreamt about a feast.
I think I'll go and sleep an hour or two,
Then wake and have some fun, that's what I'll do.'
    The first cock crew at last, and thereupon
Up rose this jolly lover Absalon
In gayest clothes, garnished with that and this;
But first he chewed a grain of liquorice
To charm his breath before he combed his hair.
Under his tongue the comfit nestling there
Would make him gracious. He began to roam
Towards the carpenter's; he reached their home
And by the casement window took his stand.
Breast-high it stood, no higher than his hand.
He gave a cough, it was a semi-sound;
'Alison, honey-comb, are you around?
Sweet cinnamon, my little pretty bird,
Sweetheart, wake up and say a little word!
You seldom think of me in all my woe,
I sweat for love of you wherever I go!
No wonder if I do, I pine and bleat
As any lambkin hungering for the teat,
Believe me, darling, I'm so deep in love
I croon with longing like a turtle-dove,
I eat as little as a girl at school.'
'You go away,' she answered, 'you Tom-fool!
There's no come-up-and-kiss-me here for you.
I love another and why shouldn't I too?
Better than you, by Jesu, Absalon!
Take yourself off or I shall throw a stone.
I want to get some sleep. You go to Hell!'
'Alas!' said Absalon. 'I knew it well;
True love is always mocked and girded at;
So kiss me, if you can't do more than that,
For Jesu's love and for the love of me!'
'And if I do, will you be off?' said she.
'Promise you, darling,' answered Absalon.
'Get ready then; wait, I'll put something on,'

20

She said and then she added under breath
To Nicholas, 'Hush . . . we shall laugh to death!'
   This Absalon went down upon his knees;
'I am a lord!' he thought, 'And by degrees
There may be more to come; the plot may thicken.'
'Mercy, my love!' he said, 'Your mouth, my chicken!'
   She flung the window open then in haste
And said, 'Have done, come on, no time to waste,
The neighbours here are always on the spy.'
   Absalon started wiping his mouth dry.
Dark was the night as pitch, as black as coal,
And at the window out she put her hole,
And Absalon, so fortune framed the farce,
Put up his mouth and kissed her naked arse
Most savorously before he knew of this.
   And back he started. Something was amiss;
He knew quite well a woman has no beard,
Yet something rough and hairy had appeared.
'What have I done?' he said. 'Can that be you?'
'Teehee!' she cried and clapped the window to.
Off went poor Absalon sadly through the dark.
'A beard! a beard!' cried Nicholas the Spark.
'God's body, that was something like a joke!'
And Absalon, overhearing what he spoke,
Bit on his lips and nearly threw a fit
In rage and thought, 'I'll pay you back for it!'
   Who's busy rubbing, scraping at his lips
With dust, with sand, with straw, with cloth, with chips,
But Absalon? He thought, 'I'll bring him down!
I wouldn't let this go for all the town.
I'd take my soul and sell it to the Devil
To be revenged upon him! I'll get level.
O God, why did I let myself be fooled?'
   The fiery heat of love by now had cooled,
For from the time he kissed her hinder parts
He didn't give a tinker's curse for tarts;
His malady was cured by this endeavour
And he defied all paramours whatever.
   So, weeping like a child that has been whipped,
He turned away; across the road he slipped
And called on Gervase. Gervase was a smith;
His forge was full of things for ploughing with

21

And he was busy sharpening a share.
    Absalon knocked, and with an easy air
Called, 'Gervase! Open up the door, come on!'
'What's that? Who's there?' 'It's me, it's Absalon.'
'What, Absalon? By Jesu's blessed tree
You're early up! Hey, *benedicite*,
What's wrong? Some jolly girl as like as not
Has coaxed you out and set you on the trot.
Blessed St Neot! You know the thing I mean.'
    But Absalon, who didn't give a bean
For all his joking, offered no debate.
He had a good deal more upon his plate
Then Gervase knew and said, 'Would it be fair
To borrow that coulter in the chimney there,
The hot one, see it? I've a job to do;
It won't take long, I'll bring it back to you.'
Gervase replied, 'Why, if you asked for gold,
A bag of sovereigns or of wealth untold,
It should be yours, as I'm an honest smith.
But, Christ, why borrow that to do it with?'
'Let that,' said Absalon, 'be as it may;
You'll hear about it all some other day.'
    He caught the coulter up—the haft was cool—
And left the smithy softly with the tool,
Crept to the little window in the wall
And coughed. He knocked and gave a little call
Under the window as he had before.
    Alison said, 'There's someone at the door.
Who's knocking there? I'll warrant it's a thief.'
'Why, no,' said he, 'my little flower-leaf,
It's your own Absalon, my sweety-thing!
Look what I've brought you—it's a golden ring
My mother gave me, as I may be saved.
It's very fine, and prettily engraved;
I'll give it to you, darling, for a kiss.'
    Now Nicholas had risen for a piss,
And thought he could improve upon the jape
And make him kiss his arse ere he escape,
And opening the window with a jerk,
Stuck out his arse, a handsome piece of work,
Buttocks and all, as far as to the haunch.
    Said Absalon, all set to make a launch,

22

'Speak, pretty bird, I know not where thou art!'
This Nicholas at once let fly a fart
As loud as if it were a thunder-clap.
He was near blinded by the blast, poor chap,
But his hot iron was ready; with a thump
He smote him in the middle of the rump.

Off went the skin a hand's breath round about
Where the hot coulter struck and burnt it out.
Such was the pain, he thought he must be dying
And, mad with agony, he started crying,
'Help! Water! Water! Help! For Heaven's love!'

The carpenter, startled from sleep above,
And hearing shouts for water and a thud,
Thought, 'Heaven help us! Here comes Nowel's Flood!'
And up he sat and with no more ado
He took his axe and smote the ropes in two
And down went everything. He didn't stop
To sell his bread and ale, but came down flop
Upon the floor and fainted right away.

Up started Alison and Nicholay
And shouted, 'Help!' and 'Murder!' in the street.
The neighbours all came running up in heat
And stood there staring at the wretched man.
He lay there fainting, pale beneath his tan;
His arm in falling had been broken double.
But still he was obliged to face his trouble,
For when he spoke he was at once borne down
By Nicholas and his wife. They told the town
That he was mad, there'd got into his blood
Some sort of nonsense about 'Nowel's Flood',
That vain imaginings and fantasy
Had made him buy the kneading-tubs, that he
Had hung them in the rafters up above
And that he'd begged them both for heaven's love
To sit up in the roof for company.

All started laughing at this lunacy
And streamed upstairs to gape and pry and poke,
And treated all his sufferings as a joke.
No matter what the carpenter asserted
It went for nothing, no one was converted;
With powerful oaths they swore the fellow down
And he was held for mad by all the town;

The students all ganged up with one another
Saying: 'The fellow's crazy, my dear brother!'
And every one among them laughed and joked.
And so the carpenter's wife was truly poked,
As if his jealousy to justify,
And Absalon has kissed her nether eye
And Nicholas is branded on the bum
And God bring all of us to Kingdom Come.

—translated by Nevill Coghill

THOMAS WYATT
(1503–42)

My galley charged with forgetfulness
Through sharp seas in winter nights doth pass
'Tween rock and rock; and eke my foe, alas,
That is my lord, steereth with cruelness;
And every oar a thought in readiness,
As though that death were light in such a case.
An endless wind doth tear the sail apace,
Of forced sighs and trusty fearfulness;
A rain of tears, a cloud of dark disdain,
Have done the wearied cords great hindrance.
Wreathed with error and eke with ignorance,
The stars be hid that led me to this pain;
Drowned is reason, that should be my comfort,
And I remain despairing of the port.

*

They flee from me, that sometime did me seek
With naked foot stalking within my chamber.
Once have I seen them gentle tame and meek
That now are wild, and do not once remember
That sometime they have put themselves in danger
To take bread at my hand; and now they range,
Busily seeking in continual change.

Thanked be fortune, it hath been otherwise
Twenty times better. But once especial,
In thin array, after a pleasant guise,
When her loose gown did from her shoulders fall,
And she me caught in her arms long and small,
And therewithal so sweetly did me kiss
And softly said, "Dear heart, how like you this?"

It was no dream, for I lay broad awaking.
But all is turned now through my gentleness
Into a bitter fashion of forsaking.
And I have leave to go of her goodness,
And she also to use newfangleness.
But since that I unkindly so am served,
How like you this? What hath she now deserved?

HENRY HOWARD,
EARL OF SURREY
(1517–47)

Set me whereas the sun doth parch the green,
Or where his beams do not dissolve the ice;
In temperate heat, where he is felt and seen;
In presence prest of people, mad or wise.
Set me in high, or yet in low degree;
In longest night, or in the shortest day;
In clearest sky, or where clouds thickest be;
In lusty youth, or when my hairs are grey.
Set me in heaven, in earth, or else in hell,
In hill or dale, or in the foaming flood;
Thrall, or at large, alive whereso I dwell,
Sick, or in health, in evil fame or good,
    Hers will I be; and only with this thought
    Content myself, although my chance be nought.

A COMPLAINT BY NIGHT
OF THE LOVER NOT BELOVED

Alas! so all things now do hold their peace!
Heaven and earth disturbed in no thing;
The beasts, the air, the birds their song do cease,
The night's car the stars about doth bring.
Calm is the sea; the waves work less and less:
So am not I, whom love, alas! doth wring,
Bringing before my face the great increase
Of my desires, whereat I weep and sing,
In joy and woe, as in a doubtful case.
For my sweet thoughts sometime do pleasure bring;
But by and by, the cause of my disease
Gives me a pang, that inwardly doth sting,

When that I think what grief it is again,
To live and lack the thing should rid my pain.

*

When raging love with extreme pain
Most cruelly distrains my heart;
When that my tears as floods of rain,
Bear witness to my woeful smart;
When sighs have wasted so my breath
That I lie at the point of death;

I call to mind the navy great
That the Greeks brought to Troy town
And how the boistous winds did beat
Their ships and rent their sails adown,
Till Agamemnon's daughter's blood
Appeased the gods that them withstood.

And how that in those ten years' war
Full many a bloody deed was done;
And many a lord that came full far
There caught his bane, alas, too soon,
And many a good knight overrun,
Before the Greeks had Helen won.

Then think I thus: sith such repair,
So long time war of valiant men,
Was all to win a lady fair,
Shall I not learn to suffer then,
And think my life well spent to be
Serving a worthier wight than she?

Therefore I never will repent,
But pains contented still endure;
For like as, when rough winter spent,
The pleasant spring straight draweth in ure,
So, after raging storms of care,
Joyful at length may be my fare.

WALTER RALEGH
(1552–1618)

THE LIE

Go, Soul, the body's guest,
    Upon a thankless arrant:
Fear not to touch the best;
    The truth shall be thy warrant.
Go, since I needs must die,
And give the world the lie.

Say to the court, it glows
    And shines like rotten wood;
Say to the church, it shows
    What's good, and doth no good.
If church and court reply,
Then give them both the lie.

Tell potentates, they live
    Acting by others' action;
Not loved unless they give,
    Not strong but by a faction:
If potentates reply,
Give potentates the lie.

Tell men of high condition,
    That manage the estate,
Their purpose is ambition,
    Their practice only hate.
And if they once reply,
Then give them all the lie.

Tell them that brave it most,
    They beg for more by spending,
Who, in their greatest cost,
    Like nothing but commending.

And if they make reply,
Then give them all the lie.

Tell zeal it wants devotion;
  Tell love it is but lust;
Tell time it is but motion;
  Tell flesh it is but dust.
And wish them not reply,
For thou must give the lie.

Tell age it daily wasteth;
  Tell honour how it alters;
Tell beauty how she blasteth;
  Tell favour how it falters.
And as they shall reply,
Give every one the lie.

Tell wit how much it wrangles
  In tickle points of niceness;
Tell wisdom she entangles
  Herself in over-wiseness.
And when they do reply,
Straight give them both the lie.

Tell physic of her boldness;
  Tell skill it is prevention;
Tell charity of coldness;
  Tell law it is contention.
And as they do reply,
So give them still the lie.

Tell fortune of her blindness;
  Tell nature of decay;
Tell friendship of unkindness;
  Tell justice of delay.
And if they will reply,
Then give them all the lie.

Tell arts they have no soundness,
  But vary by esteeming;
Tell schools they want profoundness,
  And stand too much on seeming.

If arts and schools reply,
Give arts and schools the lie.

Tell faith it's fled the city;
   Tell how the country erreth;
Tell manhood shakes off pity;
   Tell virtue least preferreth.
And if they do reply,
Spare not to give the lie.

So when thou hast, as I
   Commanded thee, done blabbing,
Although to give the lie
   Deserves no less than stabbing,
Stab at thee he that will,
No stab the soul can kill.

EDMUND SPENSER
(1552–99)

More then most faire, full of the living fire
Kindled above unto the maker neere;
No eyes but joyes, in which all powers conspire,
That to the world naught else be counted deare.
Through your bright beames doth not the blinded guest,
Shoot out his darts to base affection's wound:
But angels come to lead fraile mindes to rest
In chast desires on heavenly beauty bound.
You frame my thoughts and fashion me within,
You stop my tongue, and teach my hart to speake,
You calme the storme that passion did begin,
Strong thrugh your cause, but by your vertue weak.
  Dark is the world, where your light shined never;
  Well is he borne, that may behold you ever.

*

Let not one sparke of filthy lustfull fyre
Breake out, that may her sacred place molest:
Ne one light glance of sensuall desyre
Attempt to work her gentle mindes unrest.
But pure affections bred in spotlesse brest,
And modest thoughts breathd from wel tempred sprites
Goe visit her in her chast bowre of rest,
Accompanyde with angelick delightes.
There fill your selfe with those most joyous sights,
The which my selfe could never yet attayne:
But speak no word to her of these sad plights,
Which her too constant stiffenesse doth constrayn.
  Only behold her rare perfection,
  And blesse your fortune's fayre election.

EPITHALAMION

Ye learned sisters which have oftentimes
Beene to me ayding, others to adorne:
Whom ye thought worthy of your gracefull rymes,
That even the greatest did not greatly scorne
To heare theyr names sung in your simple layes,
But joyed in theyr prayse.
And when ye list your owne mishaps to mourne,
Which death, or love, or fortunes wreck did rayse,
Your string could soone to sadder tenor turne,
And teach the woods and waters to lament
Your dolefull dreriment.
Now lay those sorrowfull complaints aside,
And having all your heads with girland crownd,
Helpe me mine owne loves prayses to resound,
Ne let the same of any be envide.
So Orpheus did for his owne bride,
So I unto my selfe alone will sing,
The woods shall to me answer and my eccho ring.

Early before the worlds light giving lampe,
His golden beame upon the hils doth spred,
Having disperst the nights unchearefull dampe,
Doe ye awake, and with fresh lusty hed,
Go to the bowre of my beloved love,
My truest turtle dove,
Bid her awake; for Hymen is awake,
And long since ready forth his maske to move,
With his bright Tead that flames with many a flake,
And many a bachelor to waite on him
In theyr fresh garments trim.
Bid her awake therefore and soone her dight
For lo the wished day is come at last,
That shall for al the paynes and sorrowes past,
Pay to her usury of long delight:
And whylest she doth her dight
Doe ye to her of joy and solace sing,
That al the woods may answer and your eccho ring.

Bring with you all the Nymphes that you can heare
Both of the rivers and the forrests greene:
And of the sea that neighbours to her neare,
Al with gay girlands goodly wel beseene.
And let them also with them bring in hand
Another gay girland
For my fayre love of lillyes and of roses,
Bound truelove wise with a blew silke riband.
And let them make great store of bridale poses,
And let them eeke bring store of other flowers
To deck the bridale bowers.
And let the ground whereas her foot shall tread,
For feare the stones her tender foot should wrong
Be strewed with fragrant flowers all along,
And diapred lyke the discoloured mead.
Which done, doe at her chamber dore awayt,
For she will waken strayt,
The whiles doe ye this song unto her sing,
The woods shall to you answer and your eccho ring.

Ye Nymphes of Mulla which with carefull heed,
The silver scaly trouts doe tend full well,
And greedy pikes which use therein to feed,
(Those trouts and pikes all others doo excell)
And ye likewise which keepe the rushy lake,
Where none doo fishes take,
Bynd up the locks the which hang scatterd light,
And in his waters which your mirror make,
Behold your faces as the christall bright,
That when you come whereas my love doth lie,
No blemish she may spie.
And eke ye lightfoot mayds which keepe the deere,
That on the hoary mountayne use to towre,
And the wylde wolves which seeke them to devoure,
With your steele darts doo chace from comming neer
Be also present heere
To helpe to decke her and to help to sing,
That al the woods may answer and your eccho ring.

Wake, now my love, awake; for it is time,
The Rosy Morne long since left Tithones bed,
All ready to her silver coche to clyme,

And Phoebus gins to shew his glorious hed.
Hark how the cheerefull birds do chaunt theyr laies
And carroll of loves praise.
The merry Larke hir mattins sings aloft,
The thrush replyes, the Mavis descant playes
The Ouzell shrills, the Ruddock warbles soft,
So goodly al agree with sweet consent,
To this dayes merriment.
Ah my deere love why doe ye sleepe thus long,
When meeter were that ye should now awake,
T'awayt the comming of your joyous make,
And hearken to the birds lovelearned song,
The deawy leaves among.
For they of joy and pleasance to you sing,
That al the woods them answer and theyr eccho ring.

My love is now awake out of her dreame,
And her fayre eyes like stars that dimmed were
With darksome cloud, now shew theyr goodly beams
More bright then Hesperus his head doth rere.
Come now ye damzels, daughters of delight,
Helpe quickly her to dight,
But first come ye fayre houres which were begot
In Joves sweet paradice, of Day and Night,
Which doe the seasons of the yeare allot,
And al that ever in this world is fayre
Doe make and still repayre.
And ye three handmayds of the Cyprian Queene
The which doe still adorne her beauties pride,
Helpe to addorne my beautifullest bride:
And as ye her array, still throw betweene
Some graces to be seene,
And as ye use to Venus, to her sing,
The whiles the woods shal answer and your eccho ring.

Now is my love al ready forth to come,
Let all the virgins therefore well awayt,
And ye fresh boyes that tend upon her groome
Prepare your selves; for he is comming strayt.
Set all your things in seemely good aray
Fit for so joyfull day,
The joyfulst day that ever sunne did see.

Faire Sun, shew forth thy favourable ray,
And let thy lifull heat not fervent be
For feare of burning her sunshyny face,
Her beauty to disgrace.
O fayrest Phoebus, father of the Muse,
If ever I did honour thee aright,
Or sing the thing, that mote thy mind delight,
Doe not thy servants simple boone refuse,
But let this day let this one day be myne,
Let al the rest be thine.
Then I thy soverayne prayses loud wil sing,
That al the woods shal answer and theyr eccho ring.

Harke how the Minstrels gin to shrill aloud
Their merry Musick that resounds from far,
The pipe, the tabor, and the trembling Croud,
That well agree withouten breach or jar.
But most of al the Damzels doe delite,
When they their tymbrels smyte,
And thereunto doe daunce and carrol sweet,
That all the sences they doe ravish quite,
The whyles the boyes run up and downe the street,
Crying aloud with strong confused noyce,
As if it were one voyce.
Hymen iô Hymen, Hymen they do shout,
That even to the heavens theyr shouting shrill
Doth reach, and all the firmament doth fill,
To which the people standing all about
As in approvance doe thereto applaud
And loud advaunce her laud,
And evermore they *Hymen Hymen* sing,
That al the woods them answer and theyr eccho ring.

Loe where she comes along with portly pace,
Lyke Phoebe from her chamber of the East,
Arysing forth to run her mighty race,
Clad all in white, that seemes a virgin best.
So well it her beseemes that ye would weene
Some angell she had beene.
Her long loose yellow locks lyke golden wyre,
Sprinckled with perle, and perling flowres a tweene,
Doe lyke a golden mantle her attyre,

36

And being crowned with a girland greene,
Seeme lyke some mayden Queene.
Her modest eyes abashed to behold
So many gazers, as on her do stare,
Upon the lowly ground affixed are.
Ne dare lift up her countenance too bold,
But blush to heare her prayses sung so loud,
So farre from being proud.
Nathlesse doe ye still loud her prayses sing,
That al the woods may answer and your eccho ring.

Tell me ye merchants daughters did ye see
So fayre a creature in your towne before,
So sweet, so lovely, and so mild as she,
Adornd with beautyes grace and vertues store,
Her goodly eyes lyke Saphyres shining bright,
Her forehead yvory white,
Her cheekes lyke apples which the sun hath rudded,
Her lips lyke cherryes charming men to byte,
Her brest like to a bowle of creame uncrudded,
Her paps lyke lyllies budded,
Her snowie necke lyke to a marble towre,
And al her body like a pallace fayre,
Ascending uppe with many a stately stayre,
To honours seat and chastities sweet bowre.
Why stand ye still ye virgins in amaze,
Upon her so to gaze,
Whiles ye forget your former lay to sing,
To which the woods did answer and your eccho ring.

But if ye saw that which no eyes can see,
The inward beauty of her lively spright,
Garnisht with heavenly guifts of high degree,
Much more then would ye wonder at that sight,
And stand astonisht lyke to those which red
Medusaes mazeful hed.
There dwels sweet love and constant chastity,
Unspotted fayth and comely womanhood,
Regard of honour and mild modesty,
There vertue raynes as Queene in royal throne,
And giveth lawes alone.
The which the base affections doe obay

And yeeld theyr services unto her will,
Ne thought of thing uncomely ever may
Thereto approch to tempt her mind to ill.
Had ye once seene these her celestial threasures,
And unrevealed pleasures,
Then would ye wonder and her prayses sing,
That al the woods should answer and your eccho ring.

Open the temple gates unto my love,
Open them wide that she may enter in,
And al the postes adorne as doth behove,
And al the pillours deck with girlands trim,
For to recyve this Saynt with honour dew,
That commeth in to you.
With trembling steps and humble reverence,
She commeth in, before th'almighties vew,
Of her ye virgins learne obedience,
When so ye come into those holy places,
To humble your proud faces;
Bring her up to the high altar, that she may
The sacred ceremonies there partake,
The which do endlesse matrimony make,
And let the roring Organs loudly play
The praises of the Lord in lively notes,
The whiles with hollow throates
The Choristers the joyous Antheme sing,
That al the woods may answere and their eccho ring.

Behold whiles she before the altar stands
Hearing the holy priest that to her speakes
And blesseth her with his two happy hands,
How the red roses flush up in her cheekes,
And the pure snow with goodly vermill stayne,
Like crimsin dyde in grayne,
That even the Angels which continually,
About the sacred Altare doe remaine,
Forget their service and about her fly,
Ofte peeping in her face that seemes more fayre,
The more they on it stare.
But her sad eyes still fastened on the ground,
Are governed with goodly modesty,
That suffers not one looke to glaunce awry,

Which may let in a little thought unsownd.
Why blush ye love to give to me your hand,
The pledge of al our band?
Sing ye sweet Angels, Alleluya sing,
That al the woods may answere and your eccho ring.

Now al is done; bring home the bride againe,
Bring home the triumph of our victory,
Bring home with you the glory of her gaine,
With joyance bring her and with jollity.
Never had man more joyfull day then this,
Whom heaven would heape with blis.
Make feast therefore now al this live long day,
This day for ever to me holy is,
Poure out the wine without restraint or stay,
Poure not by cups, but by the belly full,
Poure out to all that wull,
And sprinkle all the postes and wals with wine,
That they may sweat, and drunken be withall.
Crowne ye God Bacchus with a coronall,
And Hymen also crowne with wreathes of vine,
And let the Graces daunce unto the rest;
For they can doo it best:
The whiles the maydens doe theyr carroll sing,
To which the woods shal answer and theyr eccho ring.

Ring ye the bels, ye yong men of the towne,
And leave your wonted labours for this day:
This day is holy; doe ye write it downe,
That ye for ever it remember may.
This day the sunne is in his chiefest hight,
With Barnaby the bright,
From whence declining daily by degrees,
He somewhat loseth of his heat and light,
When once the Crab behind his back he sees.
But for this time it ill ordained was,
To chose the longest day in all the yeare,
And shortest night, when longest fitter weare:
Yet never day so long, but late would passe.
Ring ye the bels, to make it weare away,
And bonefiers make all day,

And daunce about them, and about them sing
That al the woods may answer, and your eccho ring.

Ah when will this long weary day have end,
And lende me leave to come unto my love?
How slowly do the houres theyr numbers spend?
How slowly does sad Time his feathers move?
Hast thee O fayrest Planet to thy home
Within the Westerne fome:
Thy tyred steedes long since have need of rest.
Long though it be, at last I see it gloome,
And the bright evening star with golden creast
Appeare out of the East.
Fayre childe of beauty, glorious lampe of love
That al the host of heaven in rankes doost lead,
And guydest lovers through the nightes dread,
How chearefully thou lookest from above,
And seemst to laugh atweene thy twinkling light
As joying in the sight
Of these glad many which for joy doe sing,
That al the woods them answer and their eccho ring.

Now ceasse ye damsels your delights forepast;
Enough is it, that all the day was youres:
Now day is doen, and night is nighing fast:
Now bring the Bryde into the brydall boures.
Now night is come, now soone her disaray,
And in her bed her lay;
Lay her in lillies and in violets,
And silken courteins over her display,
And odourd sheetes, and Arras coverlets.
Behold how goodly my faire love does ly
In proud humility;
Like unto Maia, when as Jove her tooke,
In Tempe, lying on the flowry gras,
Twixt sleepe and wake, after she weary was,
With bathing in the Acidalian brooke.
Now it is night, ye damsels may be gon,
And leave my love alone,
And leave likewise your former lay to sing:
The woods no more shal answere, nor your eccho ring.

40

Now welcome night, thou night so long expected,
That long daies labour doest at last defray,
And al my cares, which cruell love collected,
Hast sumd in one, and cancelled for aye:
Spread thy broad wing over my love and me,
That no man may us see,
And in thy sable mantle us enwrap,
From feare of perrill and foule horror free.
Let no false treason seeke us to entrap,
Nor any dread disquiet once annoy
The safety of our joy:
But let the night be calme and quietsome,
Without tempestuous storms or sad afray:
Lyke as when Jove with fayre Alcmena lay,
When he begot the great Tirynthian groome:
Or lyke as when he with thy selfe did lie,
And begot Majesty.
And let the mayds and yongmen cease to sing:
Ne let the woods them answer, nor theyr eccho ring.

Let no lamenting cryes, nor dolefull teares,
Be heard all night within nor yet without:
Ne let false whispers, breeding hidden feares,
Breake gentle sleepe with misconceived dout.
Let no deluding dreames, nor dreadful sights
Make sudden sad affrights;
Ne let housefyres, nor lightnings helpelesse harmes,
Ne let the Pouke, nor other evill sprights,
Ne let mischivous witches with theyr charmes,
Ne let hob Goblins, names whose sence we see not,
Fray us with things that be not.
Let not the shriech Oule, nor the Storke be heard:
Nor the night Raven that still deadly yels,
Nor damned ghosts cald up with mighty spels,
Nor griesly vultures make us once affeard:
Ne let the unpleasant Quyre of Frogs still croking
Make us to wish theyr choking.
Let none of these theyr drery accents sing;
Ne let the woods them answer, nor theyr eccho ring.

But let stil Silence trew night watches keepe,
That sacred peace may in assurance rayne,

And tymely sleep, when it is tyme to sleepe,
May poure his limbs forth on your pleasant playne,
The whiles an hundred little winged loves,
Like divers fethered doves,
Shall fly and flutter round about your bed,
And in the secret darke, that none reproves,
Their prety stealthes shal worke, and snares shal spread
To filch away sweet snatches of delight,
Conceald through covert night.
Ye sonnes of Venus, play your sports at will,
For greedy pleasure, carelesse of your toyes,
Thinks more upon her paradise of joyes,
Then what ye do, albe it good or ill.
Al night therefore attend your merry play,
For it will soone be day:
Now none doth hinder you, that say or sing,
Ne will the woods now answer, nor your eccho ring.

Who is the same, which at my window peepes?
Or whose is that faire face, that shines so bright,
Is it not Cinthia, she that never sleepes,
But walkes about high heaven al the night?
O fayrest goddesse, do thou not envy
My love with me to spy.
For thou likewise didst love, though now unthought,
And for a fleece of woll, which privily,
The Latmian shephard once unto thee brought,
His pleasures with thee wrought.
Therefore to us be favourable now;
And sith of wemens labours thou hast charge,
And generation goodly dost enlarge,
Encline thy will t'effect our wishfull vow,
And the chast wombe informe with timely seed,
That may our comfort breed:
Till which we cease our hopefull hap to sing,
Ne let the woods us answere, nor our eccho ring.

And thou great Juno, which with awful might
The lawes of wedlock still dost patronise,
And the religion of the faith first plight
With sacred rites hast taught to solemnise:

And eeke for comfort often called art
Of women in their smart,
Eternally bind thou this lovely band,
And all thy blessings unto us impart.
And thou glad Genius, in whose gentle hand,
The bridale bowre and geniall bed remaine,
Without blemish or staine,
And the sweet pleasures of theyr loves delight
With secret ayde doest succour and supply,
Till they bring forth the fruitfull progeny,
Send us the timely fruit of this same night.
And thou fayre Hebe, and thou Hymen free,
Grant that it may so be.
Til which we cease your further prayse to sing,
Ne any woods shal answer, nor your eccho ring.

And ye high heavens, the temple of the gods,
In which a thousand torches flaming bright
Doe burne, that to us wretched earthly clods,
In dreadful darknesse lend desired light;
And al ye powers which in the same remayne,
More then we men can fayne,
Poure out your blessing on us plentiously,
And happy influence upon us raine,
That we may raise a large posterity,
Which from the earth, which they may long possesse,
With lasting happinesse,
Up to your haughty pallaces may mount,
And for the guerdon of theyr glorious merit
May heavenly tabernacles there inherit,
Of blessed Saints for to increase the count.
So let us rest, sweet love, in hope of this,
And cease till then our tymely joyes to sing,
The woods no more us answer, nor our eccho ring.

Song made in lieu of many ornaments,
With which my love should duly have bene dect,
Which cutting off through hasty accidents,

43

Ye would not stay your dew time to expect,
But promist both to recompens,
Be unto her a goodly ornament,
And for short time an endlesse moniment.

PHILIP SIDNEY
(1554–86)

Loving in truth, and fain in verse my love to show,
   That the dear she might take some pleasure of my pain;
   Pleasure might cause her read, reading might make her know;
   Knowledge might pity win, and pity grace obtain,
I sought fit words to paint the blackest face of woe,
   Studying inventions fine, her wits to entertain,
   Oft turning others' leaves to see if thence would flow
   Some fresh and fruitful showers upon my sun-burned brain.
But words came halting forth, wanting invention's stay;
   Invention, nature's child, fled step-dame Study's blows;
   And others' feet still seemed but strangers in my way.
Thus, great with child to speak, and helpless in my throes,
   Biting my truant pen, beating myself for spite,
   "Fool," said my muse to me, "look in thy heart and write."

*

Fly, fly, my friends. I have my death wound, fly;
   See there that boy, that murthering boy, I say,
   Who, like a thief hid in dark bush, doth lie
   Till bloody bullet get him wrongful prey.
So tyrant he no fitter place could spy,
   Nor so fair level in so secret stay,
   As that sweet black which veils the heavenly eye;
   There himself with his shot he close doth lay.
Poor passenger, pass now thereby I did,
   And stayed, pleased with the prospect of the place,
   While that black hue from me the bad guest hid;
But straight I saw motions of lightning grace,
   And then descried the glistering of his dart,
   But ere I could fly thence, it pierced my heart.

*

Your words, my friend, (right healthful caustics) blame
   My young mind marred, whom love doth windlass so
   That mine own writings like bad servants show
   My wits, quick in vain thoughts, in virtue lame;
That Plato I read for nought but if he tame
   Such coltish years; that to my birth I owe
   Nobler desires, lest else that friendly foe,
   Great expectation, wear a train of shame.
For since mad March great promise made of me,
   If now the May of my years much decline,
   What can be hoped my harvest time will be?
"Sure," you say well, "Your wisdom's golden mine,
   Dig deep with learning's spade." Now tell me this,
   Hath this world aught so fair as Stella is?

*

With how sad steps, O Moon, thou climbest the skies!
   How silently, and with how wan a face.
   What, may it be that even in heavenly place
   That busy archer his sharp arrows tries?
Sure, if that long-with-love-acquainted eyes
   Can judge of love, thou feelest a lover's case;
   I read it in thy looks; thy languished grace
   To me, that feel the like, thy state descries.
Then, even of fellowship, O Moon, tell me,
   Is constant love deemed there but want of wit?
   Are beauties there as proud as here they be?
Do they above love to be loved, and yet
   Those lovers scorn whom that love doth possess?
   Do they call virtue there ungratefulness?

*

Come, Sleep! O Sleep, the certain knot of peace,
   The baiting place of wit, the balm of woe,
   The poor man's wealth, the prisoner's release,
   The indifferent judge between the high and low;
With shield of proof shield me from out the prease
   Of those fierce darts despair at me doth throw;

46

Oh make in me those civil wars to cease;
    I will good tribute pay, if thou do so.
Take thou of me smooth pillows, sweetest bed,
    A chamber deaf to noise and blind to light,
    A rosy garland and a weary head;
And if these things as being thine by right,
    Move not thy heavy grace, thou shalt in me,
    Livelier than elsewhere Stella's image see.

*

"Who is it that this dark night
Underneath my window plaineth?"
    "It is one who from thy sight
    Being (ah) exiled, disdaineth
    Every other vulgar light."

"Why, alas, and are you he?
Be not yet those fancies changed?"
    "Dear, when you find change in me,
    Though from me you be estranged,
    Let my change to ruin be."

"Well, in absence this will die;
Leave to see and leave to wonder."
    "Absence sure will help, if I
    Can learn how myself to sunder
    From what in my heart doth lie."

"But time will these thoughts remove:
Time doth work what no man knoweth."
    "Time doth as the subject prove;
    With time still the affection groweth
    In the faithful turtle dove."

"What if you new beauties see?
Will not they stir new affection?"
    "I will think they pictures be,
    Image-like, of saint's perfection,
    Poorly counterfeiting thee."

"But your reason's purest light
Bids you leave such minds to nourish."
 "Dear, do reason no such spite;
 Never doth thy beauty flourish
 More than in my reason's sight."

"But the wrongs love bears will make
Love at length leave undertaking."
 "No, the more fools it do shake,
 In a ground of so firm making,
 Deeper still they drive the stake."

"Peace, I think that some give ear;
Come no more lest I get anger."
 "Bliss, I will my bliss forbear;
 Fearing, sweet, you to endanger;
 But my soul shall harbor there."

"Well, begone, begone, I say,
Lest that Argus' eyes perceive you."
 "Oh, unjust fortune's sway,
 Which can make me thus to leave you,
 And from louts to run away."

*

Ring out your bells, let mourning shows be spread,
 For Love is dead!
  All love is dead, infected
  With plague of deep disdain;
  Worth, as nought worth, rejected,
  And Faith fair scorn doth gain.
   From so ungrateful fancy,
   From such a female frenzy,
   From them that use men thus,
   Good Lord, deliver us!

Weep, neighbours, weep; do you not hear it said
 That Love is dead?
  His death-bed, peacock's folly;
  His winding-sheet is shame;

His will false-seeming holy;
His sole executor blame.
  From so ungrateful fancy,
  From such a female frenzy,
  From them that use men thus,
  Good Lord, deliver us!

Let dirge be sung, and trentals rightly read,
  For Love is dead!
  Sir Wrong his tomb ordaineth,
  My mistress' marble heart,
  Which epitaph containeth
  "Her eyes were once his dart."
  From so ungrateful fancy,
  From such a female frenzy,
  From them that use men thus,
  Good Lord, deliver us!

Alas, I lie; rage hath this error bred;
  Love is not dead.
  Love is not dead, but sleepeth
  In her unmatched mind,
  Where she his counsel keepeth,
  Till due deserts she find.
  Therefore from so vile fancy,
  To call such wit a frenzy,
  Who Love can temper thus,
  Good Lord, deliver us!

*

Leave me, O Love, which reachest but to dust;
And thou, my mind, aspire to higher things;
Grow rich in that which never taketh rust,
Whatever fades but fading pleasure brings.
Draw in thy beams, and humble all thy might
To that sweet yoke where lasting freedoms be;
Which breaks the clouds and opens forth the light,
That doth both shine and give us sight to see.
Oh, take fast hold; let that light be thy guide

In this small course which birth draws out to death,
And think how evil becometh him to slide,
Who seeketh heaven, and comes of heavenly breath.
  Then farewell, world; thy uttermost I see;
  Eternal Love, maintain thy life in me.

GEORGE PEELE
(ca. 1557–96)

When as the rye reach to the chin,
And chopcherry, chopcherry ripe within,
Strawberries swimming in the cream,
And schoolboys playing in the stream;
Then oh, then oh, then oh my true love said,
Till that time come again,
She could not live a maid.

*

Hot sun, cool fire, tempered with sweet air,
Black shade, fair nurse, shadow my white hair;
Shine, sun; burn, fire; breathe, air, and ease me.
Black shade, fair nurse, shroud me and please me.
Shadow, my sweet nurse, keep me from burning,
Make not my glad cause cause of mourning.
    Let not my beauty's fire
    Inflame unstaid desire,
    Nor pierce any bright eye
    That wandereth lightly.

ROBERT GREENE
(1558–92)

Sitting by a river side,
Where a silent stream did glide,
Muse I did of many things,
That the mind in quiet brings.
I gan think how some men deem
Gold their god, and some esteem
Honour is the chief content,
That to man in life is lent;
And some others do contend,
Quiet none, like to a friend.
Others hold, there is no wealth
Compared to a perfect health;
Some man's mind in quiet stands,
When he is lord of many lands.
But I did sigh, and said all this
Was but a shade of perfect bliss.
And in my thoughts I did approve,
Nought so sweet as is true love.
Love 'twixt lovers passeth these,
When mouth kisseth and heart 'grees,
With folded arms and lips meeting,
Each soul another sweetly greeting;
For by the breath the soul fleeteth,
And soul with soul in kissing meeteth.
If love be so sweet a thing,
That such happy bliss doth bring,
Happy is love's sugared thrall,
But unhappy maidens all,
Who esteem your virgin's blisses
Sweeter than a wife's sweet kisses.
No such quiet to the mind,
As true love with kisses kind;

But if a kiss prove unchaste,
Then is true love quite disgraced.
Though love be sweet, learn this of me:
No love sweet but honesty.

SAMUEL DANIEL
(1562–1619)

Fair is my love, and cruel as she is fair.
Her brow shades frowns, although her eyes are sunny,
Her smiles are lightning, though her pride despair,
And her disdains are gall, her favours honey.
A modest maid, decked with a blush of honour,
Whose feet do tread green paths of youth and love,
The wonder of all eyes that look upon her,
Sacred on earth, designed a saint above.
Chastity and beauty, which were deadly foes,
Live reconciled friends within her brow;
And had she pity to conjoin with those,
Then who had heard the plaints I utter now?
For had she not been fair, and thus unkind,
My Muse had slept, and none had known my mind.

*

When winter snows upon thy sable hairs,
And frost of age hath nipped thy beauties near;
When dark shall seem thy day that never clears,
And all lies withered that was held so dear;
Then take this picture which I here present thee,
Limned with a pencil not all unworthy.
Here see the gifts that God and nature lent thee;
Here read thyself, and what I suffered for thee.
This may remain thy lasting monument,
Which happily posterity may cherish;
These colours with thy fading are not spent;
These may remain when thou and I shall perish.
If they remain, then thou shalt live thereby;
They will remain, and so thou canst not die.

*

Care-charmer Sleep, son of the sable night,
Brother to death, in silent darkness born,
Relieve my languish and restore the light;
With dark forgetting of my care, return,
And let the day be time enough to mourn
The shipwreck of my ill-adventured youth.
Let waking eyes suffice to wail their scorn
Without the torment of the night's untruth.
Cease, dreams, the images of day-desires,
To model forth the passions of the morrow.
Never let rising sun approve you liars,
To add more grief to aggravate my sorrow.
Still let me sleep, embracing clouds in vain,
And never wake to feel the day's disdain.

ULYSSES AND THE SIREN

Siren: Come, worthy Greek, Ulysses, come,
          Possess these shores with me;
          The winds and seas are troublesome,
          And here we may be free.
             Here may we sit and view their toil
          That travail on the deep,
          And joy the day in mirth the while,
          And spend the night in sleep.

Ulysses: Fair nymph, if fame or honour were
          To be attained with ease,
          Then would I come and rest with thee,
          And leave such toils as these.
             But here it dwells, and here must I
          With danger seek it forth;
          To spend the time luxuriously
          Becomes not men of worth.

Siren: Ulysses, oh be not deceived
          With that unreal name;
          This honour is a thing conceived,

And rests on others' fame.
  Begotten only to molest
Our peace, and to beguile
The best thing of our life, our rest,
And give us up to toil.

Ulysses: Delicious nymph, suppose there were
Nor honour nor report,
Yet manliness would scorn to wear
The time in idle sport.
  For toil doth give a better touch,
To make us feel our joy;
And ease finds tediousness, as much
As labour, yields annoy.

Siren: Then pleasure likewise seems the shore
Whereto tends all your toil,
Which you forego to make it more,
And perish oft the while.
  Who may disport them diversly,
Find never tedious day,
And ease may have variety
As well as action may.

Ulysses: But natures of the noblest frame
These toils and dangers please,
And they take comfort in the same,
As much as you in ease,
  And with the thought of actions past,
Are recreated still;
When pleasure leaves a touch at last
To show that it was ill.

Siren: That doth opinion only cause
That's out of custom bred,
Which makes us many other laws
Than ever nature did.
  No widows wail for our delights,
Our sports are without blood;
The world, we see, by warlike wights
Receives more hurt than good.

56

Ulysses:	But yet the state of things require
	These motions of unrest,
	And these great spirits of high desire
	Seem born to turn them best,
	To purge the mischiefs that increase
	And all good order mar;
	For oft we see a wicked peace
	To be well changed for war.

Siren:	Well, well, Ulysses, then I see
	I shall not have thee here,
	And therefore I will come to thee,
	And take my fortunes there.
	I must be won that cannot win,
	Yet lost were I not won;
	For beauty hath created been
	To undo, or be undone.

MICHAEL DRAYTON
(1563–1631)

How many paltry, foolish, painted things,
That now in coaches trouble every street,
Shall be forgotten, whom no poet sings,
Ere they be well wrapped in their winding sheet!
Where I to thee eternity shall give,
When nothing else remaineth of these days,
And queens hereafter shall be glad to live
Upon the alms of thy superfluous praise.
Virgins and matrons reading these my rhymes
Shall be so much delighted with thy story
That they shall grieve they lived not in these times,
To have seen thee, their sex's only glory.
  So shalt thou fly above the vulgar throng,
  Still to survive in my immortal song.

*

If he from heaven that filched the living fire
Condemned by Jove to endless torment be,
I greatly marvel how you still go free,
That far beyond Prometheus did aspire.
The fire he stole, although of heavenly kind,
Which from above he craftily did take,
Of lifeless clods us living men to make,
He did bestow in temper of the mind.
But you broke into heaven's immortal store,
Where virtue, honour, wit, and beauty lay;
Which, taking thence, you have escaped away,
Yet stand as free as ere you did before,
  Yet old Prometheus punished for his rape.
  Thus poor thieves suffer, when the greater 'scape.

*

Since there's no help, come let us kiss and part.
Nay, I have done, you get no more of me;
And I am glad, yea glad with all my heart
That thus so cleanly I myself can free.
Shake hands forever, cancel all our vows,
And when we meet at any time again,
Be it not seen in either of our brows
That we one jot of former love retain.
Now at the last gasp of love's latest breath,
When, his pulse failing, passion speechless lies;
When faith is kneeling by his bed of death,
And innocence is closing up his eyes;
    Now if thou wouldst, when all have given him over,
    From death to life thou mightest him yet recover.

TO THE VIRGINIAN VOYAGE

You brave heroic minds,
Worthy your country's name,
    That honour still pursue,
    Go, and subdue,
Whilst loitering hinds
Lurk here at home with shame.

Britons, you stay too long;
Quickly aboard bestow you,
    And with a merry gale
    Swell your stretched sail,
With vows as strong
As the winds that blow you.

Your course securely steer,
West and by south forth keep,
    Rocks, lee shores, nor shoals,
    When Aeolus scowls,
You need not fear,
So absolute the deep.

And cheerfully at sea,
Success you still entice,
    To get the pearl and gold,
    And ours to hold,
Virginia,
Earth's only paradise,

Where nature hath in store
Fowl, venison, and fish,
    And the fruitfullest soil
    Without your toil
Three harvests more,
All greater than your wish.

And the ambitious vine
Crowns with his purple mass,
    The cedar reaching high
    To kiss the sky,
The cypress, pine,
And useful sassafras.

To whose the golden age
Still nature's laws doth give,
    No other cares that tend,
    But them to defend
From winter's age,
That long there doth not live.

Whenas the luscious smell
Of that delicious land,
    Above the seas that flows,
    The clear wind throws,
Your hearts to swell
Approaching the dear strand,

In kenning of the shore,
Thanks to God first given,
    O you, the happiest men,
    Be frolic then,
Let cannons roar,
Frighting the wide heaven.

And in regions far
Such heroes bring ye forth
  As those from whom we came,
  And plant our name
Under that star
Not known unto our north.

And as there plenty grows
Of laurel everywhere,
  Apollo's sacred tree,
  You it may see
A poet's brows
To crown, that may sing there.

Thy voyages attend,
Industrious Hakluyt,
  Whose reading shall enflame
  Men to seek fame,
And much commend
To after times thy wit.

CHRISTOPHER MARLOWE
(1564–93)

from HERO AND LEANDER

On Hellespont, guilty of true-loves' blood,
In view and opposite, two cities stood,
Sea-borderers, disjoined by Neptune's might;
The one Abydos, the other Sestos hight.
At Sestos Hero dwelt; Hero the fair,
Whom young Apollo courted for her hair
And offered as a dower his burning throne,
Where she should sit for men to gaze upon.
The outside of her garments were of lawn,
The lining purple silk, with gilt stars drawn,
Her wide sleeves green, and bordered with a grove,
Where Venus in her naked glory strove
To please the careless and disdainful eyes
Of proud Adonis, that before her lies;
Her kirtle blue, whereon was many a stain,
Made with the blood of wretched lovers slain.
Upon her head she wore a myrtle wreath,
From whence her veil reached to the ground beneath.
Her veil was artificial flowers and leaves,
Whose workmanship both man and beast deceives.
Many would praise the sweet smell as she passed,
When 'twas the odor which her breath forth cast;
And there for honey, bees have sought in vain,
And, beat from thence, have lighted there again.
About her neck hung chains of pebble-stone,
Which, lightened by her neck, like diamonds shone.
She wore no gloves, for neither sun nor wind
Would burn or parch her hands, but to her mind
Or warm or cool them, for they took delight
To play upon those hands, they were so white.
Buskins of shells all silvered used she,
And branched with blushing coral to the knee,

Where sparrows perched, of hollow pearl and gold,
Such as the world would wonder to behold.
Those with sweet water oft her handmaid fills,
Which, as she went, would chirrup through the bills.
Some say, for her the fairest Cupid pined,
And looking in her face, was strooken blind.
But this is true: so like was one the other,
As he imagined Hero was his mother,
And oftentimes into her bosom flew,
About her naked neck his bare arms threw,
And laid his childish head upon her breast,
And with still panting rocked, there took his rest.
So lovely fair was Hero, Venus' nun,
As Nature wept, thinking she was undone,
Because she took more from her than she left
And of such wondrous beauty her bereft.
Therefore, in sign her treasure suffered wrack,
Since Hero's time hath half the world been black.
Amorous Leander, beautiful and young,
Whose tragedy divine Musaeus sung,
Dwelt at Abydos; since him dwelt there none
For whom succeeding times make greater moan.
His dangling tresses that were never shorn,
Had they been cut and unto Colchos borne,
Would have allured the venturous youth of Greece
To hazard more than for the Golden Fleece.
Fair Cynthia wished his arms might be her sphere;
Grief makes her pale, because she moves not there.
His body was as straight as Circe's wand;
Jove might have sipped out nectar from his hand.
Even as delicious meat is to the taste,
So was his neck in touching, and surpassed
The white of Pelops' shoulder. I could tell ye
How smooth his breast was, and how white his belly,
And whose immortal fingers did imprint
That heavenly path, with many a curious dint,
That runs along his back. But my rude pen
Can hardly blazon forth the loves of men,
Much less of powerful gods; let it suffice
That my slack Muse sings of Leander's eyes.

. . . .

What is it now but mad Leander dares?
"O Hero, Hero!" thus he cried full oft,
And then he got him to a rock aloft,
Where, having spied her tower, long stared he on 't
And prayed the narrow toiling Hellespont
To part in twain, that he might come and go,
But still the rising billows answered "No."
With that he stripped him to the ivory skin
And crying, "Love, I come!" leapt lively in.
Whereat the sapphire-visaged god grew proud
And made his capering Triton sound aloud,
Imagining that Ganymede, displeased,
Had left the heavens, therefore on him seized.
Leander strived; the waves about him wound,
And pulled him to the bottom, where the ground
Was strewed with pearl, and in low coral groves
Sweet singing mermaids sported with their loves
On heaps of heavy gold and took great pleasure
To spurn in careless sort the shipwrack treasure.
For here the stately azure palace stood
Where kingly Neptune and his train abode.
The lusty god embraced him, called him love,
And swore he never should return to Jove.
But when he knew it was not Ganymede,
For under water he was almost dead,
He heaved him up, and looking on his face,
Beat down the bold waves with his triple mace,
Which mounted up, intending to have kissed him,
And fell in drops like tears because they missed him.
Leander being up, began to swim,
And, looking back, saw Neptune follow him.
Whereat aghast, the poor soul gan to cry,
"Oh let me visit Hero ere I die!"
The god put Helle's bracelet on his arm,
And swore the sea should never do him harm.
He clapped his plump cheeks, with his tresses played,
And, smiling wantonly, his love bewrayed.
He watched his arms, and as they opened wide,
At every stroke betwixt them he would slide
And steal a kiss, and then run out and dance
And, as he turned, cast many a lustful glance
And threw him gaudy toys to please his eye,

And dive into the water and there pry
Upon his breast, his thighs, and every limb,
And up again and close beside him swim
And talk of love. Leander made reply,
"You are deceived; I am no woman, I."
Thereat smiled Neptune and then told a tale
How that a shepherd, sitting in a vale,
Played with a boy so fair and kind
As, for his love, both earth and heaven pined;
That of the cooling river durst not drink
Lest water nymphs should pull him from the brink.
And when he sported in the fragrant lawns,
Goat-footed satyrs and up-staring fawns
Would steal him thence. Ere half this tale was done
"Ay me!" Leander cried, "the enamoured sun
That now should shine on Thetis' glassy bower
Descends upon my radiant Hero's tower.
Oh, that these tardy arms of mine were wings!"
And as he spake, upon the waves he springs.
Neptune was angry that he gave no ear,
And in his heart revenging malice bare.
He flung at him his mace, but as it went
He called it in, for love made him repent.
The mace returning back, his own hand hit,
As meaning to be venged for darting it.
When this fresh bleeding wound Leander viewed,
His color went and came, as if he rued
The grief which Neptune felt. In gentle breasts
Relenting thoughts, remorse, and pity rests,
And who have hard hearts and obdurate minds
But vicious, harebrained, and illiterate hinds?
The god, seeing him with pity to be moved,
Thereon concluded that he was beloved.
(Love is too full of faith, too credulous,
With folly and false hope deluding us.)
Wherefore Leander's fancy to surprise,
To the rich ocean for gifts he flies.
'Tis wisdom to give much; a gift prevails
When deep persuading oratory fails.
By this Leander, being near the land,
Cast down his weary feet and felt the sand.
Breathless albeit he were, he rested not

Till to the solitary tower he got.
And knocked and called; at which celestial noise,
The longing heart of Hero much more joys
Than nymphs and shepherds when the timbrel rings,
Or crooked dolphin when the sailor sings.
She stayed not for her robes, but straight arose
And, drunk with gladness, to the door she goes;
Where, seeing a naked man, she screeched for fear
(Such sights as this to tender maids are rare),
And ran into the dark herself to hide.
Rich jewels in the dark are soonest spied.
Unto her was he led, or rather drawn
By those white limbs which sparkled through the lawn.
The nearer that he came, the more she fled,
And, seeking refuge, slipped into her bed.
Whereon Leander sitting, thus began,
Through numbing cold, all feeble, faint, and wan:
"If not for love, yet, love, for pity's sake
Me in thy bed and maiden bosom take;
At least vouchsafe these arms some little room,
Who, hoping to embrace thee, cheerly swum.
This head was beat with many a churlish billow,
And therefore let it rest upon thy pillow."
Herewith affrighted Hero shrunk away
And in her lukewarm place Leander lay,
Whose lively heat, like fire from heaven fet,
Would animate gross clay, and higher set
The drooping thoughts of base declining souls
Than dreary Mars' carousing nectar bowls.
His hands he cast upon her like a snare;
She, overcome with shame and sallow fear,
Like chaste Diana when Actaeon spied her,
Being suddenly betrayed, dived down to hide her,
And as her silver body downward went,
With both her hands she made the bed a tent,
And in her own mind thought herself secure,
O'ercast with dim and darksome coverture.
And now she lets him whisper in her ear,
Flatter, entreat, promise, protest, and swear.
Yet ever as he greedily assayed
To touch those dainties, she the harpy played,
And every limb did, as a soldier stout,

Defend the fort and keep the foeman out.
For though the rising ivory mount he scaled,
Which is with azure circling lines empaled,
Much like a globe (a globe may I term this
By which love sails to regions full of bliss),
Yet there with Sisyphus he toiled in vain
Till gentle parley did the truce obtain.
Wherein Leander on her quivering breast,
Breathless spoke something and sighed out the rest;
Which so prevailed, as he, with small ado,
Enclosed her in his arms and kissed her, too.
And every kiss to her was as a charm
And to Leander as a fresh alarm.
So that the truce was broke, and she, alas,
Poor silly maiden, at his mercy was.
Love is not full of pity, as men say,
But deaf and cruel, where he means to prey.
Even as a bird which in our hands we wring
Forth plungeth and oft flutters with her wing,
She trembling strove; this strife of hers, like that
Which made the world, another world begat
Of unknown joy. Treason was in her thought,
And cunningly to yield herself she sought.
Seeming not won, yet won she was, at length.
(In such wars women use but half their strength.)
Leander now, like Theban Hercules,
Entered the orchard of the Hesperides,
Whose fruit none rightly can describe but he
That pulls or shakes it from the golden tree.
And now she wished this night were never done,
And sighed to think upon the approaching sun,
For much it grieved her that the bright daylight
Should know the pleasure of this blessed night,
And them like Mars and Erycine displayed,
Both in each other's arms chained as they laid.
Again she knew not how to frame her look
Or speak to him who in a moment took
That which so long, so charily she kept.
And fain by stealth away she would have crept,
And to some corner secretly have gone,
Leaving Leander in the bed alone.
But as her naked feet were whipping out,

67

He on the sudden clinged her so about
That mermaidlike unto the floor she slid:
One half appeared, the other half was hid.
Thus near the bed she blushing stood upright,
And from her countenance behold ye might
A kind of twilight break, which through the hair,
As from an orient cloud, gleams here and there,
And round about the chamber this false morn
Brought forth the day before the day was born.
So Hero's ruddy cheek Hero betrayed,
And her all naked to his sight displayed,
Whence his admiring eyes more pleasure took
Than Dis on heaps of gold fixing his look.
By this Apollo's golden harp began
To sound forth music to the Ocean,
Which watchful Hesperus no sooner heard
But he the day's bright-bearing car prepared,
And ran before, as harbinger of light,
And with his flaring beams mocked ugly Night,
Till she, o'ercome with anguish, shame and rage,
Danged down to hell her loathsome carriage.

WILLIAM SHAKESPEARE
(1564–1616)

When forty winters shall besiege thy brow,
And dig deep trenches in thy beauty's field,
Thy youth's proud livery, so gazed on now,
Will be a tattered weed, of small worth held:
Then, being asked where all thy beauty lies,
Where all the treasure of thy lusty days,
To say, within thine own deep-sunken eyes,
Were an all-eating shame, and thriftless praise.
How much more praise deserved thy beauty's use,
If thou couldst answer, "This fair child of mine
Shall sum my count, and make my old excuse,"
Proving his beauty by succession thine!
   This were to be new made when thou art old,
   And see thy blood warm when thou feelst it cold.

*

Those hours, that with gentle work did frame
The lovely gaze where every eye doth dwell,
Will play the tyrants to the very same,
And that unfair, which fairly doth excel:
For never-resting Time leads Summer on
To hideous Winter, and confounds him there;
Sap checked with frost, and lusty leaves quite gone,
Beauty o'er-snowed and bareness every where:
Then, were not Summer's distillation left,
A liquid prisoner pent in walls of glass,
Beauty's effect with beauty were bereft,
Nor it, nor no remembrance what it was:
   But flowers distilled, though they with Winter meet,
   Leese but their show: their substance still lives sweet.

*

When I do count the clock that tells the time,
And see the brave day sunk in hideous night;
When I behold the violet past prime,
And sable curls all silvered o'er with white;
When lofty trees I see barren of leaves,
Which erst from heat did canopy the herd,
And Summer's green all girded up in sheaves,
Borne on the bier with white and bristly beard;
Then, of thy beauty do I question make,
That thou among the wastes of time must go,
Since sweets and beauties do themselves forsake,
And die as fast as they see others grow;
  And nothing 'gainst Time's scythe can make defence,
  Save breed, to brave him when he takes thee hence.

*

Oh that you were yourself! But, love, you are
No longer yours than you yourself here live:
Against this coming end you should prepare,
And your sweet semblance to some other give:
So should that beauty which you hold in lease
Find no determination: then you were
Yourself again, after yourself's decease,
When your sweet issue your sweet form should bear.
Who lets so fair a house fall to decay,
Which husbandry in honour might uphold
Against the stormy gusts of Winter's day,
And barren rage of death's eternal cold?
  Oh, none but unthrifts. Dear my love, you know,
  You had a father: let your son say so.

*

No more be grieved at that which thou hast done:
Roses have thorns, and silver fountains mud;
Clouds and eclipses stain both moon and sun,
And loathsome canker lives in sweetest bud.
All men make faults, and even I in this,
Authorising thy trespass with compare;

Myself corrupting, salving thy amiss,
Excusing thy sins more than thy sins are:
For to thy sensual fault I bring in sense,
Thy adverse party is thy advocate,
And 'gainst myself a lawful plea commence.
Such civil war is in my love and hate,
    That I an accessary needs must be
    To that sweet thief which sourly robs from me.

*

When I consider every thing that grows
Holds in perfection but a little moment;
That this huge stage presenteth naught but shows,
Whereon the stars in secret influence comment;
When I perceive that men as plants increase,
Cheered and checked even by the selfsame sky,
Vaunt in their youthful sap, at height decrease,
And wear their brave state out of memory;
Then the conceit of this inconstant stay
Sets you most rich in youth before my sight,
Where wasteful time debateth with decay,
To change your day of youth to sullied night,
    And, all in war with Time, for love of you,
    As he takes from you, I engraft you new.

*

Shall I compare thee to a summer's day?
Thou art more lovely and more temperate:
Rough winds do shake the darling buds of May,
And summer's lease hath all too short a date.
Sometime too hot the eye of heaven shines,
And often is his gold complexion dimmed,
And every fair from fair sometime declines,
By chance, or nature's changing course, untrimmed;
But thy eternal summer shall not fade,
Nor lose possession of that fair thou owest;
Nor shall death brag thou wanderest in his shade,
When in eternal lines to time thou growest.
    So long as men can breathe, or eyes can see,
    So long lives this, and this gives life to thee.

*

When in disgrace with fortune and men's eyes,
I all alone beweep my outcast state,
And trouble deaf heaven with my bootless cries,
And look upon myself, and curse my fate,
Wishing me like to one more rich in hope,
Featured like him, like him with friends possessed,
Desiring this man's art, and that man's scope,
With what I most enjoy contented least;
Yet in these thoughts myself almost despising,
Haply I think on thee, and then my state
(Like to the lark at break of day arising
From sullen earth) sings hymns at heaven's gate:
  For thy sweet love remembered such wealth brings,
  That then I scorn to change my state with kings.

*

When to the sessions of sweet silent thought
I summon up remembrance of things past,
I sigh the lack of many a thing I sought,
And with old woes new wail my dear time's waste:
Then can I drown an eye, unused to flow,
For precious friends hid in death's dateless night,
And weep afresh love's long-since-cancelled woe,
And moan the expense of many a vanished sight.
Then can I grieve at grievances fore gone,
And heavily from woe to woe tell o'er
The sad account of fore-bemoaned moan,
Which I new pay, as if not paid before:
  But if the while I think on thee, dear friend,
  All losses are restored, and sorrows end.

*

Full many a glorious morning have I seen
Flatter the mountain tops with sovereign eye,
Kissing with golden face the meadows green,
Gilding pale streams with heavenly alchemy;

Anon permit the basest clouds to ride
With ugly rack on his celestial face,
And from the forlorn world his visage hide,
Stealing unseen to west with this disgrace.
Even so my sun one early morn did shine,
With all triumphant splendour on my brow;
But out, alack! He was but one hour mine,
The region cloud hath masked him from me now.
   Yet him for this my love no whit disdaineth;
   Suns of the world may stain when heaven's sun staineth.

*

Not marble, nor the gilded monuments
Of princes, shall outlive this powerful rhyme;
But you shall shine more bright in these contents
Than unswept stone, besmeared with sluttish time.
When wasteful war shall statues overturn,
And broils root out the work of masonry,
Nor Mars his sword, nor war's quick fire shall burn
The living record of your memory.
'Gainst death and all-oblivious enmity
Shall you pace forth; your praise shall still find room
Even in the eyes of all posterity,
That wear this world out to the ending doom.
   So, till the judgment that yourself arise,
   You live in this, and dwell in lovers' eyes.

*

Like as the waves make towards the pebbled shore,
So do our minutes hasten to their end;
Each changing place with that which goes before.
In sequent toil all forwards do contend.
Nativity, once in the main of light,
Crawls to maturity, wherewith being crowned,
Crooked eclipses 'gainst his glory fight,
And Time that gave doth now his gift confound.
Time doth transfix the flourish set on youth,
And delves the parallels in beauty's brow;
Feeds on the rarities of Nature's truth,

And nothing stands but for his scythe to mow.
   And yet to times in hope my verse shall stand,
   Praising thy worth, despite his cruel hand.

*

No longer mourn for me, when I am dead,
Than you shall hear the surly sullen bell
Give warning to the world that I am fled
From this vile world, with vilest worms to dwell:
Nay, if you read this line, remember not
The hand that writ it; for I love you so,
That I in your sweet thoughts would be forgot,
If thinking on me then should make you woe.
Oh, if (I say) you look upon this verse,
When I perhaps compounded am with clay,
Do not so much as my poor name rehearse,
But let your love even with my life decay;
   Lest the wise world should look into your moan,
   And mock you with me after I am gone.

*

That time of year thou mayst in me behold,
When yellow leaves, or none, or few, do hang
Upon those boughs which shake against the cold,
Bare ruined choirs, where late the sweet birds sang.
In me thou seest the twilight of such day
As after sunset fadeth in the west,
Which by and by black night doth take away,
Death's second self, that seals up all in rest:
In me thou seest the glowing of such fire,
That on the ashes of his youth doth lie,
As the deathbed whereon it must expire,
Consumed with that which it was nourished by.
   This thou perceivest, which makes thy love more strong
   To love that well which thou must leave ere long.

*

Was it the proud full sail of his great verse,
Bound for the prize of all too precious you,
That did my ripe thoughts in my brain inherse,
Making their tomb the womb wherein they grew?
Was it his spirit, by spirits taught to write
Above a mortal pitch, that struck me dead?
No, neither he, nor his compeers by night
Giving him aid, my verse astonished:
He, nor that affable familiar ghost,
Which nightly gulls him with intelligence,
As victors of my silence cannot boast.
I was not sick of any fear from thence;
    But when your countenance filled up his line,
    Then lacked I matter; that enfeebled mine.

*

They that have power to hurt, and will do none,
That do not do the thing they most do show,
Who, moving others, are themselves as stone,
Unmoved, cold, and to temptation slow;
They rightly do inherit heaven's graces,
And husband nature's riches from expense;
They are the lords and owners of their faces,
Others but stewards of their excellence.
The summer's flower is to the summer sweet,
Though to itself it only live and die;
But if that flower with base infection meet,
The basest weed outbraves his dignity;
    For sweetest things turn sourest by their deeds:
    Lilies that fester smell far worse than weeds.

*

How like a winter hath my absence been
From thee, the pleasure of the fleeting year!
What freezings have I felt, what dark days seen,
What old December's bareness everywhere!
And yet this time removed was summer's time;
The teeming autumn, big with rich increase,

75

Bearing the wanton burthen of the prime,
Like widowed wombs after their lords' decease:
Yet this abundant issue seemed to me
But hope of orphans, and unfathered fruit;
For summer and his pleasures wait on thee,
And, thou away, the very birds are mute;
　Or, if they sing, 'tis with so dull a cheer,
　That leaves look pale, dreading the winter's near.

*

From you have I been absent in the spring,
When proud-pied April, dressed in all his trim,
Hath put a spirit of youth in every thing,
That heavy Saturn laughed and leaped with him:
Yet nor the lays of birds, nor the sweet smell
Of different flowers in odour and in hue,
Could make me any summer's story tell,
Or from their proud lap pluck them where they grew:
Nor did I wonder at the lily's white,
Nor praise the deep vermilion in the rose;
They were but sweet, but figures of delight,
Drawn after you; you pattern of all those.
　Yet seemed it winter still, and, you away,
　As with your shadow I with these did play.

*

When in the chronicle of wasted time
I see descriptions of the fairest wights,
And beauty making beautiful old rhyme
In praise of ladies dead and lovely knights,
Then, in the blazon of sweet beauty's best,
Of hand, of foot, of lip, of eye, of brow,
I see their antique pen would have expressed
Even such a beauty as you master now.
So all their praises are but prophecies
Of this our time, all you prefiguring;
And for they looked but with divining eyes,
They had not skill enough your worth to sing:

For we, which now behold these present days,
Have eyes to wonder, but lack tongues to praise.

*

Let me not to the marriage of true minds
Admit impediments: love is not love
Which alters when it alteration finds,
Or bends with the remover to remove:
Oh no; it is an ever-fixed mark,
That looks on tempests, and is never shaken;
It is the star to every wandering bark,
Whose worth's unknown, although his height be taken.
Love's not time's fool, though rosy lips and cheeks
Within his bending sickle's compass come;
Love alters not with his brief hours and weeks,
But bears it out even to the edge of doom.
    If this be error, and upon me proved,
    I never writ, nor no man ever loved.

*

The expense of spirit in a waste of shame
Is lust in action; and till action, lust
Is perjured, murtherous, bloody, full of blame,
Savage, extreme, rude, cruel, not to trust;
Enjoyed no sooner but despised straight;
Past reason hunted, and no sooner had,
Past reason hated, as a swallowed bait,
On purpose laid to make the taker mad;
Mad in pursuit, and in possession so;
Had, having, and in quest to have, extreme;
A bliss in proof, and proved, a very woe;
Before, a joy proposed; behind, a dream.
    All this the world well knows, yet none knows well
    To shun the heaven that leads men to this hell.

*

My mistress' eyes are nothing like the sun;
Coral is far more red than her lips' red:

If snow be white, why then her breasts are dun;
If hairs be wires, black wires grow on her head.
I have seen roses damasked, red and white,
But no such roses see I in her cheeks;
And in some perfumes is there more delight
Than in the breath that from my mistress reeks.
I love to hear her speak; yet well I know
That music hath a far more pleasing sound:
I grant I never saw a goddess go;
My mistress, when she walks, treads on the ground.
   And yet, by heaven, I think my love as rare
   As any she belied with false compare.

*

When my love swears that she is made of truth,
I do believe her, though I know she lies,
That she might think me some untutored youth,
Unlearned in the world's false subtleties.
Thus vainly thinking that she thinks me young,
Although she knows my days are past the best,
Simply I credit her false-speaking tongue:
On both sides thus is simple truth suppressed.
But wherefore says she not she is unjust?
And wherefore say not I that I am old?
Oh, love's best habit is in seeming trust,
And age in love loves not to have years told:
   Therefore I lie with her, and she with me,
   And in our faults by lies we flattered be.

*

My love is as a fever, longing still
For that which longer nurseth the disease;
Feeding on that which doth preserve the ill,
The uncertain sickly appetite to please.
My reason, the physician to my love,
Angry that his prescriptions are not kept,
Hath left me, and I desperate now approve,
Desire is death, which physic did except.
Past cure I am, now reason is past care,

78

And frantic mad with ever more unrest:
My thoughts and my discourse as madmen's are,
At random from the truth vainly expressed;
   For I have sworn thee fair, and thought thee bright,
   Who art as black as hell, as dark as night.

SPRING

When daisies pied and violets blue
   And lady-smocks all silver-white
And cuckoo-buds of yellow hue
   Do paint the meadows with delight,
The cuckoo then, on every tree,
Mocks married men; for thus sings he,
         Cuckoo;
Cuckoo, cuckoo. Oh, word of fear,
Unpleasing to a married ear!

When shepherds pipe on oaten straws,
   And merry larks are ploughmen's clocks,
When turtles tread, and rooks, and daws,
   And maidens bleach their summer smocks,
The cuckoo then, on every tree,
Mocks married men; for thus sings he,
         Cuckoo;
Cuckoo, cuckoo. Oh, word of fear,
Unpleasing to a married ear!

WINTER

When icicles hang by the wall,
   And Dick the shepherd blows his nail,
And Tom bears logs into the hall,
   And milk comes frozen home in pail,
When blood is nipped, and ways be foul,
Then nightly sings the staring owl,
         Tu-who;

Tu-whit, tu-who—a merry note,
While greasy Joan doth keel the pot.

When all aloud the wind doth blow,
  And coughing drowns the parson's saw,
And birds sit brooding in the snow,
  And Marian's nose looks red and raw,
When roasted crabs hiss in the bowl,
Then nightly sings the staring owl,
                    Tu-who;
Tu-whit, tu-who—a merry note,
While greasy Joan doth keel the pot.

ARIEL'S SONG

Come unto these yellow sands,
  And then take hands:
Curtsied when you have, and kissed—
  The wild waves whist—
Foot it featly here and there,
And, sweet sprites, the burden bear.
    Hark, hark!
              Bow, wow!
  The watchdogs bark:
              Bow, wow!
  Hark, hark! I hear
The strain of strutting Chanticleer:
          Cock-a-diddle-dow.

*

Full fathom five thy father lies;
  Of his bones are coral made.
Those are pearls that were his eyes.
  Nothing of him that doth fade,
  But doth suffer a sea-change
  Into something rich and strange.
  Sea-nymphs hourly ring his kneel:
              Ding-dong.
Hark! now I hear them; ding-dong, bell.

THE PHOENIX AND THE TURTLE

Let the bird of loudest lay,
On the sole Arabian tree,
Herald sad and trumpet be,
To whose sound chaste wings obey.

But thou shrieking harbinger,
Foul precurrer of the fiend,
Augur of the fever's end,
To this troop come thou not near.

From this session interdict
Every fowl of tyrant wing,
Save the eagle, feathered king;
Keep the obsequy so strict.

Let the priest in surplice white,
That defunctive music can,
Be the death-divining swan,
Lest the requiem lack his right.

And thou, treble-dated crow,
That thy sable gender makest
With the breath thou givest and takest,
'Mongst our mourners shalt thou go.

Here the anthem doth commence;
Love and constancy is dead;
Phoenix and the turtle fled
In a mutual flame from hence.

So they loved, as love in twain
Had the essence but in one;
Two distincts, division none;
Number there in love was slain.

Hearts remote, yet not asunder;
Distance, and no space was seen
'Twixt the turtle and his queen;
But in them it were a wonder.

So between them love did shine,
That the turtle saw his right
Flaming in the phoenix' sight;
Either was the other's mine.

Property was thus appalled,
That the self was not the same;
Single nature's double name
Neither two nor one was called.

Reason, in itself confounded,
Saw division grow together;
To themselves yet either-neither,
Simple were so well compounded:

That it cried, "How true a twain
Seemeth this concordant one!
Love hath reason, reason none,
If what parts can so remain."

Whereupon it made this threne
To the phoenix and the dove,
Co-supremes and stars of love;
As chorus to their tragic scene.

THRENOS

Beauty, truth, and rarity,
Grace in all simplicity,
Here enclosed in cinders lie.

Death is now the phoenix' nest;
And the turtle's loyal breast
To eternity doth rest,

Leaving no posterity;
'Twas not their infirmity,
It was married chastity.

Truth may seem, but cannot be;
Beauty brag, but 'tis not she;
Truth and beauty buried be.

To this urn let those repair,
That are either true or fair;
For these dead birds sigh a prayer.

THOMAS CAMPION
(1567–1620)

My sweetest Lesbia, let us live and love,
And though the sager sort our deeds reprove,
Let us not weigh them; heaven's great lamps do dive
Into their west, and straight again revive;
But soon as once set is our little light,
Then must we sleep one ever-during night.

If all would lead their lives in love like me,
Then bloody swords and armor should not be;
No drum nor trumpet peaceful sleeps should move,
Unless alarm came from the camp of love.
But fools do live, and waste their little light,
And seek with pain their ever-during night.

When timely death my life and fortune ends,
Let not my hearse be vexed with mourning friends.
But let all lovers, rich in triumph, come
And with sweet pastimes grace my happy tomb,
And Lesbia, close up thou my little light,
And crown with love my ever-during night.

*

Now winter nights enlarge
The number of their hours,
And clouds their storms discharge
Upon the airy towers.

Let now the chimneys blaze
And cups o'erflow with wine;
Let well-tuned words amaze
With harmony divine.

Now yellow waxen lights
Shall wait on honey love,
While youthful revels, masks, and courtly sights
Sleep's leaden spells remove.

This time doth well dispense
With lovers' long discourse;
Much speech hath some defence,
Though beauty no remorse.

All do not all things well.
Some measures comely tread;
Some knotted riddles tell;
Some poems smoothly read.

The summer hath his joys,
And winter his delights;
Though love and all his pleasures are but toys,
They shorten tedious nights.

THOMAS NASHE
(1567–1601)

Adieu, farewell, earth's bliss;
This world uncertain is;
Fond are life's lustful joys;
Death proves them all but toys;
None from his darts can fly;
I am sick, I must die.
    Lord, have mercy on us!

Rich men, trust not in wealth;
Gold cannot buy you health;
Physic himself must fade;
All things to end are made.
The plague full swift goes by;
I am sick, I must die.
    Lord, have mercy on us!

Beauty is but a flower
Which wrinkles will devour;
Brightness falls from the air;
Queens have died young and fair;
Dust hath closed Helen's eye.
I am sick, I must die.
    Lord, have mercy on us!

Strength stoops unto the grave,
Worms feed on Hector brave;
Swords may not fight with fate,
Earth still holds ope her gate.
"Come, come," the bells do cry.
I am sick, I must die.
    Lord, have mercy on us!

Wit with his wantonness
Tasteth death's bitterness.

Hell's executioner
Hath no ears for to hear
What vain art can reply.
I am sick, I must die.
  Lord, have mercy on us!

Haste, therefore, each degree,
To welcome destiny;
Heaven is our heritage,
Earth but a player's stage;
Mount we unto the sky.
I am sick, I must die.
  Lord, have mercy on us!

JOHN DONNE
(1572–1631)

THE INDIFFERENT

I can love both fair and brown;
Her whom abundance melts, and her whom want betrays;
Her who loves loneness best, and her who masks and plays;
Her whom the country formed, and whom the town;
Her who believes, and her who tries;
Her who still weeps with spongy eyes;
And her who is dry cork, and never cries.
I can love her, and her, and you and you,
I can love any, so she be not true.

Will no other vice content you?
Will it not serve your turn to do as did your mothers?
Have you old vices spent, and now would find out others?
Or doth a fear, that men are true, torment you?
Oh we are not; be not you so,
Let me, and do you, twenty know.
Rob me, but bind me not, and let me go.
Must I, who came to travail thorough you,
Grow your fixed subject, because you are true?

Venus heard me sigh this song,
And by love's sweetest part, variety, she swore,
She heard not this till now; and that it should be so no more.
She went, examined, and returned ere long,
And said, "Alas, some two or three
Poor heretics in love there be,
Which think to establish dangerous constancy.
But I have told them, 'Since you will be true,
You shall be true to them, who are false to you.' "

*

Go, and catch a falling star,
  Get with child a mandrake root,
Tell me where all past years are,
  Or who cleft the Devil's foot;
Teach me to hear mermaids singing,
  Or to keep off envy's stinging,
        And find
        What wind
Serves to advance an honest mind.

If thou beest born to strange sights,
  Things invisible to see,
Ride ten thousand days and nights,
  Till age snow white hairs on thee;
Thou, when thou returnest, wilt tell me
All strange wonders that befell thee,
        And swear
        No where
Lives a woman true and fair.

If thou findest one, let me know;
  Such a pilgrimage were sweet,
Yet do not; I would not go,
  Though at next door we might meet.
Though she were true, when you met her,
And last, till you write your letter,
        Yet she
        Will be
False, ere I come to two or three.

THE BAIT

Come live with me, and be my love,
And we will some new pleasures prove
Of golden sands, and crystal brooks,
With silken lines and silver hooks.

There will the river whispering run
Warmed by thy eyes, more than the sun.
And there the enamoured fish will stay,
Begging themselves they may betray.

When thou wilt swim in that live bath,
Each fish, which every channel hath,
Will amorously to thee swim,
Gladder to catch thee, than thou him.

If thou, to be so seen, beest loth,
By sun or moon, thou darkenest both,
And if myself have leave to see,
I need not their light, having thee.

Let others freeze with angling reeds,
And cut their legs with shells and weeds,
Or treacherously poor fish beset,
With strangling snare, or windowy net;

Let coarse bold hands, from slimy nest
The bedded fish in banks outwrest,
Or curious traitors, sleavesilk flies
Bewitch poor fishes' wandering eyes.

For thee, thou needest no such deceit,
For thou thyself art thine own bait;
That fish that is not catched thereby,
Alas, is wiser far than I.

THE GOOD MORROW

I wonder by my troth, what thou and I
Did till we loved. Were we not weaned till then,
But sucked on country pleasures, childishly?
Or snorted we in the seven sleepers' den?
'Twas so; but this, all pleasures fancies be.
If ever any beauty I did see,
Which I desired and got, 'twas but a dream of thee.

And now good morrow to our waking souls,
Which watch not one another out of fear;
For love, all love of other sights controls,
And makes one little room an everywhere.
Let sea-discoverers to new worlds have gone,
Let maps to others, worlds on worlds have shown,
Let us possess one world; each hath one, and is one.

My face in thine eye, thine in mine appears,
And true plain hearts do in the faces rest,
Where can we find two fitter hemispheres
Without sharp north, without declining west?
What ever dies, was not mixed equally;
If our two loves be one, or, thou and I
Love so alike, that none do slacken, none can die.

THE FLEA

Mark but this flea, and mark in this,
How little that which thou deniest me is.
Me it sucked first, and now sucks thee,
And in this flea our two bloods mingled be;
Confess it, this cannot be said
A sin, nor shame, or loss of maidenhead,
  Yet this enjoys before it woo,
  And pampered swells with one blood made of two,
  And this, alas, is more than we would do.

Oh stay; three lives in one flea spare,
Where we almost, nay more than married are.
This flea is you and I, and this
Our marriage bed, and marriage temple is;
Though parents grudge, and you, we're met,
And cloistered in these living walls of jet.
  Though use make you apt to kill me,
  Let not to this, self-murder added be,
  And sacrilege; three sins in killing three.

Cruel and sudden, hast thou since
Purpled thy nail in blood of innocence?
In what could this flea guilty be,
Except in that drop which it sucked from thee?
Yet thou triumphest, and sayest that thou
Findest not thyself, nor me the weaker now.
   'Tis true; then learn how false fears be;
   Just so much honour, when thou yieldest to me,
   Will waste, as this flea's death took life from thee.

THE SUN RISING

      Busy old fool, unruly Sun,
      Why dost thou thus,
Through windows, and through curtains call on us?
Must to thy motions lovers' seasons run?
      Saucy pedantic wretch! go chide
      Late schoolboys, and sour prentices;
   Go tell court-huntsmen, that the King will ride;
   Call country ants to harvest offices.
Love, all alike, no season knows, nor clime,
Nor hours, days, months, which are the rags of time.

      Thy beams, so reverend, and strong
      Why shouldst thou think?
I could eclipse and cloud them with a wink,
But that I would not lose her sight so long.
      If her eyes have not blinded thine,
      Look, and tomorrow late, tell me,
   Whether both the Indias of spice and mine
   Be where thou leftest them, or lie here with me.
Ask for those kings whom thou sawest yesterday,
And thou shalt hear all here in one bed lay.

      She is all states, and all princes I.
      Nothing else is.
Princes do but play us; compared to this,
All honour's mimic; all wealth alchemy.
      Thou, Sun, art half as happy as we,

In that the world's contracted thus;
    Thine age asks ease, and since thy duties be
    To warm the world, that's done in warming us.
Shine here to us, and thou art everywhere;
This bed thy centre is, these walls thy sphere.

THE ECSTASY

Where, like a pillow on a bed,
    A pregnant bank swelled up, to rest
The violet's reclining head,
    Sat we two, one another's best.
Our hands were firmly cemented
    With a fast balm, which thence did spring;
Our eye-beams twisted, and did thread
    Our eyes upon one double string;
So to intergraft our hands, as yet,
    Was all our means to make us one;
And pictures in our eyes to get
    Was all our propagation.
As 'twixt two equal armies, fate
    Suspends uncertain victory,
Our souls (which to advance their state,
    Were gone out) hung 'twixt her and me.
And whilst our souls negotiate there,
    We like sepulchral statues lay;
All day the same our postures were,
    And we said nothing all the day.
If any, so by love refined,
    That he soul's language understood,
And by good love were grown all mind,
    Within convenient distance stood,
He (though he knew not which soul spake
    Because both meant, both spake the same)
Might thence a new concoction take,
    And part far purer than he came.
This ecstasy doth unperplex
    (We said) and tell us what we love.
We see by this, it was not sex,

93

We see, we saw not what did move;
But as all several souls contain
   Mixture of things, they know not what,
Love, these mixed souls doth mix again,
   And makes both one, each this and that.
A single violet transplant,
   The strength, the colour, and the size
(All which before was poor and scant)
   Redoubles still, and multiplies.
When love, with one another so
   Interinanimates two souls,
That abler soul, which thence doth flow,
   Defects of loneliness controls.
We then, who are this new soul, know
   Of what we are composed and made,
For the atomies of which we grow,
   Are souls, whom no change can invade.
But oh, alas, so long, so far
   Our bodies why do we forbear?
They are ours, though they are not we, we are
   The intelligences, they the sphere.
We owe them thanks, because they thus
   Did us to us, at first convey,
Yielded their forces, sense, to us,
   Nor are dross to us, but allay.
On man heaven's influence works not so,
   But that it first imprints the air;
So soul into the soul may flow,
   Though it to body first repair.
As our blood labours to beget
   Spirits as like souls as it can,
Because such fingers need to knit
   That subtle knot, which makes us man;
So must pure lovers' souls descend
   To affections, and to faculties,
Which sense may reach and apprehend,
   Else a great prince in prison lies.
To our bodies turn we then, that so
   Weak men on love revealed may look;
Love's mysteries in souls do grow,
   But yet the body is his book.
And if some lover, such as we,

Have heard this dialogue of one,
    Let him still mark us, he shall see
        Small change, when we're to bodies gone.

THE CANONISATION

For God's sake hold your tongue, and let me love!
    Or chide my palsy, or my gout,
My five grey hairs, or ruined fortune flout;
    With wealth your state, your mind with arts improve;
        Take you a course, get you a place,
        Observe his Honour, or his Grace,
Or the King's real, or his stamped face
    Contemplate; what you will, approve,
    So you will let me love.

Alas, alas, who's injured by my love?
    What merchant's ships have my sighs drowned?
Who says my tears have overflowed his ground?
    When did my colds a forward spring remove?
        When did the heats which my veins fill
        Add one more to the plaguey bill?
Soldiers find wars, and lawyers find out still
    Litigious men, which quarrels move,
    Though she and I do love.

Call us what you will, we are made such by love;
    Call her one, me another fly;
We are tapers too, and at our own cost die.
    And we in us find the eagle and the dove;
        The phoenix riddle hath more wit
        By us; we two being one, are it.
So to one neutral thing both sexes fit.
    We die and rise the same, and prove
    Mysterious by this love.

We can die by it, if not live by love,
    And if unfit for tombs and hearse
Our legend be, it will be fit for verse;

95

And if no piece of chronicle we prove,
　　We'll build in sonnets pretty rooms;
　　As well a well-wrought urn becomes
The greatest ashes, as half-acre tombs.
　　And by these hymns, all shall approve
　　Us canonized for love,

And thus invoke us: "You whom reverend love
　　Made one another's hermitage;
You, to whom love was peace, that now is rage;
　　Who did the whole world's soul contract, and drove
　　　　Into the glasses of your eyes
　　　　(So made such mirrors, and such spies,
That they did all to you epitomise),
　　Countries, towns, courts: beg from above
　　A pattern of your love!"

＊

Sweetest love, I do not go
　　For weariness of thee,
Nor in hope the world can show
　　A fitter love for me;
　　　　But since that I
Must die at last, 'tis best
To use my self in jest,
　　Thus by feigned deaths to die.

Yesternight the sun went hence,
　　And yet is here today;
He hath no desire nor sense,
　　Nor half so short a way.
　　　　Then fear not me,
But believe that I shall make
Speedier journeys, since I take
　　More wings and spurs than he.

Oh how feeble is man's power,
　　That if good fortune fall,
Cannot add another hour,
　　Nor a lost hour recall!

But come bad chance,
And we join to it our strength,
And we teach it art and length,
Itself o'er us to advance.

When thou sighest, thou sighest no wind,
But sighest my soul away;
When thou weepest, unkindly kind,
My life's blood doth decay.
It cannot be
That thou lovest me, as thou sayest;
If in thine my life thou waste,
Thou art the best of me.

Let not thy divining heart
Forethink me any ill;
Destiny may take thy part,
And may thy fears fulfill.
But think that we
Are but turned aside to sleep;
They who one another keep
Alive, ne'er parted be.

A VALEDICTION: FORBIDDING MOURNING

As virtuous men pass mildly away,
And whisper to their souls to go,
Whilst some of their sad friends do say,
"The breath goes now," and some say, "No!"

So let us melt, and make no noise,
No tear-floods, nor sigh-tempests move;
'Twere profanation of our joys
To tell the laity our love.

Moving of the earth brings harms and fears;
Men reckon what it did and meant,
But trepidation of the spheres,
Though greater far, is innocent.

Dull sublunary lovers' love
   (Whose soul is sense) cannot admit
Absence, because it doth remove
   Those things which elemented it.

But we by a love, so much refined,
   That our selves know not what it is,
Inter-assured of the mind,
   Care less, eyes, lips, and hands to miss.

Our two souls, therefore, which are one,
   Though I must go, endure not yet
A breach, but an expansion,
   Like gold to airy thinness beat.

If they be two, they are two so
   As stiff twin compasses are two;
Thy soul the fixed foot, makes no show
   To move, but doth, if the other do.

And though it in the centre sit,
   Yet when the other far doth roam,
It leans and hearkens after it,
   And grows erect, as that comes home.

Such wilt thou be to me, who must
   Like the other foot, obliquely run;
Thy firmness makes my circle just,
   And makes me end where I begun.

A LECTURE UPON THE SHADOW

Stand still, and I will read to thee
A lecture, love, in love's philosophy.
    These three hours that we have spent,
    Walking here, two shadows went
Along with us, which we ourselves produced;
But now the sun is just above our head,
    We do those shadows tread,
    And to brave clearness all things are reduced.

So whilst our infant loves did grow,
    Disguises did, and shadows, flow,
    From us, and our care; but now 'tis not so.

That love hath not attained the highest degree,
    Which is still diligent lest others see.

Except our loves at this noon stay,
We shall new shadows make the other way.
        As the first were made to blind
        Others, these which come behind
Will work upon ourselves, and blind our eyes.
If our loves faint, and westwardly decline,
        To me thou, falsely, thine,
        And I to thee mine actions shall disguise.
    The morning shadows wear away,
    But these grow longer all the day,
    But oh, love's day is short, if love decay.

Love is a growing, or full constant light;
And his first minute after noon is night.

TWICKENHAM GARDEN

Blasted with sighs, and surrounded with tears,
    Hither I come to seek the spring,
    And at mine eyes and at mine ears,
Receive such balms, as else cure everything;
    But oh, self-traitor, I do bring
The spider love, which transubstantiates all,
    And can convert manna to gall;
And that this place may thoroughly be thought
    True paradise, I have the serpent brought.

'Twere wholesomer for me, that winter did
    Benight the glory of this place,
    And that a grave frost did forbid
These trees to laugh, and mock me to my face.
    But that I may not this disgrace

Endure, nor yet leave loving, love, let me
    Some senseless piece of this place be;
Make me a mandrake, so I may groan here,
    Or a stone fountain weeping out my year.

Hither with crystal vials, lovers come,
    And take my tears, which are love's wine,
And try your mistress' tears at home,
For all are false, that taste not just like mine.
    Alas, hearts do not in eyes shine,
Nor can you more judge woman's thoughts by tears,
    Than by her shadow, what she wears.
O perverse sex, where none is true but she,
    Who's therefore true, because her truth kills me.

A NOCTURNAL UPON ST. LUCY'S DAY, BEING THE SHORTEST DAY

'Tis the year's midnight, and it is the day's,
Lucy's, who scarce seven hours herself unmasks;
    The sun is spent, and now his flasks
    Send forth light squibs, no constant rays;
        The world's whole sap is sunk;
The general balm the hydroptic earth hath drunk,
Whither, as to the bed's feet, life is shrunk,
Dead and interred. Yet all these seem to laugh
Compared with me, who am their epitaph.

Study me then, you who shall lovers be
At the next world, that is, at the next spring;
    For I am every dead thing
    In whom love wrought new alchemy.
        For his art did express
A quintessence even from nothingness,
From dull privations, and lean emptiness
He ruined me, and I am re-begot
Of absence, darkness, death; things which are not.

100

All others, from all things, draw all that's good:
Life, soul, form, spirit; whence they being have.
   I, by love's limbeck, am the grave
    Of all that's nothing. Oft a flood
      Have we two wept, and so
Drowned the whole world, us two; oft did we grow
To be two chaoses, when we did show
Care to aught else; and often absences
Withdrew our souls, and made us carcasses.

But I am by her death (which word wrongs her)
Of the first nothing the elixir grown;
   Were I a man, that I were one,
    I needs must know; I should prefer
      If I were any beast,
Some ends, some means; yea plants, yea stones detest
And love; all, all some properties invest;
If I an ordinary nothing were,
As shadow, a light, and body must be here.

But I am none; nor will my sun renew.
You lovers, for whose sake the lesser sun
   At this time to the Goat is run
    To fetch new lust, and give it you,
      Enjoy your summer all;
Since she enjoys her long night's festival,
Let me prepare towards her, and let me call
This hour her vigil, and her eve, since this
Both the year's, and the day's deep midnight is.

THE COMPARISON

As the sweet sweat of roses in a still,
As that which from chafed musk cat's pores doth trill,
As the almighty balm of the early east,
Such are the sweat drops of my mistress' breast.
And on her neck her skin such lustre sets,
They seem no sweat drops, but pearl carcanets.
Rank sweaty froth thy mistress' brow defiles,

Like spermatic issue of ripe menstruous boils;
Or like that scum, which, by need's lawless law
Enforced, Sanserra's starved men did draw
From parboiled shoes, and boots, and all the rest
Which were with any sovereign fatness blessed,
And like vile lying stones in saffroned tin,
Or warts, or weals, they hang upon her skin.
Round as the world's her head, on every side,
Like to the fatal ball which fell on Ide,
Or that whereof God had such jealousy,
As for the ravishing thereof we die.
Thy head is like a rough-hewn statue of jet,
Where marks for eye, nose, mouth, are yet scarce set;
Like the first Chaos, or flat seeming face
Of Cynthia, when the earth's shadows her embrace;
Like Proserpine's white beauty-keeping chest,
Or Jove's best fortune's urn, is her fair breast.
Thine's like worm-eaten trunks, clothed in seal's skin,
Or grave, that's dust without, and stink within.
And like that slender stalk, at whose end stands
The woodbine quivering, are her arms and hands.
Like rough-barked elmboughs, or the russet skin
Of men late scourged for madness, or for sin,
Like sun-parched quarters on the city gate,
Such is thy tanned skin's lamentable state.
And like a bunch of ragged carrots stand
The short swollen fingers of thy gouty hand.
Then like the chemic's masculine equal fire,
Which in the limbeck's warm womb doth inspire
Into the earth's worthless dirt a soul of gold,
Such cherishing heat her best-loved part doth hold.
Thine's like the dread mouth of a fired gun,
Or like hot liquid metals newly run
Into clay moulds; or like to that Etna
Where round about the grass is burnt away.
Are not your kisses then as filthy, and more,
As a worm sucking an envenomed sore?
Doth not thy fearful hand in feeling quake,
As one which gathering flowers, still fears a snake?
Is not your last act harsh, and violent,
As where a plough a stony ground doth rent?
So kiss good turtles, so devoutly nice

Are priests in handling reverent sacrifice,
And such in searching wounds the surgeon is
As we, when we embrace, or touch, or kiss.
Leave her, and I will leave comparing thus;
She, and comparisons are odious.

THE AUTUMNAL

No spring, nor summer beauty hath such grace,
    As I have seen in one autumnal face.
Young beauties force our love, and that's a rape,
    This doth but counsel, yet you cannot scape.
If 'twere a shame to love, here 'twere no shame;
    Affection here takes reverence's name.
Were her first years the Golden Age; that's true,
    But now she's gold oft tried, and ever new.
That was her torrid and inflaming time,
    This is her tolerable tropic clime.
Fair eyes, who asks more heat than comes from hence,
    He in a fever wishes pestilence.
Call not these wrinkles graves; if graves they were,
    They were Love's graves; for else he is nowhere.
Yet lies not Love dead here, but here doth sit
    Vowed to this trench, like an anchorite.
And here, till hers, which must be his death, come,
    He doth not dig a grave, but build a tomb.
Here dwells he, though he sojourn everywhere,
    In progress, yet his standing house is here.
Here, where still evening is; not noon, nor night;
    Where no voluptuousness, yet all delight.
In all her words, unto all hearers fit,
    You may at revels, you at council, sit.
This is Love's timber, youth his underwood;
    There he, as wine in June, enrages blood,
Which then comes seasonabliest, when our taste
    And appetite to other things is past.
Xerxes' strange Lydian love, the platan tree,
    Was loved for age, none being so large as she,
Or else because, being young, nature did bless

Her youth with age's glory, barrenness.
If we love things long sought, age is a thing
   Which we are fifty years in compassing.
If transitory things, which soon decay,
   Age must be loveliest at the latest day.
But name not winter-faces, whose skin's slack;
   Lank, as an unthrift's purse; but a soul's sack;
Whose eyes seek light within, for all here's shade;
   Whose mouths are holes, rather worn out, than made;
Whose every tooth to a several place is gone,
   To vex their souls at Resurrection.
Name not these living death's-heads unto me,
   For these, not ancient, but antiques be.
I hate extremes; yet I had rather stay
   With tombs, than cradles, to wear out a day.
Since such love's natural station is, may still
   My love descend, and journey down the hill,
Not panting after growing beauties, so,
   I shall ebb out with them, who homeward go.

TO HIS MISTRESS GOING TO BED

Come, Madam, come; all rest my powers defy;
Until I labour, I in labour lie.
The foe oft-times having the foe in sight,
Is tired with standing though they never fight.
Off with that girdle, like heaven's zone glittering,
But a far fairer world encompassing.
Unpin that spangled breastplate which you wear,
That the eyes of busy fools may be stopped there.
Unlace yourself, for that harmonious chime
Tells me from you, that now 'tis your bed time.
Off with that happy busk, which I envy,
That still can be, and still can stand so nigh.
Your gown going off, such beauteous state reveals,
As when from flowery meads the hill's shadow steals.
Off with that wiry coronet and show
The hairy diadem which on you doth grow.
Now off with those shoes, and then safely tread

In this love's hallowed temple, this soft bed.
In such white robes heaven's angels used to be
Received by men; thou angel bringest with thee
A heaven like Mahomet's paradise; and though
Ill spirits walk in white, we easily know
By this these angels from an evil sprite;
Those set our hairs, but these our flesh upright.

License my roving hands, and let them go
Before, behind, between, above, below!
O my America! my new found land!
My kingdom, safeliest when with one man manned!
My mine of precious stones, my empery,
How blessed am I in this discovering thee!
To enter in these bonds, is to be free;
Then where my hand is set, my seal shall be.

Full nakedness, all joys are due to thee.
As souls unbodied, bodies unclothed must be,
To taste whole joys. Gems which you women use
Are as Atlanta's balls, cast in men's views,
That when a fool's eye lighteth on a gem,
His earthly soul may covet theirs, not them.
Like pictures, or like books' gay coverings made
For laymen, are all women thus arrayed;
Themselves are mystic books, which only we
Whom their imputed grace will dignify
Must see revealed. Then since I may know,
As liberally, as to a midwife, show
Thyself! Cast all, yea, this white linen hence;
Here is no penance, much less innocence.

To teach thee, I am naked first. Why, then,
What needst thou have more covering than a man?

*

Thou hast made me; and shall thy work decay?
Repair me now, for now mine end doth haste;
I run to death, and death meets me as fast,
And all my pleasures are like yesterday.
I dare not move my dim eyes any way,
Despair behind, and death before doth cast
Such terror; and my feeble flesh doth waste

By sin in it, which it towards hell doth weigh.
Only thou art above, and when towards thee
By thy leave I can look, I rise again;
But our old subtle foe so tempteth me,
That not one hour I can myself sustain.
Thy Grace may wing me to prevent his art,
And thou like adamant draw mine iron heart.

*

O my black soul! Now thou art summoned
By sickness, death's herald, and champion;
Thou art like a pilgrim, which abroad hath done
Treason, and durst not turn to whence he is fled;
Or like a thief, which till death's doom be read,
Wisheth himself delivered from prison,
But damned and haled to execution,
Wisheth that still he might be imprisoned.
Yet grace, if thou repent, thou canst not lack.
But who shall give thee that grace to begin?
Oh, make thyself with holy mourning black,
And red with blushing, as thou art with sin!
Or wash thee in Christ's blood, which hath this might
That being red, it dyes red souls to white.

*

I am a little world made cunningly
Of elements, and an angelic sprite,
But black sin hath betrayed to endless night
My world's both parts, and, oh, both parts must die.
You which beyond that heaven which was most high
Have found new spheres, and of new land can write,
Pour new seas in mine eyes, that so I might
Drown my world with my weeping earnestly;
Or wash it if it must be drowned no more.
But oh it must be burnt; alas, the fire
Of lust and envy burnt it heretofore,
And made it fouler; let their flames retire,
And burn me, O Lord, with a fiery zeal
Of thee and thy house, which doth in eating heal.

This is my play's last scene; here heavens appoint
My pilgrimage's last mile; and my race
Idly, yet quickly run, hath this last pace;
My span's last inch, my minute's latest point,
And gluttonous death will instantly unjoint
My body and soul, and I shall sleep a space;
But my ever-waking part shall see that face,
Whose fear already shakes my every joint.
Then, as my soul to heaven, her first seat, takes flight,
And earth-born body in the earth shall dwell,
So fall my sins, that all may have their right,
To where they are bred, and would press me, to hell.
Impute me righteous, thus purged of evil,
For thus I leave the world, the flesh, and devil.

*

At the round earth's imagined corners, blow
Your trumpets, angels, and arise, arise
From death, you numberless infinities
Of souls, and to your scattered bodies go;
All whom the flood did, and fire shall o'erthrow;
All whom war, dearth, age, agues, tyrannies,
Despair, law, chance, hath slain; and you whose eyes
Shall behold God, and never taste death's woe.
But let them sleep, Lord, and me mourn a space;
For, if above all these, my sins abound,
'Tis late to ask abundance of thy grace
When we are there. Here on this lowly ground,
Teach me how to repent; for that's as good
As if thou hadst sealed my pardon with thy blood.

*

Death be not proud, though some have called thee
Mighty and dreadful, for thou art not so,
For those whom thou thinkest thou dost overthrow
Die not, poor Death, nor yet canst thou kill me;

From rest and sleep, which but thy pictures be,
Much pleasure; then from thee, much more must flow,
And soonest our best men with thee do go,
Rest of their bones, and soul's delivery.
Thou art slave to fate, chance, kings, and desperate men,
And dost with poison, war and sickness dwell,
And poppy, or charms can make us sleep as well,
And better than thy stroke. Why swellest thou then?
One short sleep past, we wake eternally,
And death shall be no more. Death, thou shalt die.

*

What if this present were the world's last night?
Mark in my heart, O soul, where thou dost dwell,
The picture of Christ crucified, and tell
Whether his countenance can thee affright.
Tears in his eyes quench the amazing light;
Blood fills his frowns, which from his pierced head fell;
And can that tongue adjudge thee unto hell,
Which prayed forgiveness for his foes' fierce spite?
No, no. But as in my idolatry
I said to all my profane mistresses,
Beauty, of pity, foulness only is
A sign of rigour, so I say to thee,
To wicked spirits are horrid shapes assigned;
This beauteous form assures a piteous mind.

*

Batter my heart, three-personed God; for you
As yet but knock, breathe, shine, and seek to mend.
That I may rise and stand, o'erthrow me, and bend
Your force to break, blow, burn, and make me new.
I, like an usurped town, to another due,
Labour to admit you; but oh, to no end!
Reason, your viceroy in me, me should defend,
But is captived, and proves weak or untrue.
Yet dearly I love you, and would be loved fain,
But am betrothed unto your enemy.

Divorce me, untie, or break that knot again;
Take me to you, imprison me, for I
Except you enthral me, never shall be free;
Nor ever chaste, except you ravish me.

GOOD FRIDAY, 1613: RIDING WESTWARD

Let man's soul be a sphere, and then, in this,
The intelligence that moves, devotion is;
And as the other spheres, by being grown
Subject to foreign motion, lose their own,
And being by others hurried every day,
Scarce in a year their natural form obey;
Pleasure or business so our souls admit
For their first mover, and are whirled by it.
Hence is it, that I am carried towards the west
This day, when my soul's form bends toward the east.
There I should see a sun, by rising set,
And by that setting endless day beget;
But that Christ on his cross did rise and fall,
Sin had eternally benighted all.
Yet dare I almost be glad, I do not see
That spectacle of too much weight for me.
Who sees God's face, that is self life, must die;
What a death were it then to see God die?
It made his own lieutenant Nature shrink,
It made his footstool crack, and the sun wink.
Could I behold those hands which span the poles,
And turn all spheres at once, pierced with those holes?
Could I behold that endless height which is
Zenith to us, and to our antipodes,
Humbled below us? Or that blood which is
The seat of all our souls, if not of his,
Made dirt of dust; or that flesh which was worn
By God, for his apparel, ragged, and torn?
If on these things I durst not look, durst I
Upon his miserable mother cast mine eye,
Who was God's partner here, and furnished thus
Half of that sacrifice, which ransomed us?

Though these things, as I ride, be from mine eye,
They are present yet unto my memory,
For that looks towards them; and thou lookest towards me,
O Saviour, as thou hangest upon the tree;
I turn my back to thee but to receive
Corrections, till thy mercies bid thee leave.
Oh think me worth thine anger; punish me,
Burn off my rusts and my deformity,
Restore thine image so much, by thy grace,
That thou mayst know me, and I'll turn my face.

BEN JONSON
(1572–1637)

Come, my Celia, let us prove,
While we may, the sports of love;
Time will not be ours for ever:
He at length our good will sever.
Spend not then his gifts in vain.
Suns that set, may rise again;
But if once we lose this light,
'Tis with us perpetual night.
Why should we defer our joys?
Fame and rumour are but toys.
Cannot we delude the eyes
Of a few poor household spies;
Or his easier ears beguile,
So removed by our wile?
'Tis no sin love's fruit to steal,
But the sweet theft to reveal:
To be taken, to be seen,
These have crimes accounted been.

*

Still to be neat, still to be dressed,
As you were going to a feast;
Still to be powdered, still perfumed:
Lady, it is to be presumed,
Though art's hid causes are not found,
All is not sweet, all is not sound.

Give me a look, give me a face
That makes simplicity a grace;
Robes loosely flowing, hair as free:
Such sweet neglect more taketh me

Than all the adulteries of art;
They strike mine eyes, but not my heart.

*

The faery beam upon you,
The stars to glister on you;
   A moon of light,
   In the noon of night,
Till the fire-drake hath o'ergone you!
The wheel of fortune guide you,
The boy with the bow beside you;
   Run aye in the way,
   Till the bird of day,
And the luckier lot betide you!

*

"Buzz," quoth the blue fly.
  "Hum," quoth the bee.
"Buzz" and "hum" they cry,
  And so do we.
In his ear, in his nose,
  Thus, do you see?
  He ate the dormouse,
  Else it was he.

*

Though I am young and cannot tell
Either what death or love is well,
Yet I have heard they both bear darts,
And both do aim at human hearts:
And then again, I have been told,
Love wounds with heat, as death with cold;
So that I fear they do but bring
Extremes to touch, and mean one thing.

As in a ruin we it call
One thing to be blown up or fall;
Or to our end, like way may have

By flash of lightning, or a wave:
So love's inflamed shaft or brand
May kill as soon as death's cold hand,
Except love's fires the virtue have
To fright the frost out of the grave.

A FIT OF RHYME AGAINST RHYME

Rhyme, the rack of finest wits,
That expresseth but by fits
     True conceit,
Spoiling senses of their treasure,
Cozening judgment with a measure,
     But false weight;
Wresting words from their true calling;
Propping verse for fear of falling
     To the ground;
Jointing syllables, drowning letters,
Fastening vowels, as with fetters
     They were bound!
Soon as lazy thou wert known,
All good poetry hence was flown,
     And art banished:
For a thousand years together,
All Parnassus' green did wither,
     And wit vanished!
Pegasus did fly away,
At the wells no Muse did stay,
     But bewailed,
So to see the fountain dry,
And Apollo's music die,
     All light failed!
Starveling rhymes did fill the stage,
Not a poet in an age
     Worthy crowning.
Not a work deserving bays,
Nor a line deserving praise,
     Pallas frowning:
Greek was free from rhyme's infection,

Happy Greek, by this protection,
                    Was not spoiled.
Whilst the Latin, queen of tongues,
Is not yet free from rhyme's wrongs,
                    But rests foiled.
Scarce the hill again doth flourish,
Scarce the world a wit doth nourish
                    To restore
Phoebus to his crown again,
And the Muses to their brain,
                    As before.
Vulgar languages that want
Words, and sweetness, and be scant
                    Of true measure,
Tyrant rhyme hath so abused,
That they long since have refused
                    Other caesure.
He that first invented thee,
May his joints tormented be,
                    Cramped for ever;
Still may syllabes jar with time,
Still may reason war with rhyme,
                    Resting never!
May his sense when it would meet
The cold tumor in his feet,
                    Grow unsounder;
And his title be long fool,
That in rearing such a school
                    Was the founder!

AN EPISTLE TO A FRIEND,
TO PERSUADE HIM TO THE WARS

Wake, friend, from forth thy lethargy! The drum
Beats brave and loud in Europe, and bids come
All that dare rouse: or are not loth to quit
Their vicious ease, and be o'erwhelmed with it.
It is a call to keep the spirits alive
That gasp for action, and would yet revive
Man's buried honour, in his sleepy life:

Quickning dead nature to her noblest strife.
All other acts of worldlings are but toil
In dreams, begun in hope, and end in spoil.
Look on the ambitious man, and see him nurse
His unjust hopes with praises begged, or, worse,
Bought flatteries, the issue of his purse,
Till he become both their and his own curse!
Look on the false and cunning man, that loves
No person, nor is loved: what ways he proves
To gain upon his belly; and at last
Crushed in the snaky brakes that he had past!
See the grave, sour, and supercilious sir,
In outward face, but inward, light as fur,
Or feathers, lay his fortune out to show,
Till envy wound or maim it at a blow!
See him that's called, and thought the happiest man
Honoured at once, and envied (if it can
Be honour is so mixed) by such as would
For all their spite, be like him, if they could;
No part or corner man can look upon,
But there are objects bid him to be gone
As far as he can fly, or follow day,
Rather than here so bogged in vices stay.
The whole world here leavened with madness swells;
And being a thing blown out of nought, rebels
Against his Maker, high alone with weeds,
And impious rankness of all sects and seeds:
Not to be checked or frighted now with fate,
But more licentious made and desperate!
Our delicacies are grown capital,
And even our sports are dangers! What we call
Friendship, is now masked hatred! Justice fled,
And shamefacedness together! All laws dead
That kept man living! Pleasures only sought!
Honour and honesty, as poor things thought
As they are made! Pride and stiff clownage mixed
To make up greatness! And man's whole good fixed
In bravery, or gluttony, or coin,
All which he makes the servants of the groin!
Thither it flows: how much did Stallion spend
To have his court-bred filly there commend
His lace and starch; and fall upon her back

In admiration, stretched upon the rack
Of lust, to his rich suit, and title, Lord?
Ay, that's a charm and half! She must afford
That all respect, she must lie down; nay, more,
'Tis there civility to be a whore:
He's one of blood and fashion! And with these
The bravery makes she can no honour leese:
To do't with cloth, or stuffs, lust's name might merit,
With velvet, plush, and tissues, it is spirit.
   Oh these so ignorant monsters, light, as proud!
Who can behold their manners, and not cloud-
Like, on them lighten? If that nature could
Not make a verse, anger or laughter would,
To see them aye discoursing with their glass,
How they may make some one that day an ass,
Planting their purls and curls, spread forth like net,
And every dressing for a pit-fall set
To catch the flesh in, and to pound a ——
Be at their visits, see them squeamish, sick,
Ready to cast at one whose band sits ill,
And then leap mad on a neat picardill,
As if a brize were gotten in their tail;
And firk, and jerk, and for the coachman rail,
And jealous each of other, yet think long
To be abroad chanting some bawdy song,
And laugh, and measure thighs, then squeak, spring, itch,
Do all the tricks of a salt lady bitch!
For t'other pound of sweetmeats, he shall feel
That pays, or what he will: the dame is steel.
For these with her young company she'll enter,
Where Pitts, or Wright, or Modet would not venture;
And comes by these degrees the style t' inherit
Of woman of fashion, and a lady of spirit.
Nor is the title questioned with our proud,
Great, brave, and fashioned folk, these are allowed;
Adulteries now are not so hid, or strange,
They're grown commodity upon Exchange:
He that will follow but another's wife,
Is loved, though he let out his own for life;
The husband now's called churlish, or a poor
Nature, that will not let his wife be a whore;
Or use all arts, or haunt all companies

116

That may corrupt her, even in his eyes.
The brother trades a sister, and the friend
Lives to the lord, but to the lady's end.
Less must not be thought on than mistress; or
If it be thought, killed like her embrions; for
Whom no great mistress hath as yet infamed
A fellow of coarse lechery, is named,
The servant of the serving-woman, in scorn,
Ne'er came to taste the plenteous marriage-horn.

Thus they do talk. And are these objects fit
For man to spend his money on? his wit?
His time? health? soul? Will he for these go throw
Those thousands on his back, shall after blow
His body to the Counters, or the Fleet?
Is it for these that Fine-man meets the street
Coached, or on foot-cloth, thrice changed every day,
To teach each suit he has, the ready way
From Hyde Park to the stage, where at the last
His dear and borrowed bravery he must cast?
When not his combs, his curling-irons, his glass,
Sweet bags, sweet powders, nor sweet words will pass
For less security. O heavens! For these
Is it that man pulls on himself disease,
Surfeit, and quarrel? Drinks the t'other health?
Or by damnation voids it, or by stealth?

What fury of late is crept into our feasts?
What honour given to the drunkenest guests?
What reputation to bear one glass more,
When oft the bearer is born out of door?
This hath our ill-used freedom, and soft peace
Brought on us, and will every hour increase.
Our vices do not tarry in a place,
But being in motion still, or rather in race,
Tilt one upon another, and now bear
This way, now that, as if their number were
More than themselves, or than our lives could take,
But both fell pressed under the load they make.

I'll bid thee look no more, but flee, flee, friend,
This precipice, and rocks that have no end,
Or side, but threatens ruin. The whole day
Is not enough, now, but the nights to play:
And whilst our states, strength, body, and mind we waste,

Go make ourselves the usurers at a cast.
He that no more for age, cramps, palsies can
Now use the bones, we see doth hire a man
To take the box up for him; and pursues
The dice with glassen eyes, to the glad views
Of what he throws: like lechers grown content
To be beholders, when their powers are spent.
   Can we not leave this worm? Or will we not?
Is that the truer excuse? Or have we got
In this, and like, an itch of vanity,
That scratching now's our best felicity?
Well, let it go. Yet this is better, then
To lose the forms and dignities of men,
To flatter my good lord, and cry his bowl
Runs sweetly, as it had his lordship's soul:
Although, perhaps it has, what's that to me,
That may stand by, and hold my peace? Will he,
When I am hoarse with praising his each cast,
Give me but that again, that I must waste
In sugar candied, or in buttered beer,
For the recovery of my voice? No, there
Pardon his lordship; flattery's grown so cheap
With him, for he is followed with that heap,
That watch and catch, at what they may applaud,
As a poor single flatterer, without bawd
Is nothing, such scarce meat and drink he'll give;
But he that's both, and slave to both, shall live
And be beloved, while the whores last. O times!
Friend, fly from hence, and let these kindled rhymes
Light thee from hell on earth; where flatterers, spies,
Informers, masters both of arts and lies;
Lewd slanderers, soft whisperers, that let blood
The life, and fame-veins, yet not understood
Of the poor sufferers; where the envious, proud,
Ambitious, factious, superstitious, loud
Boasters, and perjured, with the infinite more
Prevaricators swarm: of which the store
(Because they're every where amongst mankind
Spread through the world) is easier far to find,
Than once to number, or bring forth to hand,
Though thou wert Muster-master of the land.
   Go, quit them all! And take along with thee,

Thy true friend's wishes, Colby, which shall be,
That thine be just and honest, that thy deeds
Not wound thy conscience, when thy body bleeds;
That thou dost all things more for truth than glory
And never but for doing wrong be sorry;
That by commanding first thyself, thou makest
Thy person fit for any charge thou takest:
That fortune never make thee to complain,
But what she gives, thou darest give her again;
That whatsoever face thy fate puts on,
Thou shrink or start not; but be always one;
That thou think nothing great but what is good;
And from that thought strive to be understood.
So, 'live or dead, thou wilt preserve a fame
Still precious with the odour of thy name.
And last, blaspheme not; we did never hear
Man thought the valianter, 'cause he durst swear;
No more, than we should think a lord had had
More honour in him, 'cause we've known him mad:
These take, and now go seek thy peace in war,
Who falls for love of God, shall rise a star.

*

Oh, do not wanton with those eyes,
 Lest I be sick with seeing;
Nor cast them down, but let them rise,
 Lest shame destroy their being.

Oh, be not angry with those fires,
 For then their threats will kill me;
Nor look too kind on my desires,
 For then my hopes will spill me.

Oh, do not steep them in thy tears,
 For so will sorrow slay me;
Nor spread them as distract with fears;
 Mine own enough betray me.

*

Drink to me only with thine eyes,
    And I will pledge with mine;
Or leave a kiss but in the cup
    And I'll not look for wine.
The thirst that from the soul doth rise
    Doth ask a drink divine;
But might I of Jove's nectar sup,
    I would not change for thine.

I sent thee late a rosy wreath,
    Not so much honouring thee
As giving it a hope that there
    It could not withered be;
But thou thereon didst only breathe
    And sentest it back to me;
Since when it grows, and smells, I swear,
    Not of itself but thee!

TO PENSHURST

Thou art not, Penshurst, built to envious show
Of touch or marble; nor canst boast a row
Of polished pillars, or a roof of gold:
Thou hast no lantern, whereof tales are told;
Or stair, or courts; but standest an ancient pile,
And these grudged at, art reverenced the while.
Thou joyest in better marks, of soil, of air,
Of wood, of water; therein thou art fair.
Thou has thy walks for health, as well as sport:
Thy mount, to which thy Dryads do resort,
Where Pan and Bacchus their high feasts have made,
Beneath the broad beech, and the chestnut shade;
That taller tree, which of a nut was set,
At his great birth, where all the Muses met.
There, in the writhed bark, are cut the names
Of many a sylvan, taken with his flames;
And thence the ruddy satyrs oft provoke
The lighter fauns, to reach thy lady's oak.

Thy copse too, named of Gamage, thou hast there,
That never fails to serve thee seasoned deer,
When thou wouldst feast or exercise thy friends.
The lower land, that to the river bends,
Thy sheep, thy bullocks, kine, and calves do feed;
The middle grounds thy mares and horses breed.
Each bank doth yield thee conies; and the tops
Fertile of wood, Ashore and Sidney's copse,
To crown thy open table, doth provide
The purpled pheasant, with the speckled side:
The painted partridge lies in every field,
And for thy mess is willing to be killed.
And if the high-swollen Medway fail thy dish,
Thou hast thy ponds, that pay thee tribute fish,
Fat aged carps that run into thy net,
And pikes, now weary their own kind to eat,
As loth the second draught or cast to stay,
Officiously at first themselves betray.
Bright eels that emulate them, and leap on land,
Before the fisher, or into his hand,
Then hath thy orchard fruit, thy garden flowers,
Fresh as the air, and new as are the hours.
The early cherry, with the later plum,
Fig, grape, and quince, each in his time doth come:
The blushing apricot, and woolly peach
Hang on thy walls, that every child may reach.
And though thy walls be of the country stone,
They're reared with no man's ruin, no man's groan;
There's none, that dwell about them, wish them down;
But all come in, the farmer and the clown;
And no one empty-handed, to salute
Thy lord and lady, though they have no suit.
Some bring a capon, some a rural cake,
Some nuts, some apples; some that think they make
The better cheeses, bring them; or else send
By their ripe daughters, whom they would commend
This way to husbands; and whose baskets bear
An emblem of themselves in plum, or pear.
But what can this (more than express their love)
Add to thy free provisions, far above
The need of such? Whose liberal board doth flow
With all that hospitality doth know!

Where comes no guest, but is allowed to eat,
Without his fear, and of thy lord's own meat:
Where the same beer and bread, and self-same wine,
That is his lordship's, shall be also mine.
And I not fain to sit (as some this day,
At great men's tables) and yet dine away.
Here no man tells my cups; nor standing by,
A waiter, doth my gluttony envy:
But gives me what I call, and lets me eat,
He knows, below, he shall find plenty of meat;
Thy tables hoard not up for the next day,
Nor, when I take my lodging, need I pray
For fire, or lights, or livery; all is there;
As if thou then wert mine, or I reigned here:
There's nothing I can wish, for which I stay.
That found King James, when hunting late, this way,
With his brave son, the prince; they saw thy fires
Shine bright on every hearth, as the desires
Of thy Penates had been set on flame,
To entertain them; or the country came,
With all their zeal, to warm their welcome here.
What (great, I will not say, but) sudden cheer
Didst thou then make 'em! and what praise was heaped
On thy good lady, then! who therein reaped
The just reward of her high huswifry;
To have her linen, plate, and all things nigh,
When she was far; and not a room, but dressed,
As if it had expected such a guest!
These, Penshurst, are thy praise, and yet not all.
Thy lady's noble, fruitful, chaste withal.
His children thy great lord may call his own;
A fortune, in this age, but rarely known.
They are, and have been taught religion; thence
Their gentler spirits have sucked innocence.
Each morn, and even, they are taught to pray,
With the whole household, and may, every day,
Read in their virtuous parents' noble parts,
The mysteries of manners, arms, and arts.
Now, Penshurst, they that will proportion thee
With other edifices, when they see
Those proud ambitious heaps, and nothing else,
May say, their lords have built, but thy lord dwells.

ON MY FIRST SON

Farewell, thou child of my right hand, and joy.
My sin was too much hope of thee, loved boy:
Seven years thou wert lent to me, and I thee pay,
Exacted by thy fate, on the just day.
Oh, could I lose all father, now! For why,
Will man lament the state he should envy?
To have so soon 'scaped world's, and flesh's rage,
And, if no other misery, yet age!
Rest in soft peace, and asked, say here doth lie
Ben Jonson his best piece of poetry:
For whose sake henceforth all his vows be such,
As what he loves may never like too much.

*

Who says that Giles and Joan at discord be?
The observing neighbours no such mood can see.
Indeed, poor Giles repents he married ever;
But that his Joan doth too. And Giles would never,
By his free will, be in Joan's company:
No more would Joan he should. Giles riseth early,
And having got him out of doors is glad;
The like is Joan: but turning home is sad;
And so is Joan. Oftimes when Giles doth find
Harsh sights at home, Giles wisheth he were blind;
All this doth Joan: or that his long-yearned life
Were quite out-spun; the like wish hath his wife.
The children that he keeps, Giles swears are none
Of his getting; and so swears his Joan.
In all affections she concurreth still.
If now, with man and wife, to will and nill
The self-same things, a note of concord be:
I know no couple better can agree!

ON MY FIRST DAUGHTER

Here lies, to each her parents, ruth,
Mary, the daughter of their youth;
Yet all heaven's gifts being heaven's due,
It makes the father less to rue.
At six months' end she parted hence
With safety of her innocence;
Whose soul heaven's Queen, whose name she bears,
In comfort of her mother's tears,
Hath placed amongst her virgin-train:
Where while that, severed, doth remain,
This grave partakes the fleshly birth;
Which cover lightly, gentle earth!

ROBERT HERRICK
(1591–1674)

I sing of brooks, of blossoms, birds, and bowers,
Of April, May, of June, and July flowers;
I sing of may-poles, hock-carts, wassails, wakes,
Of bridegrooms, brides, and of their bridal cakes.
I write of youth, of love; and have access
By these to sing of cleanly wantonness.
I sing of dews, of rains, and piece by piece
Of balm, of oil, of spice, and ambergris.
I sing of times trans-shifting, and I write
How roses first came red, and lilies white.
I write of groves, of twilights, and I sing
The court of Mab, and of the Fairy King.
I write of hell; I sing, and ever shall,
Of heaven, and hope to have it after all.

*

A sweet disorder in the dress
Kindles in clothes a wantonness.
A lawn about the shoulders thrown
Into a fine distraction,
An erring lace, which here and there
Enthralls the crimson stomacher;
A cuff neglectful, and thereby
Ribands to flow confusedly;
A winning wave, deserving note,
In the tempestuous petticoat;
A careless shoe string, in whose tie
I see a wild civility;
Do more bewitch me than when art
Is too precise in every part.

*

Gather ye rosebuds while ye may,
　　Old time is still a-flying,
And that same flower that smiles today,
　　Tomorrow will be dying.

The glorious lamp of heaven, the sun,
　　The higher he's a-getting,
The sooner will his race be run,
　　And nearer he's to setting.

That age is best which is the first,
　　When youth and blood are warmer;
But being spent, the worse, and worst
　　Times still succeed the former.

Then be not coy, but use your time,
　　And while ye may, go marry;
For having lost but once your prime,
　　You may forever tarry.

*

Her eyes the glow-worm lend thee;
The shooting stars attend thee;
　　And the elves also,
　　Whose little eyes glow
Like the sparks of fire, befriend thee.

No will-o'-th'-wisp mis-light thee;
Nor snake, or slow-worm bite thee;
　　But on, on thy way
　　Not making a stay,
Since ghost there's none to affright thee.

Let not the dark thee cumber;
What though the moon does slumber?
　　The stars of the night
　　Will lend thee their light,
Like tapers clear without number.

Then, Julia, let me woo thee,
Thus, thus to come unto me;
   And when I shall meet
   Thy silvery feet,
My soul I'll pour into thee.

*

Whenas in silks my Julia goes,
Then, then, methinks, how sweetly flows
That liquefaction of her clothes.
Next, when I cast mine eyes and see
That brave vibration each way free,
Oh, how that glittering taketh me!

CORINNA'S GOING A-MAYING

Get up, get up for shame, the blooming morn
Upon her wings presents the god unshorn!
   See how Aurora throws her fair
   Fresh-quilted colours through the air.
   Get up, sweet slug-a-bed, and see
   The dew bespangling herb and tree.
Each flower has wept and bowed toward the east
Above an hour since, yet you not dressed,
   Nay, not so much as out of bed.
   When all the birds have matins said,
   And sung their thankful hymns, 'tis sin,
   Nay, profanation, to keep in,
Whenas a thousand virgins on this day
Spring, sooner than the lark, to fetch in May.

Rise, and put on your foliage, and be seen
To come forth like the springtime, fresh and green,
   And sweet as Flora. Take no care
   For jewels for your gown or hair.
   Fear not, the leaves will strew
   Gems in abundance upon you.
Besides, the childhood of the day has kept,

Against you come, some orient pearls unwept;
   Come and receive them while the light
   Hangs on the dew-locks of the night,
   And Titan on the eastern hill
   Retires himself, or else stands still,
Till you come forth. Wash, dress, be brief in praying;
Few beads are best when once we go a-maying.

Come, my Corinna, come; and coming, mark
How each field turns a street, each street a park
   Made green and trimmed with trees; see how
   Devotion gives each house a bough
   Or branch; each porch, each door, ere this,
   An ark, a tabernacle is,
Made up of whitethorn neatly interwove,
As if here were those cooler shades of love.
   Can such delights be in the street
   And open fields, and we not see't?
   Come, we'll abroad; and let's obey
   The proclamation made for May
And sin no more, as we have done, by staying;
But, my Corinna, come, let's go a-maying.

There's not a budding boy or girl this day
But is got up, and gone to bring in May!
   A deal of youth, ere this, is come
   Back, and with whitethorn laden, home.
   Some have despatched their cakes and cream
   Before that we have left to dream;
And some have wept, and wooed, and plighted troth,
And chose their priest, ere we can cast off sloth;
   Many a green-gown has been given,
   Many a kiss, both odd and even,
   Many a glance too has been sent
   From out the eye, love's firmament;
Many a jest told of the keys betraying
This night, and locks picked, yet we're not a-maying.

Come, let us go while we are in our prime,
And take the harmless folly of the time.
   We shall grow old apace, and die
      Before we know our liberty.

Our life is short, and our days run
As fast away as does the sun.
And as a vapour, or a drop of rain
Once lost, can ne'er be found again,
So when or you or I are made
A fable, song, or fleeting shade,
All love, all liking, all delight
Lies drowned with us in endless night.
Then while time serves, and we are but decaying,
Come, my Corinna, come, let's go a-maying.

CHERRY-RIPE

Cherry-ripe, ripe, ripe, I cry,
Full and fair ones; come and buy!
If so be you ask me where
They do grow, I answer: there,
Where my Julia's lips do smile;
There's the land, or cherry-isle
Whose plantations fully show
All the year where cherries grow.

*

Here, here I live with what my board
Can with the smallest cost afford.
Though ne'er so mean the viands be,
They well content my Prue and me.
Or pea, or bean, or wort, or beet,
Whatever comes, content makes sweet.
Here we rejoice because no rent
We pay for our poor tenement,
Wherein we rest, and never fear
The landlord or the usurer;
The quarter-day does ne'er affright
Our peaceful slumbers in the night.
We eat our own and batten more
Because we feed on no man's score,
But pity those whose flanks grow great,

Swelled with the lard of others' meat.
We bless our fortunes when we see
Our own beloved privacy,
And like our living, where we're known
To very few, or else to none.

CEREMONIES FOR CHRISTMAS

Come, bring with a noise,
My merry merry boys,
The Christmas log to the firing;
While my good dame, she
Bids ye all be free,
And drink to your heart's desiring!
With the last year's brand
Light the new block, and
For good success in his spending,
On your psalteries play,
That sweet luck may
Come while the log is a-tending.
Drink now the strong beer,
Cut the white loaf here;
The while the meat is a-shredding
For the rare mince pie,
And the plums stand by
To fill the paste that's a-kneading.

HIS LITANY TO THE HOLY SPIRIT

In the hour of my distress,
When temptations me oppress,
And when I my sins confess,
　　　Sweet Spirit, comfort me!

When I lie within my bed,
Sick in heart and sick in head,

And with doubts discomforted,
    Sweet Spirit, comfort me!

When the house doth sigh and weep,
And the world is drowned in sleep,
Yet mine eyes the watch do keep,
    Sweet Spirit, comfort me!

When the artless doctor sees
No one hope, but of his fees,
And his skill runs on the lees,
    Sweet Spirit, comfort me!

When his potion and his pill
Has, or none, or little skill,
Meet for nothing but to kill,
    Sweet Spirit, comfort me!

When the passing bell doth toll,
And the furies in a shoal
Come to fright a parting soul,
    Sweet Spirit, comfort me!

When the tapers now burn blue,
And the comforters are few,
And that number more than true,
    Sweet Spirit, comfort me!

When the priest his last hath prayed,
And I nod to what is said,
'Cause my speech is now decayed,
    Sweet Spirit, comfort me!

When, God knows, I'm tossed about,
Either with despair, or doubt,
Yet before the glass be out,
    Sweet Spirit, comfort me!

When the tempter me pursueth
With the sins of all my youth,
And half damns me with untruth,
    Sweet Spirit, comfort me!

When the flames and hellish cries
Fright mine ears, and fright mine eyes,
And all terrors me surprise,
    Sweet Spirit, comfort me!

When the judgment is revealed,
And that opened which was sealed,
When to thee I have appealed,
    Sweet Spirit, comfort me!

HENRY KING
(1592–1669)

THE EXEQUY

Accept, thou shrine of my dead saint,
Instead of dirges, this complaint;
And for sweet flowers to crown thy hearse
Receive a strew of weeping verse
From thy grieved friend, whom thou mightest see
Quite melted into tears for thee.
Dear loss! Since thy untimely fate
My task hath been to meditate
On thee, on thee; thou art the book,
The library whereon I look,
Though almost blind. For thee, loved clay,
I languish out, not live, the day,
Using no other exercise
But what I practice with mine eyes;
By which wet glasses I find out
How lazily time creeps about
To one that mourns; this, only this,
My exercise and business is.
So I compute the weary hours
With sighs dissolved into showers,
Nor wonder if my time go thus
Backward and most preposterous;
Thou hast benighted me; thy set
This eve of blackness did beget,
Who wast my day, though overcast
Before thou hadst thy noontide passed;
And I remember must in tears,
Thou scarce hadst seen so many years
As day tells hours. By thy clear sun
My love and fortune first did run.
But thou wilt never more appear
Folded within my hemisphere,

Since both thy light and motion
Like a fled star is fallen and gone;
And 'twixt me and my soul's dear wish
An earth now interposed is,
Which such a strange eclipse doth make
As ne'er was read in almanac.
I could allow thee for a time
To darken me and my sad clime.
Were it a month, a year, or ten,
I would thy exile live till then,
And all that space my mirth adjourn,
So thou wouldst promise to return;
And putting off thy ashy shroud,
At length disperse this sorrow's cloud.
But woe is me! the longest date
Too narrow is to calculate
These empty hopes; never shall I
Be so much blest as to descry
A glimpse of thee, till that day come
Which shall the earth to cinders doom,
And a fierce fever must calcine
The body of this world like thine,
My little world. That fit of fire
Once off, our bodies shall aspire
To our souls' bliss; then we shall rise
And view ourselves with clearer eyes
In that calm region where no night
Can hide us from each other's sight.
Meantime, thou hast her, earth; much good
May my harm do thee. Since it stood
With Heaven's will I might not call
Her longer mine, I give thee all
My short-lived right and interest
In her whom living I loved best.
With a most free and bounteous grief,
I give thee what I could not keep.
Be kind to her, and prithee look
Thou write into thy doomsday book
Each parcel of this rarity,
Which in thy casket shrined doth lie.
See that thou make thy reckoning straight,
And yield her back again by weight;

For thou must audit on thy trust
Each grain and atom of this dust,
As thou wilt answer Him that lent,
Not gave thee, my dear monument.
So close the ground, and 'bout her shade
Black curtains draw; my bride is laid.
Sleep on, my love, in thy cold bed,
Never to be disquieted.
My last good-night! Thou wilt not wake
Till I thy fate shall overtake;
Till age, or grief, or sickness must
Marry my body to that dust
It so much loves, and fill the room
My heart keeps empty in thy tomb.
Stay for me there, I will not fail
To meet thee in that hollow vale.
And think not much of my delay;
I am already on the way,
And follow thee with all the speed
Desire can make, or sorrows breed.
Each minute is a short degree,
And every hour a step towards thee.
At night when I betake to rest,
Next morn I rise nearer my west
Of life, almost by eight hours' sail,
Than when sleep breathed his drowsy gale.
Thus from the sun my bottom steers,
And my day's compass downward bears:
Nor labor I to stem the tide
Through which to thee I swiftly glide.
'Tis true, with shame and grief I yield,
Thou like the van first tookest the field,
And gotten hath the victory
In thus adventuring to die
Before me, whose more years might crave
A just precedence in the grave.
But hark! My pulse like a soft drum
Beats my approach, tells thee I come;
And slow howe'er my marches be,
I shall at last sit down by thee.
The thought of this bids me go on,
And wait my dissolution

With hope and comfort. Dear, forgive
The crime, I am content to live
Divided, with but half a heart,
Till we shall meet and never part.

GEORGE HERBERT
(1593–1633)

REDEMPTION

Having been tenant long to a rich lord,
  Not thriving, I resolved to be bold,
  And make a suit unto him, to afford
A new small-rented lease, and cancel the old.
In heaven at his manor I him sought:
  They told me there that he was lately gone
  About some land, which he had dearly bought
Long since on earth, to take possession.
I straight returned, and knowing his great birth,
  Sought him accordingly in great resorts,
  In cities, theatres, gardens, parks, and courts.
At length I heard a ragged noise and mirth
  Of thieves and murderers: there I him espied,
  Who straight "Your suit is granted," said, and died.

EASTER WINGS

Lord, who createdest man in wealth and store,
  Though foolishly he lost the same,
    Decaying more and more,
      Till he became
      Most poor;
      With thee
      Oh let me rise
    As larks, harmoniously,
   And sing this day thy victories;
Then shall the fall further the flight in me.

My tender age in sorrow did begin,
And still with sicknesses and shame
Thou didst so punish sinne,
That I became
Most thin.
With thee
Let me combine
And feel this day thy victory;
For, if I imp my wing on thine,
Affliction shall advance the flight in me.

JORDAN

Who says that fictions only and false hair
Become a verse? Is there in truth no beauty?
Is all good structure in a winding stair?
May no lines pass, except they do their duty
    Not to a true, but painted chair?

Is it no verse, except enchanted groves
And sudden arbours shadow coarse-spun lines?
Must purling streams refresh a lover's loves?
Must all be veiled, while he that reads divines,
    Catching the sense at two removes?

Shepherds are honest people; let them sing.
Riddle who list, for me, and pull for prime.
I envy no man's nightingale or spring;
Nor let them punish me with loss of rhyme,
    Who plainly say, "My God, My King."

AFFLICTION

Kill me not every day,
Thou Lord of life, since thy one death for me
Is more than all my deaths can be,

Though I in broken pay
Die over each hour of Methuselah's stay.

If all men's tears were let
Into one common sewer, sea, and brine;
What were they all, compared to thine,
Wherein if they were set,
They would discolour thy most bloody sweat?

Thou art my grief alone.
Thou, Lord, conceal it not; and as thou art
All my delight, so all my smart.
Thy cross took up in one,
By way of impress, all my future moan.

EMPLOYMENT

He that is weary, let him sit.
My soul would stir
And trade in courtesies and wit,
Quitting the fur
To cold complexions needing it.
Man is no star, but a quick coal
Of mortal fire;
Who blows it not, nor doth control
A faint desire,
Lets his own ashes choke his soul.
When the elements did for place contest
With him whose will
Ordained the highest to be best,
The earth sat still,
And by the others is oppressed.
Life is a business, not good cheer,
Ever in wars.
The sun still shineth there or here,
Whereas the stars
Watch an advantage to appear.
Oh that I were an orange tree,
That busy plant!

Then should I ever laden be,
        And never want
Some fruit for him that dressed me.
But we are still too young or old.
        The man is gone,
Before we do our wares unfold.
        So we freeze on,
Untill the grave increase our cold.

VIRTUE

Sweet day, so cool, so calm, so bright,
The bridal of the earth and sky,
The dew shall weep thy fall tonight,
        For thou must die.

Sweet rose, whose hue, angry and brave,
Bids the rash gazer wipe his eye,
Thy root is ever in its grave,
        And thou must die.

Sweet spring, full of sweet days and roses,
A box where sweets compacted lie,
My music shows ye have your closes,
        And all must die.

Only a sweet and virtuous soul,
Like seasoned timber, never gives,
But though the whole world turn to coal,
        Then chiefly lives.

TIME

Meeting with Time, "Slack thing!" said I,
"Thy scythe is dull; whet it for shame!"
"No marvel, sir," he did reply,
"If it at length deserve some blame.

But where one man would have me grind it,
Twenty for one too sharp do find it."

"Perhaps some such of old did pass,
Who above all things loved this life,
To whom thy scythe a hatchet was,
Which now is but a pruning knife.
    Christ's coming hath made man thy debtor,
    Since by thy cutting he grows better,

And in his blessing thou art blessed.
For where thou only were before
An executioner at best,
Thou art a gardner now, and more,
    An usher to convey our souls
    Beyond the utmost stars and poles.

And this is that makes life so long,
While it detains us from our God.
Even pleasures here increase the wrong,
And length of days lengthen the rod.
    Who wants the place, where God doth dwell,
    Partakes already half of hell.

Of what strange length must that needs be,
Which even eternity excludes!"
Thus far Time heard me patiently,
Then chafing said, "This man deludes.
    What do I here before his door?
    He doth not crave less time, but more."

PEACE

Sweet Peace, where dost thou dwell? I humbly crave,
    Let me once know.
  I sought thee in a secret cave,
    And asked, if Peace were there.
A hollow wind did seem to answer, "No;
    Go seek elsewhere."

I did; and going did a rainbow note.
          Surely, thought I,
This is the lace of Peace's coat;
          I will search out the matter.
But while I looked, the clouds immediately
          Did break and scatter.

Then went I to a garden, and did spy
          A gallant flower,
The Crown Imperial. "Sure," said I,
          "Peace at the root must dwell."
But when I digged, I saw a worm devour
          What showed so well.

At length I met a reverend good old man,
          Whom when for Peace
I did demand, he thus began:
          "There was a Prince of old
At Salem dwelt, who lived with good increase
          Of flock and fold.

He sweetly lived; yet sweetness did not save
          His life from foes.
But after death out of his grave
          There sprang twelve stalks of wheat,
Which many wondering at, got some of those
          To plant and set.

It prospered strangely, and did soon disperse
          Through all the earth,
For they that taste it do rehearse,
          That virtue lies therein,
A secret virtue bringing peace and mirth
          By flight of sin.

Take of this grain, which in my garden grows,
          And grows for you;
Make bread of it; and that repose
          And peace, which everywhere
With so much earnestness you do pursue,
          Is only there."

THE COLLAR

I struck the board, and cried, "No more.
        I will abroad.
What? shall I ever sigh and pine?
My lines and life are free; free as the road,
    Loose as the wind, as large as store.
        Shall I be still in suit?
Have I no harvest but a thorn
To let me blood, and not restore
What I have lost with cordial fruit?
        Sure there was wine
Before my sighs did dry it; there was corn
    Before my tears did drown it.
    Is the year only lost to me?
        Have I no bays to crown it?
No flowers, no garlands gay? All blasted?
        All wasted?
Not so, my heart; but there is fruit,
        And thou hast hands.
Recover all thy sigh-blown age
On double pleasures; leave thy cold dispute
Of what is fit and not. Forsake thy cage,
        Thy rope of sands,
Which petty thoughts have made, and made to thee
    Good cable, to enforce and draw,
        And be thy law,
While thou didst wink and wouldst not see.
        Away, take heed;
        I will abroad.
Call in thy death's head there: tie up thy fears.
        He that forbears
    To suit and serve his need,
        Deserves his load."
But as I raved and grew more fierce and wild
        At every word,
Methought I heard one calling, "Child!"
        And I replied, "My Lord."

THE PULLEY

When God at first made man,
Having a glass of blessings standing by,
"Let us" (said he) "pour on him all we can;
Let the world's riches, which dispersed lie,
Contract into a span."

So strength first made a way;
Then beauty flowed, then wisdom, honour, pleasure.
When almost all was out, God made a stay,
Perceiving that alone of all his treasure
Rest in the bottom lay.

"For if I should" (said he)
"Bestow this jewel also on my creature,
He would adore my gifts instead of me,
And rest in Nature, not the God of Nature;
So both should losers be.

Yet let him keep the rest,
But keep them with repining restlessness.
Let him be rich and weary, that at least,
If goodness lead him not, yet weariness
May toss him to my breast."

THE ANSWER

My comforts drop and melt away like snow.
I shake my head, and all the thoughts and ends
Which my fierce youth did bandy, fall and flow
Like leaves about me; or like summer friends,
Flies of estates and sunshine. But to all,
Who think me eager, hot, and undertaking,
But in my prosecutions slack and small;
As a young exhalation, newly waking,

Scorns his first bed of dirt, and means the sky;
But cooling by the way, grows pursy and slow,
And settling to a cloud, doth live and die
In that dark state of tears; to all, that so
Show me, and set me, I have one reply,
Which they that know the rest, know more than I.

LOVE

Love bade me welcome; yet my soul drew back,
      Guilty of dust and sin.
But quick-eyed Love, observing me grow slack
      From my first entrance in,
Drew nearer to me, sweetly questioning,
      If I lacked any thing.

"A guest," I answered, "worthy to be here."
      Love said, "You shall be he."
"I the unkind, ungrateful? Ah my dear,
      I cannot look on thee."
Love took my hand, and smiling did reply,
      "Who made the eyes but I?"

"Truth, Lord, but I have marred them; let my shame
      Go where it doth deserve."
"And know you not," says Love, "who bore the blame?
      My dear, then I will serve.
You must sit down," says Love, "and taste my meat."
      So I did sit and eat.

THOMAS CAREW
(ca. 1594–1639)

THE SPRING

Now that the winter's gone, the earth hath lost
Her snow-white robes, and now no more the frost
Candies the grass, or casts an icy cream
Upon the silver lake or crystal stream,
But the warm sun thaws the benumbed earth,
And makes it tender; gives a sacred birth
To the dead swallow; wakes in hollow tree
The drowsy cuckoo and the humble-bee.
Now do a choir of chirping minstrels bring
In triumph to the world the youthful spring.
The valleys, hills, and woods in rich array
Welcome the coming of the longed-for May.
Now all things smile; only my love doth lour,
Nor hath the scalding noonday sun the power
To melt that marble ice, which still doth hold
Her heart congealed, and makes her pity cold.
The ox, which lately did for shelter fly
Into the stall, doth now securely lie
In open fields; and love no more is made
By the fireside, but in the cooler shade.
Amyntas now doth with his Chloris sleep
Under a sycamore, and all things keep
Time with the season. Only she doth carry
June in her eyes, in her heart January.

MEDIOCRITY IN LOVE REJECTED

Give me more love or more disdain;
  The torrid or the frozen zone

Bring equal ease unto my pain,
   The temperate affords me none.
Either extreme of love or hate
Is sweeter than a calm estate.

Give me a storm; if it be love,
   Like Danaë in that golden shower,
I swim in pleasure; if it prove
   Disdain, that torrent will devour
My vulture-hopes; and he's possessed
Of heaven, that's but from hell released.
   Then crown my joys or cure my pain;
   Give me more love or more disdain.

*

Ask me no more where Jove bestows,
When June is past, the fading rose,
For in your beauty's orient deep
These flowers, as in their causes, sleep.

Ask me no more whither doth stray
The golden atoms of the day,
For in pure love heaven did prepare
Those powders to enrich your hair.

Ask me no more whither doth haste
The nightingale when May is past,
For in your sweet dividing throat
She winters and keeps warm her note.

Ask me no more where those stars light
That downwards fall in dead of night,
For in your eyes they sit, and there
Fixed become as in their sphere.

Ask me no more if east or west
The phoenix builds her spicy nest,
For unto you at last she flies,
And in your fragrant bosom dies.

DISDAIN RETURNED

He that loves a rosy cheek,
   Or a coral lip admires,
Or from star-like eyes doth seek
   Fuel to maintain his fires;
As old time makes these decay,
So his flames must waste away.

But a smooth and steadfast mind,
   Gentle thoughts and calm desires,
Hearts with equal love combined,
   Kindle never-dying fires.
Where these are not, I despise
Lovely cheeks, or lips, or eyes.

No tears, Celia, now shall win
   My resolved heart to return;
I have searched thy soul within,
   And find nought but pride and scorn;
I have learned thy arts, and now
   Can disdain as much as thou.
Some power, in my revenge, convey
That love to her I cast away.

EDMUND WALLER
(1606–87)

Go, lovely rose;
Tell her that wastes her time and me,
That now she knows,
When I resemble her to thee,
How sweet and fair she seems to be.

Tell her that's young,
And shuns to have her graces spied,
That hadst thou sprung
In deserts, where no men abide,
Thou must have uncommended died.

Small is the worth
Of beauty from the light retired.
Bid her come forth,
Suffer herself to be desired,
And not blush so to be admired.

Then die, that she
The common fate of all things rare
May read in thee;
How small a part of time they share
That are so wondrous sweet and fair!

JOHN MILTON
(1608–74)

L'ALLEGRO

Hence, loathed Melancholy,
  Of Cerberus and blackest Midnight born,
In Stygian cave forlorn
  'Mongst horrid shapes, and shrieks, and sights unholy,
Find out some uncouth cell,
  Where brooding Darkness spreads his jealous wings,
And the night-raven sings;
  There under ebon shades, and low-browed rocks,
As ragged as thy locks,
  In dark Cimmerian desert ever dwell.
But come, thou Goddess fair and free,
In heaven ycleped Euphrosyne,
And by men, heart-easing Mirth,
Whom lovely Venus at a birth
With two sister Graces more
To ivy-crowned Bacchus bore;
Or whether (as some sager sing)
The frolic Wind that breathes the spring,
Zephyr with Aurora playing,
As he met her once a-Maying,
There on beds of violets blue,
And fresh-blown roses washed in dew,
Filled her with thee, a daughter fair,
So buxom, blithe and debonair.
  Haste thee, Nymph, and bring with thee
Jest and youthful Jollity,
Quips, and Cranks, and wanton Wiles,
Nods, and Becks, and wreathed Smiles,
Such as hang on Hebe's cheek,
And love to live in dimple sleek;
Sport that wrinkled Care derides,
And Laughter holding both his sides.

Come, and trip it as ye go,
On the light fantastic toe;
And in thy right hand lead with thee
The mountain Nymph, sweet Liberty;
And, if I give thee honour due,
Mirth, admit me of thy crew,
To live with her, and live with thee,
In unreproved pleasures free;
To hear the lark begin his flight,
And singing startle the dull night,
From his watch-tower in the skies,
Till the dappled Dawn doth rise;
Then to come, in spite of sorrow,
And at my window bid good-morrow,
Through the sweet-briar or the vine,
Or the twisted eglantine;
While the cock with lively din
Scatters the rear of Darkness thin;
And to the stack, or the barn-door,
Stoutly struts his dames before:
Oft listening how the hounds and horn
Cheerly rouse the slumbering Morn,
From the side of some hoar hill,
Through the high wood echoing shrill:
Sometime walking, not unseen,
By hedgerow elms, on hillocks green,
Right against the eastern gate,
Where the great Sun begins his state,
Robed in flames and amber light,
The clouds in thousand liveries dight;
While the ploughman, near at hand,
Whistles o'er the furrowed land,
And the milkmaid singeth blithe,
And the mower whets his scythe,
And every shepherd tells his tale
Under the hawthorn in the dale.

   Straight mine eye hath caught new pleasures,
Whilst the lantskip round it measures:
Russet lawns, and fallows grey,
Where the nibbling flocks do stray;
Mountains on whose barren breast

The labouring clouds do often rest;
Meadows trim with daisies pied;
Shallow brooks, and rivers wide.
Towers and battlements it sees
Bosomed high in tufted trees,
Where perhaps some Beauty lies,
The Cynosure of neighbouring eyes.
Hard by, a cottage chimney smokes
From betwixt two aged oaks,
Where Corydon and Thyrsis met
Are at their savoury dinner set
Of hearbs and other country messes,
Which the neat-handed Phillis dresses;
And then in haste her bower she leaves,
With Thestylis to bind the sheaves;
Or, if the earlier season lead,
To the tanned haycock in the mead.
    Sometimes with secure delight
The upland hamlets will invite,
When the merry bells ring round,
And the jocond rebecks sound
To many a youth and many a maid
Dancing in the chequered shade;
And young and old come forth to play
On a sunshine holyday,
Till the livelong daylight fail:
Then to the spicy nut-brown ale,
With stories told of many a feat,
How fairy Mab the junkets eat:
She was pinched and pulled, she said;
And he, by Friar's lanthorn led,
Tells how the drudging Goblin sweat
To earn his cream-bowl duly set,
When in one night, ere glimpse of morn,
His shadowy flail hath threshed the corn
That ten day-labourers could not end;
Then lies him down, the lubbar fend,
And, stretched out all the chimney's length,
Basks at the fire his hairy strength,
And crop-full out of doors he flings,
Ere the first cock his matin rings.

Thus done the tales, to bed they creep,
By whispering winds soon lulled asleep.
Towered cities please us then,
And the busy hum of men,
Where throngs of Knights and Barons bold,
In weeds of peace, high triumphs hold,
With store of Ladies, whose bright eyes
Rain influence, and judge the prize
Of wit or arms, while both contend
To win her grace whom all commend.
There let Hymen oft appear
In saffron robe, with taper clear,
And pomp, and feast, and revelry,
With mask and antique pageantry;
Such sights as youthful Poets dream
On summer eves by haunted stream.
Then to the well-trod stage anon,
If Jonson's learned sock be on,
Or sweetest Shakespeare, Fancy's child,
Warble his native wood-notes wild.
And ever, against eating cares,
Lap me in soft Lydian airs,
Married to immortal verse,
Such as the meeting soul may pierce,
In notes with many a winding bout
Of linked sweetness long drawn out
With wanton heed and giddy cunning,
The melting voice through mazes running,
Untwisting all the chains that tie
The hidden soul of harmony;
That Orpheus' self may heave his head
From golden slumber on a bed
Of heaped Elysian flowers, and hear
Such strains as would have won the ear
Of Pluto to have quite set free
His half-regained Eurydice.
These delights if thou canst give,
Mirth, with thee I mean to live.

IL PENSEROSO

Hence, vain deluding Joys,
    The brood of Folly without father bred!
How little you bested,
    Or fill the fixed mind with all your toys!
Dwell in some idle brain,
    And fancies fond with gaudy shapes possess,
As thick and numberless
    As the gay motes that people the sunbeams,
Or likest hovering dreams,
    The fickle pensioners of Morpheus' train.
But hail! thou Goddess sage and holy!
Hail, divinest Melancholy!
Whose saintly visage is too bright
To hit the sense of human sight,
And therefore to our weaker view
O'erlaid with black, staid Wisdom's hue;
Black, but such as in esteem
Prince Memnon's sister might beseem,
Or that starred Ethiop Queen that strove
To set her beauty's praise above
The Sea-Nymphs, and their powers offended.
Yet thou art higher far descended:
Thee bright-haired Vesta long of yore
To solitary Saturn bore;
His daughter she; in Saturn's reign
Such mixture was not held a stain.
Oft in glimmering bowers and glades
He met her, and in secret shades
Of woody Ida's inmost grove,
Whilst yet there was no fear of Jove.
Come, pensive Nun, devout and pure,
Sober, steadfast, and demure,
All in a robe of darkest grain,
Flowing with majestic train,
And sable stole of cypress lawn
Over thy decent shoulders drawn.
Come; but keep thy wonted state,
With even step, and musing gait,
And looks commercing with the skies,

Thy rapt soul sitting in thine eyes:
There, held in holy passion still,
Forget thyself to marble, till
With a sad leaden downward cast
Thou fix them on the earth as fast.
And join with thee calm Peace and Quiet,
Spare Fast, that oft with gods doth diet,
And hears the Muses in a ring
Aye round about Jove's altar sing;
And add to these retired Leisure,
That in trim gardens takes his pleasure;
But, first and chieftest, with thee bring
Him that yon soars on golden wing,
Guiding the fiery-wheeled throne,
The Cherub Contemplation;
And the mute Silence hist along,
'Less Philomel will deign a song,
In her sweetest saddest plight,
Smoothing the rugged brow of Night,
While Cynthia checks her dragon yoke
Gently o'er the accustomed oak.
Sweet bird, that shunn'st the noise of folly,
Most musical, most melancholy!
Thee, Chauntress, oft the woods among
I woo, to hear thy even-song;
And, missing thee, I walk unseen
On the dry smooth-shaven green,
To behold the wandering Moon,
Riding near her highest noon,
Like one that had been led astray
Through the heaven's wide pathless way,
And oft, as if her head she bowed,
Stooping through a fleecy cloud.
Oft, on a plat of rising ground,
I hear the far-off curfew sound,
Over some wide-watered shore,
Swinging slow with sullen roar;
Or, if the air will not permit,
Some still removed place will fit,
Where glowing embers through the room
Teach light to counterfeit a gloom,
Far from all resort of mirth,

Save the cricket on the hearth,
Or the Bellman's drowsy charm
To bless the doors from nightly harm.
Or let my lamp, at midnight hour,
Be seen in some high lonely tower,
Where I may oft outwatch the Bear,
With thrice-great Hermes, or unsphere
The spirit of Plato, to unfold
What worlds or what vast regions hold
The immortal mind that hath forsook
Her mansion in this fleshly nook;
And of those Daemons that are found
In fire, air, flood, or underground,
Whose power hath a true consent
With planet or with element.
Sometime let gorgeous Tragedy
In sceptred pall come sweeping by,
Presenting Thebs, or Pelops' line,
Or the tale of Troy divine,
Or what (though rare) of later age
Ennobled hath the buskined stage.
But, O sad Virgin! that thy power
Might raise Musaeus from his bower;
Or bid the soul of Orpheus sing
Such notes as, warbled to the string,
Drew iron tears down Pluto's cheek,
And made Hell grant what Love did seek;
Or call up him that left half-told
The story of Cambuscan bold,
Of Camball, and of Algarsife,
And who had Canace to wife,
That owned the virtuous ring and glass,
And of the wondrous horse of brass
On which the Tartar King did ride;
And if aught else great Bards beside
In sage and solemn tunes have sung,
Of turneys, and of trophies hung,
Of forests, and inchantments drear,
Where more is meant than meets the ear.
Thus, Night, oft see me in thy pale career,
Till civil-suited Morn appear,
Not tricked and frounced, as she wont

With the Attic boy to hunt,
But kerchieft in a comely cloud,
While rocking winds are piping loud,
Or ushered with a shower still,
When the gust hath blown his fill,
Ending on the rustling leaves,
With minute drops from off the eaves.
And, when the sun begins to fling
His flaring beams, me, Goddess, bring
To arched walks of twilight groves,
And shadows brown, that Sylvan loves,
Of pine, or monumental oak,
Where the rude axe with heaved stroke
Was never heard the Nymphs to daunt,
Or fright them from their hallowed haunt.
There, in close covert, by some brook,
Where no profaner eye may look,
Hide me from Day's garish eye,
While the bee with honeyed thigh,
That at her flowery work doth sing,
And the waters murmuring,
With such consort as they keep,
Entice the dewey-feathered Sleep.
And let some strange mysterious dream,
Wave at his wings in airy stream,
Of lively portraiture displayed,
Softly on my eyelids laid.
And as I wake, sweet music breathe
Above, about, or underneath,
Sent by some Spirit to mortals good,
Or the unseen Genius of the wood.
But let my due feet never fail
To walk the studious cloister's pale,
And love the high embowed roof,
With antick pillars massy proof,
And storied windows richly dight,
Casting a dim religious light.
There let the pealing organ blow,
To the full voiced Quire below,
In service high and anthems clear,
As may with sweetness, through mine ear,
Dissolve me into ecstasies,

And bring all Heaven before mine eyes.
And may at last my weary age
Find out the peaceful hermitage,
The hairy gown and mossy cell,
Where I may sit and rightly spell,
Of every star that Heaven doth shew,
And every hearb that sips the dew;
Till old experience do attain
To something like prophetic strain.
These pleasures, Melancholy, give,
And I with thee will choose to live.

ON HIS BLINDNESS

When I consider how my light is spent
  Ere half my days in this dark world and wide,
  And that one Talent which is death to hide
  Lodged with me useless, though my soul more bent
To serve therewith my Maker, and present
  My true account, lest He returning chide,
  "Doth God exact day-labour, light denied?"
  I fondly ask. But Patience, to prevent
That murmur, soon replies, "God doth not need
  Either man's work or his own gifts. Who best
  Bear his mild yoke, they serve him best. His state
Is kingly: thousands at his bidding speed,
  And post o'er land and ocean without rest;
  They also serve who only stand and wait."

ON HIS DECEASED WIFE

Methought I saw my late espoused saint
  Brought to me like Alcestis from the grave,
  Whom Jove's great son to her glad husband gave,
  Rescued from Death by force, though pale and faint.
Mine, as whom washed from spot of childbed taint
  Purification in the Old Law did save,

And such as yet once more I trust to have
Full sight of her in Heaven without restraint,
Came vested all in white, pure as her mind.
Her face was veiled; yet to my fancied sight
Love, sweetness, goodness, in her person shined
So clear as in no face with more delight.
But, oh! as to embrace me she inclined,
I waked, she fled, and day brought back my night.

from PARADISE LOST

Of man's first disobedience, and the fruit
Of that forbidden tree whose mortal taste
Brought death into the World, and all our woe,
With loss of Eden, till one greater Man
Restore us, and regain the blissful Seat,
Sing, Heavenly Muse, that, on the secret top
Of Oreb, or of Sinai, didst inspire
That Shepherd who first taught the chosen seed
In the beginning how the heavens and earth
Rose out of Chaos: or, if Sion hill
Delight thee more, and Siloa's brook that flowed
Fast by the oracle of God, I thence
Invoke thy aid to my adventrous song,
That with no middle flight intends to soar
Above the Aonian mount, while it pursues
Things unattempted yet in prose or rhyme.
And chiefly Thou, O Spirit, that dost prefer
Before all temples the upright heart and pure,
Instruct me, for Thou knowest; Thou from the first
Wast present, and, with mighty wings outspread,
Dove-like sat'st brooding on the vast Abyss,
And madest it pregnant: what in me is dark
Illumine, what is low raise and support;
That, to the highth of this great argument,
I may assert Eternal Providence,
And justify the ways of God to men.
Say first—for Heaven hides nothing from thy view,
Nor the deep tract of Hell—say first what cause

Moved our grand Parents, in that happy state,
Favoured of Heaven so highly, to fall off
From their Creator, and transgress his will
For one restraint, lords of the World besides.
Who first seduced them to that foul revolt?

The infernal Serpent; he it was whose guile,
Stirred up with envy and revenge, deceived
The mother of mankind, what time his pride
Had cast him out from Heaven, with all his host
Of rebel Angels, by whose aid, aspiring
To set himself in glory above his peers,
He trusted to have equalled the Most High,
If he opposed, and, with ambitious aim
Against the throne and monarchy of God,
Raised impious war in Heaven and battle proud,
With vain attempt. Him the Almighty Power
Hurled headlong flaming from the ethereal sky,
With hideous ruin and combustion, down
To bottomless perdition, there to dwell
In adamantine chains and penal fire,
Who durst defy the Omnipotent to arms.

Nine times the space that measures day and night
To mortal men, he, with his horrid crew,
Lay vanquished, rowling in the fiery gulf,
Confounded, though immortal. But his doom
Reserved him to more wrath; for now the thought
Both of lost happiness and lasting pain
Torments him: round he throws his baleful eyes,
That witnessed huge affliction and dismay,
Mixed with obdurate pride and steadfast hate.
At once, as far as Angel's ken, he views
The dismal situation waste and wild.
A dungeon horrible, on all sides round,
As one great furnace flamed; yet from those flames
No light; but rather darkness visible
Served only to discover sights of woe,
Regions of sorrow, doleful shades, where peace
And rest can never dwell, hope never comes
That comes to all, but torture without end
Still urges, and a fiery deluge, fed
With ever-burning sulphur unconsumed
Such place Eternal Justice had prepared

For those rebellious; here their prison ordained
In utter darkness, and their portion set,
As far removed from God and light of Heaven
As from the centre thrice to the utmost pole.
Oh how unlike the place from whence they fell!
. . . .
So stretched out huge in length the Arch-Fiend lay,
Chained on the burning lake; nor ever thence
Had risen, or heaved his head, but that the will
And high permission of all-ruling Heaven
Left him at large to his own dark designs,
That with reiterated crimes he might
Heap on himself damnation, while he sought
Evil to others, and enraged might see
How all his malice served but to bring forth
Infinite goodness, grace, and mercy, shown
On Man by him seduced, but on himself
Treble confusion, wrath, and vengeance poured.
    Forthwith upright he rears from off the pool
His mighty stature; on each hand the flames
Driven backward slope their pointing spires, and, rowled
In billows, leave i' the midst a horrid vale.
Then with expanded wings he steers his flight
Aloft, incumbent on the dusky air,
That felt unusual weight; till on dry land
He lights—if it were land that ever burned
With solid, as the lake with liquid fire,
And such appeared in hue as when the force
Of subterranean wind transports a hill
Torn from Pelorus, or the shattered side
Of thundering Aetna, whose combustible
And fuelled entrails, thence conceiving fire,
Sublimed with mineral fury, aid the winds,
And leave a singed bottom all involved
With stench and smoke. Such resting found the soles
Of unblest feet.
. . . .
    "Is this the region, this the soil, the clime,"
Said then the lost Archangel, "this the seat
That we must change for Heaven? this mournful gloom
For that celestial light? Be it so, since He
Who now is sovran can dispose and bid

161

What shall be right. Fardest from Him is best,
Whom reason hath equalled, force hath made supreme
Above his equals. Farewell, happy fields,
Where joy forever dwells! Hail, horrors! Hail,
Infernal world! and thou, profoundest Hell,
Receive thy new possessor—one who brings
A mind not to be changed by place or time.
The mind is its own place, and in itself
Can make a Heaven of Hell, a Hell of Heaven.
What matter where, if I be still the same,
And what I should be, all but the less than he
Whom thunder hath made greater? Here at least
We shall be free; the Almighty hath not built
Here for his envy, will not drive us hence:
Here we may reign secure; and, in my choice,
To reign is worth ambition, though in Hell:
Better to reign in Hell than serve in Heaven.
But wherefore let we then our faithful friends,
The associates and co-partners of our loss,
Lie thus astonished on the oblivious pool,
And call them not to share with us their part
In this unhappy mansion, or once more
With rallied arms to try what may be yet
Regained in Heaven, or what more lost in Hell?"

. . . .

O for that warning voice, which he who saw
The Apocalypse heard cry in Heaven aloud,
Then when the Dragon, put to second rout,
Came furious down to be revenged on men,
Woe to the inhabitants on Earth! That now,
While time was, our first parents had been warned
The coming of their secret Foe, and scaped,
Haply so scaped, his mortal snare! For now
Satan, now first inflamed with rage, came down,
The tempter, ere the accuser, of mankind;
To wreak on innocent frail Man his loss
Of that first battle, and his flight to Hell.
Yet not rejoicing in his speed, though bold
Far off and fearless, nor with cause to boast,
Begins his dire attempt; which, nigh the birth
Now rowling, boils in his tumultuous breast,
And like a devilish engine back recoils

Upon himself. Horror and doubt distract
His troubled thoughts, and from the bottom stir
The hell within him; for within him Hell
He brings, and round about him, nor from Hell
One step, no more than from Himself, can fly
By change of place. Now conscience wakes despair
That slumbered; wakes the bitter memory
Of what he was, what is, and what must be
Worse; of worse deeds worse sufferings must ensue!
Sometimes towards Eden, which now in his view
Lay pleasant, his grieved look he fixes sad;
Sometimes towards Heaven and the full-blazing Sun,
Which now sat high in his meridian tower:
Then, much revolving, thus in sighs began:
    "O thou that, with surpassing glory crowned,
Lookest from thy sole dominion like the god
Of this new World—at whose sight all the stars
Hide their diminished heads—to thee I call,
But with no friendly voice, and add thy name,
O Sun, to tell thee how I hate thy beams,
That bring to my remembrance from what state
I fell, how glorious once above thy sphere,
Till pride and worse ambition threw me down,
Warring in Heaven against Heaven's matchless King!
Ah, wherefore? He deserved no such return
From me, whom he created what I was
In that bright eminence, and with his good
Upbraided none; nor was his service hard.
What could be less than to afford him praise,
The easiest recompense, and pay him thanks,
How due? Yet all his good proved ill in me,
And wrought but malice. Lifted up so high,
I 'sdained subjection, and thought one step higher
Would set me highest, and in a moment quit
The debt immense of endless gratitude,
So burthensome, still paying, still to owe;
Forgetful what from him I still received;
And understood not that a grateful mind
By owing owes not, but still pays, at once
Indebted and discharged—what burden then?
Oh, had his powerful destiny ordained
Me some inferior Angel, I had stood

163

Then happy; no unbounded hope had raised
Ambition. Yet why not? Some other Power
As great might have aspired, and me, though mean,
Drawn to his part. But other Powers as great
Fell not, but stand unshaken, from within
Or from without to all temptations armed!
Hadst thou the same free will and power to stand?
Thou hadst. Whom hast thou then, or what, to accuse,
But Heaven's free love dealt equally to all?
Be then his love accursed, since, love or hate,
To me alike it deals eternal woe.
Nay, cursed be thou; since against his thy will
Chose freely what it now so justly rues.
Me miserable! which way shall I fly
Infinite wrath and infinite despair?
Which way I fly is Hell; myself am Hell;
And, in the lowest deep, a lower deep
Still threatening to devour me opens wide,
To which the Hell I suffer seems a Heaven.
O, then, at last relent! Is there no place
Left for repentance, none for pardon left?
None left but by submission; and that word
Disdain forbids me, and my dread of shame
Among the Spirits beneath, whom I seduced
With other promises and other vaunts
Than to submit, boasting I could subdue
The Omnipotent. Aye me! they little know
How dearly I abide that boast so vain,
Under what torments inwardly I groan.
While they adore me on the throne of Hell,
With diadem and sceptre high advanced,
The lower still I fall, only supreme
In misery: such joy ambition finds!
But say I could repent, and could obtain,
By act of grace, my former state; how soon
Would highth recall high thoughts, how soon unsay
What feigned submission swore! Ease would recant
Vows made in pain, as violent and void
(For never can true reconcilement grow
Where wounds of deadly hate have pierced so deep);
Which would but lead me to a worse relapse
And heavier fall: so should I purchase dear

Short intermission, bought with double smart.
This knows my Punisher; therefore as far
From granting he, as I from begging, peace.
All hope excluded thus, behold, instead
Of us, outcast, exiled, his new delight,
Mankind, created, and for him this World!
So farewell hope, and, with hope, farewell fear,
Farewell remorse! All good to me is lost;
Evil, be thou my Good: by thee at least
Divided empire with Heaven's King I hold,
By thee, and more than half perhaps will reign;
As Man ere long, and this new World, shall know."
    Thus while he spake, each passion dimmed his face,
Thrice changed with pale—ire, envy, and despair;
Which marred his borrowed visage, and betrayed
Him counterfeit, if any eye beheld:
For Heavenly minds from such distempers foul
Are ever clear. Whereof he soon aware
Each perturbation smoothed with outward calm,
Artificer of fraud; and was the first
That practised falsehood under saintly show,
Deep malice to conceal, couched with revenge:
Yet not enough had practised to deceive
Uriel, once warned; whose eye pursued him down
The way he went, and on the Assyrian mount
Saw him disfigured, more than could befall
Spirit of happy sort: his gestures fierce
He marked and mad demeanour, then alone,
As he supposed, all unobserved, unseen.
    So on he fares, and to the border comes
Of Eden, where delicious Paradise,
Now nearer, crowns with her enclosure green,
As with a rural mound, the champain head
Of a steep wilderness whose hairy sides
With thicket overgrown, grotesque and wild,
Access denied; and overhead up-grew
Insuperable highth of loftiest shade,
Cedar, and pine, and fir, and branching palm,
A sylvan scene, and, as the ranks ascend
Shade above shade, a woody theatre
Of stateliest view. Yet higher than their tops
The verdurous wall of Paradise up-sprung;

Which to our general Sire gave prospect large
Into his nether empire neighbouring round.
And higher than that wall a circling row
Of goodliest trees, loaden with fairest fruit,
Blossoms and fruits at once of golden hue,
Appeared, with gay enamelled colours mixed;
On which the sun more glad impressed his beams
Than in fair evening cloud, or humid bow,
When God hath showered the earth; so lovely seemed
That lantskip. And of pure now purer air
Meets his approach, and to the heart inspires
Vernal delight and joy, able to drive
All sadness but despair. Now gentle gales,
Fanning their odoriferous wings, dispense
Native perfumes, and whisper whence they stole
Those balmy spoils. As when to them who sail
Beyond the Cape of Hope, and now are past
Mozambic, off at sea north-east winds blow
Sabean odours from the spicy shore
Of Araby the Blest, with such delay
Well pleased they slack their course, and many a league
Cheered with the grateful smell old Ocean smiles;
So entertained those odorous sweets the Fiend
Who came their bane, though with them better pleased
Than Asmodëus with the fishy fume
That drove him, though enamoured, from the spouse
Of Tobit's son, and with a vengeance sent
From Media post to Egypt, there fast bound.
    Now to the ascent of that steep savage hill
Satan had journeyed on, pensive and slow;
But further way found none; so thick entwined,
As one continued brake, the undergrowth
Of shrubs and tangling bushes had perplexed
All path of man or beast that passed that way.
One gate there only was, and that looked east
On the other side. Which when the Arch-Felon saw,
Due entrance he disdained, and, in contempt,
At one slight bound high overleaped all bound
Of hill or highest wall, and sheer within
Lights on his feet. As when a prowling wolf,
Whom hunger drives to seek new haunt for prey,
Watching where shepherds pen their flocks at eve,

In hurdled cotes amid the field secure,
Leaps o'er the fence with ease into the fold;
Or as a thief, bent to unhoard the cash
Of some rich burgher, whose substantial doors,
Cross-barred and bolted fast, fear no assault,
In at the window climbs, or o'er the tiles;
So clomb this first grand Thief into God's fold:
So since into his Church lewd hirelings climb.
Thence up he flew, and on the Tree of Life,
The middle tree and highest there that grew,
Sat like a Cormorant; yet not true life
Thereby regained, but sat devising death
To them who lived; nor on the virtue thought
Of that life-giving plant, but only used
For prospect what, well used, had been the pledge
Of immortality. So little knows
Any, but God alone, to value right
The good before him, but perverts best things
To worst abuse, or to their meanest use.
Beneath him, with new wonder, now he views,
To all delight of human sense exposed,
In narrow room Nature's whole wealth; yea, more—
A Heaven on Earth: for blissful Paradise
Of God the garden was, by him in the east
Of Eden planted. Eden stretched her line
From Auran eastward to the royal towers
Of great Seleucia, built by Grecian kings,
Or where the sons of Eden long before
Dwelt in Telassar. In this pleasant soil
His far more pleasant garden God ordained.
Out of the fertile ground he caused to grow
All trees of noblest kind for sight, smell, taste;
And all amid them stood the Tree of Life,
High eminent, blooming ambrosial fruit
Of vegetable gold; and next to life,
Our death, the Tree of Knowledge, grew fast by—
Knowledge of good, bought dear by knowing ill.
Southward through Eden went a river large,
Nor changed his course, but through the shaggy hill
Passed underneath ingulfed; for God had thrown
That mountain, as his garden-mould, high raised
Upon the rapid current, which, through veins

167

Of porous earth with kindly thirst updrawn,
Rose a fresh fountain, and with many a rill
Watered the garden; thence united fell
Down the steep glade, and met the nether flood,
Which from his darksome passage now appears,
And now, divided into four main streams,
Runs diverse, wandering many a famous realm
And country whereof here needs no account;
But rather to tell how, if Art could tell
How, from that sapphire fount the crisped brooks,
Rowling on orient pearl and sands of gold,
With mazy error under pendent shades
Ran nectar, visiting each plant, and fed
Flowers worthy of Paradise, which not nice Art
In beds and curious knots, but Nature boon
Poured forth profuse on hill, and dale, and plain,
Both where the morning sun first warmly smote
The open field, and where the unpierced shade
Imbrowned the noontide bowers. Thus was this place,
A happy rural seat of various view:
Groves whose rich trees wept odorous gums and balm;
Others whose fruit, burnished with golden rind,
Hung amiable—Hesperian fables true,
If true, here only—and of delicious taste.
Betwixt them lawns, or level downs, and flocks
Grazing the tender herb, were interposed,
Or palmy hillock; or the flowery lap
Of some irriguous valley spread her store,
Flowers of all hue, and without thorn the rose.
Another side, umbrageous grots and caves
Of cool recess, o'er which the mantling vine
Lays forth her purple grape, and gently creeps
Luxuriant; meanwhile murmuring waters fall
Down the slope hills dispersed, or in a lake,
That to the fringed bank with myrtle crowned
Her crystal mirror holds, unite their streams.
The birds their quire apply; airs, vernal airs,
Breathing the smell of field and grove, attune
The trembling leaves, while universal Pan,
Knit with the Graces and the Hours in dance,
Led on the eternal Spring. Not that fair field
Of Enna, where Proserpin gathering flowers,

Herself a fairer flower, by gloomy Dis
Was gathered—which cost Ceres all that pain
To seek her through the world—nor that sweet grove
Of Daphne, by Orontes and the inspired
Castalian spring, might with this Paradise
Of Eden strive; nor that Nyseian isle,
Girt with the river Triton, where old Cham,
Whom Gentiles Ammon call and Libyan Jove,
Hid Amalthea, and her florid son,
Young Bacchus, from his stepdame Rhea's eye;
Nor, where Abassin kings their issue guard,
Mount Amara (though this by some supposed
True Paradise) under the Ethiop line
By Nilus' head, enclosed with shining rock,
A whole day's journey high, but wide remote
From this Assyrian garden, where the Fiend
Saw undelighted all delight, all kind
Of living creatures, new to sight and strange.
Two of far nobler shape, erect and tall,
God-like erect, with native honour clad
In naked majesty, seemed lords of all,
And worthy seemed; for in their looks divine
The image of their glorious Maker shon,
Truth, wisdom, sanctitude severe and pure—
Severe, but in true filial freedom placed,
Whence true authority in men: though both
Not equal, as their sex not equal seemed;
For contemplation he and valour formed,
For softness she and sweet attractive grace;
He for God only, she for God in him.
His fair large front and eye sublime declared
Absolute rule; and Hyacinthin locks
Round from his parted forelock manly hung
Clustering, but not beneath his shoulders broad:
She, as a veil down to the slender waist,
Her unadorned golden tresses wore
Dishevelled, but in wanton ringlets waved
As the vine curls her tendrils—which implied
Subjection, but required with gentle sway,
And by her yielded, by him best received—
Yielded, with coy submission, modest pride,
And sweet, reluctant, amorous delay.

Nor those mysterious parts were then concealed;
Then was not guilty shame. Dishonest shame
Of Nature's works, honour dishonourable,
Sin-bred, how have ye troubled all mankind
With shows instead, mere shows of seeming pure,
And banished from man's life his happiest life,
Simplicity and spotless innocence!
So passed they naked on, nor shunned the sight
Of God or Angel; for they thought no ill:
So hand in hand they passed, the loveliest pair
That ever since in love's embraces met—
Adam the goodliest man of men since born
His sons; the fairest of her daughters Eve.

. . . .

In bower and field he sought, where any tuft
Of grove or garden-plot more pleasant lay,
Their tendance or plantation for delight;
By fountain or by shady rivulet
He sought them both, but wished his hap might find
Eve separate; he wished, but not with hope
Of what so seldom chanced, when to his wish,
Beyond his hope, Eve separate he spies,
Veiled in a cloud of fragrance, where she stood,
Half-spied, so thick the roses bushing round
About her glowed, oft stooping to support
Each flower of tender stalk, whose head, though gay
Carnation, purple, azure, or specked with gold,
Hung drooping unsustained. Them she upstays
Gently with myrtle band, mindless the while
Herself, though fairest unsupported flower,
From her best prop so far, and storm so nigh.
Nearer he drew, and many a walk traversed
Of stateliest covert, cedar, pine, or palm;
Then voluble and bold, now hid, now seen
Among thick-woven arborets, and flowers
Imbordered on each bank, the hand of Eve:
Spot more delicious than those gardens feigned
Or of revived Adonis, or renowned
Alcinoüs, host of old Laertes' son,
Or that, not mystic, where the sapient king
Held dalliance with his fair Egyptian spouse.
Much he the place admired, the person more.

As one who, long in populous city pent,
Where houses thick and sewers annoy the air,
Forth issuing on a summer's morn, to breathe
Among the pleasant villages and farms
Adjoined, from each thing met conceives delight—
The smell of grain, or tedded grass, or kine,
Or dairy, each rural sight, each rural sound—
If chance with nymph-like step fair virgin pass,
What pleasing seemed for her now pleases more,
She most, and in her look sums all delight:
Such pleasure took the Serpent to behold
This flowery plat, the sweet recess of Eve
Thus early, thus alone. Her heavenly form
Angelic, but more soft and feminine,
Her graceful innocence, her every air
Of gesture or least action, overawed
His malice, and with rapine sweet bereaved
His fierceness of the fierce intent it brought.
That space the Evil One abstracted stood
From his own evil, and for the time remained
Stupidly good, of enmity disarmed,
Of guile, of hate, of envy, of revenge.
But the hot hell that always in him burns,
Though in mid Heaven, soon ended his delight,
And tortures him now more, the more he sees
Of pleasure not for him ordained. Then soon
Fierce hate he recollects, and all his thoughts
Of mischief, gratulating, thus excites:
　　"Thoughts, whither have ye led me? with what sweet
Compulsion thus transported to forget
What hither brought us? hate, not love, nor hope
Of Paradise for Hell, here to taste
Of pleasure, but all pleasure to destroy,
Save what is in destroying; other joy
To me is lost. Then let me not let pass
Occasion which now smiles. Behold alone
The Woman, opportune to all attempts—
Her husband, for I view far round, not nigh,
Whose higher intellectual more I shun,
And strength, of courage haughty, and of limb
Heroic built, though of terrestrial mould;
Foe not informidable, exempt from wound—

171

I not; so much hath Hell debased, and pain
Infeebled me, to what I was in Heaven.
She fair, divinely fair, fit love for Gods,
Not terrible, though terror be in love,
And beauty, not approached by stronger hate,
Hate stronger under show of love well feigned—
The way which to her ruin now I tend."

So spake the Enemy of Mankind, enclosed
In serpent, inmate bad, and toward Eve
Addressed his way—not with indented wave,
Prone on the ground, as since, but on his rear,
Circular base of rising folds, that towered
Fold above fold, a surging maze; his head
Crested aloft, and carbuncle his eyes;
With burnished neck of verdant gold, erect
Amidst his circling spires, that on the grass
Floated redundant. Pleasing was his shape
And lovely; never since the serpent kind
Lovelier—not those that in Illyria changed
Hermione and Cadmus, or the God
In Epidaurus; nor to which transformed
Ammonian Jove, or Capitoline, was seen,
He with Olympias, this with her who bore
Scipio, the highth of Rome. With tract oblique
At first, as one who sought access but feared
To interrupt, sidelong he works his way.
As when a ship, by skilful steersman wrought
Nigh river's mouth or foreland, where the wind
Veers oft, as oft so steers, and shifts her sail,
So varied he, and of his tortuous train
Curled many a wanton wreath in sight of Eve,
To lure her eye. She, busied, heard the sound
Of rustling leaves, but minded not, as used
To such disport before her through the field
From every beast, more duteous at her call
Than at Circean call the herd disguised.
He, bolder now, uncalled before her stood,
But as in gaze admiring. Oft he bowed
His turret crest and sleek enamelled neck,
Fawning, and licked the ground whereon she trod.
His gentle dumb expression turned at length
The eye of Eve to mark his play; he, glad

Of her attention gained, with serpent-tongue
Organic, or impulse of vocal air,
His fraudulent temptation thus began:
  "Wonder not, sovran mistress (if perhaps
Thou canst who art sole wonder), much less arm
Thy looks, the heaven of mildness, with disdain,
Displeased that I approach thee thus, and gaze
Insatiate, I thus single, nor have feared
Thy awful brow, more awful thus retired.
Fairest resemblance of thy Maker fair,
Thee all things living gaze on, all things thine
By gift, and thy celestial beauty adore,
With ravishment beheld—there best beheld
Where universally admired. But here,
In this enclosure wild, these beasts among,
Beholders rude, and shallow to discern
Half what in thee is fair, one man except,
Who sees thee (and what is one?) who shouldst be seen
A Goddess among Gods, adored and served
By Angels numberless, thy daily train?"
  So glozed the Tempter, and his proem tuned.
Into the heart of Eve his words made way,
Though at the voice much marvelling; at length,
Not unamazed, she thus in answer spake:
  "What may this mean? Language of Man pronounced
By tongue of brute, and human sense expressed!
The first at least of these I thought denied
To beasts, whom God on their creation-day
Created mute to all articulate sound;
The latter I demur, for in their looks
Much reason, and in their actions, oft appears.
Thee, Serpent, subtlest beast of all the field
I knew, but not with human voice endued;
Redouble, then, this miracle, and say,
How camest thou speakable of mute, and how
To me so friendly grown above the rest
Of brutal kind that daily are in sight:
Say, for such wonder claims attention due."
  To whom the guileful Tempter thus replied:
"Empress of this fair World, resplendent Eve!
Easy to me it is to tell thee all
What thou commandest, and right thou shouldst be obeyed.

173

I was at first as other beasts that graze
The trodden herb, of abject thoughts and low,
As was my food, nor aught but food discerned
Or sex, and apprehended nothing high:
Till on a day, roving the field, I chanced
A goodly tree far distant to behold,
Loaden with fruit of fairest colours mixed,
Ruddy and gold. I nearer drew to gaze;
When from the boughs a savoury odour blown,
Grateful to appetite, more pleased my sense
Than smell of sweetest fennel, or the teats
Of ewe or goat dropping with milk at even,
Unsucked of lamb or kid, that tend their play.
To satisfy the sharp desire I had
Of tasting those fair Apples, I resolved
Not to defer; hunger and thirst at once,
Powerful persuaders, quickened at the scent
Of that alluring fruit, urged me so keen.
About the mossy trunk I wound me soon;
For, high from ground, the branches would require
Thy utmost reach, or Adam's; round the Tree
All other beasts that saw, with like desire
Longing and envying stood, but could not reach.
Amid the tree now got, where plenty hung
Tempting so nigh, to pluck and eat my fill
I spared not; for such pleasure till that hour
At feed or fountain never had I found.
Sated at length, ere long I might perceive
Strange alteration in me, to degree
Of Reason in my inward powers, and Speech
Wanted not long, though to this shape retained.
Thenceforth to speculations high or deep
I turned my thoughts, and with capacious mind
Considered all things visible in Heaven,
Or Earth, or Middle, all things fair and good.
But all that fair and good in thy divine
Semblance, and in thy beauty's heavenly ray,
United I beheld—no fair to thine
Equivalent or second; which compelled
Me thus, though importune perhaps, to come
And gaze, and worship thee of right declared
Sovran of creatures, universal Dame!"

So talked the spirited sly Snake; and Eve,
Yet more amazed, unwary thus replied:
  "Serpent, thy overpraising leaves in doubt
The virtue of that Fruit, in thee first proved.
But say, where grows the Tree? from hence how far?
For many are the trees of God that grow
In Paradise, and various, yet unknown
To us; in such abundance lies our choice
As leaves a greater store of fruit untouched,
Still hanging incorruptible, till men
Grow up to their provision, and more hands
Help to disburden Nature of her bearth."
  To whom the wily Adder, blithe and glad:
"Empress, the way is ready, and not long—
Beyond a row of myrtles, on a flat,
Fast by a fountain, one small thicket past
Of blowing myrrh and balm. If thou accept
My conduct, I can bring thee thither soon."
  "Lead, then," said Eve. He, leading, swiftly rowled
In tangles, and made intricate seem straight,
To mischief swift. Hope elevates, and joy
Brightens his crest. As when a wandering fire,
Compact of unctuous vapour, which the night
Condenses, and the cold invirons round,
Kindled through agitation to a flame
(Which oft, they say, some evil Spirit attends),
Hovering and blazing with delusive light,
Misleads the amazed night-wanderer from his way
To bogs and mires, and oft through pond or pool,
There swallowed up and lost, from succour far:
So glistered the dire Snake, and into fraud
Led Eve, our credulous mother, to the Tree
Of Prohibition, root of all our woe;
Which when she saw, thus to her guide she spake:
  "Serpent, we might have spared our coming hither,
Fruitless to me, though fruit be here to excess,
The credit of whose virtue rest with thee—
Wondrous, indeed, if cause of such effects!
But of this tree we may not taste nor touch;
God so commanded, and left that command
Sole daughter of his voice: the rest, we live
Law to ourselves; our Reason is our Law."

To whom the Tempter guilefully replied:
"Indeed! Hath God then said that of the fruit
Of all these garden-trees ye shall not eat,
Yet lords declared of all in Earth or Air?"
     To whom thus Eve, yet sinless: "Of the fruit
Of each tree in the garden we may eat;
But of the fruit of this fair Tree, amidst
The Garden, God hath said, 'Ye shall not eat
Thereof, nor shall ye touch it, lest ye die.' "
     She scarce had said, though brief, when now more bold
The Tempter, but, with show of zeal and love
To Man, and indignation at his wrong,
New part puts on, and, as to passion moved,
Fluctuates disturbed, yet comely, and in act
Raised, as of some great matter to begin.
As when of old some orator renowned
In Athens or free Rome, where eloquence
Flourished, since mute, to some great cause addressed,
Stood in himself collected, while each part,
Motion, each act, won audience ere the tongue
Sometimes in highth began, as no delay
Of preface brooking through his zeal of right:
So standing, moving, or to highth upgrown,
The Tempter, all impassioned, thus began:
     "O sacred, wise, and wisdom-giving Plant,
Mother of science! Now I feel thy power
Within me clear, not only to discern
Things in their causes, but to trace the ways
Of highest agents, deemed however wise.
Queen of this Universe! Do not believe
Those rigid threats of death. Ye shall not die.
How should ye? By the Fruit? It gives you life
To knowledge. By the Threatener? Look on me,
Me who have touched and tasted, yet both live,
And life more perfet have attained than Fate
Meant me, by ventring higher than my lot.
Shall that be shut to Man which to the Beast
Is open? or will God incense his ire
For such a petty trespass, and not praise
Rather your dauntless virtue, whom the pain
Of death denounced, whatever thing Death be,
Deterred not from achieving what might lead

176

To happier life, knowledge of Good and Evil?
Of good, how just! Of evil—if what is evil
Be real, why not known, since easier shunned?
God, therefore, cannot hurt ye and be just;
Not just, not God; not feared then, nor obeyed:
Your fear itself of death removes the fear.
Why, then, was this forbid? Why but to awe,
Why but to keep ye low and ignorant,
His worshipers? He knows that in the day
Ye eat thereof your eyes, that seem so clear,
Yet are but dim, shall perfectly be then
Opened and cleared, and ye shall be as Gods,
Knowing both good and evil, as they know.
That ye should be as Gods, since I as Man,
Internal Man, is but proportion meet—
I, of brute, human; ye, of human, Gods.
So ye shall die perhaps, by putting off
Human, to put on Gods—death to be wished,
Though threatened, which no worse than this can bring!
And what are Gods, that Man may not become
As they, participating godlike food?
The Gods are first, and that advantage use
On our belief, that all from them proceeds.
I question it; for this fair Earth I see,
Warmed by the Sun, producing every kind;
Them nothing. If they all things, who enclosed
Knowledge of Good and Evil in this Tree,
That whoso eats thereof forthwith attains
Wisdom without their leave? And wherein lies
The offence, that Man should thus attain to know?
What can your knowledge hurt him, or this Tree
Impart against his will, if all be his?
Or is it envy? And can envy dwell
In Heavenly breasts? These, these and many more
Causes import your need of this fair Fruit.
Goddess humane, reach, then, and freely taste!"
   He ended; and his words, replete with guile,
Into her heart too easy entrance won.
Fixed on the Fruit she gazed, which to behold
Might tempt alone; and in her ears the sound
Yet rung of his persuasive words, impregned
With reason, to her seeming, and with truth.

Meanwhile the hour of noon drew on, and waked
An eager appetite, raised by the smell
So savoury of that Fruit, which with desire,
Inclinable now grown to touch or taste,
Solicited her longing eye; yet first,
Pausing a while, thus to herself she mused:
"Great are thy virtues, doubtless, best of Fruits,
Though kept from Man, and worthy to be admired,
Whose taste, too long forborne, at first assay
Gave elocution to the mute, and taught
The tongue not made for speech to speak thy praise.
Thy praise he also who forbids thy use
Conceals not from us, naming thee the Tree
Of Knowledge, knowledge both of Good and Evil;
Forbids us then to taste. But his forbidding
Commends thee more, while it infers the good
By thee communicated, and our want;
For good unknown sure is not bad, or, had
And yet unknown, is as not had at all.
In plain, then, what forbids he but to know?
Forbids us good, forbids us to be wise!
Such prohibitions bind not. But, if Death
Bind us with after-bands, what profits then
Our inward freedom? In the day we eat
Of this fair Fruit, our doom is we shall die!
How dies the Serpent? He hath eaten, and lives,
And knows, and speaks, and reasons, and discerns,
Irrational till then. For us alone
Was death invented? Or to us denied
This intellectual food, for beasts reserved?
For beasts it seems; yet that one beast which first
Hath tasted envies not, but brings with joy
The good befallen him, author unsuspect,
Friendly to Man, far from deceit or guile.
What fear I, then? Rather, what know to fear
Under this ignorance of Good and Evil,
Of God or Death, of law or penalty?
Here grows the cure of all, this Fruit divine,
Fair to the eye, inviting to the taste,
Of virtue to make wise. What hinders, then,
To reach, and feed at once both body and mind?"
　　So saying, her rash hand in evil hour

Forth-reaching to the Fruit, she plucked, she eat.
Earth felt the wound, and Nature from her seat,
Sighing through all her works, gave signs of woe
That all was lost. Back to the thicket slunk
The guilty Serpent, and well might, for Eve,
Intent now only on her taste, naught else
Regarded; such delight till then, as seemed,
In fruit she never tasted, whether true,
Or fancied so through expectation high
Of knowledge; nor was Godhead from her thought.
Greedily she ingorged without restraint,
And knew not eating death.

JOHN SUCKLING
(1609–42)

Out upon it, I have loved
  Three whole days together;
And am like to love three more,
  If it prove fair weather.

Time shall moult away his wings,
  Ere he shall discover
In the whole wide world again
  Such a constant lover.

But the spite on't is, no praise
  Is due at all to me:
Love with me had made no stays,
  Had it any been but she.

Had it any been but she,
  And that very face,
There had been at least ere this
  A dozen dozen in her place.

*

Why so pale and wan, fond lover?
    Prithee, why so pale?
Will, when looking well can't move her,
    Looking ill prevail?
    Prithee, why so pale?

Why so dull and mute, young sinner?
    Prithee, why so mute?
Will, when speaking well can't win her,
    Saying nothing do 't?
    Prithee, why so mute?

Quit, quit, for shame, this will not move:
This cannot take her.
If of herself she will not love,
Nothing can make her:
The devil take her!

RICHARD CRASHAW
(1613–49)

THE FLAMING HEART

Upon the book and picture of the seraphical Saint Teresa,
as she is usually expressed with a seraphim beside her.

Well-meaning readers, you that come as friends
And catch the precious name this piece pretends;
Make not too much haste to admire
That fair-cheeked fallacy of fire.
That is a seraphim, they say,
And this the great Teresia.
Readers, be ruled by me, and make
Here a well-placed and wise mistake.
You must transpose the picture quite,
And spell it wrong to read it right;
Read him for her and her for him;
And call the saint the seraphim.
   Painter, what didst thou understand
To put her dart into his hand?
See, even the years and size of him
Show this the mother seraphim.
This is the mistress-flame; and duteous he
Her happy fireworks, here, comes down to see.
O most poor-spirited of men!
Had thy cold pencil kissed her pen,
Thou couldst not so unkindly err
To show us this faint shade for her.
Why man, this speaks pure mortal frame,
And mocks with female frost love's manly flame.
One would suspect thou meantest to paint
Some weak, inferior, woman saint.
But had thy pale-faced purple took
Fire from the burning cheeks of that bright book,
Thou wouldst on her have heaped up all

182

That could be found seraphical;
Whate'er this youth of fire wears fair,
Rosy fingers, radiant hair,
Glowing cheeks, and glistering wings,
All those fair and flagrant things,
But before all that fiery dart
Had filled the hand of this great heart.
　Do then as equal right requires,
Since his the blushes be, and hers the fires;
Resume and rectify thy rude design;
Undress thy seraphim into mine.
Redeem this injury of thy art;
Give him the veil, give her the dart.
　Give him the veil, that he may cover
The red cheeks of a rivalled lover,
Ashamed that our world now can show
Nests of new seraphims here below.
　Give her the dart, for it is she
(Fair youth) shoots both thy shaft and thee.
Say, all ye wise and well-pierced hearts,
That live and die amidst her darts,
What is it your tasteful spirits prove
In that rare life of her and love?
Say and bear witness. Sends she not
A seraphim at every shot?
What magazines of immortal arms there shine!
Heaven's great artillery in each love-spun line.
Give then the dart to her who gives the flame;
Give him the veil, who kindly takes the shame.
　But if it be the frequent fate
Of worse faults to be fortunate;
If all's prescription; and proud wrong
Harkens not to an humble song;
For all the gallantry of him,
Give me the suffering seraphim.
His be the bravery of all those bright things,
The glowing cheeks, the glittering wings;
The rosy hand, the radiant dart;
Leave her alone the flaming heart.
　Leave her that; and thou shalt leave her
Not one loose shaft, but love's whole quiver.
For in love's field was never found

A nobler weapon than a wound.
Love's passives are his activest part.
The wounded is the wounding heart.
O heart! the equal poise of love's both parts,
Big like with wounds and darts,
Live in these conquering leaves; live all the same,
And walk through all tongues one triumphant flame.
Live here, great heart, and love and die and kill,
And bleed and wound, and yield and conquer still.
Let this immortal life, where'er it comes,
Walk in a crowd of loves and martyrdoms.
Let mystic deaths wait on't, and wise souls be
The love-slain witnesses of this life of thee.
O sweet incendiary! show here thy art,
Upon this carcass of a hard cold heart.
Let all thy scattered shafts of light, that play
Among the leaves of thy large books of day,
Combined against this breast, at once break in
And take away from me myself and sin!
This gracious robbery shall thy bounty be,
And my best fortunes such fair spoils of me.
O thou undaunted daughter of desires,
By all thy dower of lights and fires,
By all the eagle in thee, all the dove,
By all thy lives and deaths of love,
By thy large draughts of intellectual day
And by thy thirsts of love more large than they,
By all thy brim-filled bowls of fierce desire,
By thy last morning's draught of liquid fire,
By the full kingdom of that final kiss
That seized thy parting soul, and sealed thee His,
By all the heavens thou hast in Him,
Fair sister of the seraphim,
By all of Him we have in thee,
Leave nothing of myself in me!
Let me so read thy life that I
Unto all life of mine may die!

RICHARD LOVELACE
(1618–57)

TO ALTHEA, FROM PRISON

When love with unconfined wings
Hovers within my gates,
And my divine Althea brings
To whisper at the grates;
When I lie tangled in her hair
And fettered to her eye,
The gods that wanton in the air
Know no such liberty.

When flowing cups run swiftly round
With no allaying Thames,
Our careless heads with roses bound,
Our hearts with loyal flames;
When thirsty grief in wine we steep,
When healths and draughts go free,
Fishes that tipple in the deep
Know no such liberty.

When (like committed linnets) I
With shriller throat shall sing
The sweetness, mercy, majesty,
And glories of my King;
When I shall voice aloud how good
He is, how great should be,
Enlarged winds, that curl the flood,
Know no such liberty.

Stone walls do not a prison make,
Nor iron bars a cage;
Minds innocent and quiet take
That for an hermitage.

If I have freedom in my love,
And in my soul am free,
Angels alone that soar above
Enjoy such liberty.

ANDREW MARVELL
(1621–78)

ON A DROP OF DEW

See how the orient dew,
Shed from the bosom of the morn
  Into the blowing roses,
Yet careless of its mansion new,
For the clear region where 'twas born
  Round in itself incloses,
  And in its little globe's extent
Frames as it can its native element;
  How it the purple flower does slight,
  Scarce touching where it lies,
But gazing back upon the skies,
  Shines with a mournful light
    Like its own tear,
Because so long divided from the sphere.
  Restless it rolls and unsecure,
    Trembling lest it grow impure,
  Till the warm sun pity its pain,
And to the skies exhale it back again.
  So the soul, that drop, that ray
Of the clear fountain of eternal day,
Could it within the human flower be seen,
  Remembering still its former height,
  Shuns the sweet leaves and blossoms green;
  And recollecting its own light,
Does, in its pure and circling thoughts, express
The greater heaven in an heaven less.
  In how coy a figure wound,
  Every way it turns away;
  So the world excluding round,
  Yet receiving in the day;
  Dark beneath but bright above,
  Here disdaining, there in love;

How loose and easy hence to go,
How girt and ready to ascend;
Moving but on a point below,
It all about does upwards bend.
Such did the manna's sacred dew distill,
White and entire, though congealed and chill;
Congealed on earth, but does, dissolving, run
Into the glories of the almighty sun.

A DIALOGUE BETWEEN THE SOUL
AND BODY

SOUL

Oh, who shall from this dungeon raise
A soul enslaved so many ways?
With bolts of bones, that fettered stands
In feet, and manacled in hands;
Here blinded with an eye and there
Deaf with the drumming of an ear;
A soul hung up, as 'twere, in chains
Of nerves and arteries and veins;
Tortured, besides each other part,
In a vain head and double heart.

BODY

Oh, who shall me deliver whole
From bonds of this tyrannic soul?
Which stretched upright, impales me so
That mine own precipice I go;
And warms and moves this needless frame,
A fever could but do the same.
And, wanting where its spite to try,
Has made me live to let me die.
A body that could never rest,
Since this ill spirit it possessed.

188

SOUL

What magic could me thus confine
Within another's grief to pine,
Where whatsoever it complain,
I feel, that cannot feel, the pain?
And all my care itself employs,
That to preserve which me destroys.
Constrained not only to endure
Diseases, but, what's worse, the cure;
And ready oft the port to gain,
Am shipwrecked into health again.

BODY

But physic yet could never reach
The maladies thou me dost teach:
Whom first the cramp of hope does tear,
And then the palsy shakes of fear;
The pestilence of love does heat,
Or hatred's hidden ulcer eat.
Joy's cheerful madness does perplex,
Or sorrow's other madness vex;
Which knowledge forces me to know,
And memory will not forego.
What but a soul could have the wit
To build me up for sin so fit?
So architects do square and hew
Green trees that in the forest grew.

TO HIS COY MISTRESS

Had we but world enough, and time,
This coyness, Lady, were no crime.
We would sit down, and think which way
To walk, and pass our long love's day.
Thou by the Indian Ganges' side
Shouldst rubies find; I by the tide
Of Humber would complain. I would
Love you ten years before the Flood,

And you should, if you please, refuse
Till the conversion of the Jews.
My vegetable love should grow
Vaster than empires and more slow.
An hundred years should go to praise
Thine eyes, and on thy forehead gaze;
Two hundred to adore each breast,
But thirty thousand to the rest;
An age at least to every part,
And the last age should show your heart.
For, Lady, you deserve this state,
Nor would I love at lower rate.

But at my back I always hear
Time's winged chariot hurrying near;
And yonder all before us lie
Deserts of vast eternity.
Thy beauty shall no more be found,
Nor, in thy marble vault, shall sound
My echoing song; then worms shall try
That long-preserved virginity,
And your quaint honour turn to dust,
And into ashes all my lust:
The grave's a fine and private place,
But none, I think, do there embrace.

Now therefore, while the youthful hue
Sits on thy skin like morning dew,
And while thy willing soul transpires
At every pore with instant fires,
Now let us sport us while we may,
And now, like amorous birds of prey,
Rather at once our time devour
Than languish in his slow-chapped power.
Let us roll all our strength and all
Our sweetness up into one ball,
And tear our pleasures with rough strife
Through the iron gates of life;
Thus, though we cannot make our sun
Stand still, yet we will make him run.

THE DEFINITION OF LOVE

My love is of a birth as rare
As 'tis, for object, strange and high;
It was begotten by Despair
Upon Impossibility.

Magnanimous Despair alone
Could show me so divine a thing,
Where feeble Hope could ne'er have flown,
But vainly flapped its tinsel wing.

And yet I quickly might arrive
Where my extended soul is fixed;
But Fate does iron wedges drive,
And always crowds itself betwixt.

For Fate with jealous eyes does see
Two perfect loves, nor lets them close;
Their union would her ruin be,
And her tyrannic power depose.

And therefore her decrees of steel
Us as the distant poles have placed
(Though Love's whole world on us doth wheel),
Not by themselves to be embraced;

Unless the giddy heaven fall,
And earth some new convulsion tear,
And, us to join, the world should all
Be cramped into a planisphere.

As lines, so loves, oblique may well
Themselves in every angle greet;
But ours, so truly parallel,
Though infinite, can never meet.

Therefore the love which us doth bind,
But Fate so enviously debars,
Is the conjunction of the mind,
And opposition of the stars.

THE GARDEN

How vainly men themselves amaze
To win the palm, the oak, or bays,
And their incessant labours see
Crowned from some single herb, or tree,
Whose short and narrow-verged shade
Does prudently their toils upbraid;
While all flowers and all trees do close
To weave the garlands of repose!

Fair Quiet, have I found thee here,
And Innocence, thy sister dear?
Mistaken long, I sought you then
In busy companies of men.
Your sacred plants, if here below,
Only among the plants will grow;
Society is all but rude
To this delicious solitude.

No white nor red was ever seen
So amorous as this lovely green.
Fond lovers, cruel as their flame,
Cut in these trees their mistress' name:
Little, alas, they know or heed
How far these beauties hers exceed!
Fair trees, wheresoe'er your barks I wound,
No name shall but your own be found!

When we have run our passion's heat,
Love hither makes his best retreat.
The gods, that mortal beauty chase,
Still in a tree did end their race.
Apollo hunted Daphne so,
Only that she might laurel grow;
And Pan did after Syrinx speed,
Not as a nymph, but for a reed.

What wondrous life in this I lead!
Ripe apples drop about my head;
The luscious clusters of the vine
Upon my mouth do crush their wine;
The nectarine and curious peach
Into my hands themselves do reach;
Stumbling on melons, as I pass,
Ensnared with flowers, I fall on grass.

Meanwhile the mind from pleasure less
Withdraws into its happiness;
The mind, that ocean where each kind
Does straight its own resemblance find;
Yet it creates, transcending these,
Far other worlds and other seas,
Annihilating all that's made
To a green thought in a green shade.

Here at the fountain's sliding foot,
Or at some fruit-tree's mossy root,
Casting the body's vest aside,
My soul into the boughs does glide:
There, like a bird, it sits and sings,
Then whets and combs its silver wings,
And, till prepared for longer flight,
Waves in its plumes the various light.

Such was that happy garden-state,
While man there walked without a mate:
After a place so pure and sweet,
What other help could yet be meet!
But 'twas beyond a mortal's share
To wander solitary there:
Two paradises 'twere in one
To live in Paradise alone.

How well the skillful gardener drew,
Of flowers and herbs, this dial new!
Where, from above, the milder sun
Does through a fragrant zodiac run;

And, as it works, the industrious bee
Computes its time as well as we!
How could such sweet and wholesome hours
Be reckoned but with herbs and flowers?

HENRY VAUGHAN
(1621–95)

PEACE

My soul, there is a country
   Far beyond the stars,
Where stands a winged sentry
   All skilful in the wars.
There, above noise and danger,
   Sweet Peace sits crowned with smiles,
And one born in a manger
   Commands the beauteous files.
He is thy gracious friend,
   And (O my soul awake!)
Did in pure love descend
   To die here for thy sake.
If thou canst get but thither,
   There grows the flower of peace,
The rose that cannot wither,
   Thy fortress and thy ease.
Leave, then, thy foolish ranges;
   For none can thee secure
But one who never changes,
   Thy God, thy life, thy cure.

THE WORLD

I saw Eternity the other night,
Like a great ring of pure and endless light,
   All calm, as it was bright;
And round beneath it, time in hours, days, years,
   Driven by the spheres
Like a vast shadow moved; in which the world

And all her train were hurled.
The doting lover in his quaintest strain
    Did there complain;
Near him, his lute, his fancy, and his slights,
    Wit's sour delights,
With gloves, and knots, the silly snares of pleasure,
    Yet his dear treasure,
All scattered lay, while he his eyes did pour
    Upon a flower.

The darksome statesman, hung with weights and woe,
Like a thick midnight-fog, moved there so slow,
    He did not stay, nor go;
Condemning thoughts—like sad eclipses—scowl
    Upon his soul,
And clouds of crying witnesses without
    Pursued him with one shout.
Yet digged the mole, and lest his ways be found,
    Worked under ground,
Where he did clutch his prey; but one did see
    That policy;
Churches and altars fed him; perjuries
    Were gnats and flies;
It rained about him blood and tears, but he
    Drank them as free.

The fearful miser on a heap of rust
Sat pining all his life there, did scarce trust
    His own hands with the dust,
Yet would not place one piece alone, but lives
    In fear of thieves.
Thousands there were as frantic as himself,
    And hugged each one his pelf;
The downright epicure placed heaven in sense,
    And scorned pretence;
While others, slipt into a wide excess,
    Said little less;
The weaker sort, slight, trivial wares enslave,
    Who think them brave;
And poor despised Truth sate counting by
    Their victory.

Yet some, who all this while did weep and sing,
And sing, and weep, soared up into the ring;
    But most would use no wing.
O fools—said I—thus to prefer dark night
    Before true light!
To live in grots, and caves, and hate the day
    Because it shows the way,
The way, which from this dead and dark abode
    Leads up to God;
A way where you might tread the sun, and be
    More bright than he!
But as I did their madness so discuss
    One whispered thus,
"This ring the Bridegroom did for none provide,
    But for His bride."

JOHN DRYDEN
(1631–1700)

Poor mortals that are clogged with earth below
    Sink under love and care,
    While we that dwell in air
Such heavy passions never know.
    Why then should mortals be
    Unwilling to be free
    From blood, that sullen cloud
    Which shining souls does shroud?
      Then they'll show bright,
      And like us light,
When leaving bodies with their care,
    They slide to us and air.

MAC FLECKNOE

Or, a Satire upon the True-Blue-Protestant Poet T.S.

All human things are subject to decay,
And when fate summons, monarchs much obey.
This Flecknoe found, who, like Augustus, young
Was called to empire, and had governed long;
In prose and verse, was owned, without dispute,
Through all the realms of *Nonsense,* absolute.
This aged prince, now flourishing in peace,
And blest with issue of a large increase;
Worn out with business, did at length debate
To settle the succession of the State;
And, pondering which of all his sons was fit
To reign, and wage immortal war with wit,
Cried: " 'Tis resolved; for nature pleads, that he
Should only rule, who most resembles me.

Sh—— alone my perfect image bears,
Mature in dulness from his tender years:
Sh—— alone, of all my sons, is he
Who stands confirmed in full stupidity.
The rest to some faint meaning make pretense,
But Sh—— never deviates into sense.
Some beams of wit on other souls may fall,
Strike through, and make a lucid interval,
But Sh——'s genuine night admits no ray,
His rising fogs prevail upon the day.
Besides, his goodly fabric fills the eye
And seems designed for thoughtless majesty:
Thoughtless as monarch oaks that shade the plain,
And, spread in solemn state, supinely reign.
Heywood and Shirley were but types of thee,
Thou last great prophet of tautology.
Even I, a dunce of more renown than they,
Was sent before but to prepare thy way:
And, coarsely clad in Norwich drugget came
To teach the nations in thy greater name.
My warbling lute, the lute I whilom strung,
When to King John of Portugal I sung,
Was but the prelude to that glorious day,
When thou on silver Thames didst cut thy way,
With well-timed oars before the royal barge,
Swelled with the pride of thy celestial charge;
And big with hymn, commander of a host,
The like was ne'er in Epsom blankets tossed.
Methinks I see the new Arion sail,
The lute still trembling underneath thy nail.
At thy well-sharpened thumb from shore to shore
The treble squeaks for fear, the basses roar;
Echoes from Pissing Alley Sh—— call,
And Sh—— they resound from Aston Hall.
About thy boat the little fishes throng,
As at the morning toast that floats along.
Sometimes, as prince of thy harmonious band,
Thou wieldest thy papers in thy threshing hand.
St. André's feet ne'er kept more equal time,
Not even the feet of thy own *Psyche's* rhyme;
Though they in number as in sense excel:
So just, so like tautology, they fell,

199

That, pale with envy, Singleton forswore
The lute and sword, which he in triumph bore,
And vowed he ne'er would act Villerius more."
Here stopped the good old sire, and wept for joy
In silent raptures of the hopeful boy.
All arguments, but most his plays, persuade,
That for anointed dulness he was made.

  Close to the walls which fair Augusta bind,
(The fair Augusta much to fears inclined,)
An ancient fabric raised t' inform the sight,
There stood of yore, and Barbican it hight:
A watchtower once; but now, so fate ordains,
Of all the pile an empty name remains.
From its old ruins brothel-houses rise,
Scenes of lewd loves, and of polluted joys,
Where their vast courts the mother-strumpets keep,
And, undisturbed by watch, in silence sleep.
Near these a nursery erects its head,
Where queens are formed, and future heroes bred;
Where unfledged actors learn to laugh and cry,
Where infant punks their tender voices try,
And little Maximins the gods defy.
Great Fletcher never treads in buskins here,
Nor greater Jonson dares in socks appear;
But gentle Simkin just reception finds
Amidst this monument of vanished minds:
Pure clinches the suburbian Muse affords,
And Panton waging harmless war with words.
Here Flecknoe, as a place to fame well known,
Ambitiously designed his Sh——'s throne;
For ancient Dekker prophesied long since,
That in this pile should reign a mighty prince,
Born for a scourge of wit, and flail of sense;
To whom true dulness should some *Psyches* owe,
But worlds of *Misers* from his pen should flow;
Humourists and hypocrites it should produce,
Whole Raymond families, and tribes of Bruce.

  Now Empress Fame had published the renown
Of Sh——'s coronation through the town.
Roused by report of Fame, the nations meet,
From near Bunhill, and distant Watling Street.

No Persian carpets spread the imperial way,
But scattered limbs of mangled poets lay;
From dusty shops neglected authors come,
Martyrs of pies, and relics of the bum.
Much Heywood, Shirley, Ogleby there lay,
But loads of Sh—— almost choked the way.
Bilked stationers for yeomen stood prepared,
And Herringman was captain of the guard.
The hoary prince in majesty appeared,
High on a throne of his own labours reared.
At his right hand our young Ascanius sate,
Rome's other hope, and pillar of the State.
His brows thick fogs, instead of glories, grace,
And lambent dulness played around his face.
As Hannibal did to the altars come,
Sworn by his sire a mortal foe to Rome;
So Sh—— swore, nor should his vow be vain,
That he till death true dulness would maintain;
And, in his father's right, and realm's defence,
Ne'er to have peace with wit, nor truce with sense.
The king himself the sacred unction made,
As king by office, and as priest by trade.
In his sinister hand, instead of ball,
He placed a mighty mug of potent ale;
Love's Kingdom to his right he did convey,
At once his sceptre, and his rule of sway;
Whose righteous lore the prince had practiced young,
And from whose loins recorded *Psyche* sprung.
His temples, last, with poppies were o'erspread,
That nodding seemed to consecrate his head.
Just at that point of time, if fame not lie,
On his left hand twelve reverend owls did fly.
So Romulus, 'tis sung, by Tiber's brook,
Presage of sway from twice six vultures took.
The admiring throng loud acclamations make,
And omens of his future empire take.
The sire then shook the honours of his head,
And from his brows damps of oblivion shed
Full on the filial dulness: long he stood,
Repelling from his breast the raging god;
At length burst out in this prophetic mood:

201

"Heavens bless my son, from Ireland let him reign
To far Barbadoes on the western main;
Of his dominion may no end be known,
And greater than his father's be his throne;
Beyond *Love's Kingdom* let him stretch his pen!"
He paused, and all the people cried, "Amen."
Then thus continued he: "My son, advance
Still in new impudence, new ignorance.
Success let others teach, learn thou from me
Pangs without birth, and fruitless industry.
Let *Virtuosos* in five years be writ;
Yet not one thought accuse thy toil of wit.
Let gentle George in triumph tread the stage,
Make Dorimant betray, and Loveit rage;
Let Cully, Cockwood, Fopling, charm the pit,
And in their folly show the writer's wit.
Yet still thy fools shall stand in thy defence,
And justify their author's want of sense.
Let 'em be all by thy own model made
Of dulness, and desire no foreign aid;
That they to future ages may be known,
Not copies drawn, but issue of thy own.
Nay, let thy men of wit too be the same,
All full of thee, and differing but in name.
But let no alien S—dl—y interpose,
To lard with wit thy hungry *Epsom* prose.
And when false flowers of rhetoric thou wouldst cull,
Trust nature, do not labour to be dull;
But write thy best, and top; and, in each line,
Sir Formal's oratory will be thine:
Sir Formal, though unsought, attends thy quill,
And does thy northern dedications fill.
Nor let false friends seduce thy mind to fame,
By arrogating Jonson's hostile name.
Let father Flecknoe fire thy mind with praise,
And uncle Ogleby thy envy raise.
Thou art my blood, where Jonson has no part:
What share have we in nature, or in art?
Where did his wit on learning fix a brand,
And rail at arts he did not understand?
Where made he love in Prince Nicander's vein,

202

Or swept the dust in *Psyche's* humble strain?
Where sold he bargains, 'whip-stitch, kiss my arse,'
Promised a play and dwindled to a farce?
When did his Muse from Fletcher scenes purloin,
As thou whole Eth'rege dost transfuse to thine?
But so transfused, as oil on water's flow,
His always floats above, thine sinks below.
This is thy province, this thy wondrous way,
New humours to invent for each new play:
This is that boasted bias of thy mind,
By which one way, to dulness, 'tis inclined;
Which makes thy writings lean on one side still,
And, in all changes, that way bends thy will.
Nor let thy mountain-belly make pretense
Of likeness; thine's a tympany of sense.
A tun of man in thy large bulk is writ,
But sure thou art but a kilderkin of wit.
Like mine, thy gentle numbers feebly creep;
Thy tragic Muse gives smiles, thy comic sleep.
With whate'er gall thou settest thyself to write,
Thy inoffensive satires never bite.
In thy felonious heart though venom lies,
It does but touch thy Irish pen, and dies.
Thy genius calls thee not to purchase fame
In keen iambics, but mild anagram.
Leave writing plays, and choose for thy command
Some peaceful province in acrostic land.
There thou mayest wings display and altars raise,
And torture one poor word ten thousand ways.
Or, if thou wouldst thy different talents suit,
Set thy own songs, and sing them to thy lute."

    He said: but his last words were scarcely heard;
For Bruce and Longvil had a trap prepared,
And down they sent the yet declaiming bard.
Sinking he left his drugget robe behind,
Borne upwards by a subterranean wind.
The mantle fell to the young prophet's part,
With double portion of his father's art.

SONG FOR ST. CECILIA'S DAY

From harmony, from heavenly harmony
 This universal frame began:
 When Nature underneath a heap
  Of jarring atoms lay
 And could not heave her head,
The tuneful voice was heard from high,
  Arise, ye more than dead!
Then cold, and hot, and moist, and dry
In order to their stations leap,
  And music's power obey.

From harmony, from heavenly harmony
 This universal frame began:
 From harmony to harmony
Through all the compass of the notes it ran,
The diapason closing full in man.

What passion cannot music raise and quell?
 When Jubal struck the chorded shell
His listening brethren stood around,
 And, wondering, on their faces fell
To worship that celestial sound.
Less than a god they thought there could not dwell
 Within the hollow of that shell
 That spoke so sweetly and so well.
What passion cannot music raise and quell?

The trumpet's loud clangour
 Excites us to arms,
With shrill notes of anger
 And mortal alarms.
The double double double beat
 Of the thundering drum
 Cries "Hark! the foes come;
Charge, charge, 'tis too late to retreat!"

The soft complaining flute
 In dying notes discovers

204

The woes of hopeless lovers,
Whose dirge is whispered by the warbling lute.

Sharp violins proclaim
Their jealous pangs and desperation,
Fury, frantic indignation,
Depth of pains, and height of passion
For the fair disdainful dame.

But oh! what art can teach,
What human voice can reach
The sacred organ's praise?
Notes inspiring holy love,
Notes that wing their heavenly ways
To mend the choirs above.
Orpheus could lead the savage race,
And trees unrooted left their place
Sequacious of the lyre:
But bright Cecilia raised the wonder higher;
When to her organ vocal breath was given
An angel heard, and straight appeared—
Mistaking earth for heaven.

Grand Chorus

As from the power of sacred lays
The spheres began to move,
And sung the great Creator's praise
To all the blest above;
So when the last and dreadful hour
This crumbling pageant shall devour,
The trumpet shall be heard on high,
The dead shall live, the living die,
And music shall untune the sky.

THOMAS TRAHERNE
(1637–74)

POVERTY

As in the house I sat
Alone and desolate,
No creature but the fire and I,
The chimney and the stool, I lift mine eye
Up to the wall,
And in the silent hall
Saw nothing mine
But some few cups and dishes shine,
The table and the wooden stools
Where people used to dine;
A painted cloth there was
Wherein some ancient story wrought
A little entertained my thought
Which light discovered through the glass.

I wondered much to see
That all my wealth should be
Confined in such a little room,
Yet hope for more I scarcely durst presume.
It grieved me sore
That such a scanty store
Should be my all;
For I forgot my ease and health;
Nor did I think of hands or eyes,
Nor soul nor body prize;
I neither thought the sun,
Nor moon, nor stars, nor people mine,
Though they did round about me shine;
And therefore I was quite undone.

Some greater things, I thought,
Must needs for me be wrought,

Which, till my craving mind should see,
I ever should lament my poverty.
          I fain would have
          Whatever bounty gave;
               Nor could there be
Without, or love, or deity.
For, should not He be infinite,
          Whose hand created me?
          Ten thousand absent things
Did vex my poor and wanting mind,
Which, till I be no longer blind,
Let me not see the King of Kings.

          His love must surely be
          Rich, infinite and free;
Nor can He be thought a God
Of grace and power, that fills not his abode,
          His holy court,
          In kind and liberal sort.
          Joys and pleasures,
Plenty of jewels and goods and treasures
To enrich the poor, cheer the forlorn,
          His palace must adorn,
          And given all to me!
For, till His works my wealth became,
No love or peace did me inflame.
But now I have a Deity.

JOHN WILMOT,
EARL OF ROCHESTER
(1647–80)

As Chloris full of harmless thought
    Beneath the willows lay,
Kind love a comely shepherd brought
    To pass the time away.

She blushed to be encountered so
    And chid the amorous swain,
But as she strove to rise and go,
    He pulled her back again.

A sudden passion seized her heart
    In spite of her disdain;
She found a pulse in every part,
    And love in every vein.

"Ah, youth!" quoth she, "What charms are these
    That conquer and surprise?
Ah, let me—for unless you please,
    I have no power to rise."

She faintly spoke, and trembling lay,
    For fear he should comply,
But virgins' eyes their hearts betray
    And give their tongues the lie.

Thus she, who princes had denied
    With all their pompous train,
Was in the lucky minute tried
    And yielded to the swain.

*

Love a woman? You're an ass!
  'Tis a most insipid passion
To choose out for your happiness
  The silliest part of God's creation.

Let the porter and the groom,
  Things designed for dirty slaves,
Drudge in fair Aurelia's womb
  To get supplies for age and graves.

Farewell, woman! I intend
  Henceforth every night to sit
With my lewd, well-natured friend,
  Drinking to engender wit.

Then give me health, wealth, mirth, and wine,
  And, if busy love entrenches,
There's a sweet, soft page of mine
  Does the trick worth forty wenches.

UPON HIS LEAVING HIS MISTRESS

'Tis not that I am weary grown
Of being yours, and yours alone;
But with what face can I incline
To damn you to be only mine?
  You, whom some kinder power did fashion,
  By merit and by inclination,
  The joy at least of one whole nation.

Let meaner spirits of your sex
With humbler aims their thoughts perplex,
And boast if by their arts they can
Contrive to make *one* happy man;
  Whilst, moved by an impartial sense,
  Favors like nature you dispense
  With universal influence.

See, the kind seed-receiving earth
To every grain affords a birth.
On her no showers unwelcome fall;
Her willing womb retains 'em all.
   And shall my Celia be confined?
   No! Live up to thy mighty mind,
  And be the mistress of mankind.

MATTHEW PRIOR
(1664–1721)

TO A YOUNG GENTLEMAN IN LOVE:
A TALE

"From public noise and factious strife,
From all the busy ills of life,
Take me, my Celia, to thy breast,
And lull my wearied soul to rest!
Forever in this humble cell,
Let thee and I, my fair one, dwell;
None enter else but Love, and he
Shall bar the door and keep the key.
   To painted roofs and shining spires
(Uneasy seats of high desires)
Let the unthinking many crowd,
That dare be covetous and proud!
In golden bondage let them wait,
And barter happiness for state.
But oh, my Celia, when thy swain
Desires to see a court again,
May heaven around this destined head
The choicest of its curses shed!
To sum up all the rage of fate
In the two things I dread and hate,
Mayst thou be false, and I be great!"
   Thus, on his Celia's panting breast
Fond Celadon his soul expressed.
While with delight the lovely maid
Received the vows, she thus repaid:
   "Hope of my age, joy of my youth,
Blessed miracle of love and truth!
All that could ever be counted mine,
My love and life, long since are thine.
A real joy I never knew,

211

Till I believed thy passion true.
A real grief I ne'er can find,
Till thou provest perjured or unkind.
Contempt, and poverty, and care
All we abhor, and all we fear,
Blessed with thy presence, I can bear.
Through waters and through flames I'll go,
Sufferer and solace of thy woe!
Trace me some yet unheard-of way,
That I thy ardour may repay,
And make my constant passion known,
By more than woman yet has done!

    Had I a wish that did not bear
The stamp and image of my dear,
I'd pierce my heart through every vein,
And die to let it out again.
No! Venus shall my witness be
(If ever Venus loved like me)
That for one hour I would not quit
My shepherd's arms, and this retreat,
To be the Persian monarch's bride,
Partner of all his power and pride;
Or rule in regal state above,
Mother of gods, and wife of Jove!"

        Oh, happy these of human race!
But soon, alas, our pleasures pass!
He thanked her on his bended knee;
Then drank a quart of milk and tea.
And, leaving her adored embrace,
Hastened to court to beg a place;
While she, his absence to bemoan,
The very moment he was gone,
Called Thyrsis from beneath the bed,
Where all this time he had been hid.

MORAL

While men have these ambitious fancies,
And wanton wenches read romances,
Our sex will— "What? Out with it." —lie;
And theirs in equal strains reply.

The moral of the tale I sing
(A posy for a wedding ring)
In this short verse will be confined:
Love is a jest and vows are wind.

JONATHAN SWIFT
(1667–1745)

A DESCRIPTION OF THE MORNING

Now hardly here and there a hackney coach
Appearing, showed the ruddy morn's approach.
Now Betty from her master's bed had flown,
And softly stole to discompose her own;
The slip-shod 'prentice from his master's door
Had pared the dirt and sprinkled round the floor.
Now Moll had whirled her mop with dexterous airs,
Prepared to scrub the entry and the stairs.
The youth with broomy stumps began to trace
The kennel's edge, where wheels had worn the place.
The small-coal man was heard with cadence deep,
Till drowned in shriller notes of chimney-sweep:
Duns at his lordship's gate began to meet;
And brickdust Moll had screamed through half the street.
The turnkey now his flock returning sees,
Duly let out a-nights to steal for fees:
The watchful bailiffs take their silent stands,
And schoolboys lag with satchels in their hands.

A DESCRIPTION OF A CITY SHOWER

Careful observers may foretell the hour
(By sure prognostics) when to dread a shower:
While rain depends, the pensive cat gives o'er
Her frolics, and pursues her tail no more.
Returning home at night, you'll find the sink
Strike your offended sense with double stink.
If you be wise, then go not far to dine;
You'll spend in coach-hire more than save in wine.

A coming shower your shooting corns presage,
Old aches throb, your hollow tooth will rage.
Sauntering in coffeehouse is Dulman seen;
He damns the climate and complains of spleen.

Meanwhile the South, rising with dabbled wings,
A sable cloud athwart the welkin flings,
That swilled more liquor than it could contain,
And, like a drunkard, gives it up again.
Brisk Susan whips her linen from the rope,
While the first drizzling shower is borne aslope:
Such is that sprinkling which some careless quean
Flirts on you from her mop, but not so clean:
You fly, invoke the gods; then, turning, stop
To rail; she singing, still whirls on her mop.
Not yet the dust had shunned the unequal strife,
But, aided by the wind, fought still for life,
And wafted with its foe by violent gust,
'Twas doubtful which was rain and which was dust.
Ah, where must needy poet seek for aid,
When dust and rain at once his coat invade?
Sole coat, where dust cemented by the rain
Erects the nap, and leaves a mingled stain.

Now in contiguous drops the flood comes down,
Threatening with deluge this devoted town.
To shops in crowds the daggled females fly,
Pretend to cheapen goods, but nothing buy.
The Templar spruce, while every spout's abroach,
Stays till 'tis fair, yet seems to call a coach.
The tucked-up sempstress walks with hasty strides,
While streams run down her oiled umbrella's sides.
Here various kinds, by various fortunes led,
Commence acquaintance underneath a shed.
Triumphant Tories and desponding Whigs
Forget their feuds, and join to save their wigs.
Boxed in a chair, the beau impatient sits,
While spouts run clattering o'er the roof by fits,
And ever and anon with frightful din
The leather sounds; he trembles from within.
So when Troy chairmen bore the wooden steed,
Pregnant with Greeks impatient to be freed
(Those bully Greeks, who, as the moderns do,
Instead of paying chair-men, run them through),

Laocoon struck the outside with his spear,
And each imprisoned hero quaked for fear.
    Now from all parts the swelling kennels flow,
And bear their trophies with them as they go:
Filth of all hues and odours seem to tell
What street they sailed from, by their sight and smell.
They, as each torrent drives with rapid force,
From Smithfield or St. Pulchre's shape their course,
And in huge confluence joined at Snow Hill ridge,
Fall from the conduit prone to Holborn Bridge.
Sweepings from butchers' stalls, dung, guts, and blood,
Drowned puppies, stinking sprats, all drenched in mud,
Dead cats and turnip-tops come tumbling down the flood.

THE LADY'S DRESSING-ROOM

Five hours (and who can do it less in?)
By haughty Celia spent in dressing,
The goddess from her chamber issues,
Arrayed in lace, brocades, and tissues.
    Strephon, who found the room was void,
And Betty otherwise employed,
Stole in and took a strict survey
Of all the litter as it lay:
Whereof, to make the matter clear,
An inventory follows here.
    And first, a dirty smock appeared,
Beneath the armpits well besmeared;
Strephon, the rogue, displayed it wide,
And turned it round on every side:
On such a point few words are best,
And Strephon bids us guess the rest;
But swears how damnably the men lie
In calling Celia sweet and cleanly.
    Now listen, while he next produces
The various combs for various uses;
Filled up with dirt so closely fixed,
No brush could force a way betwixt;
A paste of composition rare,

Sweat, dandruff, powder, lead, and hair:
A forehead cloth with oil upon't,
To smooth the wrinkles on her front:
Here alum-flour, to stop the steams
Exhaled from sour unsavoury streams:
There night-gloves made of Tripsey's hide,
Bequeathed by Tripsey when she died;
With puppy-water, beauty's help,
Distilled from Tripsey's darling whelp.
Here gallipots and vials placed,
Some filled with washes, some with paste;
Some with pomatums, paints, and slops,
And ointments good for scabby chaps.
Hard by a filthy basin stands,
Fouled with the scouring of her hands:
The basin takes whatever comes,
The scrapings from her teeth and gums,
A nasty compound of all hues,
For here she spits and here she spews.

But oh! it turned poor Strephon's bowels
When he beheld and smelt the towels,
Begummed, bemattered, and beslimed,
With dirt, and sweat, and ear-wax grimed;
No object Strephon's eye escapes;
Her petticoats in frouzy heaps;
Nor be the handkerchiefs forgot,
All varnished o'er with snuff and snot.
The stockings why should I expose,
Stained with the moisture of her toes,
Or greasy coifs, or pinners reeking,
Which Celia slept at least a week in?
A pair of tweezers next he found,
To pluck her brows in arches round;
Or hairs that sink the forehead low,
Or on her chin like bristles grow.

The virtues we must not let pass
Of Celia's magnifying glass;
When frighted Strephon cast his eye on it,
It showed the visage of a giant:
A glass that can to sight disclose
The smallest worm in Celia's nose,

And faithfully direct her nail
To squeeze it out from head to tail;
For, catch it nicely by the head,
It must come out, alive or dead.

   Why, Strephon, will you tell the rest?
And must you needs describe the chest?
That careless wench! no creature warn her
To move it out from yonder corner!
But leave it standing full in sight,
For you to exercise your spite?
In vain the workman showed his wit,
With rings and hinges counterfeit,
To make it seem in this disguise
A cabinet to vulgar eyes:
Which Strephon ventured to look in,
Resolved to go through thick and thin.
He lifts the lid: there needs no more,
He smelt it all the time before.

   As, from within Pandora's box,
When Epimetheus oped the locks,
A sudden universal crew
Of human evils upward flew;
He still was comforted to find
That hope at last remained behind:
So Strephon, lifting up the lid,
To view what in the chest was hid,
The vapours flew from out the vent;
But Strephon, cautious, never meant
The bottom of the pan to grope,
And foul his hands in search of hope.
Oh! Ne'er may such a vile machine
Be once in Celia's chamber seen!
Oh! May she better learn to keep
Those "secrets of the hoary deep."

   As mutton-cutlets, prime of meat,
Which, though with art you salt and beat,
As laws of cookery require,
And roast them at the clearest fire;
If from adown the hopeful chops
The fat upon the cinder drops,
To stinking smoke it turns the flame,

Poisoning the flesh from whence it came,
And up exhales a greasy stench,
For which you curse the careless wench:
So things which must not be expressed,
When plumped into the reeking chest,
Send up an excremental smell
To taint the parts from whence they fell:
The petticoats and gown perfume,
And waft a stink round every room.
 Thus finishing his grand survey,
Disgusted Strephon stole away;
Repeating in his amorous fits,
"Oh! Celia, Celia, Celia shits!"
But Vengeance, goddess never sleeping,
Soon punished Strephon for his peeping:
His foul imagination links
Each dame he sees with all her stinks;
And, if unsavoury odours fly,
Conceives a lady standing by.
All women his description fits,
And both ideas jump like wits;
By vicious fancy coupled fast,
And still appearing in contrast.
 I pity wretched Strephon, blind
To all the charms of womankind.
Should I the queen of love refuse
Because she rose from stinking ooze?
To him that looks behind the scene,
Statira's but some pocky quean.
 When Celia all her glory shows,
If Strephon would but stop his nose,
(Who now so impiously blasphemes
Her ointments, daubs, and paints, and creams,
Her washes, slops, and every clout,
With which he makes so foul a rout,)
He soon will learn to think like me,
And bless his ravished eyes to see
Such order from confusion sprung,
Such gaudy tulips raised from dung.

VERSES ON THE DEATH OF DR. SWIFT

As Rochefoucauld his maxims drew
From nature, I believe 'em true:
They argue no corrupted mind
In him; the fault is in mankind.

This maxim more than all the rest
Is thought too base for human breast:
"In all distresses of our friends
We first consult our private ends,
While Nature, kindly bent to ease us,
Points out some circumstance to please us."

If this perhaps your patience move,
Let reason and experience prove.

We all behold with envious eyes
Our equal raised above our size.
Who would not at a crowded show
Stand high himself, keep others low?
I love my friend as well as you,
But why should he obstruct my view?
Then let me have the higher post;
Suppose it but an inch at most.

If in a battle you should find
One, whom you love of all mankind,
Had some heroic action done,
A champion killed, or trophy won;
Rather than thus be overtopped,
Would you not wish his laurels cropped?

Dear honest Ned is in the gout,
Lies racked with pain, and you without:
How patiently you hear him groan!
How glad the case is not your own!

What poet would not grieve to see
His brethren write as well as he?
But, rather than they should excel,
He'd wish his rivals all in hell.

Her end when emulation misses,
She turns to envy, stings, and hisses:
The strongest friendship yields to pride,
Unless the odds be on our side.

Vain humankind! Fantastic race!
Thy various follies who can trace?

Self-love, ambition, envy, pride,
Their empire in our hearts divide.
Give others riches, power, and station;
'Tis all on me a usurpation;
I have no title to aspire,
Yet, when you sink, I seem the higher.
In Pope I cannot read a line,
But with a sigh I wish it mine:
When he can in one couplet fix
More sense than I can do in six,
It gives me such a jealous fit,
I cry, Pox take him and his wit!
   Why must I be outdone by Gay
In my own humorous biting way?
   Arbuthnot is no more my friend,
Who dares to irony pretend,
Which I was born to introduce,
Refined it first, and showed its use.
   St. John as well as Pulteney knows
That I had some repute for prose;
And, till they drove me out of date,
Could maul a minister of state.
If they have mortified my pride,
And made me throw my pen aside;
If with such talents Heaven hath blessed 'em,
Have I not reason to detest 'em?
   To all my foes, dear Fortune, send
Thy gifts, but never to my friend:
I tamely can endure the first,
But this with envy makes me burst.
   Thus much may serve by way of proem;
Proceed we therefore to our poem.
   The time is not remote, when I
Must by the course of nature die:
When, I foresee, my special friends
Will try to find their private ends;
Though it is hardly understood
Which way my death can do them good;
Yet thus, methinks, I hear 'em speak:
See how the Dean begins to break!
Poor gentleman! He droops apace!
You plainly find it in his face.

That old vertigo in his head
Will never leave him till he's dead.
Besides, his memory decays;
He recollects not what he says;
He cannot call his friends to mind;
Forgets the place where last he dined;
Plies you with stories o'er and o'er,
He told them fifty times before.
How does he fancy we can sit
To hear his out-of-fashion wit?
But he takes up with younger folks,
Who for his wine will bear his jokes.
Faith, he must make his stories shorter,
Or change his comrades once a quarter;
In half the time he talks them round,
There must another set be found.

  For poetry, he's past his prime;
He takes an hour to find a rhyme;
His fire is out, his wit decayed,
His fancy sunk, his Muse a jade.
I'd have him throw away his pen—
But there's no talking to some men.

  And then their tenderness appears,
By adding largely to my years:

  He's older than he would be reckoned,
And well remembers Charles the Second.
He hardly drinks a pint of wine;
And that, I doubt, is no good sign.
His stomach, too, begins to fail;
Last year we thought him strong and hale;
But now he's quite another thing;
I wish he may hold out till spring.
They hug themselves, and reason thus:
It is not yet so bad with us.

  In such a case they talk in tropes,
And by their fears express their hopes.
Some great misfortune to portend
No enemy can match a friend.
With all the kindness they profess,
The merit of a lucky guess
(When daily how-d'y's come of course,
And servants answer, "Worse and worse!")

222

Would please 'em better, than to tell
That, God be praised, the Dean is well.
Then he who prophesied the best,
Approves his foresight to the rest:
    You know I always feared the worst,
And often told you so at first.
He'd rather choose that I should die,
Than his prediction prove a lie.
Not one foretells I shall recover,
But all agree to give me over.
    Yet, should some neighbour feel a pain
Just in the parts where I complain,
How many a message would he send!
What hearty prayers that I should mend!
Inquire what regimen I kept;
What gave me ease, and how I slept,
And more lament, when I was dead,
Than all the snivellers round my bed.
    My good companions, never fear;
For though you may mistake a year,
Though your prognostics run too fast,
They must be verified at last.
    Behold the fatal day arrive!
How is the Dean?—He's just alive.
Now the departing prayer is read.
He hardly breathes—The Dean is dead.
Before the passing bell begun,
The news through half the town has run.
Oh! may we all for death prepare!
What has he left? And who's his heir?
I know no more than what the news is;
'Tis all bequeathed to public uses.
To public use! a perfect whim!
What had the public done for him?
Mere envy, avarice, and pride:
He gave it all—but first he died.
And had the Dean in all the nation
No worthy friend, no poor relation?
So ready to do strangers good,
Forgetting his own flesh and blood?
Now Grub Street wits are all employed;
With elegies the town is cloyed;

Some paragraph in every paper
To curse the Dean, or bless the Drapier.
 The doctors, tender of their fame,
Wisely on me lay all the blame.
"We must confess his case was nice;
But he would never take advice.
Had he been ruled, for aught appears,
He might have lived these twenty years:
For, when we opened him, we found,
That all his vital parts were sound."
 From Dublin soon to London spread,
'Tis told at court: The Dean is dead.
Kind Lady Suffolk, in the spleen,
Runs laughing up to tell the queen.
The queen, so gracious, mild and good,
Cries, "Is he gone? 'Tis time he should.
He's dead, you say; why, let him rot:
I'm glad the medals were forgot.
I promised him, I own; but when?
I only was the princess then;
But now, as consort of the king,
You know, 'tis quite a different thing."
 Now Chartres, at Sir Robert's levee,
Tells with a sneer the tidings heavy:
"Why, is he dead without his shoes?"
Cries Bob, "I'm sorry for the news:
Oh, were the wretch but living still,
And in his place my good friend Will!
Or had a miter on his head,
Provided Bolingbroke were dead!"
 Now Curll his shop from rubbish drains:
Three genuine tomes of Swift's remains!
And then, to make them pass the glibber,
Revised by Theobald, Moore, and Cibber.
He'll treat me as he does my betters,
Publish my will, my life, my letters;
Revive the libels born to die,
Which Pope must bear, as well as I.
 Here shift the scene, to represent
How those I love my death lament.
Poor Pope will grieve a month, and Gay,
A week, and Arbuthnot, a day.

St. John himself will scarce forbear
To bite his pen, and drop a tear.
The rest will give a shrug, and cry,
"I'm sorry—but we all must die!"
  Indifference clad in wisdom's guise
All fortitude of mind supplies:
For how can stony bowels melt
In those who never pity felt?
When we are lashed, they kiss the rod,
Resigning to the will of God.
  The fools, my juniors by a year,
Are tortured with suspense and fear;
Who wisely thought my age a screen,
When death approached, to stand between:
The screen removed, their hearts are trembling;
They mourn for me without dissembling.
  My female friends, whose tender hearts
Have better learned to act their parts,
Receive the news in doleful dumps:
"The Dean is dead (and what is trumps?)
Then, Lord have mercy on his soul!
(Ladies, I'll venture for the vole.)
Six deans, they say, must bear the pall.
(I wish I knew what king to call.)
Madam, your husband will attend
The funeral of so good a friend?"
"No, madam, 'tis a shocking sight;
And he's engaged tomorrow night:
My Lady Club would take it ill,
If he should fail her at quadrille.
He loved the Dean—(I lead a heart)
But dearest friends, they say, must part.
His time was come; he ran his race;
We hope he's in a better place."
  Why do we grieve that friends should die?
No loss more easy to supply.
One year is past; a different scene!
No further mention of the Dean,
Who now, alas, no more is missed,
Than if he never did exist.
Where's now this favourite of Apollo?
Departed—and his works must follow,

Must undergo the common fate;
His kind of wit is out of date.

    Some country squire to Lintot goes,
Inquires for Swift in verse and prose.
Says Lintot, "I have heard the name;
He died a year ago." "The same."
He searches all the shop in vain.
"Sir, you may find them in Duck Lane:
I sent them, with a load of books,
Last Monday to the pastry-cook's.
To fancy they could live a year!
I find you're but a stranger here.
The Dean was famous in his time,
And had a kind of knack at rhyme.
His way of writing now is past:
The town has got a better taste.
I keep no antiquated stuff;
But spick and span I have enough.
Pray do but give me leave to show 'em:
Here's Colley Cibber's birthday poem.
This ode you never yet have seen
By Stephen Duck upon the Queen.
Then here's a letter finely penned
Against the Craftsman and his friend;
It clearly shows that all reflection
On ministers is disaffection.
Next, here's Sir Robert's vindication,
And Mr. Henley's last oration.
The hawkers have not got them yet:
Your Honour please to buy a set?
Here's Woolston's tracts, the twelfth edition;
'Tis read by every politician:
The country members, when in town,
To all their boroughs send them down;
You never met a thing so smart;
The courtiers have them all by heart;
Those maids of honour (who can read)
Are taught to use them for their creed.
The reverend author's good intention
Has been rewarded with a pension.
He does an honour to his gown,
By bravely running priestcraft down;

He shows, as sure as God's in Gloucester,
That Jesus was a grand impostor;
That all his miracles were cheats,
Performed as jugglers do their feats:
The church had never such a writer;
A shame he has not got a miter!"
    Suppose me dead; and then suppose
A club assembled at the Rose;
Where, from discourse of this and that,
I grow the subject of their chat.
And while they toss my name about,
With favour some, and some without,
One, quite indifferent in the cause,
My character impartial draws:
    "The Dean, if we believe report,
Was never ill received at court.
As for his works in verse and prose,
I own myself no judge of those;
Nor can I tell what critics thought 'em:
But this I know, all people bought 'em,
As with a moral view designed
To cure the vices of mankind.
    His vein, ironically grave,
Exposed the fool and lashed the knave,
To steal a hint was never known,
But what he wrote was all his own.
    He never thought an honour done him,
Because a duke was proud to own him,
Would rather slip aside and choose
To talk with wits in dirty shoes;
Despised the fools with stars and garters,
So often seen caressing Chartres.
He never courted men in station,
Nor persons held in admiration;
Of no man's greatness was afraid,
Because he sought for no man's aid.
Though trusted long in great affairs,
He gave himself no haughty airs;
Without regarding private ends,
Spent all his credit for his friends;
And only chose the wise and good;
No flatterers, no allies in blood;

But succoured virtue in distress,
And seldom failed of good success;
As numbers in their hearts must own,
Who, but for him, had been unknown.

With princes kept a due decorum,
But never stood in awe before 'em.
He followed David's lesson just:
In princes never put thy trust;
And would you make him truly sour,
Provoke him with a slave in power;
The Irish senate if you named,
With what impatience he declaimed!
Fair Liberty was all his cry,
For her he stood prepared to die;
For her he boldly stood alone;
For her he oft exposed his own.
Two kingdoms, just as faction led,
Had set a prince upon his head,
But not a traitor could be found,
To sell him for six hundred pound.

Had he but spared his tongue and pen,
He might have rose like other men;
But power was never in his thought,
And wealth he valued not a groat:
Ingratitude he often found,
And pitied those who meant the wound;
But kept the tenor of his mind,
To merit well of human kind:
Nor made a sacrifice of those
Who still were true, to please his foes.
He laboured many a fruitless hour,
To reconcile his friends in power;
Saw mischief by a faction brewing,
While they pursued each other's ruin.
But finding vain was all his care,
He left the court in mere despair.

And, oh! How short are human schemes!
Here ended all our golden dreams.
What St. John's skill in state affairs,
What Ormonde's valour, Oxford's cares,
To save their sinking country lent,
Was all destroyed by one event.

Too soon that precious life was ended,
On which alone our weal depended.
When up a dangerous faction starts,
With wrath and vengeance in their hearts;
By solemn league and covenant bound,
To ruin, slaughter, and confound;
To turn religion to a fable,
And make the government a Babel;
Pervert the laws, disgrace the gown,
Corrupt the senate, rob the crown;
To sacrifice old England's glory,
And make her infamous in story;
When such a tempest shook the land,
How could unguarded virtue stand?
With horror, grief, despair, the Dean
Beheld the dire destructive scene:
His friends in exile, or the Tower,
Himself within the frown of power,
Pursued by base envenomed pens,
Far to the land of slaves and fens;
A servile race in folly nursed,
Who truckle most, when treated worst.

By innocence and resolution,
He bore continual persecution;
While numbers to preferment rose,
Whose merits were to be his foes;
When even his own familiar friends,
Intent upon their private ends,
Like renegadoes now he feels,
Against him lifting up their heels.

The Dean did, by his pen, defeat
An infamous destructive cheat;
Taught fools their interest how to know,
And gave them arms to ward the blow.
Envy has owned it was his doing,
To save that hapless land from ruin;
While they who at the steerage stood,
And reaped the profit, sought his blood.

To save them from their evil fate,
In him was held a crime of state.
A wicked monster on the bench,
Whose fury blood could never quench;

As vile and profligate a villain,
As modern Scroggs, or old Tresilian;
Who long all justice had discarded,
Nor feared he God, nor man regarded;
Vowed on the Dean his rage to vent,
And make him of his zeal repent:
But heaven his innocence defends,
The grateful people stand his friends;
Not strains of law, nor judge's frown,
Nor topics brought to please the crown,
Nor witness hired, nor jury picked,
Prevail to bring him in convict.

In exile, with a steady heart,
He spent his life's declining part;
Where folly, pride, and faction sway
Remote from St. John, Pope, and Gay.

His friendships there, to few confined,
Were always of the middling kind;
No fools of rank, a mongrel breed,
Who fain would pass for lords indeed:
Where titles give no right or power,
And peerage is a withered flower;
He would have held it a disgrace,
If such a wretch had known his face.
On rural squires, that kingdom's bane,
He vented oft his wrath in vain;
Biennial squires to market brought:
Who sell their souls, and votes for naught;
The nation stripped, go joyful back,
To rob the church, their tenants rack,
Go snacks with rogues and rapparees;
And keep the peace to pick up fees;
In every job to have a share,
A jail or barrack to repair;
And turn the tax for public roads,
Commodious to their own abodes.

Perhaps I may allow the Dean
Had too much satire in his vein;
And seemed determined not to starve it,
Because no age could more deserve it.
Yet malice never was his aim;
He lashed the vice, but spared the name;

No individual could resent,
Where thousands equally were meant;
His satire points at no defect,
But what all mortals may correct;
For he abhorred that senseless tribe
Who call it humour when they gibe:
He spared a hump, or crooked nose,
Whose owners set not up for beaux.
True genuine dulness moved his pity,
Unless it offered to be witty.
Those who their ignorance confessed,
He ne'er offended with a jest;
But laughed to hear an idiot quote
A verse from Horace learned by rote.

He knew a hundred pleasant stories,
With all the turns of Whigs and Tories:
Was cheerful to his dying day;
And friends would let him have his way.

He gave the little wealth he had
To build a house for fools and mad;
And showed by one satiric touch,
No nation wanted it so much.
That kingdom he hath left his debtor,
I wish it soon may have a better."

JOHN GAY
(1685–1732)

THE POET AND THE ROSE

I hate the man who builds his name
On ruins of another's fame.
Thus prudes by characters overthrown
Imagine that they raise their own;
Thus scribblers, covetous of praise,
Think slander can transplant the bays.
Beauties and bards have equal pride,
With both all rivals are decried.
Who praises Lesbia's eyes and feature,
Must call her sister, awkward creature;
For the kind flattery's sure to charm,
When we some other nymph disarm.

As in the cool of early day
A poet sought the sweets of May,
The garden's fragrant breath ascends,
And every stalk with odour bends.
A rose he plucked, he gazed, admired,
Thus singing as the Muse inspired.

Go, rose, my Chloe's bosom grace;
  How happy should I prove,
Might I supply that envied place
  With never-fading love!
There, Phoenix-like, beneath her eye,
Involved in fragrance, burn and die!

Know, hapless flower, that thou shalt find
  More fragrant roses there;
I see thy withering head reclined
  With envy and despair!

One common fate we both must prove;
You die with envy, I with love.

Spare your comparisons, replied
An angry rose, who grew beside;
Of all mankind you should not flout us;
What can a poet do without us!
In every love-song roses bloom;
We lend you colour and perfume.
Does it to Chloe's charms conduce,
To found her praise on our abuse?
Must we, to flatter her, be made
To wither, envy, pine and fade?

from *THE BEGGAR'S OPERA*

WHAT SHALL I DO TO SHOW HOW MUCH I LOVE HER?

Virgins are like the fair flower in its lustre,
    Which in the garden enamels the ground;
Near it the bees in play flutter and cluster,
    And gaudy butterflies frolic around.
But, when once plucked, 'tis no longer alluring,
    To *Covent-garden* 'tis sent (as yet sweet),
There fades, and shrinks, and grows past all enduring,
    Rots, stinks, and dies, and is trod under feet.

A SOLDIER AND A SAILOR

A fox may steal your hens, sir,
A whore your health and pence, sir,
Your daughter rob your chest, sir,
Your wife may steal your rest, sir,
    A thief your goods and plate.

But this is all but picking,
With rest, pence, chest and chicken;

It ever was decreed, sir,
If lawyer's hand is feed, sir,
  He steals your whole estate.

WOULD YOU HAVE A YOUNG VIRGIN?

If the heart of a man is depressed with cares,
The mist is dispelled when a woman appears;
Like the notes of a fiddle, she sweetly, sweetly
Raises the spirits, and charms our ears.
  Roses and lilies her cheeks disclose,
  But her ripe lips are more sweet than those.
    Press her,
    Caress her,
    With blisses,
    Her kisses
Dissolve us in pleasure, and soft repose.

ALEXANDER POPE
(1688–1744)

THE RAPE OF THE LOCK

Canto I

What dire offense from amorous causes springs,
What mighty contests rise from trivial things,
I sing—This verse to Caryll, Muse, is due:
This, even Belinda may vouchsafe to view:
Slight is the subject, but not so the praise,
If she inspire, and he approve my lays.
Say what strange motive, Goddess, could compel
A well-bred lord to assault a gentle belle?
Oh, say what stranger cause, yet unexplored,
Could make a gentle belle reject a lord?
In tasks so bold can little men engage,
And in soft bosoms dwells such mighty rage?
Sol through white curtains shot a timorous ray,
And oped those eyes that must eclipse the day.
Now lapdogs give themselves the rousing shake,
And sleepless lovers, just at twelve, awake:
Thrice rung the bell, the slipper knocked the ground,
And the pressed watch returned a silver sound.
Belinda still her downy pillow pressed,
Her guardian sylph prolonged the balmy rest:
'Twas he had summoned to her silent bed
The morning-dream that hovered o'er her head.
A youth more glittering than a birth-night beau
(That even in slumber caused her cheek to glow)
Seemed to her ear his winning lips to lay,
And thus in whispers said, or seemed to say.
"Fairest of mortals, thou distinguished care
Of thousand bright inhabitants of air!
If e'er one vision touched thy infant thought,
Of all the nurse and all the priest have taught,

Of airy elves by moonlight shadows seen,
The silver token, and the circled green,
Or virgins visited by angel powers,
With golden crowns and wreaths of heavenly flowers,
Hear and believe! thy own importance know,
Nor bound thy narrow views to things below.
Some secret truths, from learned pride concealed,
To maids alone and children are revealed:
What though no credit doubting wits may give?
The fair and innocent shall still believe.
Know, then, unnumbered spirits round thee fly,
The light militia of the lower sky:
These, though unseen, are ever on the wing,
Hang o'er the box, and hover round the ring.
Think what an equipage thou hast in air,
And view with scorn two pages and a chair.
As now your own, our beings were of old,
And once enclosed in woman's beauteous mould;
Thence, by a soft transition, we repair
From earthly vehicles to these of air.
Think not, when woman's transient breath is fled,
That all her vanities at once are dead:
Succeeding vanities she still regards,
And though she plays no more, o'erlooks the cards.
Her joy in gilded chariots, when alive,
And love of ombre, after death survive.
For when the fair in all their pride expire,
To their first elements their souls retire:
The sprites of fiery termagants in flame
Mount up, and take a salamander's name.
Soft yielding minds to water glide away,
And sip, with nymphs, their elemental tea.
The graver prude sinks downward to a gnome,
In search of mischief still on earth to roam.
The light coquettes in sylphs aloft repair,
And sport and flutter in the fields of air.
　　Know further yet; whoever fair and chaste
Rejects mankind, is by some sylph embraced:
For spirits, freed from mortal laws, with ease
Assume what sexes and what shapes they please.
What guards the purity of melting maids,
In courtly balls, and midnight masquerades,

Safe from the treacherous friend, and daring spark,
The glance by day, the whisper in the dark,
When kind occasion prompts their warm desires,
When music softens, and when dancing fires?
'Tis but their sylph, the wise celestials know,
Though Honour is the word with men below.
　　Some nymphs there are, too conscious of their face,
For life predestined to the gnomes' embrace,
Who swell their prospects and exalt their pride,
When offers are disdained, and love denied:
Then gay ideas crowd the vacant brain,
While peers, and dukes, and all their sweeping train,
And garters, stars, and coronets appear,
And in soft sounds, 'your grace' salutes their ear.
'Tis these that early taint the female soul,
Instruct the eyes of young coquettes to roll,
Teach infants' cheeks a bidden blush to know,
And little hearts to flutter at a beau.
　　Oft, when the world imagine women stray,
The sylphs through mystic mazes guide their way,
Through all the giddy circle they pursue,
And old impertinence expel by new.
What tender maid but must a victim fall
To one man's treat, but for another's ball?
When Florio speaks what virgin could withstand,
If gentle Damon did not squeeze her hand?
With varying vanities, from every part,
They shift the moving toyshop of their heart;
Where wigs with wigs, with sword-knots sword-knots strive,
Beaux banish beaux, and coaches coaches drive.
This erring mortals levity may call;
Oh, blind to truth! the sylphs contrive it all.
　　Of these am I, who thy protection claim,
A watchful sprite, and Ariel is my name.
Late, as I ranged the crystal wilds of air,
In the clear mirror of thy ruling star
I saw, alas! some dread event impend,
Ere to the main this morning sun descend,
But Heaven reveals not what, or how, or where:
Warned by the sylph, O pious maid, beware!
This to disclose is all thy guardian can:
Beware of all, but most beware of man!"

He said; when Shock, who thought she slept too long,
Leapt up, and waked his mistress with his tongue.
'Twas then, Belinda, if report say true,
Thy eyes first opened on a billet-doux;
Wounds, charms, and ardors were no sooner read,
But all the vision vanished from thy head.

And now, unveiled, the toilet stands displayed,
Each silver vase in mystic order laid.
First, robed in white, the nymph intent adores,
With head uncovered, the cosmetic powers.
A heavenly image in the glass appears;
To that she bends, to that her eyes she rears.
The inferior priestess, at her altar's side,
Trembling begins the sacred rites of pride.
Unnumbered treasures ope at once, and here
The various offerings of the world appear;
From each she nicely culls with curious toil,
And decks the goddess with the glittering spoil.
This casket India's glowing gems unlocks,
And all Arabia breathes from yonder box.
The tortoise here and elephant unite,
Transformed to combs, the speckled and the white.
Here files of pins extend their shining rows,
Puffs, powders, patches, bibles, billet-doux.
Now awful Beauty puts on all its arms;
The fair each moment rises in her charms,
Repairs her smiles, awakens every grace,
And calls forth all the wonders of her face;
Sees by degrees a purer blush arise,
And keener lightnings quicken in her eyes.
The busy sylphs surround their darling care,
These set the head, and those divide the hair,
Some fold the sleeve, while others plait the gown;
And Betty's praised for labours not her own.

Canto II

Not with more glories, in the ethereal plain,
The sun first rises o'er the purpled main,
Than, issuing forth, the rival of his beams
Launched on the bosom of the silver Thames.
Fair nymphs and well-dressed youths around her shone,

But every eye was fixed on her alone.
On her white breast a sparkling cross she wore,
Which Jews might kiss, and infidels adore.
Her lively looks a sprightly mind disclose,
Quick as her eyes, and as unfixed as those:
Favours to none, to all she smiles extends;
Oft she rejects, but never once offends.
Bright as the sun, her eyes the gazers strike,
And, like the sun, they shine on all alike.
Yet graceful ease, and sweetness void of pride,
Might hide her faults, if belles had faults to hide:
If to her share some female errors fall,
Look on her face, and you'll forget 'em all.

 This nymph, to the destruction of mankind,
Nourished two locks which graceful hung behind
In equal curls, and well conspired to deck
With shining ringlets her smooth ivory neck.
Love in these labyrinths his slaves detains,
And mighty hearts are held in slender chains.
With hairy springes we the birds betray,
Slight lines of hair surprise the finny prey,
Fair tresses man's imperial race ensnare,
And beauty draws us with a single hair.

 The adventurous baron the bright locks admired,
He saw, he wished, and to the prize aspired.
Resolved to win, he meditates the way,
By force to ravish, or by fraud betray;
For when success a lover's toil attends,
Few ask if fraud or force attained his ends.

 For this, ere Phoebus rose, he had implored
Propitious Heaven, and every power adored,
But chiefly Love—to Love an altar built,
Of twelve vast French romances, neatly gilt.
There lay three garters, half a pair of gloves,
And all the trophies of his former loves.
With tender billet-doux he lights the pyre,
And breathes three amorous sighs to raise the fire.
Then prostrate falls, and begs with ardent eyes
Soon to obtain, and long possess the prize:
The powers gave ear, and granted half his prayer,
The rest the winds dispersed in empty air.

 But now secure the painted vessel glides,

The sunbeams trembling on the floating tides,
While melting music steals upon the sky,
And softened sounds along the waters die.
Smooth flow the waves, the zephyrs gently play,
Belinda smiled, and all the world was gay.
All but the sylph—with careful thoughts oppressed,
The impending woe sat heavy on his breast.
He summons straight his denizens of air;
The lucid squadrons round the sails repair:
Soft o'er the shrouds aerial whispers breathe
That seemed but zephyrs to the train beneath.
Some to the sun their insect-wings unfold,
Waft on the breeze, or sink in clouds of gold.
Transparent forms too fine for mortal sight,
Their fluid bodies half dissolved in light,
Loose to the wind their airy garments flew,
Thin glittering textures of the filmy dew,
Dipped in the richest tincture of the skies,
Where light disports in ever-mingling dyes,
While every beam new transient colours flings,
Colours that change whene'er they wave their wings.
Amid the circle, on the gilded mast,
Superior by the head was Ariel placed;
His purple pinions opening to the sun,
He raised his azure wand, and thus begun:
    "Ye sylphs and sylphids, to your chief give ear!
Fays, fairies, genii, elves, and daemons, hear!
Ye know the spheres and various tasks assigned
By laws eternal to the aerial kind.
Some in the fields of purest aether play,
And bask and whiten in the blaze of day.
Some guide the course of wandering orbs on high,
Or roll the planets through the boundless sky.
Some less refined, beneath the moon's pale light,
Pursue the stars that shoot athwart the night,
Or suck the mists in grosser air below,
Or dip their pinions in the painted bow,
Or brew fierce tempests on the wintry main,
Or on the glebe distill the kindly rain.
Others on earth o'er human race preside,
Watch all their ways, and all their actions guide:
Of these the chief the care of nations own,

And guard with arms divine the British throne.
   Our humbler province is to tend the fair,
Not a less pleasing, though less glorious care:
To save the powder from too rude a gale,
Nor let the imprisoned essences exhale;
To draw fresh colours from the vernal flowers;
To steal from rainbows e'er they drop in showers
A brighter wash; to curl their waving hairs,
Assist their blushes, and inspire their airs;
Nay oft, in dreams invention we bestow,
To change a flounce, or add a furbelow.
   This day black omens threat the brightest fair,
That e'er deserved a watchful spirit's care;
Some dire disaster, or by force or slight,
But what, or where, the Fates have wrapped in night:
Whether the nymph shall break Diana's law,
Or some frail china jar receive a flaw,
Or stain her honour or her new brocade,
Forget her prayers, or miss a masquerade,
Or lose her heart, or necklace, at a ball;
Or whether Heaven has doomed that Shock must fall.
Haste, then, ye spirits! to your charge repair:
The fluttering fan be Zephyretta's care;
The drops to thee, Brillante, we consign;
And, Momentilla, let the watch be thine;
Do thou, Crispissa, tend her favorite lock;
Ariel himself shall be the guard of Shock.
   To fifty chosen sylphs, of special note,
We trust the important charge, the petticoat;
Oft have we known that sevenfold fence to fail,
Though stiff with hoops, and armed with ribs of whale.
Form a strong line about the silver bound,
And guard the wide circumference around.
   Whatever spirit, careless of his charge,
His post neglects, or leaves the fair at large,
Shall feel sharp vengeance soon o'ertake his sins,
Be stopped in vials, or transfixed with pins,
Or plunged in lakes of bitter washes lie,
Or wedged whole ages in a bodkin's eye;
Gums and pomatums shall his flight restrain,
While clogged he beats his silken wings in vain,
Or alum styptics with contracting power

Shrink his thin essence like a riveled flower:
Or, as Ixion fixed, the wretch shall feel
The giddy motion of the whirling mill,
Midst fumes of burning chocolate shall glow,
And tremble at the sea that froths below!"

He spoke; the spirits from the sails descend;
Some, orb in orb, around the nymph extend;
Some thread the mazy ringlets of her hair;
Some hang upon the pendants of her ear:
With beating hearts the dire event they wait,
Anxious, and trembling for the birth of Fate.

Canto III

Close by those meads, forever crowned with flowers,
Where Thames with pride surveys his rising towers,
There stands a structure of majestic frame,
Which from the neighbouring Hampton takes its name.
Here Britain's statesmen oft the fall foredoom
Of foreign tyrants and of nymphs at home;
Here thou, great Anna, whom three realms obey,
Dost sometimes counsel take—and sometimes tea.

Hither the heroes and the nymphs resort,
To taste awhile the pleasures of a court;
In various talk the instructive hours they passed,
Who gave a ball or paid the visit last;
One speaks the glory of the British queen,
And one describes a charming Indian screen;
A third interprets motions, looks, and eyes;
At every word a reputation dies.
Snuff, or the fan, supply each pause of chat,
With singing, laughing, ogling, and all that.

Meanwhile, declining from the noon of day,
The sun obliquely shoots his burning ray;
The hungry judges soon the sentence sign,
And wretches hang that jurymen may dine;
The merchant from the Exchange returns in peace,
And the long labours of the toilet cease.
Belinda now, whom thirst of fame invites,
Burns to encounter two adventurous knights,
At ombre singly to decide their doom,
And swells her breast with conquests yet to come.

Straight the three bands prepare in arms to join,
Each band the number of the sacred nine.
Soon as she spreads her hand, the aerial guard
Descend, and sit on each important card:
First Ariel perched upon a matador,
Then each according to the rank they bore;
For sylphs, yet mindful of their ancient race,
Are, as when women, wondrous fond of place.

Behold, four kings in majesty revered,
With hoary whiskers and a forky beard;
And four fair queens whose hands sustain a flower,
The expressive emblem of their softer power;
Four knaves in garbs succinct, a trusty band,
Caps on their heads, and halberts in their hand;
And parti-coloured troops, a shining train,
Draw forth to combat on the velvet plain.

The skillful nymph reviews her force with care;
"Let spades be trumps!" she said, and trumps they were.
Now move to war her sable matadors,
In show like leaders of the swarthy Moors.
Spadillio first, unconquerable lord!
Led off two captive trumps, and swept the board.
As many more Manillio forced to yield,
And marched a victor from the verdant field.
Him Basto followed, but his fate more hard
Gained but one trump and one plebeian card.
With his broad sabre next, a chief in years,
The hoary majesty of spades appears,
Puts forth one manly leg, to sight revealed,
The rest his many-coloured robe concealed.
The rebel knave, who dares his prince engage,
Proves the just victim of his royal rage.
Even mighty Pam, that kings and queens o'erthrew
And mowed down armies in the fights of loo,
Sad chance of war! now destitute of aid,
Falls undistinguished by the victor Spade.

Thus far both armies to Belinda yield;
Now to the baron fate inclines the field.
His warlike Amazon her host invades,
The imperial consort of the crown of spades.
The club's black tyrant first her victim died,
Spite of his haughty mien and barbarous pride.

243

What boots the regal circle on his head,
His giant limbs, in state unwieldy spread?
That long behind he trails his pompous robe,
And of all monarchs only grasps the globe?
    The baron now his diamonds pours apace;
The embroidered king who shows but half his face,
And his refulgent queen, with powers combined
Of broken troops an easy conquest find.
Clubs, diamonds, hearts, in wild disorder seen,
With throngs promiscuous strew the level green.
Thus when dispersed a routed army runs,
Of Asia's troops, and Afric's sable sons,
With like confusion different nations fly,
Of various habit, and of various dye,
The pierced battalions disunited fall
In heaps on heaps; one fate o'erwhelms them all.
    The knave of diamonds tries his wily arts,
And wins (oh, shameful chance!) the queen of hearts.
At this, the blood the virgin's cheek forsook,
A livid paleness spreads o'er all her look;
She sees, and trembles at the approaching ill,
Just in the jaws of ruin, and Codille,
And now (as oft in some distempered state)
On one nice trick depends the general fate.
An ace of hearts steps forth: the king unseen
Lurked in her hand, and mourned his captive queen.
He springs to vengeance with an eager pace,
And falls like thunder on the prostrate ace.
The nymph exulting fills with shouts the sky,
The walls, the woods, and long canals reply.
    O thoughtless mortals, ever blind to fate,
Too soon dejected, and too soon elate!
Sudden these honours shall be snatched away,
And cursed forever this victorious day.
    For lo! The board with cups and spoons is crowned,
The berries crackle, and the mill turns round;
On shining altars of Japan they raise
The silver lamp; the fiery spirits blaze:
From silver spouts the grateful liquors glide,
While China's earth receives the smoking tide.
At once they gratify their scent and taste,
And frequent cups prolong the rich repast.

Straight hover round the fair her airy band;
Some, as she sipped, the fuming liquor fanned,
Some o'er her lap their careful plumes displayed,
Trembling, and conscious of the rich brocade.
Coffee (which makes the politician wise,
And see through all things with his half-shut eyes)
Sent up in vapours to the baron's brain
New stratagems, the radiant lock to gain.
Ah, cease, rash youth, desist ere 'tis too late,
Fear the just gods, and think of Scylla's fate!
Changed to a bird, and sent to flit in air,
She dearly pays for Nisus' injured hair!

But when to mischief mortals bend their will,
How soon they find fit instruments of ill!
Just then, Clarissa drew with tempting grace
A two-edged weapon from her shining case:
So ladies in romance assist their knight,
Present the spear, and arm him for the fight.
He takes the gift with reverence, and extends
The little engine on his fingers' ends;
This just behind Belinda's neck he spread,
As o'er the fragrant steams she bends her head.
Swift to the lock a thousand sprites repair,
A thousand wings, by turns, blow back the hair,
And thrice they twitched the diamond in her ear,
Thrice she looked back, and thrice the foe drew near.
Just in that instant, anxious Ariel sought
The close recesses of the virgin's thought;
As on the nosegay in her breast reclined,
He watched the ideas rising in her mind,
Sudden he viewed, in spite of all her art,
An earthly lover lurking at her heart.
Amazed, confused, he found his power expired,
Resigned to fate, and with a sigh retired.

The peer now spreads the glittering forfex wide,
To enclose the lock; now joins it, to divide.
Even then, before the fatal engine closed,
A wretched sylph too fondly interposed;
Fate urged the shears, and cut the sylph in twain
(But airy substance soon unites again):
The meeting points the sacred hair dissever
From the fair head, forever, and forever!

Then flashed the living lightnings from her eyes,
And screams of horror rend the affrighted skies.
Not louder shrieks to pitying heaven are cast,
When husbands, or when lapdogs breathe their last;
Or when rich china vessels fallen from high,
In glittering dust and painted fragments lie!
"Let wreaths of triumph now my temples twine,"
The victor cried, "the glorious prize is mine!
While fish in streams, or birds delight in air,
Or in a coach and six the British fair,
As long as *Atalantis*" shall be read,
Or the small pillow grace a lady's bed,
While visits shall be paid on solemn days,
When numerous wax-lights in bright order blaze,
While nymphs take treats, or assignations give,
So long my honour, name, and praise shall live!
What time would spare, from steel receives its date,
And monuments, like men, submit to fate!
Steel could the labour of the gods destroy,
And strike to dust the imperial towers of Troy;
Steel could the works of mortal pride confound,
And hew triumphal arches to the ground.
What wonder then, fair nymph! thy hairs should feel,
The conquering force of unresisted steel?"

Canto IV

But anxious cares the pensive nymph oppressed,
And secret passions laboured in her breast.
Not youthful kings in battle seized alive,
Not scornful virgins who their charms survive,
Not ardent lovers robbed of all their bliss,
Not ancient ladies when refused a kiss,
Not tyrants fierce that unrepenting die,
Not Cynthia when her manteau's pinned awry,
E'er felt such rage, resentment, and despair,
As thou, sad virgin! for thy ravished hair.
For, that sad moment, when the sylphs withdrew
And Ariel weeping from Belinda flew,
Umbriel, a dusky, melancholy sprite
As ever sullied the fair face of light,
Down to the central earth, his proper scene,

Repaired to search the gloomy cave of Spleen.
Swift on his sooty pinions flits the gnome,
And in a vapour reached the dismal dome.
No cheerful breeze this sullen region knows,
The dreaded east is all the wind that blows.
Here in a grotto, sheltered close from air,
And screened in shades from day's detested glare,
She sighs forever on her pensive bed,
Pain at her side, and megrim at her head.
Two handmaids wait the throne: alike in place
But differing far in figure and in face.
Here stood Ill-Nature like an ancient maid,
Her wrinkled form in black and white arrayed;
With store of prayers for mornings, nights, and noons,
Her hand is filled; her bosom with lampoons.
There Affectation, with a sickly mien,
Shows in her cheek the roses of eighteen,
Practiced to lisp, and hang the head aside,
Faints into airs, and languishes with pride,
On the rich quilt sinks with becoming woe,
Wrapped in a gown, for sickness and for show.
The fair ones feel such maladies as these,
When each new nightdress gives a new disease.
A constant vapour o'er the palace flies,
Strange phantoms rising as the mists arise;
Dreadful as hermit's dreams in haunted shades,
Or bright as visions of expiring maids.
Now glaring fiends, and snakes on rolling spires,
Pale spectres, gaping tombs, and purple fires;
Now lakes of liquid gold, Elysian scenes,
And crystal domes, and angels in machines.
Unnumbered throngs on every side are seen
Of bodies changed to various forms by Spleen.
Here living teapots stand, one arm held out,
One bent; the handle this, and that the spout:
A pipkin there, like Homer's tripod, walks;
Here sighs a jar, and there a goose pie talks;
Men prove with child, as powerful fancy works,
And maids, turned bottles, call aloud for corks.
Safe passed the gnome through this fantastic band,
A branch of healing spleenwort in his hand.
Then thus addressed the power: "Hail, wayward queen!

247

Who rule the sex to fifty from fifteen:
Parent of vapours and of female wit,
Who give the hysteric or poetic fit,
On various tempers act by various ways,
Make some take physic, others scribble plays;
Who cause the proud their visits to delay,
And send the godly in a pet to pray.
A nymph there is that all your power disdains,
And thousands more in equal mirth maintains.
But oh! If e'er thy gnome could spoil a grace,
Or raise a pimple on a beauteous face,
Like citron-waters matrons' cheeks inflame,
Or change complexions at a losing game;
If e'er with airy horns I planted heads,
Or rumpled petticoats, or tumbled beds,
Or caused suspicion when no soul was rude,
Or discomposed the headdress of a prude,
Or e'er to costive lapdog gave disease,
Which not the tears of brightest eyes could ease,
Hear me, and touch Belinda with chagrin:
That single act gives half the world the spleen."
    The goddess with a discontented air
Seems to reject him though she grants his prayer.
A wondrous bag with both her hands she binds,
Like that where once Ulysses held the winds;
There she collects the force of female lungs,
Sighs, sobs, and passions, and the war of tongues.
A vial next she fills with fainting fears,
Soft sorrows, melting griefs, and flowing tears.
The gnome rejoicing bears her gifts away,
Spreads his black wings, and slowly mounts to day.
    Sunk in Thalestris' arms the nymph he found,
Her eyes dejected and her hair unbound.
Full o'er their heads the swelling bag he rent,
And all the Furies issued at the vent.
Belinda burns with more than mortal ire,
And fierce Thalestris fans the rising fire.
"O wretched maid!" she spread her hands, and cried
(While Hampton's echoes, "Wretched maid!" replied),
"Was it for this you took such constant care
The bodkin, comb, and essence to prepare?
For this your locks in paper durance bound,

For this with torturing irons wreathed around?
For this with fillets strained your tender head,
And bravely bore the double loads of lead?
Gods! shall the ravisher display your hair,
While the fops envy, and the ladies stare!
Honour forbid! at whose unrivaled shrine
Ease, pleasure, virtue, all our sex resign.
Methinks already I your tears survey,
Already hear the horrid things they say,
Already see you a degraded toast,
And all your honour in a whisper lost!
How shall I, then, your helpless fame defend?
'Twill then be infamy to seem your friend!
And shall this prize, the inestimable prize,
Exposed through crystal to the gazing eyes,
And heightened by the diamond's circling rays,
On that rapacious hand forever blaze?
Sooner shall grass in Hyde Park Circus grow,
And wits take lodgings in the sound of Bow;
Sooner let earth, air, sea, to chaos fall,
Men, monkeys, lapdogs, parrots, perish all!"
    She said; then raging to Sir Plume repairs,
And bids her beau demand the precious hairs
(Sir Plume of amber snuffbox justly vain,
And the nice conduct of a clouded cane),
With earnest eyes, and round unthinking face,
He first the snuffbox opened, then the case,
And thus broke out—"My Lord, why, what the devil!
Zounds! damn the lock! 'Fore Gad, you must be civil!
Plague on't! 'tis past a jest—nay prithee, pox!
Give her the hair"—he spoke, and rapped his box.
    "It grieves me much," replied the peer again,
"Who speaks so well should ever speak in vain.
But by this lock, this sacred lock I swear
(Which never more shall join its parted hair;
Which never more its honours shall renew,
Clipped from the lovely head where late it grew),
That while my nostrils draw the vital air,
This hand, which won it, shall forever wear."
He spoke, and speaking, in proud triumph spread
The long-contended honours of her head.
    But Umbriel, hateful gnome, forbears not so;

He breaks the vial whence the sorrows flow.
Then see! The nymph in beauteous grief appears,
Her eyes half languishing, half drowned in tears;
On her heaved bosom hung her drooping head,
Which with a sigh she raised, and thus she said:
    "Forever cursed be this detested day,
Which snatched my best, my favourite curl away!
Happy! ah, ten times happy had I been,
If Hampton Court these eyes had never seen!
Yet am not I the first mistaken maid,
By love of courts to numerous ills betrayed.
Oh, had I rather unadmired remained
In some lone isle, or distant northern land;
Where the gilt chariot never marks the way,
Where none learn ombre, none e'er taste bohea!
There kept my charms concealed from mortal eye,
Like roses that in deserts bloom and die.
What moved my mind with youthful lords to roam?
Oh, had I stayed, and said my prayers at home!
'Twas this the morning omens seemed to tell,
Thrice from my trembling hand the patch-box fell;
The tottering china shook without a wind,
Nay, Poll sat mute, and Shock was most unkind!
A sylph too warned me of the threats of fate,
In mystic visions, now believed too late!
See the poor remnants of these slighted hairs!
My hands shall rend what e'en thy rapine spares.
These in two sable ringlets taught to break,
Once gave new beauties to the snowy neck;
The sister lock now sits uncouth, alone,
And in its fellow's fate foresees its own;
Uncurled it hangs, the fatal shears demands,
And tempts once more thy sacrilegious hands.
Oh, hadst thou, cruel! been content to seize
Hairs less in sight, or any hairs but these!"

Canto V

    She said; the pitying audience melt in tears.
But Fate and Jove had stopped the baron's ears.
In vain Thalestris with reproach assails,
For who can move when fair Belinda fails?

Not half so fixed the Trojan could remain,
While Anna begged and Dido raged in vain.
Then grave Clarissa graceful waved her fan;
Silence ensued, and thus the nymph began:
    "Say why are beauties praised and honoured most,
The wise man's passion, and the vain man's toast?
Why decked with all that land and sea afford,
Why angels called, and angel-like adored?
Why round our coaches crowd the white-gloved beaux,
Why bows the side box from its inmost rows?
How vain are all these glories, all our pains,
Unless good sense preserve what beauty gains;
That men may say when we the front box grace,
'Behold the first in virtue as in face!'
Oh! if to dance all night, and dress all day,
Charmed the smallpox, or chased old age away,
Who would not scorn what housewife's cares produce,
Or who would learn one earthly thing of use?
To patch, nay ogle, might become a saint,
Nor could it sure be such a sin to paint.
But since, alas! frail beauty must decay,
Curled or uncurled, since locks will turn to grey;
Since painted, or not painted, all shall fade,
And she who scorns a man must die a maid;
What then remains but well our power to use,
And keep good humour still whate'er we lose?
And trust me, dear, good humour can prevail
When airs, and flights, and screams, and scolding fail.
Beauties in vain their pretty eyes may roll;
Charms strike the sight, but merit wins the soul."
    So spoke the dame, but no applause ensued;
Belinda frowned, Thalestris called her prude.
"To arms, to arms!" the fierce virago cries,
And swift as lightning to the combat flies.
All side in parties, and begin the attack;
Fans clap, silks rustle, and tough whalebones crack;
Heroes' and heroines' shouts confusedly rise,
And bass and treble voices strike the skies.
No common weapons in their hands are found,
Like gods they fight, nor dread a mortal wound.
    So when bold Homer makes the gods engage,
And heavenly breasts with human passions rage;

'Gainst Pallas, Mars; Latona, Hermes arms;
And all Olympus rings with loud alarms:
Jove's thunder roars, heaven trembles all around,
Blue Neptune storms, the bellowing deeps resound:
Earth shakes her nodding towers, the ground gives way,
And the pale ghosts start at the flash of day!

    Triumphant Umbriel on a sconce's height
Clapped his glad wings, and sat to view the fight:
Propped on the bodkin spears, the sprites survey
The growing combat, or assist the fray.

    While through the press enraged Thalestris flies,
And scatters death around from both her eyes,
A beau and witling perished in the throng,
One died in metaphor, and one in song.
"O cruel nymph! a living death I bear,"
Cried Dapperwit, and sunk beside his chair.
A mournful glance Sir Fopling upwards cast,
"Those eyes are made so killing"—was his last.
Thus on Maeander's flowery margin lies
The expiring swan, and as he sings he dies.

    When bold Sir Plume had drawn Clarissa down,
Chloe stepped in, and killed him with a frown;
She smiled to see the doughty hero slain,
But, at her smile, the beau revived again.

    Now Jove suspends his golden scales in air,
Weighs the men's wits against the lady's hair;
The doubtful beam long nods from side to side;
At length the wits mount up, the hairs subside.

    See, fierce Belinda on the baron flies,
With more than usual lightning in her eyes;
Nor feared the chief the unequal fight to try,
Who sought no more than on his foe to die.

    But this bold lord with manly strength endued,
She with one finger and a thumb subdued:
Just where the breath of life his nostrils drew,
A charge of snuff the wily virgin threw;
The gnomes direct, to every atom just,
The pungent grains of titillating dust.
Sudden, with starting tears each eye o'erflows,
And the high dome re-echoes to his nose.

    "Now meet thy fate," incensed Belinda cried,
And drew a deadly bodkin from her side.

(The same, his ancient personage to deck,
Her great-great-grandsire wore about his neck,
In three seal rings; which after, melted down,
Formed a vast buckle for his widow's gown:
Her infant grandame's whistle next it grew,
The bells she jingled, and the whistle blew;
Then in a bodkin graced her mother's hairs,
Which long she wore, and now Belinda wears).
  "Boast not my fall," he cried, "insulting foe!
Thou by some other shalt be laid as low.
Nor think to die dejects my lofty mind:
All that I dread is leaving you behind!
Rather than so, ah, let me still survive,
And burn in Cupid's flames—but burn alive."
  "Restore the lock!" she cries; and all around
"Restore the lock!" the vaulted roofs rebound.
Not fierce Othello in so loud a strain
Roared for the handkerchief that caused his pain.
But see how oft ambitious aims are crossed,
And chiefs contend till all the prize is lost!
The lock, obtained with guilt, and kept with pain,
In every place is sought, but sought in vain:
With such a prize no mortal must be blessed,
So Heaven decrees! With Heaven who can contest?
  Some thought it mounted to the lunar sphere,
Since all things lost on earth are treasured there.
There heroes' wits are kept in ponderous vases,
And beaux' in snuffboxes and tweezer cases.
There broken vows and deathbed alms are found,
And lovers' hearts with ends of riband bound,
The courtier's promises, and sick man's prayers,
The smiles of harlots, and the tears of heirs,
Cages for gnats, and chains to yoke a flea,
Dried butterflies, and tomes of casuistry.
  But trust the Muse—she saw it upward rise,
Though marked by none but quick, poetic eyes
(So Rome's great founder to the heavens withdrew,
To Proculus alone confessed in view);
A sudden star, it shot through liquid air,
And drew behind a radiant trail of hair.
Not Berenice's locks first rose so bright,
The heavens bespangling with disheveled light.

The sylphs behold it kindling as it flies,
And pleased pursue its progress through the skies.
    This the beau monde shall from the Mall survey,
And hail with music its propitious ray.
This the blest lover shall for Venus take,
And send up vows from Rosamonda's lake.
This Partridge soon shall view in cloudless skies,
When next he looks through Galileo's eyes;
And hence the egregious wizard shall foredoom
The fate of Louis, and the fall of Rome.
    Then cease, bright nymph! to mourn thy ravished hair,
Which adds new glory to the shining sphere!
Not all the tresses that fair head can boast,
Shall draw such envy as the lock you lost.
For, after all the murders of your eye,
When, after millions slain, yourself shall die:
When those fair suns shall set, as set they must,
And all those tresses shall be laid in dust,
This lock the Muse shall consecrate to fame,
And 'midst the stars inscribe Belinda's name.

ODE ON SOLITUDE

Happy the man whose wish and care
    A few paternal acres bound,
Content to breathe his native air,
        In his own ground.

Whose herds with milk, whose fields with bread,
    Whose flocks supply him with attire,
Whose trees in summer yield him shade,
        In winter, fire.

Blest, who can unconcernedly find
    Hours, days, and years slide soft away,
In health of body, peace of mind,
        Quiet by day,

Sound sleep by night; study and ease,
    Together mixed; sweet recreation;
And innocence, which most does please
        With meditation.

Thus let me live, unseen, unknown;
    Thus unlamented let me die;
Steal from the world, and not a stone
        Tell where I lie.

ELOISA TO ABELARD

In these deep solitudes and awful cells,
Where heavenly-pensive contemplation dwells,
And ever-musing melancholy reigns;
What means this tumult in a vestal's veins?
Why rove my thoughts beyond this last retreat?
Why feels my heart its long-forgotten heat?
Yet, yet I love! From Abelard it came,
And Eloisa yet must kiss the name.
    Dear fatal name! rest ever unrevealed,
Nor pass these lips in holy silence sealed.
Hide it, my heart, within that close disguise,
Where mixed with God's, his loved idea lies.
Oh write it not, my hand—the name appears
Already written—wash it out, my tears!
In vain lost Eloisa weeps and prays;
Her heart still dictates, and her hand obeys.
    Relentless walls, whose darksome round contains
Repentant sighs, and voluntary pains!
Ye rugged rocks, which holy knees have worn;
Ye grots and caverns shagged with horrid thorn!
Shrines, where their vigils pale-eyed virgins keep,
And pitying saints, whose statues learn to weep!
Though cold like you, unmoved, and silent grown,
I have not yet forgot myself to stone.
All is not heaven's while Abelard has part,
Still rebel nature holds out half my heart;
Nor prayers nor fasts its stubborn pulse restrain,

Nor tears, for ages taught to flow in vain.
　Soon as thy letters trembling I unclose,
That well-known name awakens all my woes.
Oh name forever sad! Forever dear!
Still breathed in sighs, still ushered with a tear.
I tremble, too, where'er my own I find,
Some dire misfortune follows close behind.
Line after line my gushing eyes o'erflow,
Led through a sad variety of woe:
Now warm in love, now withering in my bloom,
Lost in a convent's solitary gloom!
There stern religion quenched the unwilling flame,
There died the best of passions, love and fame.
　Yet write, oh write me all, that I may join
Griefs to thy griefs, and echo sighs to thine.
Nor foes nor fortune take this power away.
And is my Abelard less kind than they?
Tears still are mine, and those I need not spare,
Love but demands what else were shed in prayer;
No happier task these faded eyes pursue,
To read and weep is all they now can do.
　Then share thy pain, allow that sad relief;
Ah, more than share it! Give me all thy grief.
Heaven first taught letters for some wretch's aid,
Some banished lover, or some captive maid;
They live, they speak, they breathe what love inspires,
Warm from the soul, and faithful to its fires,
The virgin's wish without her fears impart,
Excuse the blush, and pour out all the heart,
Speed the soft intercourse from soul to soul,
And waft a sigh from Indus to the Pole.
　Thou knowest how guiltless first I met thy flame,
When love approached me under friendship's name;
My fancy formed thee of angelic kind,
Some emanation of the all-beauteous mind.
Those smiling eyes, attempering every ray,
Shone sweetly lambent with celestial day:
Guiltless I gazed; heaven listened while you sung;
And truths divine came mended from that tongue.
From lips like those what precept failed to move?
Too soon they taught me 'twas no sin to love.
Back through the paths of pleasing sense I ran,

256

Nor wished an angel whom I loved a man.
Dim and remote the joys of saints I see,
Nor envy them that heaven I lose for thee.
How oft, when pressed to marriage, have I said,
Curse on all laws but those which love has made!
Love, free as air, at sight of human ties,
Spreads his light wings, and in a moment flies.
Let wealth, let honour, wait the wedded dame,
August her deed, and sacred be her fame;
Before true passion all those views remove,
Fame, wealth, and honour! What are you to love?
The jealous god, when we profane his fires,
Those restless passions in revenge inspires,
And bids them make mistaken mortals groan,
Who seek in love for aught but love alone.
Should at my feet the world's great master fall,
Himself, his throne, his world, I'd scorn 'em all:
Not Caesar's empress would I deign to prove;
No, make me mistress to the man I love;
If there be yet another name more free,
More fond than mistress, make me that to thee!
Oh happy state, when souls each other draw,
When love is liberty, and nature, law:
All then is full, possessing, and possessed,
No craving void left aching in the breast:
Even thought meets thought ere from the lips it part,
And each warm wish springs mutual from the heart.
This sure is bliss (if bliss on earth there be)
And once the lot of Abelard and me.
Alas how changed! What sudden horrors rise!
A naked lover bound and bleeding lies!
Where, where was Eloise? Her voice, her hand,
Her poniard, had opposed the dire command.
Barbarian, stay! That bloody hand restrain;
The crime was common; common be the pain.
I can no more; by shame, by rage suppressed,
Let tears, and burning blushes speak the rest.
Canst thou forget that sad, that solemn day,
When victims at yon altar's foot we lay?
Canst thou forget what tears that moment fell,
When, warm in youth, I bade the world farewell?
As with cold lips I kissed the sacred veil,

257

The shrines all trembled, and the lamps grew pale:
Heaven scarce believed the conquest it surveyed,
And saints with wonder heard the vows I made.
Yet then, to those dread altars as I drew,
Not on the cross my eyes were fixed, but you;
Not grace, or zeal, love only was my call,
And if I lose thy love, I lose my all.
Come! With thy looks, thy words, relieve my woe;
Those still, at least, are left thee to bestow.
Still on that breast enamoured let me lie,
Still drink delicious poison from thy eye,
Pant on thy lip, and to thy heart be pressed;
Give all thou canst—and let me dream the rest.
Ah no! Instruct me other joys to prize,
With other beauties charm my partial eyes,
Full in my view set all the bright abode,
And make my soul quit Abelard for God.
   Ah, think at least thy flock deserve thy care,
Plants of thy hand, and children of thy prayer.
From the false world in early youth they fled,
By thee to mountains, wilds, and deserts led.
You raised these hallowed walls; the desert smiled,
And paradise was opened in the wild.
No weeping orphan saw his father's stores
Our shrines irradiate, or emblaze the floors;
No silver saints, by dying misers given,
Here bribed the rage of ill-requited heaven:
But such plain roofs as piety could raise,
And only vocal with the Maker's praise.
In these lone walls (their days eternal bound)
These moss-grown domes with spiry turrets crowned,
Where awful arches make a noonday night,
And the dim windows shed a solemn light,
Thy eyes diffused a reconciling ray,
And gleams of glory brightened all the day.
But now no face divine contentment wears,
'Tis all blank sadness, or continual tears.
See how the force of others' prayers I try,
(O pious fraud of amorous charity!)
But why should I on others' prayers depend?
Come thou, my father, brother, husband, friend!
Ah, let thy handmaid, sister, daughter move,

258

And all those tender names in one, thy love!
The darksome pines that o'er yon rocks reclined
Wave high, and murmur to the hollow wind,
The wandering streams that shine between the hills,
The grots that echo to the tinkling rills,
The dying gales that pant upon the trees,
The lakes that quiver to the curling breeze;
No more these scenes my meditation aid,
Or lull to rest the visionary maid:
But o'er the twilight groves and dusky caves,
Long-sounding isles, and intermingled graves,
Black Melancholy sits, and round her throws
A death-like silence, and a dread repose:
Her gloomy presence saddens all the scene,
Shades every flower, and darkens every green,
Deepens the murmur of the falling floods,
And breathes a browner horror on the woods.
    Yet here forever, ever must I stay;
Sad proof how well a lover can obey!
Death, only death, can break the lasting chain;
And here, even then, shall my cold dust remain,
Here all its frailties, all its flames resign,
And wait, till 'tis no sin to mix with thine.
    Ah wretch! Believed the spouse of God in vain,
Confessed within the slave of love and man.
Assist me, heaven! But whence arose that prayer?
Sprung it from piety, or from despair?
Even here, where frozen chastity retires,
Love finds an altar for forbidden fires.
I ought to grieve, but cannot what I ought;
I mourn the lover, not lament the fault;
I view my crime, but kindle at the view,
Repent old pleasures, and solicit new;
Now turned to heaven, I weep my past offence,
Now think of thee, and curse my innocence.
Of all affliction taught a lover yet,
'Tis sure the hardest science to forget!
How shall I lose the sin, yet keep the sense,
And love the offender, yet detest the offence?
How the dear object from the crime remove,
Or how distinguish penitence from love?
Unequal task! A passion to resign,

For hearts so touched, so pierced, so lost as mine.
Ere such a soul regains its peaceful state,
How often must it love, how often hate!
How often hope, despair, resent, regret,
Conceal, disdain—do all things but forget.
But let heaven seize it, all at once 'tis fired,
Not touched, but rapt; not wakened, but inspired!
Oh come! oh teach me nature to subdue,
Renounce my love, my life, myself—and you.
Fill my fond heart with God alone, for he
Alone can rival, can succeed to thee.

   How happy is the blameless vestal's lot!
The world forgetting, by the world forgot.
Eternal sunshine of the spotless mind!
Each prayer accepted, and each wish resigned;
Labour and rest, that equal periods keep;
"Obedient slumbers that can wake and weep;"
Desires composed, affections ever even;
Tears that delight, and sighs that waft to heaven.
Grace shines around her with serenest beams,
And whispering angels prompt her golden dreams.
For her the unfading rose of Eden blooms,
And wings of seraphs shed divine perfumes,
For her the spouse prepares the bridal ring,
For her white virgins hymeneals sing,
To sounds of heavenly harps she dies away,
And melts in visions of eternal day.

   Far other dreams my erring soul employ,
Far other raptures, of unholy joy:
When at the close of each sad, sorrowing day,
Fancy restores what vengeance snatched away,
Then conscience sleeps, and, leaving nature free,
All my loose soul unbounded springs to thee.
O cursed, dear horrors of all-conscious night!
How glowing guilt exalts the keen delight!
Provoking demons all restraint remove,
And stir within me every source of love.
I hear thee, view thee, gaze o'er all thy charms,
And round thy phantom glue my clasping arms.
I wake—no more I hear, no more I view,
The phantom flies me, as unkind as you.
I call aloud; it hears not what I say;

I stretch my empty arms; it glides away:
To dream once more I close my willing eyes;
Ye soft illusions, dear deceits, arise!
Alas, no more! Methinks we wandering go
Through dreary wastes, and weep each other's woe;
Where round some mouldering tower pale ivy creeps,
And low-browed rocks hang nodding o'er the deeps.
Sudden you mount! You beckon from the skies;
Clouds interpose, waves roar, and winds arise.
I shriek, start up, the same sad prospect find,
And wake to all the griefs I left behind.

For thee the fates, severely kind, ordain
A cool suspense from pleasure and from pain;
Thy life a long dead calm of fixed repose;
No pulse that riots, and no blood that glows.
Still as the sea, ere winds were taught to blow,
Or moving spirit bade the waters flow;
Soft as the slumbers of a saint forgiven,
And mild as opening gleams of promised heaven.

Come, Abelard! For what hast thou to dread?
The torch of Venus burns not for the dead.
Nature stands checked; religion disapproves;
Even thou art cold—yet Eloisa loves.
Ah hopeless, lasting flames! Like those that burn
To light the dead, and warm the unfruitful urn.

What scenes appear where'er I turn my view!
The dear ideas, where I fly, pursue,
Rise in the grove, before the altar rise,
Stain all my soul, and wanton in my eyes!
I waste the matin lamp in sighs for thee,
Thy image steals between my God and me,
Thy voice I seem in every hymn to hear,
With every bead I drop too soft a tear.
When from the censer clouds of fragrance roll,
And swelling organs lift the rising soul,
One thought of thee puts all the pomp to flight,
Priests, tapers, temples swim before my sight:
In seas of flame my plunging soul is drowned,
While altars blaze, and angels tremble round.

While prostrate here in humble grief I lie,
Kind, virtuous drops just gathering in my eye,
While praying, trembling, in the dust I roll,

And dawning grace is opening on my soul:
Come, if thou darest, all charming as thou art!
Oppose thyself to heaven; dispute my heart;
Come, with one glance of those deluding eyes
Blot out each bright idea of the skies.
Take back that grace, those sorrows, and those tears,
Take back my fruitless penitence and prayers,
Snatch me, just mounting, from the blest abode,
Assist the fiends and tear me from my God!

No, fly me, fly me! far as pole from pole;
Rise Alps between us and whole oceans roll!
Ah come not, write not, think not once of me,
Nor share one pang of all I felt for thee.
Thy oaths I quit, thy memory resign,
Forget, renounce me, hate whate'er was mine.
Fair eyes, and tempting looks (which yet I view!)
Long loved, adored ideas! All adieu!
O grace serene! O virtue heavenly fair!
Divine oblivion of low-thoughted care!
Fresh blooming hope, gay daughter of the sky!
And faith, our early immortality!
Enter each mild, each amicable guest;
Receive, and wrap me in eternal rest!

See in her cell sad Eloisa spread,
Propped on some tomb, a neighbor of the dead!
In each low wind methinks a spirit calls,
And more than echoes talk along the walls.
Here, as I watched the dying lamps around,
From yonder shrine I heard a hollow sound.
"Come, sister, come!" (it said, or seemed to say)
"Thy place is here, sad sister, come away!
Once like thyself, I trembled, wept, and prayed,
Love's victim then, though now a sainted maid:
But all is calm in this eternal sleep;
Here grief forgets to groan, and love to weep,
Even superstition loses every fear:
For God, not man, absolves our frailties here."

I come, I come! Prepare your roseate bowers,
Celestial palms, and ever-blooming flowers.
Thither, where sinners may have rest, I go,
Where flames refined in breasts seraphic glow.
Thou, Abelard! The last sad office pay,

And smooth my passage to the realms of day:
See my lips tremble, and my eyeballs roll,
Suck my last breath, and catch my flying soul!
Ah no—in sacred vestments mayest thou stand,
The hallowed taper trembling in thy hand,
Present the cross before my lifted eye,
Teach me at once, and learn of me to die.
Ah then, thy once-loved Eloisa see!
It will be then no crime to gaze on me.
See from my cheek the transient roses fly!
See the last sparkle languish in my eye!
Till every motion, pulse, and breath be o'er;
And even my Abelard beloved no more.
O Death all-eloquent! You only prove
What dust we doat on, when 'tis man we love.

Then too, when fate shall thy fair frame destroy
(That cause of all my guilt, and all my joy),
In trance ecstastic may thy pangs be drowned,
Bright clouds descend, and angels watch thee round,
From opening skies may streaming glories shine,
And saints embrace thee with a love like mine.

May one kind grave unite each hapless name,
And graft my love immortal on thy fame!
Then, ages hence, when all my woes are o'er,
When this rebellious heart shall beat no more;
If ever chance two wandering lovers brings
To Paraclete's white walls, and silver springs,
O'er the pale marble shall they join their heads,
And drink the falling tears each other sheds,
Then sadly say, with mutual pity moved,
O may we never love as these have loved!
From the full choir when loud hosannas rise,
And swell the pomp of dreadful sacrifice,
Amid that scene if some relenting eye
Glance on the stone where our cold relics lie,
Devotion's self shall steal a thought from heaven,
One human tear shall drop, and be forgiven.
And sure if fate some future bard shall join
In sad similitude of griefs to mine,
Condemned whole years in absence to deplore,
And image charms he must behold no more,
Such if there be, who loves so long, so well,

Let him our sad, our tender story tell;
The well-sung woes shall soothe my pensive ghost;
He best can paint 'em who shall feel 'em most.

ELEGY TO THE MEMORY OF
AN UNFORTUNATE LADY

What beckoning ghost, along the moonlight shade
Invites my steps, and points to yonder glade?
'Tis she! But why that bleeding bosom gored,
Why dimly gleams the visionary sword?
Oh ever beauteous, ever friendly! Tell,
Is it, in heaven, a crime to love too well?
To bear too tender, or too firm a heart,
To act a lover's or a Roman's part?
Is there no bright reversion in the sky,
For those who greatly think, or bravely die?

Why bade ye else, ye powers! her soul aspire
Above the vulgar flight of low desire?
Ambition first sprung from your blest abodes;
The glorious fault of angels and of gods:
Thence to their images on earth it flows,
And in the breasts of kings and heroes glows!
Most souls, 'tis true, but peep out once an age,
Dull sullen prisoners in the body's cage:
Dim lights of life that burn a length of years,
Useless, unseen, as lamps in sepulchres;
Like eastern kings a lazy state they keep,
And close confined in their own palace sleep.

From these perhaps (ere nature bade her die)
Fate snatched her early to the pitying sky.
As into air the purer spirits flow,
And separate from their kindred dregs below;
So flew the soul to its congenial place,
Nor left one virtue to redeem her race.

But thou, false guardian of a charge too good,
Thou, mean deserter of thy brother's blood!
See on these ruby lips the trembling breath,
These cheeks, now fading at the blast of death:

Cold is that breast which warmed the world before,
And those love-darting eyes must roll no more.
Thus, if eternal justice rules the ball,
Thus shall your wives, and thus your children fall:
On all the line a sudden vengeance waits,
And frequent hearses shall besiege your gates.
There passengers shall stand, and pointing say,
(While the long funerals blacken all the way)
Lo these were they, whose souls the Furies steeled,
And cursed with hearts unknowing how to yield.
Thus unlamented pass the proud away,
The gaze of fools, and pageant of a day!
So perish all, whose breast ne'er learned to glow
For others' good, or melt at others' woe.

What can atone (oh ever-injured shade!)
Thy fate unpitied, and thy rites unpaid?
No friend's complaint, no kind domestic tear
Pleased thy pale ghost, or graced thy mournful bier;
By foreign hands thy dying eyes were closed,
By foreign hands thy decent limbs composed,
By foreign hands thy humble grave adorned,
By strangers honoured, and by strangers mourned!
What though no friends in sable weeds appear,
Grieve for an hour, perhaps, then mourn a year,
And bear about the mockery of woe
To midnight dances, and the public show?
What though no weeping loves thy ashes grace,
Nor polished marble emulate thy face?
What though no sacred earth allow thee room,
Nor hallowed dirge be muttered o'er thy tomb?
Yet shall thy grave with rising flowers be drest,
And the green turf lie lightly on thy breast:
There shall the morn her earliest tears bestow,
There the first roses of the year shall blow;
While angels with their silver wings o'ershade
The ground, now sacred by thy relics made.

So peaceful rests, without a stone, a name,
What once had beauty, titles, wealth, and fame.
How loved, how honoured once, avails thee not,
To whom related, or by whom begot;
A heap of dust alone remains of thee;
'Tis all thou art, and all the proud shall be!

Poets themselves must fall, like those they sung;
Deaf the praised ear, and mute the tuneful tongue.
Even he, whose soul now melts in mournful lays,
Shall shortly want the generous tear he pays;
Then from his closing eyes thy form shall part,
And the last pang shall tear thee from his heart,
Life's idle business at one gasp be o'er,
The Muse forgot, and thou beloved no more!

LADY MARY WORTLEY MONTAGU
(1689–1762)

AN ANSWER TO A LADY ADVISING
ME TO RETIREMENT

You little know the heart that you advise;
I view this various scene with equal eyes.
In crowded court I find myself alone,
And pay my worship to a nobler throne.

Long since the value of this world I know,
Pity the madness, and despise the show.
Well as I can my tedious part I bear
And wait dismission without painful fear.

Seldom I mark mankind's detested ways,
Not hearing censure, nor affecting praise,
And unconcerned my future fate I trust
To that sole Being, merciful and just.

JAMES THOMSON
(1700–48)

from WINTER

See, Winter comes, to rule the varied year,
Sullen, and sad, with all his rising train;
Vapours, and clouds, and storms. Be these my theme,
These, that exalt the soul to solemn thought,
And heavenly musing. Welcome, kindred glooms!
Congenial horrors, hail! With frequent foot,
Pleased have I, in my cheerful morn of life,
When nursed by careless solitude I lived,
And sung of nature with unceasing joy,
Pleased have I wandered through your rough domain;
Trod the pure virgin snows, myself as pure;
Heard the winds roar, and the big torrent burst;
Or seen the deep fermenting tempest brewed,
In the grim evening-sky. Thus passed the time,
Till through the lucid chambers of the south
Looked out the joyous spring, looked out and smiled.

. . . .

Now when the cheerless empire of the sky
To Capricorn the Centaur-Archer yields,
And fierce Aquarius stains the inverted year;
Hung o'er the farthest verge of heaven, the sun
Scarce spreads o'er ether the dejected day.
Faint are his gleams, and ineffectual shoot
His struggling rays, in horizontal lines,
Through the thick air; as clothed in cloudy storm,
Weak, wan, and broad, he skirts the southern sky;
And, soon-descending, to the long dark night,
Wide-shading all, the prostrate world resigns.
Nor is the night unwished; while vital heat,
Light, life, and joy, the dubious day forsake.
Meantime, in sable cincture, shadows vast,
Deep-tinged and damp, and congregated clouds,

And all the vapoury turbulence of heaven
Involve the face of things. Thus Winter falls,
A heavy gloom oppressive o'er the world,
Through Nature shedding influence malign,
And rouses up the seeds of dark disease.
The soul of man dies in him, loathing life,
And black with more than melancholy views.
The cattle droop; and o'er the furrowed land,
Fresh from the plow, the dun discoloured flocks,
Untended spreading, crop the wholesome root.
Along the woods, along the moorish fens,
Sighs the sad genius of the coming storm;
And up among the loose, disjointed cliffs,
And fractured mountains wild, the brawling brook
And cave, presageful, send a hollow moan,
Resounding long in listening fancy's ear.

SAMUEL JOHNSON
(1709–84)

LONDON

Though grief and fondness in my breast rebel,
When injured Thales bids the town farewell,
Yet still my calmer thoughts his choice commend,
I praise the hermit, but regret the friend,
Resolved at length, from vice and London far,
To breathe in distant fields a purer air,
And, fixed on Cambria's solitary shore,
Give to St. David one true Briton more.

    For who would leave, unbribed, Hibernia's land,
Or change the rocks of Scotland for the Strand?
There none are swept by sudden fate away,
But all whom hunger spares, with age decay:
Here malice, rapine, accident, conspire,
And now a rabble rages, now a fire;
Their ambush here relentless ruffians lay,
And here the fell attorney prowls for prey;
Here falling houses thunder on your head,
And here a female atheist talks you dead.

    While Thales waits the wherry that contains
Of dissipated wealth the small remains,
On Thames's banks, in silent thought we stood,
Where Greenwich smiles upon the silver flood:
Struck with the seat that gave Eliza birth,
We kneel, and kiss the consecrated earth;
In pleasing dreams the blissful age renew,
And call Britannia's glories back to view;
Behold her cross triumphant on the main,
The guard of commerce, and the dread of Spain,
Ere masquerades debauched, excise oppressed,
Or English honour grew a standing jest.

    A transient calm the happy scenes bestow,
And for a moment lull the sense of woe.

At length awaking, with contemptuous frown,
Indignant Thales eyes the neighbouring town.

   Since worth, he cries, in these degenerate days,
Wants even the cheap reward of empty praise;
In those cursed walls, devote to vice and gain,
Since unrewarded science toils in vain;
Since hope but soothes to double my distress,
And every moment leaves my little less;
While yet my steady steps no staff sustains,
And life still vigorous revels in my veins;
Grant me, kind heaven, to find some happier place,
Where honesty and sense are no disgrace;
Some pleasing bank where verdant osiers play,
Some peaceful vale with nature's paintings gay;
Where once the harassed Briton found repose,
And safe in poverty defied his foes;
Some secret cell, ye powers, indulgent give!
Let —— live here, for —— has learned to live.
Here let those reign, whom pensions can incite
To vote a patriot black, a courtier white;
Explain their country's dear-bought rights away,
And plead for pirates in the face of day;
With slavish tenets taint our poisoned youth,
And lend a lie the confidence of truth.

   Let such raise palaces, and manors buy,
Collect a tax, or farm a lottery,
With warbling eunuchs fill a licensed stage,
And lull to servitude a thoughtless age.

   Heroes, proceed! what bounds your pride shall hold?
What check restrain your thirst of power and gold?
Behold rebellious virtue quite o'erthrown,
Behold our fame, our wealth, our lives your own.

   To such, a groaning nation's spoils are given,
When public crimes inflame the wrath of heaven:
But what, my friend, what hope remains for me,
Who start at theft, and blush at perjury?
Who scarce forbear, though Britain's court he sing,
To pluck a titled poet's borrowed wing;
A Statesman's logic unconvinced can hear,
And dare to slumber o'er the Gazetteer;
Despise a fool in half his pension dressed,
And strive in vain to laugh at H—y's jest.

Others with softer smiles, and subtler art,
Can sap the principles, or taint the heart;
With more address a lover's note convey,
Or bribe a virgin's innocence away.
Well may they rise, while I, whose rustic tongue
Ne'er knew to puzzle right, or varnish wrong,
Spurned as a beggar, dreaded as a spy,
Live unregarded, unlamented die.

For what but social guilt the friend endears?
Who shares Orgilio's crimes, his fortune shares.
But thou, should tempting villainy present
All Marlborough hoarded, or all Villiers spent,
Turn from the glittering bribe thy scornful eye,
Nor sell for gold, what gold could never buy,
The peaceful slumber, self-approving day,
Unsullied fame, and conscience ever gay.

The cheated nation's happy favourites, see!
Mark whom the great caress, who frown on me!
London! the needy villain's general home,
The common shore of Paris and of Rome;
With eager thirst, by folly or by fate,
Sucks in the dregs of each corrupted state.
Forgive my transports on a theme like this,
I cannot bear a French metropolis.

Illustrious Edward! From the realms of day,
The land of heroes and of saints survey;
Nor hope the British lineaments to trace,
The rustic grandeur, or the surly grace,
But lost in thoughtless ease, and empty show,
Behold the warrior dwindled to a beau;
Sense, freedom, piety, refined away,
Of France the mimic, and of Spain the prey.

All that at home no more can beg or steal,
Or like a gibbet better than a wheel;
Hissed from the stage, or hooted from the court,
Their air, their dress, their politics import;
Obsequious, artful, voluble and gay,
On Britain's fond credulity they prey.
No gainful trade their industry can 'scape,
They sing, they dance, clean shoes, or cure a clap;
All sciences a fasting monsieur knows,
And bid him go to hell, to hell he goes.

Ah! what avails it, that, from slavery far,
I drew the breath of life in English air;
Was early taught a Briton's right to prize,
And lisp the tale of Henry's victories;
If the gulled conqueror receives the chain,
And flattery subdues when arms are vain?

Studious to please, and ready to submit,
The supple Gaul was born a parasite:
Still to his interest true, where'er he goes,
Wit, bravery, worth, his lavish tongue bestows;
In every face a thousand graces shine,
From every tongue flows harmony divine.
These arts in vain our rugged natives try,
Strain out with faltering diffidence a lie,
And get a kick for awkward flattery.

Besides, with justice, this discerning age
Admires their wondrous talents for the stage:
Well may they venture on the mimic's art,
Who play from morn to night a borrowed part;
Practised their master's notions to embrace,
Repeat his maxims, and reflect his face;
With every wild absurdity comply,
And view each object with another's eye;
To shake with laughter ere the jest they hear,
To pour at will the counterfeited tear,
And as their patron hints the cold or heat,
To shake in dog-days, in December sweat.

How, when competitors like these contend,
Can surly virtue hope to fix a friend?
Slaves that with serious impudence beguile,
And lie without a blush, without a smile;
Exalt each trifle, every vice adore,
Your taste in snuff, your judgment in a whore;
Can Balbo's eloquence applaud, and swear
He gropes his breeches with a monarch's air.

For arts like these preferred, admired, caressed,
They first invade your table, then your breast;
Explore your secrets with insidious art,
Watch the weak hour, and ransack all the heart;
Then soon your ill-placed confidence repay,
Commence your lords, and govern or betray.

By numbers here from shame or censure free,

273

All crimes are safe, but hated poverty.
This, only this, the rigid law pursues,
This, only this, provokes the snarling muse.
The sober trader at a tattered cloak,
Wakes from his dream, and labours for a joke;
With brisker air the silken courtiers gaze,
And turn the varied taunt a thousand ways.
Of all the griefs that harass the distressed,
Sure the most bitter is a scornful jest;
Fate never wounds more deep the generous heart,
Than when a blockhead's insult points the dart.

Has heaven reserved, in pity to the poor,
No pathless waste, or undiscovered shore;
No secret island in the boundless main?
No peaceful desert yet unclaimed by Spain?
Quick let us rise, the happy seats explore,
And bear oppression's insolence no more.
This mournful truth is everywhere confessed,
"Slow rises worth, by poverty depressed":
But here more slow, where all are slaves to gold,
Where looks are merchandise, and smiles are sold;
Where won by bribes, by flatteries implored,
The groom retails the favours of his lord.

But hark! The affrighted crowd's tumultuous cries
Roll through the streets, and thunder to the skies;
Raised from some pleasing dream of wealth and power,
Some pompous palace, or some blissful bower,
Aghast you start, and scarce with aching sight
Sustain the approaching fire's tremendous light;
Swift from pursuing horrors take your way,
And leave your little all to flames a prey;
Then through the world a wretched vagrant roam,
For where can starving merit find a home?
In vain your mournful narrative disclose,
While all neglect, and most insult your woes.

Should heaven's just bolts Orgilio's wealth confound,
And spread his flaming palace on the ground,
Swift o'er the land the dismal rumour flies,
And public mournings pacify the skies;
The laureate tribe in servile verse relate,
How virtue wars with persecuting fate;
With well-feigned gratitude the pensioned band

Refund the plunder of the beggared land.
See! While he builds, the gaudy vassals come,
And crowd with sudden wealth the rising dome;
The price of boroughs and of souls restore,
And raise his treasures higher than before.
Now blessed with all the baubles of the great,
The polished marble, and the shining plate,
Orgilio sees the golden pile aspire,
And hopes from angry heaven another fire.
    Couldst thou resign the park and play content,
For the fair banks of Severn or of Trent;
There mightst thou find some elegant retreat,
Some hireling senator's deserted seat;
And stretch thy prospects o'er the smiling land,
For less than rent the dungeons of the Strand;
There prune thy walks, support thy drooping flowers,
Direct thy rivulets, and twine thy bowers;
And, while thy grounds a cheap repast afford,
Despise the dainties of a venal lord:
There every bush with nature's music rings,
There every breeze bears health upon its wings;
On all thy hours security shall smile,
And bless thine evening walk and morning toil.
    Prepare for death, if here at night you roam,
And sign your will before you sup from home.
Some fiery fop, with new commission vain,
Who sleeps on brambles till he kills his man;
Some frolic drunkard, reeling from a feast,
Provokes a broil, and stabs you for a jest.
Yet even these heroes, mischievously gay,
Lords of the street, and terrors of the way;
Flushed as they are with folly, youth and wine,
Their prudent insults to the poor confine;
Afar they mark the flambeau's bright approach,
And shun the shining train, and golden coach.
    In vain, these dangers past, your doors you close,
And hope the balmy blessings of repose:
Cruel with guilt, and daring with despair,
The midnight murderer bursts the faithless bar;
Invades the sacred hour of silent rest,
And leaves, unseen, a dagger in your breast.
Scarce can our fields, such crowds at Tyburn die,

With hemp the gallows and the fleet supply.
Propose your schemes, ye senatorian band,
Whose ways and means support the sinking land;
Lest ropes be wanting in the tempting spring,
To rig another convoy for the king.

    A single jail, in Alfred's golden reign,
Could half the nation's criminals contain;
Fair Justice then, without constraint adored,
Held high the steady scale, but deeped the sword;
No spies were paid, no special juries known,
Blest age! But ah! How different from our own!

    Much could I add—but see the boat at hand,
The tide retiring, calls me from the land:
Farewell! When youth, and health, and fortune spent,
Thou fliest for refuge to the wilds of Kent;
And tired like me with follies and with crimes,
In angry numbers warnst succeeding times;
Then shall thy friend, nor thou refuse his aid,
Still foe to vice, forsake his Cambrian shade;
In virtue's cause once more exert his rage,
Thy satire point, and animate thy page.

THE VANITY OF HUMAN WISHES

    Let observation, with extensive view,
Survey mankind, from China to Peru;
Remark each anxious toil, each eager strife,
And watch the busy scenes of crowded life;
Then say how hope and fear, desire and hate,
O'erspread with snares the clouded maze of fate,
Where wavering man, betrayed by venturous pride
To tread the dreary paths without a guide,
As treacherous phantoms in the mist delude,
Shuns fancied ills, or chases airy good;
How rarely reason guides the stubborn choice,
Rules the bold hand, or prompts the suppliant voice,
How nations sink, by darling schemes oppressed,
When Vengeance listens to the fool's request.
Fate wings with every wish the afflictive dart,
Each gift of nature, and each grace of art;

With fatal heat impetuous courage glows,
With fatal sweetness elocution flows,
Impeachment stops the speaker's powerful breath,
And restless fire precipitates on death.

But scarce observed, the knowing and the bold
Fall in the general massacre of gold;
Wide-wasting pest! that rages unconfined,
And crowds with crimes the records of mankind;
For gold his sword the hireling ruffian draws,
For gold the hireling judge distorts the laws;
Wealth heaped on wealth, nor truth nor safety buys,
The dangers gather as the treasures rise.

Let history tell where rival kings command,
And dubious title shakes the madded land,
When statutes glean the refuse of the sword,
How much more safe the vassal than the lord,
Low skulks the hind beneath the rage of power,
And leaves the wealthy traitor in the Tower,
Untouched his cottage, and his slumbers sound,
Though confiscation's vultures hover round.

The needy traveller, serene and gay,
Walks the wild heath and sings his toil away.
Does envy seize thee? Crush the upbraiding joy,
Increase his riches and his peace destroy;
New fears in dire vicissitude invade,
The rustling brake alarms, and quivering shade,
Nor light nor darkness bring his pain relief;
One shows the plunder, and one hides the thief.

Yet still one general cry the skies assails,
And gain and grandeur load the tainted gales;
Few know the toiling statesman's fear or care,
The insidious rival and the gaping heir.

Once more, Democritus, arise on earth,
With cheerful wisdom and instructive mirth,
See motley life in modern trappings dressed,
And feed with varied fools the eternal jest:
Thou who couldst laugh where want enchained caprice,
Toil crushed conceit, and man was of a piece;
Where Wealth unloved without a mourner died;
And scarce a sycophant was fed by Pride;
Where ne'er was known the form of mock debate,
Or seen a new-made mayor's unwieldy state;

Where change of favourites made no change of laws,
And senates heard before they judged a cause;
How wouldst thou shake at Britain's modish tribe,
Dart the quick taunt, and edge the piercing gibe!
Attentive truth and nature to descry,
And pierce each scene with philosophic eye,
To thee were solemn toys or empty show
The robes of pleasures and the veils of woe:
All aid the farce, and all thy mirth maintain,
Whose joys are causeless, or whose griefs are vain.

Such was the scorn that filled the sage's mind,
Renewed at every glance on human kind.
How just that scorn ere yet thy voice declare,
Search every state, and canvass every prayer.

Unnumbered suppliants crowd Preferment's gate,
Athirst for wealth, and burning to be great;
Delusive Fortune hears the incessant call,
They mount, they shine, evaporate, and fall.
On every stage the foes of peace attend,
Hate dogs their flight, and Insult mocks their end.
Love ends with hope, the sinking statesman's door
Pours in the morning worshipper no more;
For growing names the weekly scribbler lies,
To growing wealth the dedicator flies;
From every room descends the painted face,
That hung the bright palladium of the place;
And smoked in kitchens, or in auctions sold,
To better features yields the frame of gold;
For now no more we trace in every line
Heroic worth, benevolence divine:
The form distorted justifies the fall,
And detestation rids the indignant wall.

But will not Britain hear the last appeal,
Sign her foes' doom, or guard her favourites' zeal?
Through Freedom's sons no more remonstrance rings,
Degrading nobles and controlling kings;
Our supple tribes repress their patriot throats,
And ask no questions but the price of votes,
With weekly libels and septennial ale.
Their wish is full to riot and to rail.

In full-blown dignity, see Wolsey stand,
Law in his voice, and fortune in his hand:

To him the church, the realm, their powers consign,
Through him the rays of regal bounty shine;
Turned by his nod the stream of honour flows,
His smile alone security bestows:
Still to new heights his restless wishes tower,
Claim leads to claim, and power advances power;
Till conquest unresisted ceased to please,
And rights submitted, left him none to seize.
At length his sovereign frowns—the train of state
Mark the keen glance, and watch the sign to hate.
Where'er he turns, he meets a stranger's eye,
His suppliants scorn him, and his followers fly;
At once is lost the pride of awful state,
The golden canopy, the glittering plate,
The regal palace, the luxurious board,
The liveried army, and the menial lord.
With age, with cares, with maladies oppressed,
He seeks the refuge of monastic rest.
Grief aids disease, remembered folly stings,
And his last sighs reproach the faith of kings.

Speak thou, whose thoughts at humble peace repine,
Shall Wolsey's wealth, with Wolsey's end be thine?
Or livest thou now, with safer pride content,
The wisest justice on the banks of Trent?
For why did Wolsey, near the steeps of fate,
On weak foundations raise the enormous weight?
Why but to sink beneath misfortune's blow,
With louder ruin to the gulfs below?

What gave great Villiers to the assassin's knife,
And fixed disease on Harley's closing life?
What murdered Wentworth, and what exiled Hyde,
By kings protected and to kings allied?
What but their wish indulged in courts to shine,
And power too great to keep or to resign?

When first the college rolls receive his name,
The young enthusiast quits his ease for fame;
Resistless burns the fever of renown
Caught from the strong contagion of the gown:
O'er Bodley's dome his future labours spread,
And Bacon's mansion trembles o'er his head.
Are these thy views? proceed, illustrious youth,
And Virtue guard thee to the throne of Truth!

Yet should thy soul indulge the generous heat,
Till captive science yields her last retreat;
Should reason guide thee with her brightest ray,
And pour on misty doubt resistless day;
Should no false kindness lure to loose delight,
Nor praise relax, nor difficulty fright;
Should tempting novelty thy cell refrain,
And sloth effuse her opiate fumes in vain;
Should beauty blunt on fops her fatal dart,
Nor claim the triumph of a lettered heart;
Should no disease thy torpid veins invade,
Nor melancholy's phantoms haunt thy shade;
Yet hope not life from grief or danger free,
Nor think the doom of man reversed for thee:
Deign on the passing world to turn thine eyes,
And pause a while from letters, to be wise;
There mark what ills the scholar's life assail,
Toil, envy, want, the patron and the jail.
See nations slowly wise, and meanly just,
To buried merit raise the tardy bust.
If dreams yet flatter, once again attend,
Hear Lydiat's life, and Galileo's end.
    Nor deem, when learning her last prize bestows,
The glittering eminence exempt from foes;
See when the vulgar 'scapes, despised or awed,
Rebellion's vengeful talons seize on Laud.
From meaner minds though smaller fines content,
The plundered palace, or sequestered rent;
Marked out by dangerous parts he meets the shock,
And fatal learning leads him to the block:
Around his tomb let art and genius weep,
But hear his death, ye blockheads, hear and sleep.
    The festal blazes, the triumphal show,
The ravished standard, and the captive foe,
The senate's thanks, the gazette's pompous tale,
With force resistless o'er the brave prevail.
Such bribes the rapid Greek o'er Asia whirled,
For such the steady Romans shook the world;
For such in distant lands the Britons shine,
And stain with blood the Danube or the Rhine;
This power has praise that virtue scarce can warm,
Till fame supplies the universal charm.

Yet reason frowns on war's unequal game,
Where wasted nations raise a single name,
And mortgaged states their grandsires' wreaths regret
From age to age in everlasting debt;
Wreaths which at last the dear-bought right convey
To rust on medals, or on stones decay.
On what foundation stands the warrior's pride,
How just his hopes, let Swedish Charles decide;
A frame of adamant, a soul of fire,
No dangers fright him, and no labours tire;
O'er love, o'er fear, extends his wide domain,
Unconquered lord of pleasure and of pain;
No joys to him pacific sceptres yield,
War sounds the trump, he rushes to the field;
Behold surrounding kings their powers combine,
And one capitulate, and one resign;
Peace courts his hand, but spreads her charms in vain;
"Think nothing gained," he cries, "till naught remain,
On Moscow's walls till Gothic standards fly,
And all be mine beneath the polar sky."
The march begins in military state,
And nations on his eye suspended wait;
Stern famine guards the solitary coast,
And winter barricades the realms of frost;
He comes, nor want nor cold his course delay—
Hide, blushing glory, hide Pultowa's day:
The vanquished hero leaves his broken bands,
And shows his miseries in distant lands;
Condemned a needy supplicant to wait,
While ladies interpose, and slaves debate.
But did not Chance at length her error mend?
Did no subverted empire mark his end?
Did rival monarchs give the fatal wound?
Or hostile millions press him to the ground?
His fall was destined to a barren strand,
A petty fortress, and a dubious hand;
He left the name at which the world grew pale,
To point a moral, or adorn a tale.
All times their scenes of pompous woes afford,
From Persia's tyrant to Bavaria's lord.
In gay hostility, and barbarous pride,
With half mankind embattled at his side,

Great Xerxes comes to seize the certain prey,
And starves exhausted regions in his way;
Attendant Flattery counts his myriads o'er,
Till counted myriads soothe his pride no more;
Fresh praise is tried till madness fires his mind,
The waves he lashes, and enchains the wind;
New powers are claimed, new powers are still bestowed,
Till rude resistance lops the spreading god;
The daring Greeks deride the martial show,
And heap their valleys with the gaudy foe;
The insulted sea with humbler thought he gains,
A single skiff to speed his flight remains;
The encumbered oar scarce leaves the dreaded coast,
Through purple billows and a floating host.

   The bold Bavarian, in a luckless hour,
Tries the dread summits of Caesarean power,
With unexpected legions bursts away,
And sees defenceless realms receive his sway;
Short sway! Fair Austria spreads her mournful charms,
The queen, the beauty, sets the world in arms;
From hill to hill the beacon's rousing blaze
Spreads wide the hope of plunder and of praise;
The fierce Croatian, and the wild Hussar,
With all the sons of ravage crowd the war;
The baffled prince, in honour's flattering bloom
Of hasty greatness finds the fatal doom;
His foes' derision, and his subjects' blame,
And steals to death from anguish and from shame.

   Enlarge my life with multitude of days!
In health, in sickness, thus the suppliant prays;
Hides from himself his state, and shuns to know,
That life protracted is protracted woe.
Time hovers o'er, impatient to destroy,
And shuts up all the passages of joy;
In vain their gifts the bounteous seasons pour,
The fruit autumnal, and the vernal flower;
With listless eyes the dotard views the store,
He views, and wonders that they please no more;
Now pall the tasteless meats, and joyless wines,
And Luxury with sighs her slave resigns.
Approach, ye minstrels, try the soothing strain,
Diffuse the tuneful lenitives of pain:

No sounds, alas, would touch the impervious ear,
Though dancing mountains witnessed Orpheus near;
Nor lute nor lyre his feeble powers attend,
Nor sweeter music of a virtuous friend,
But everlasting dictates crowd his tongue,
Perversely grave, or positively wrong.
The still returning tale, and lingering jest,
Perplex the fawning niece and pampered guest,
While growing hopes scarce awe the gathering sneer,
And scarce a legacy can bribe to hear;
The watchful guests still hint the last offense;
The daughter's petulance, the son's expense,
Improve his heady rage with treacherous skill,
And mould his passions till they make his will.
  Unnumbered maladies his joints invade,
Lay siege to life and press the dire blockade;
But unextinguished avarice still remains,
And dreaded losses aggravate his pains;
He turns, with anxious heart and crippled hands,
His bonds of debt, and mortgages of lands;
Or views his coffers with suspicious eyes,
Unlocks his gold, and counts it till he dies.
But grant, the virtues of a temperate prime
Bless with an age exempt from scorn or crime;
An age that melts with unperceived decay,
And glides in modest innocence away;
Whose peaceful day benevolence endears,
Whose night congratulating conscience cheers;
The general favourite as the general friend:
Such age there is, and who shall wish its end?
  Yet even on this her load misfortune flings,
To press the weary minutes' flagging wings;
New sorrow rises as the day returns,
A sister sickens, or a daughter mourns.
Now kindred merit fills the sable bier,
Now lacerated friendship claims a tear;
Year chases year, decay pursues decay,
Still drops some joy from withering life away;
New forms arise, and different views engage,
Superfluous lags the veteran on the stage,
Till pitying Nature signs the last release,
And bids afflicted worth retire to peace.

But few there are whom hours like these await,
Who set unclouded in the gulfs of fate.
From Lydia's monarch should the search descend,
By Solon cautioned to regard his end,
In life's last scene what prodigies surprise,
Fears of the brave, and follies of the wise!
From Marlborough's eyes the streams of dotage flow,
And Swift expires a driveller and a show.

The teeming mother, anxious for her race,
Begs for each birth the fortune of a face:
Yet Vane could tell what ills from beauty spring,
And Sedley cursed the form that pleased a king.
Ye nymphs of rosy lips and radiant eyes,
Whom pleasure keeps too busy to be wise,
Whom joys with soft varieties invite,
By day the frolic, and the dance by night;
Who frown with vanity, who smile with art,
And ask the latest fashion of the heart;
What care, what rules your heedless charms shall save,
Each nymph your rival, and each youth your slave?
Against your fame with fondness hate combines,
The rival batters, and the lover mines.
With distant voice neglected virtue calls,
Less heard and less, the faint remonstrance falls;
Tired with contempt, she quits the slippery reign,
And pride and prudence take her seat in vain.
In crowd at once, where none the pass defend,
The harmless freedom, and the private friend.
The guardians yield, by force superior plied:
To interest, prudence; and to flattery, pride.
Now beauty falls betrayed, despised, distressed,
And hissing infamy proclaims the rest.

Where then shall hope and fear their objects find?
Must dull suspense corrupt the stagnant mind?
Must helpless man, in ignorance sedate,
Roll darkling down the torrent of his fate?
Must no dislike alarm, no wishes rise,
No cries invoke the mercies of the skies?
Inquirer, cease; petitions yet remain,
Which heaven may hear, nor deem religion vain.
Still raise for good the supplicating voice,
But leave to heaven the measure and the choice.

Safe in His power, whose eyes discern afar
The secret ambush of a specious prayer.
Implore His aid, in His decisions rest,
Secure, whate'er He gives, He gives the best.
Yet when the sense of sacred presence fires,
And strong devotion to the skies aspires,
Pour forth thy fervours for a healthful mind,
Obedient passions, and a will resigned;
For love, which scarce collective man can fill;
For patience sovereign o'er transmuted ill;
For faith, that panting for a happier seat,
Counts death kind Nature's signal of retreat:
These goods for man the laws of heaven ordain,
These goods He grants, who grants the power to gain;
With these celestial Wisdom calms the mind,
And makes the happiness she does not find.

ON THE DEATH OF DR. ROBERT LEVET

Condemned to Hope's delusive mine,
    As on we toil from day to day,
By sudden blasts, or slow decline,
    Our social comforts drop away.

Well tried through many a varying year,
    See Levet to the grave descend;
Officious, innocent, sincere,
    Of every friendless name the friend.

Yet still he fills Affection's eye,
    Obscurely wise, and coarsely kind;
Nor, lettered Arrogance, deny
    Thy praise to merit unrefined.

When fainting Nature called for aid,
    And hovering Death prepared the blow.
His vigorous remedy displayed
    The power of art without the show.

In Misery's darkest cavern known,
   His useful care was ever nigh,
Where hopeless Anguish poured his groan,
   And lonely Want retired to die.

No summons mocked by chill delay,
   No petty gain disdained by pride,
The modest wants of every day
   The toil of every day supplied.

His virtues walked their narrow round,
   Nor made a pause, nor left a void;
And sure the eternal Master found
   The single talent well employed.

The busy day, the peaceful night,
   Unfelt, uncounted, glided by;
His frame was firm, his powers were bright,
   Though now his eightieth year was nigh.

Then with no throbbing fiery pain,
   No cold gradations of decay,
Death broke at once the vital chain,
   And freed his soul the nearest way.

A SHORT SONG OF CONGRATULATION

Long-expected one and twenty
   Lingering year at last is flown,
Pomp and pleasure, pride and plenty,
   Great Sir John, are all your own.

Loosened from the minor's tether,
   Free to mortgage or to sell,
Wild as wind, and light as feather,
   Bid the slaves of thrift farewell.

Call the Bettys, Kates, and Jennys,
   Every name that laughs at care,

Lavish of your grandsire's guineas,
  Show the spirit of an heir.

All that prey on vice and folly
  Joy to see their quarry fly,
Here the gamester light and jolly,
  There the lender grave and sly.

Wealth, Sir John, was made to wander,
  Let it wander as it will;
See the jockey, see the pander,
  Bid them come, and take their fill.

When the bonny blade carouses,
  Pockets full, and spirits high,
What are acres? What are houses?
  Only dirt, or wet or dry.

If the guardian or the mother
  Tell the woes of wilful waste,
Scorn their counsel and their pother,
  You can hang or drown at last.

THOMAS GRAY
(1716–71)

ELEGY WRITTEN IN A COUNTRY CHURCHYARD

The curfew tolls the knell of parting day,
    The lowing herd winds slowly o'er the lea,
The plowman homeward plods his weary way,
    And leaves the world to darkness and to me.

Now fades the glimmering landscape on the sight,
    And all the air a solemn stillness holds,
Save where the beetle wheels his droning flight,
    And drowsy tinklings lull the distant folds;

Save that from yonder ivy-mantled tower
    The moping owl does to the moon complain
Of such as, wandering near her secret bower,
    Molest her ancient solitary reign.

Beneath those rugged elms, that yew tree's shade,
    Where heaves the turf in many a mouldering heap,
Each in his narrow cell forever laid,
    The rude forefathers of the hamlet sleep.

The breezy call of incense-breathing morn,
    The swallow twittering from the straw-built shed,
The cock's shrill clarion, or the echoing horn,
    No more shall wake them from their lowly bed.

For them no more the blazing hearth shall burn,
    Or busy housewife ply her evening care;
No children run to lisp their sire's return,
    Or climb his knees the envied kiss to share.

Oft did the harvest to their sickle yield,
    Their furrow oft the stubborn glebe has broke.

288

How jocund did they drive their team afield!
    How bowed the woods beneath their sturdy stroke!

Let not ambition mock their useful toil,
    Their homely joys, and destiny obscure;
Nor grandeur hear with a disdainful smile
    The short and simple annals of the poor.

The boast of heraldry, the pomp of power,
    And all that beauty, all that wealth e'er gave,
Awaits alike the inevitable hour.
    The paths of glory lead but to the grave.

Forgive, ye proud, the involuntary fault,
    If memory to these no trophies raise,
Where through the long-drawn aisle and fretted vault
    The pealing anthem swells the note of praise.

Can storied urn or animated bust
    Back to its mansion call the fleeting breath?
Can honour's voice provoke the silent dust,
    Or flattery soothe the dull cold ear of death?

Perhaps in this neglected spot is laid
    Some heart once pregnant with celestial fire;
Hands that the reins of empire might have swayed,
    Or waked to ecstasy the living lyre.

But Knowledge to their eyes her ample page
    Rich with the spoils of time did ne'er unroll;
Chill penury repressed their noble rage,
    And froze the genial current of the soul.

Full many a gem of purest ray serene,
    The dark unfathomed caves of ocean bear:
Full many a flower is born to blush unseen,
    And waste its sweetness on the desert air.

Some village Hampden, that with dauntless breast
    The little tyrant of his fields withstood;
Some mute inglorious Milton here may rest,
    Some Cromwell guiltless of his country's blood.

The applause of listening senates to command,
  The threats of pain and ruin to despise,
To scatter plenty o'er a smiling land,
  And read their history in a nation's eyes,

Their lot forbade: nor circumscribed alone
  Their growing virtues, but their crimes confined;
Forbade to wade through slaughter to a throne,
  And shut the gates of mercy on mankind,

The struggling pangs of conscious truth to hide,
  To quench the blushes of ingenuous shame,
Or heap the shrine of luxury and pride
  With incense kindled at the Muse's flame.

Far from the madding crowd's ignoble strife,
  Their sober wishes never learned to stray;
Along the cool sequestered vale of life
  They kept the noiseless tenor of their way.

Yet even those bones from insult to protect,
  Some frail memorial still erected nigh,
With uncouth rhymes and shapeless sculpture decked,
  Implores the passing tribute of a sigh.

Their name, their years, spelt by the unlettered Muse,
  The place of fame and elegy supply:
And many a holy text around she strews,
  That teach the rustic moralist to die.

For who to dumb forgetfulness a prey,
  This pleasing anxious being e'er resigned,
Left the warm precincts of the cheerful day,
  Nor cast one longing lingering look behind?

On some fond breast the parting soul relies,
  Some pious drops the closing eye requires;
Even from the tomb the voice of Nature cries,
  Even in our ashes live their wonted fires.

For thee, who mindful of the unhonoured dead
  Dost in these lines their artless tale relate;

If chance, by lonely contemplation led,
  Some kindred spirit shall inquire thy fate,

Haply some hoary-headed swain may say,
  Oft have we seen him at the peep of dawn
Brushing with hasty steps the dews away.
  To meet the sun upon the upland lawn.

There at the foot of yonder nodding beech
  That wreathes its old fantastic roots so high,
His listless length at noontide would he stretch,
  And pore upon the brook that babbles by.

Hard by yon wood, now smiling as in scorn,
  Muttering his wayward fancies he would rove,
Now drooping, woeful wan, like one forlorn,
  Or crazed with care, or crossed in hopeless love.

One morn I missed him on the customed hill,
  Along the heath and near his favourite tree;
Another came; nor yet beside the rill,
  Nor up the lawn, not at the wood was he;

The next with dirges due in sad array
  Slow through the churchway path we saw him borne.
Approach and read (for thou canst read) the lay,
  Graved on the stone beneath yon aged thorn.

THE EPITAPH

Here rests his head upon the lap of Earth
  A youth to fortune and to fame unknown.
Fair Science frowned not on his humble birth,
  And Melancholy marked him for her own.

Large was his bounty, and his soul sincere,
  Heaven did a recompense as largely send:
He gave to misery all he had, a tear,
  He gained from heaven ('twas all he wished) a friend.

No farther seek his merits to disclose,
  Or draw his frailties from their dread abode

(There they alike in trembling hope repose),
The bosom of his Father and his God.

ODE ON THE DEATH OF A FAVOURITE CAT

'Twas on a lofty vase's side,
Where China's gayest art had dyed
    The azure flowers that blow;
Demurest of the tabby kind,
The pensive Selima reclined,
    Gazed on the lake below.

Her conscious tail her joy declared;
The fair round face, the snowy beard,
    The velvet of her paws,
Her coat, that with the tortoise vies,
Her ears of jet, and emerald eyes,
    She saw; and purred applause.

Still had she gazed; but, midst the tide,
Two angel forms were seen to glide,
    The genii of the stream:
Their scaly armour's Tyrian hue
Through richest purple to the view
    Betrayed a golden gleam.

The hapless nymph with wonder saw
A whisker first and then a claw;
    With many an ardent wish,
She stretched in vain to reach the prize.
What female heart can gold despise?
    What cat's averse to fish?

Presumptuous maid! With looks intent,
Again she stretched, again she bent,
    Nor knew the gulf between.
(Malignant Fate sat by and smiled)
The slippery verge her feet beguiled,
    She tumbled headlong in.

Eight times emerging from the flood,
She mewed to every watery god,
  Some speedy aid to send.
No dolphin came, no nereid stirred;
Nor cruel Tom, nor Susan heard.
  A favourite has no friend!

From hence, ye beauties, undeceived,
Know, one false step is ne'er retrieved,
  And be with caution bold.
Not all that tempts your wandering eyes
And heedless hearts is lawful prize;
  Nor all that glisters, gold.

WILLIAM COLLINS
(1721–59)

ODE ON THE POETICAL CHARACTER

As once, if not with light regard,
I read aright that gifted bard
(Him whose school above the rest
His loveliest elfin queen has blest),
One, only one, unrivalled fair,
Might hope the magic girdle wear,
At solemn tourney hung on high,
The wish of each love-darting eye;
Lo! To each other nymph in turn applied,
   As if, in air unseen, some hovering hand,
Some chaste and angel-friend to virgin-fame,
   With whispered spell had burst the starting band,
It left unblessed her loathed dishonoured side;
   Happier, hopeless fair, if never
   Her baffled hand with vain endeavour
Had touched that fatal zone to her denied
Young fancy thus, to me divinest name,
   To whom, prepared and bathed in heaven
   The cest of amplest power is given:
   To few the godlike gift assigns,
   To gird their blessed, prophetic loins,
And gaze her visions wild, and feel unmixed her flame!

The band, as fairy legends say,
Was wove on that creating day,
When He, who called with thought to birth
Yon tented sky, this laughing earth,
And dressed with springs, and forests tall,
And poured the main engirting all,
Long by the loved enthusiast wooed,
Himself in some diviner mood,
Retiring, sat with her alone,

And placed her on his sapphire throne;
The whiles, the vaulted shrine around,
Seraphic wires were heard to sound,
Now sublimest triumph swelling,
Now on love and mercy dwelling;
And she, from out the veiling cloud,
Breathed her magic notes aloud:
And thou, thou rich-haired youth of morn,
And all thy subject life was born!
The dangerous passions kept aloof,
Far from the sainted growing woof:
But near it sat ecstatic Wonder,
Listening the deep applauding thunder:
And truth, in sunny vest arrayed,
By whose the tarsel's eyes were made;
All the shadowy tribes of mind,
In braided dance their murmurs joined,
And all the bright uncounted powers
Who feed on heaven's ambrosial flowers.
Where is the bard, whose soul can now
Its high presuming hopes avow?
Where he who thinks, with rapture blind,
This hallowed work for him designed?

High on some cliff, to heaven up-piled,
Of rude access, of prospect wild,
Where, tangled round the jealous steep,
Strange shades o'erbrow the valleys deep,
And holy genii guard the rock,
It glooms embrown, its springs unlock,
While on its rich ambitious head,
An Eden, like his own, lies spread:
I view that oak, the fancied glades among,
By which, as Milton lay, his evening ear,
From many a cloud that dropped ethereal dew,
Nigh sphered in heaven its native strains could hear:
On which that ancient trump he reached was hung;
   Thither oft, his glory greeting,
   From Waller's myrtle shades retreating,
With many a vow from hope's aspiring tongue,
My trembling feet his guiding steps pursue;
   In vain—such bliss to one alone,

Of all the sons of soul was known,
And heaven, and fancy, kindred powers,
Have now o'erturned the inspiring bowers,
Or curtained close such scene from every future view.

ODE TO SIMPLICITY

O thou by Nature taught
To breathe her genuine thought,
In numbers warmly pure and sweetly strong:
Who first on mountains wild
In Fancy, loveliest child,
Thy babe and Pleasure's, nursed the powers of song!

Thou, who with hermit heart
Disdainst the wealth of art,
And gauds and pageant weeds and trailing pall:
But comst a decent maid
In Attic robe arrayed,
O chaste unboastful nymph, to thee I call!

By all the honeyed store
On Hybla's thymy shore,
By all her blooms and mingled murmurs dear;
By her, whose love-lorn woe
In evening musings slow
Soothed sweetly sad Electra's poet's ear;

By old Cephisus deep,
Who spread his wavy sweep
In warbled wanderings round thy green retreat,
On whose enamelled side
When holy Freedom died
No equal haunt allured thy future feet.

O sister meek of truth,
To my admiring youth
Thy sober aid and native charms infuse!
The flowers that sweetest breathe,

Though beauty culled the wreath,
Still ask thy hand to range their ordered hues.

While Rome could none esteem
But virtue's patriot theme,
You loved her hills and led her laureate band;
But stayed to sing alone
To one distinguished throne,
And turned thy face, and fled her altered land.

No more, in hall or bower,
The passions own thy power,
Love, only love, her forceless numbers mean;
For thou hast left her shrine,
Nor olive more nor vine
Shall gain thy feet to bless the servile scene.

Though taste, though genius bless
To some divine excess,
Faint's the cold work till thou inspire the whole;
What each, what all supply
May court, may charm our eye,
Thou, only thou canst raise the meeting soul!

Of these let others ask
To aid some mighty task:
I only seek to find thy temperate vale,
Where oft my reed might sound
To maids and shepherds round,
And all thy sons, O Nature, learn my tale.

OLIVER GOLDSMITH
(ca. 1730–74)

THE DESERTED VILLAGE

Sweet Auburn! Loveliest village of the plain,
Where health and plenty cheered the labouring swain,
Where smiling spring its earliest visit paid,
And parting summer's lingering blooms delayed;
Dear, lovely bowers of innocence and ease,
Seats of my youth, when every sport could please,
How often have I loitered o'er thy green,
Where humble happiness endeared each scene;
How often have I paused on every charm,
The sheltered cot, the cultivated farm,
The never-failing brook, the busy mill,
The decent church that topped the neighbouring hill,
The hawthorn bush, with seats beneath the shade,
For talking age and whispering lovers made;
How often have I blessed the coming day,
When toil remitting lent its turn to play,
And all the village train, from labour free,
Led up their sports beneath the spreading tree,
While many a pastime circled in the shade,
The young contending as the old surveyed;
And many a gambol frolicked o'er the ground,
And sleights of art and feats of strength went round;
And still as each repeated pleasure tired,
Succeeding sports the mirthful band inspired;
The dancing pair that simply sought renown,
By holding out to tire each other down;
The swain mistrustless of his smutted face,
While secret laughter tittered round the place;
The bashful virgin's sidelong looks of love,
The matron's glance that would those looks reprove:
These were thy charms, sweet village! Sports like these,
With sweet succession, taught even toil to please;

These round thy bowers their cheerful influence shed,
These were thy charms, but all these charms are fled.
    Sweet, smiling village, loveliest of the lawn,
Thy sports are fled, and all thy charms withdrawn;
Amidst thy bowers the tyrant's hand is seen,
And desolation saddens all thy green:
One only master grasps the whole domain,
And half a tillage stints thy smiling plain;
No more thy glassy brook reflects the day,
But choked with sedges, works its weedy way;
Along thy glades, a solitary guest,
The hollow-sounding bittern guards its nest;
Amidst thy desert walks the lapwing flies,
And tires their echoes with unvaried cries.
Sunk are thy bowers, in shapeless ruin all,
And the long grass o'ertops the mouldering wall,
And, trembling, shrinking from the spoiler's hand,
Far, far away thy children leave the land.
    Ill fares the land, to hastening ills a prey,
Where wealth accumulates and men decay;
Princes and lords may flourish, or may fade;
A breath can make them, as a breath has made;
But a bold peasantry, their country's pride,
When once destroyed, can never be supplied.
    A time there was, ere England's griefs began,
When every rood of ground maintained its man;
For him, light labour spread her wholesome store,
Just gave what life required, but gave no more:
His best companions, innocence and health;
And his best riches, ignorance of wealth.
    But times are altered; trade's unfeeling train
Usurp the land and dispossess the swain;
Along the lawn, where scattered hamlets rose,
Unwieldy wealth, and cumbrous pomp repose;
And every want to luxury allied,
And every pang that folly pays to pride.
These gentle hours that plenty bade to bloom,
Those calm desires that asked but little room,
Those healthful sports that graced the peaceful scene,
Lived in each look, and brightened all the green;
These, far departing, seek a kinder shore,
And rural mirth and manners are no more.

Sweet Auburn! Parent of the blissful hour,
Thy glades forlorn confess the tyrant's power.
Here, as I take my solitary rounds,
Amidst thy tangling walks, and ruined grounds,
And, many a year elapsed, return to view
Where once the cottage stood, the hawthorn grew,
Remembrance wakes with all her busy train,
Swells at my breast, and turns the past to pain.

In all my wanderings round this world of care,
In all my griefs—and God has given my share—
I still had hopes my latest hours to crown,
Amidst these humble bowers to lay me down;
To husband out life's taper at the close,
And keep the flame from wasting by repose.
I still had hopes, for pride attends us still,
Amidst the swains to show my book-learned skill,
Around my fire an evening group to draw,
And tell of all I felt, and all I saw;
And as a hare whom hounds and horns pursue,
Pants to the place from whence at first she flew,
I still had hopes, my long vexations past,
Here to return—and die at home at last.

O blessed retirement, friend to life's decline,
Retreats from care that never must be mine,
How blessed is he who crowns in shades like these,
A youth of labour with an age of ease;
Who quits a world where strong temptations try,
And, since 'tis hard to combat, learns to fly!
For him, no wretches, born to work and weep,
Explore the mine, or tempt the dangerous deep;
No surly porter stands in guilty state
To spurn imploring famine from his gate;
But on he moves to meet his latter end,
Angels around befriending virtue's friend;
Sinks to the grave with unperceived decay,
While resignation gently slopes the way;
And, all his prospects brightening to the last,
His heaven commences ere the world be passed!

Sweet was the sound when oft at evening's close,
Up yonder hill the village murmur rose;
There, as I passed with careless steps and slow,
The mingling notes came softened from below;

The swain responsive as the milkmaid sung,
The sober herd that lowed to meet their young,
The noisy geese that gabbled o'er the pool,
The playful children just let loose from school;
The watchdog's voice that bayed the whispering wind,
And the loud laugh that spoke the vacant mind;
These all in soft confusion sought the shade,
And filled each pause the nightingale had made.
But now the sounds of population fail,
No cheerful murmurs fluctuate in the gale,
No busy steps the grass-grown footway tread,
For all the bloomy flush of life is fled.
All but yon widowed, solitary thing
That feebly bends beside the plashy spring;
She, wretched matron, forced, in age, for bread,
To strip the brook with mantling cresses spread,
To pick her wintry faggot from the thorn,
To seek her nightly shed, and weep till morn;
She only left of all the harmless train,
The sad historian of the pensive plain.

    Near yonder copse, where once the garden smiled,
And still where many a garden flower grows wild,
There, where a few torn shrubs the place disclose,
The village preacher's modest mansion rose.
A man he was, to all the country dear,
And passing rich with forty pounds a year;
Remote from towns he ran his godly race,
Nor e'er had changed, nor wished to change his place;
Unpractised he to fawn, or seek for power,
By doctrines fashioned to the varying hour;
Far other aims his heart had learned to prize,
More skilled to raise the wretched than to rise.
His house was known to all the vagrant train,
He chid their wanderings but relieved their pain;
The long-remembered beggar was his guest,
Whose beard, descending, swept his aged breast;
The ruined spendthrift, now no longer proud,
Claimed kindred there, and had his claims allowed;
The broken soldier, kindly bade to stay,
Sat by his fire, and talked the night away;
Wept o'er his wounds, or tales of sorrow done,
Shouldered his crutch, and showed how fields were won.

Pleased with his guests, the good man learned to glow,
And quite forgot their vices in their woe;
Careless their merits, or their faults to scan,
His pity gave ere charity began.

Thus to relieve the wretched was his pride,
And even his failings leaned to virtue's side;
But in his duty, prompt at every call,
He watched and wept, he prayed and felt, for all.
And, as a bird each fond endearment tries,
To tempt its new-fledged offspring to the skies,
He tried each art, reproved each dull delay,
Allured to brighter worlds, and led the way.

Beside the bed where parting life was laid,
And sorrow, guilt, and pain, by turns dismayed,
The reverend champion stood. At his control,
Despair and anguish fled the struggling soul;
Comfort came down, the trembling wretch to raise,
And his last faltering accents whispered praise.

At church, with meek and unaffected grace,
His looks adorned the venerable place;
Truth from his lips prevailed with double sway,
And fools, who came to scoff, remained to pray.
The service past, around the pious man,
With steady zeal each honest rustic ran;
Even children followed with endearing wile,
And plucked his gown, to share the good man's smile.
His ready smile a parent's warmth expressed;
Their welfare pleased him, and their cares distressed;
To them his heart, his love, his griefs were given,
But all his serious thoughts had rest in heaven.
As some tall cliff that lifts its awful form,
Swells from the vale, and midway leaves the storm,
Though round its breast the rolling clouds are spread,
Eternal sunshine settles on its head.

Beside yon straggling fence that skirts the way,
With blossomed furze unprofitably gay,
There, in his noisy mansion, skilled to rule,
The village master taught his little school;
A man severe he was and stern to view;
I knew him well, and every truant knew;
Well had the boding tremblers learned to trace
The day's disasters in his morning face;

Full well they laughed with counterfeited glee,
At all his jokes, for many a joke had he;
Full well the busy whisper circling round,
Conveyed the dismal tidings when he frowned;
Yet he was kind, or if severe in aught,
The love he bore to learning was in fault;
The village all declared how much he knew;
'Twas certain he could write, and cipher, too;
Lands he could measure, terms and tides presage,
And even the story ran that he could gauge.
In arguing, too, the parson owned his skill,
For, even though vanquished, he could argue still;
While words of learned length, and thundering sound,
Amazed the gazing rustics ranged around;
And still they gazed, and still the wonder grew,
That one small head could carry all he knew.

But past is all his fame. The very spot,
Where many a time he triumphed, is forgot.
Near yonder thorn that lifts its head on high,
Where once the signpost caught the passing eye,
Low lies that house where nut-brown draughts inspired,
Where graybeard Mirth and smiling Toil retired,
Where village statesmen talked with looks profound,
And news much older than their ale went round.
Imagination fondly stoops to trace
The parlour splendours of that festive place:
The whitewashed wall, the nicely sanded floor,
The varnished clock that clicked behind the door;
The chest contrived a double debt to pay,
A bed by night, a chest of drawers by day;
The pictures placed for ornament and use,
The twelve good rules, the royal game of goose;
The hearth, except when winter chilled the day,
With aspen boughs, and flowers, and fennel gay,
While broken teacups, wisely kept for show,
Ranged o'er the chimney, glistened in a row.

Vain transitory splendours! Could not all
Reprieve the tottering mansion from its fall!
Obscure it sinks, nor shall it more impart
An hour's importance to the poor man's heart;
Thither no more the peasant shall repair
To sweet oblivion of his daily care;

No more the farmer's news, the barber's tale,
No more the woodman's ballad shall prevail;
No more the smith his dusky brow shall clear,
Relax his ponderous strength, and lean to hear;
The host himself no longer shall be found
Careful to see the mantling bliss go round;
Nor the coy maid, half willing to be pressed,
Shall kiss the cup to pass it to the rest.

Yes! Let the rich deride, the proud disdain,
These simple blessings of the lowly train,
To me more dear, congenial to my heart,
One native charm, than all the gloss of art;
Spontaneous joys, where nature has its play,
The soul adopts, and owns their first-born sway;
Lightly they frolic o'er the vacant mind,
Unenvied, unmolested, unconfined.
But the long pomp, the midnight masquerade,
With all the freaks of wanton wealth arrayed:
In these, ere triflers half their wish obtain,
The toiling pleasure sickens into pain;
And, even while fashion's brightest arts decoy,
The heart distrusting asks if this be joy.

Ye friends to truth, ye statesmen, who survey
The rich man's joys increase, the poor's decay,
'Tis yours to judge how wide the limits stand
Between a splendid and a happy land.
Proud swells the tide with loads of freighted ore,
And shouting Folly hails them from her shore;
Hoards, even beyond the miser's wish, abound,
And rich men flock from all the world around.
Yet count our gains. This wealth is but a name,
That leaves our useful products still the same.
Not so the loss. The man of wealth and pride
Takes up a space that many poor supplied;
Space for his lake, his park's extended bounds,
Space for his horses, equipage, and hounds;
The robe that wraps his limbs in silken sloth
Has robbed the neighbouring fields of half their growth;
His seat, where solitary sports are seen,
Indignant spurns the cottage from the green;
Around the world each needful product flies,
For all the luxuries the world supplies.

While thus the land adorned for pleasure, all
In barren splendour feebly waits the fall.
　　As some fair female, unadorned and plain,
Secure to please while youth confirms her reign,
Slights every borrowed charm that dress supplies,
Nor shares with art the triumph of her eyes:
But when those charms are past, for charms are frail,
When time advances, and when lovers fail,
She then shines forth, solicitous to bless,
In all the glaring impotence of dress.
Thus fares the land, by luxury betrayed;
In nature's simplest charms at first arrayed;
But, verging to decline, its splendours rise,
Its vistas strike, its palaces surprise;
While scourged by famine from the smiling land,
The mournful peasant leads his humble band;
And while he sinks without one arm to save,
The country blooms—a garden, and a grave.
　　Where then, ah where, shall poverty reside,
To 'scape the pressure of contiguous pride?
If, to some common's fenceless limits strayed,
He drives his flock to pick the scanty blade,
Those fenceless fields the sons of wealth divide,
And even the bare-worn common is denied.
　　If to the city sped, what waits him there?
To see profusion that he must not share;
To see ten thousand baneful arts combined
To pamper luxury, and thin mankind;
To see those joys the sons of pleasure know,
Extorted from his fellow creature's woe.
Here, while the courtier glitters in brocade,
There the pale artist plies the sickly trade;
Here, while the proud their long-drawn pomps display,
There the black gibbet glooms beside the way.
The dome where Pleasure holds her midnight reign,
Here, richly decked, admits the gorgeous train;
Tumultuous grandeur crowds the blazing square,
The rattling chariots clash, the torches glare.
Sure scenes like these no troubles e'er annoy!
Sure these denote one universal joy!
Are these thy serious thoughts? Ah, turn thine eyes
Where the poor, houseless, shivering female lies.

305

She once, perhaps, in village plenty blessed,
Has wept at tales of innocence distressed;
Her modest looks the cottage might adorn,
Sweet as the primrose peeps beneath the thorn;
Now lost to all; her friends, her virtue fled,
Near her betrayer's door she lays her head,
And, pinched with cold, and shrinking from the shower,
With heavy heart deplores that luckless hour,
When idly first, ambitious of the town,
She left her wheel and robes of country brown.

Do thine, sweet Auburn, thine, the loveliest train,
Do thy fair tribes participate her pain?
Even now, perhaps, by cold and hunger led,
At proud men's doors they ask a little bread!

Ah, no! To distant climes, a dreary scene,
Where half the convex world intrudes between,
Through torrid tracts with fainting steps they go,
Where wild Altama murmurs to their woe.
Far different there from all that charmed before,
The various terrors of that horrid shore;
Those blazing suns that dart a downward ray,
And fiercely shed intolerable day;
Those matted woods where birds forget to sing,
But silent bats in drowsy clusters cling;
Those poisonous fields with rank luxuriance crowned,
Where the dark scorpion gathers death around;
Where at each step the stranger fears to wake
The rattling terrors of the vengeful snake;
Where crouching tigers wait their hapless prey,
And savage men, more murderous still than they;
While oft in whirls the mad tornado flies,
Mingling the ravaged landscape with the skies.
Far different these from every former scene,
The cooling brook, the grassy vested green,
The breezy covert of the warbling grove,
That only sheltered thefts of harmless love.

Good heaven! What sorrows gloomed that parting day,
That called them from their native walks away;
When the poor exiles, every pleasure past,
Hung round their bowers, and fondly looked their last,
And took a long farewell, and wished in vain
For seats like these beyond the western main;

And shuddering still to face the distant deep,
Returned and wept, and still returned to weep.
The good old sire, the first prepared to go
To new-found worlds, and wept for other's woe.
But for himself, in conscious virtue brave,
He only wished for worlds beyond the grave.
His lovely daughter, lovelier in her tears,
The fond companion of his helpless years,
Silent went next, neglectful of her charms,
And left a lover's for a father's arms.
With louder plaints, the mother spoke her woes,
And blessed the cot where every pleasure rose;
And kissed her thoughtless babes with many a tear,
And clasped them close in sorrow doubly dear;
Whilst her fond husband strove to lend relief
In all the decent manliness of grief.

O luxury! Thou cursed by heaven's decree,
How ill exchanged are things like these for thee!
How do thy potions, with insidious joy,
Diffuse their pleasures only to destroy!
Kingdoms, by thee, to sickly greatness grown,
Boast of a florid vigour not their own.
At every draught more large and large they grow,
A bloated mass of rank, unwieldy woe;
Till sapped their strength, and every part unsound,
Down, down they sink, and spread a ruin round.

Even now the devastation is begun,
And half the business of destruction done;
Even now, methinks, as pondering here I stand,
I see the rural virtues leave the land.
Down where yon anchoring vessel spreads the sail,
That, idly waiting, flaps with every gale,
Downward they move, a melancholy band,
Pass from the shore, and darken all the strand.
Contented Toil, and hospitable Care,
And kind connubial Tenderness are there;
And Piety, with wishes placed above,
And steady Loyalty, and faithful Love:
And thou, sweet Poetry, thou loveliest maid,
Still first to fly where sensual joys invade;
Unfit, in these degenerate times of shame,
To catch the heart, or strike for honest fame;

Dear charming nymph, neglected and decried,
My shame in crowds, my solitary pride;
Thou source of all my bliss, and all my woe,
That foundest me poor at first, and keepest me so;
Thou guide by which the nobler arts excel,
Thou nurse of every virtue, fare thee well.
Farewell, and Oh! Where'er thy voice be tried,
On Torno's cliffs, or Pambamarca's side,
Whether where equinoctial fervours glow,
Or winter wraps the polar world in snow,
Still let thy voice, prevailing over time,
Redress the rigours of the inclement clime;
Aid slighted truth; with thy persuasive strain
Teach erring man to spurn the rage of gain:
Teach him that states of native strength possessed,
Though very poor, may still be very blessed;
That trade's proud empire hastes to swift decay,
As ocean sweeps the laboured mole away;
While self-dependent power can time defy,
As rocks resist the billows and the sky.

ELEGY ON THE DEATH OF A MAD DOG

Good people all, of every sort,
   Give ear unto my song;
And if you find it wondrous short,
   It cannot hold you long.

In Islington there was a man,
   Of whom the world might say,
That still a godly race he ran,
   Whene'er he went to pray.

A kind and gentle heart he had,
   To comfort friends and foes;
The naked every day he clad,
   When he put on his clothes.

And in that town a dog was found,
  As many dogs there be,
Both mongrel, puppy, whelp, and hound,
  And curs of low degree.

This dog and man at first were friends;
  But when a pique began,
The dog, to gain some private ends,
  Went mad and bit the man.

Around from all the neighbouring streets
  The wondering neighbours ran,
And swore the dog had lost his wits,
  To bite so good a man.

The wound it seemed both sore and sad
  To every Christian eye;
And while they swore the dog was mad,
  They swore the man would die.

But soon a wonder came to light,
  That showed the rogues they lied:
The man recovered of the bite,
  The dog it was that died.

WILLIAM COWPER
(1731–1800)

WALKING WITH GOD

Oh! For a closer walk with God,
    A calm and heavenly frame;
A light to shine upon the road
    That leads me to the lamb!

Where is the blessedness I knew
    When first I saw the Lord?
Where is the soul-refreshing view
    Of Jesus, and his word?

What peaceful hours I once enjoyed!
    How sweet their memory still!
But they have left an aching void
    The world can never fill.

Return, O holy dove, return,
    Sweet messenger of rest;
I hate the sins that made thee mourn
    And drove thee from my breast.

The dearest idol I have known,
    Whate'er that idol be;
Help me to tear it from thy throne,
    And worship only thee.

So shall my walk be close with God,
    Calm and serene my frame;
So purer light shall mark the road
    That leads me to the lamb.

from *THE TASK*

EASE

Like a coy maiden, ease, when courted most,
Farthest retires—an idol, at whose shrine
Who oftenest sacrifice are favoured least.
The love of Nature, and the scenes she draws,
Is Nature's dictate. Strange! there should be found
Who self-imprisoned in their proud saloons,
Renounce the odours of the open field
For the unscented fictions of the loom.
Who satisfied with only pencilled scenes,
Prefer to the performance of a god
The inferior wonders of an artist's hand.
Lovely indeed the mimic works of art,
But Nature's works far lovelier. I admire—
None more admires the painter's magic skill,
Who shows me that which I shall never see,
Conveys a distant country into mine,
And throws Italian light on English walls.
But imitative strokes can do no more
Than please the eye, sweet Nature every sense.
The air salubrious of her lofty hills,
The cheering fragrance of her dewy vales
And music of her woods—no works of man
May rival these; these all bespeak a power
Peculiar, and exclusively her own.
Beneath the open sky she spreads the feast;
'Tis free to all—'tis every day renewed,
Who scorns it, starves deservedly at home.
He does not scorn it, who imprisoned long
In some unwholesome dungeon, and a prey
To sallow sickness, which the vapours dank
And clammy of his dark abode have bred,
Escapes at last to liberty and light.
His cheek recovers soon its healthful hue,
His eye relumines its extinguished fires,
He walks, he leaps, he runs—is winged with joy,
And riots in the sweets of every breeze.
He does not scorn it, who has long endured

A fever's agonies, and fed on drugs.
Nor yet the mariner, his blood inflamed
With acrid salts; his very heart athirst
To gaze at Nature in her green array.
Upon the ship's tall side he stands, possessed
With visions prompted by intense desire;
Fair fields appear below, such as he left,
Far distant, such as he would die to find—
He seeks them headlong, and is seen no more.
　　The spleen is seldom felt where Flora reigns;
The lowering eye, the petulance, the frown,
And sullen sadness that o'ershade, distort,
And mar the face of beauty, when no cause
For such immeasurable woe appears;
These Flora banishes, and gives the fair
Sweet smiles and bloom less transient than her own.
It is the constant revolution, stale
And tasteless, of the same repeated joys,
That palls and satiates, and makes languid life
A pedlar's pack, that bows the bearer down.
Health suffers, and the spirits ebb; the heart
Recoils from its own choice—at the full feast
Is famished—finds no music in the song,
No smartness in the jest, and wonders why.
Yet thousands still desire to journey on,
Though halt and weary of the path they tread.
The paralytic who can hold her cards
But cannot play them, borrows a friend's hand
To deal and shuffle, to divide and sort
Her mingled suits and sequences, and sits,
Spectatress both and spectacle, a sad
And silent cipher, while her proxy plays.
Others are dragged into the crowded room
Between supporters; and once seated, sit
Through downright inability to rise,
Till the stout bearers lift the corpse again.
These speak a loud memento. Yet even these
Themselves love life, and cling to it, as he
That overhangs a torrent, to a twig.
They love it, and yet loath it; fear to die,
Yet scorn the purposes for which they live.
Then wherefore not renounce them? No—the dread,

The slavish dread of solitude, that breeds
Reflection and remorse, the fear of shame,
And their inveterate habits, all forbid.

A WINTER WALK AT NOON

The night was winter in his roughest mood,
The morning sharp and clear. But now at noon
Upon the southern side of the slant hills,
And where the woods fence off the northern blast,
The season smiles resigning all its rage
And has the warmth of May. The vault is blue
Without a cloud, and white without a speck
The dazzling splendour of the scene below.
Again the harmony comes o'er the vale,
And through the trees I view the embattled tower
Whence all the music. I again perceive
The soothing influence of the wafted strains,
And settle in soft musings as I tread
The walk still verdant under oaks and elms
Whose outspread branches overarch the glade.
The roof though moveable through all its length
As the wind sways it, has yet well sufficed,
And intercepting in their silent fall
The frequent flakes, has kept a path for me.
No noise is here, or none that hinders thought.
The red-breast warbles still, but is content
With slender notes and more than half suppressed.
Pleased with his solitude, and flitting light
From spray to spray, where'er he rests he shakes
From many a twig the pendent drops of ice,
That twinkle in the withered leaves below.
Stillness accompanied with sounds so soft
Charms more than silence. Meditation here
May think down hours to moments. Here the heart
May give a useful lesson to the head,
And learning wiser grow without his books.
Knowledge and wisdom, far from being one,
Have oft times no connexion. Knowledge dwells
In heads replete with thoughts of other men,
Wisdom in minds attentive to their own.
Knowledge, a rude unprofitable mass,

The mere materials with which wisdom builds,
Till smoothed and squared and fitted to its place
Does but incumber whom it seems to enrich.
Knowledge is proud that he has learned so much,
Wisdom is humble that he knows no more.
Books are not seldom talismans and spells
By which the magic art of shrewder wits
Holds an unthinkable multitude enthralled.
Some to the fascination of a name
Surrender judgment hoodwinked. Some the style
Infatuates, and through labyrinths and wilds
Of error, leads them by a tune entranced.
While sloth seduces more, too weak to bear
The insupportable fatigue of thought,
And swallowing therefore without pause or choice
The total grist unsifted, husks and all.
But trees, and rivulets whose rapid course
Defies the check of winter, haunts of deer,
And sheep-walks populous with bleating lambs,
And lanes in which the primrose ere her time
Peeps through the moss that clothes the hawthorn root,
Deceive no student. Wisdom there, and truth,
Not shy as in the world, and to be won
By slow solicitation, seize at once
The roving thought, and fix it on themselves.

GEORGE CRABBE
(1754–1832)

PETER GRIMES

Old Peter Grimes made fishing his employ,
His wife he cabined with him and his boy,
And seemed that life laborious to enjoy:
To town came quiet Peter with his fish,
And had of all a civil word and wish.
He left his trade upon the sabbath-day,
And took young Peter in his hand to pray:
But soon the stubborn boy from care broke loose,
At first refused, then added his abuse;
His father's love he scorned, his power defied,
But being drunk, wept sorely when he died.
　　Yes! Then he wept, and to his mind there came
Much of his conduct, and he felt the shame—
How he had oft the good old man reviled,
And never paid the duty of a child;
How, when the father in his Bible read,
He in contempt and anger left the shed:
"It is the word of life," the parent cried;
"This is the life itself," the boy replied;
And while old Peter in amazement stood,
Gave the hot spirit to his boiling blood;
How he, with oath and furious speech, began
To prove his freedom and assert the man;
And when the parent checked his impious rage,
How he had cursed the tyranny of age—
Nay, once had dealt the sacrilegious blow
On his bare head, and laid his parent low;
The father groaned. "If thou art old," said he,
"And hast a son, thou wilt remember me.
Thy mother left me in a happy time,
Thou killedst not her. Heaven spares the double crime."
　　On an inn-settle, in his maudlin grief,

This he revolved, and drank for his relief.

Now lived the youth in freedom, but debarred
From constant pleasure, and he thought it hard;
Hard that he could not every wish obey,
But must awhile relinquish ale and play;
Hard that he could not to his cards attend,
But must acquire the money he would spend.

With greedy eye he looked on all he saw,
He knew not justice, and he laughed at law;
On all he marked he stretched his ready hand;
He fished by water, and he filched by land.
Oft in the night has Peter dropped his oar,
Fled from his boat and sought for prey on shore;
Oft up the hedgerow glided, on his back
Bearing the orchard's produce in a sack,
Or farm-yard load, tugged fiercely from the stack;
And as these wrongs to greater numbers rose,
The more he looked on all men as his foes.

He built a mud-walled hovel, where he kept
His various wealth, and there he ofttimes slept;
But no success could please his cruel soul,
He wished for one to trouble and control;
He wanted some obedient boy to stand
And bear the blow of his outrageous hand,
And hoped to find in some propitious hour
A feeling creature subject to his power.

Peter had heard there were in London then—
Still have they being!—workhouse-clearing men,
Who, undisturbed by feelings just or kind,
Would parish-boys to needy tradesmen bind;
They in their want a trifling sum would take,
And toiling slaves of piteous orphans make.

Such Peter sought, and when a lad was found,
The sum was dealt him, and the slave was bound.
Some few in town observed in Peter's trap
A boy, with jacket blue and woolen cap;
But none inquired how Peter used the rope,
Or what the bruise, that made the stripling stoop;
None could the ridges on his back behold,
None sought him shivering in the winter's cold;
None put the question—"Peter, dost thou give
The boy his food?—What, man! the lad must live!

Consider, Peter, let the child have bread;
He'll serve thee better if he's stroked and fed."
None reasoned thus—and some, on hearing cries,
Said calmly, "Grimes is at his exercise."
  Pinned, beaten, cold, pinched, threatened, and abused—
His efforts punished and his food refused—
Awake tormented—soon aroused from sleep—
Struck if he wept, and yet compelled to weep,
The trembling boy dropped down and strove to pray,
Received a blow, and trembling turned away,
Or sobbed and hid his piteous face; while he,
The savage master, grinned in horrid glee;
He'd now the power he ever loved to show,
A feeling being subject to his blow.
  Thus lived the lad, in hunger, peril, pain,
His tears despised, his supplications vain;
Compelled by fear to lie, by need to steal,
His bed uneasy and unblessed his meal,
For three sad years the boy his tortures bore,
And then his pains and trials were no more.
  "How died he, Peter?" when the people said,
He growled—"I found him lifeless in his bed,"
Then tried for softer tone, and sighed, "Poor Sam is dead."
Yet murmurs were there, and some questions asked.
How he was fed, how punished, and how tasked?
Much they suspected, but they little proved,
And Peter passed untroubled and unmoved.
  Another boy with equal ease was found,
The money granted, and the victim bound.
And what his fate? One night it chanced he fell
From the boat's mast and perished in her well,
Where fish were living kept, and where the boy
(So reasoned men) could not himself destroy.
  "Yes, so it was," said Peter, "in his play
(For he was idle both by night and day),
He climbed the mainmast and then fell below"—
Then showed his corpse and pointed to the blow.
What said the jury? They were long in doubt,
But sturdy Peter faced the matter out;
So they dismissed him, saying at the time,
"Keep fast your hatchway when you've boys who climb."
This hit the conscience, and he coloured more

317

Than for the closest questions put before.

Thus all his fears the verdict set aside,
And at the slave-shop Peter still applied.

Then came a boy of manners soft and mild.
Our seamen's wives with grief beheld the child;
All thought (the poor themselves) that he was one
Of gentle blood, some noble sinner's son,
Who had, belike, deceived some humble maid,
Whom he had first seduced and then betrayed.
However this, he seemed a gracious lad,
In grief submissive and with patience sad.

Passive he laboured, till his slender frame
Bent with his loads, and he at length was lame;
Strange that a frame so weak could bear so long
The grossest insult and the foulest wrong!
But there were causes: in the town they gave
Fire, food, and comfort to the gentle slave,
And though stern Peter, with a cruel hand
And knotted rope, enforced the rude command,
Yet he considered what he'd lately felt,
And his vile blows with selfish pity dealt.

One day such drafts the cruel fisher made,
He could not vend them in his borough trade,
But sailed for London mart; the boy was ill,
But ever humbled to his master's will;
And on the river, where they smoothly sailed,
He strove with terror and awhile prevailed;
But new to danger on the angry sea,
He clung affrightened to his master's knee.
The boat grew leaky and the wind was strong,
Rough was the passage and the time was long;
His liquor failed, and Peter's wrath arose—
No more is known—the rest we must suppose,
Or learn of Peter; Peter says he "spied
The stripling's danger and for harbour tried;
Meantime the fish, and then the apprentice died."

The pitying women raised a clamour round,
And weeping said, "Thou hast thy 'prentice drowned."

Now the stern man was summoned to the hall,
To tell his tale before the burghers all;
He gave the account, professed the lad he loved,
And kept his brazen features all unmoved.

The mayor himself with tone severe replied,
"Henceforth with thee shall never boy abide;
Hire thee a freeman, whom thou durst not beat,
But who, in thy despite, will sleep and eat;
Free thou art now! Again shouldst thou appear,
Thou'lt find thy sentence, like thy soul, severe."
    Alas! for Peter, not a helping hand,
So was he hated, could he now command.
Alone he rowed his boat, alone he cast
His nets beside, or made his anchor fast;
To hold a rope or hear a curse was none—
He toiled and railed, he groaned and swore alone.
    Thus by himself compelled to live each day,
To wait for certain hours the tide's delay;
At the same times the same dull views to see,
The bounding marsh-bank and the blighted tree;
The water only, when the tides were high,
When low, the mud half-covered and half-dry;
The sunburnt tar that blisters on the planks,
And bank-side stakes in their uneven ranks,
Heaps of entangled weeds that slowly float,
As the tide rolls by the impeded boat.
    When tides were neap and, in the sultry day,
Through the tall bounding mudbanks made their way,
Which on each side rose swelling, and below
The dark warm flood ran silently and slow;
There anchoring, Peter chose from man to hide,
There hang his head, and view the lazy tide
In its hot slimy channel slowly glide;
Where the small eels that left the deeper way
For the warm shore within the shallows play;
Where gaping mussels, left upon the mud,
Slope their slow passage to the fallen flood.
Here dull and hopeless he'd lie down and trace
How sidelong crabs had scrawled their crooked race,
Or sadly listen to the tuneless cry
Of fishing gull or clanging goldeneye;
What time the seabirds to the marsh would come,
And the loud bittern, from the bulrush home,
Gave from the salt-ditch side the bellowing boom.
He nursed the feelings these dull scenes produce,
And loved to stop beside the opening sluice;

319

Where the small stream, confined in narrow bound,
Ran with a dull, unvaried, saddening sound;
Where all, presented to the eye or ear,
Oppressed the soul with misery, grief, and fear.

Besides these objects, there were places three,
Which Peter seemed with certain dread to see;
When he drew near them he would turn from each,
And loudly whistle till he passed the reach.

A change of scene to him brought no relief;
In town, 'twas plain, men took him for a thief.
The sailors' wives would stop him in the street,
And say, "Now, Peter, thou'st no boy to beat!"
Infants at play, when they perceived him, ran,
Warning each other, "That's the wicked man!"
He growled an oath, and in an angry tone
Cursed the whole place and wished to be alone.

Alone he was, the same dull scenes in view,
And still more gloomy in his sight they grew;
Though man he hated, yet employed alone
At bootless labor, he would swear and groan,
Cursing the shoals that glided by the spot,
And gulls that caught them when his arts could not.

Cold nervous tremblings shook his sturdy frame,
And strange disease—he couldn't say the name;
Wild were his dreams, and oft he rose in fright,
Waked by his view of horrors in the night,
Horrors that would the sternest minds amaze,
Horrors that demons might be proud to raise;
And though he felt forsaken, grieved at heart
To think he lived from all mankind apart,
Yet, if a man approached, in terrors he would start.

A winter passed since Peter saw the town,
And summer lodgers were again come down.
These, idly curious, with their glasses spied
The ships in bay, as anchored for the tide—
The river's craft—the bustle of the quay—
And seaport views, which landmen love to see.

One, up the river, had a man and boat
Seen day by day, now anchored, now afloat;
Fisher he seemed; yet used no net nor hook,
Of seafowl swimming by no heed he took,
But on the gliding waves still fixed his lazy look.

At certain stations he would view the stream,
As if he stood bewildered in a dream,
Or that some power had chained him for a time,
To feel a curse or meditate on crime.

This known, some curious, some in pity went,
And others questioned, "Wretch, dost thou repent?"
He heard, he trembled, and in fear resigned
His boat; new terror filled his restless mind;
Furious he grew, and up on the country ran,
And there they seized him—a distempered man.
Him we received, and to a parish-bed,
Followed and cursed, the groaning man was led.

Here when they saw him whom they used to shun,
A lost, lone man, so harassed and undone,
Our gentle females, ever prompt to feel,
Perceived compassion on their anger steal;
His crimes they could not from their memories blot,
But they were grieved, and trembled at his lot.

A priest, too, came, to whom his words are told;
And all the signs they shuddered to behold.

"Look! look!" they cried, "His limbs with horror shake,
And as he grinds his teeth, what noise they make!
How glare his angry eyes, and yet he's not awake.
See! what cold drops upon his forehead stand,
And how he clenches that broad bony hand."

The priest, attending, found he spoke at times
As one alluding to his fears and crimes:
"It was the fall," he muttered. "I can show
The manner how—I never struck a blow"—
And then aloud—"Unhand me, free my chain!
On oath, he fell—it struck him to the brain—
Why ask my father?—that old man will swear
Against my life; besides, he wasn't there—
What, all agreed?—Am I to die today?—
My Lord, in mercy, give me time to pray."

Then, as they watched him, calmer he became,
And grew so weak he couldn't move his frame,
But murmuring spake—while they could see and hear
The start of terror and the groan of fear;
See the large dew-beads on his forehead rise,
And the cold death-drop glaze his sunken eyes;
Nor yet he died, but with unwonted force

321

Seemed with some fancied being to discourse.
He knew not us, or with accustomed art
He hid the knowledge, yet exposed his heart;
'Twas part confession and the rest defence,
A madman's tale, with gleams of waking sense.

"I'll tell you all," he said, "the very day
When the old man first placed them in my way,
My father's spirit—he who always tried
To give me trouble, when he lived and died—
When he was gone, he could not be content
To see my days in painful labour spent,
But would appoint his meetings, and he made
Me watch at these, and so neglect my trade.

'Twas one hot noon, all silent, still, serene,
No living being had I lately seen;
I paddled up and down and dipped my net,
But (such his pleasure) I could nothing get—
A father's pleasure, when his toil was done,
To plague and torture thus an only son!
And so I sat and looked upon the stream,
How it ran on and felt as in a dream,
But dream it was not; no!—I fixed my eyes
On the midstream and saw the spirits rise;
I saw my father on the water stand,
And hold a thin pale boy in either hand;
And there they glided ghastly on the top
Of the salt flood, and never touched a drop;
I would have struck them, but they knew the intent,
And smiled upon the oar, and down they went.

Now, from that day, whenever I began
To dip my net, there stood the hard old man—
He and those boys. I humbled me and prayed
They would be gone—they heeded not, but stayed;
Nor could I turn, nor would the boat go by,
But gazing on the spirits, there was I;
They bade me leap to death, but I was loath to die.
And every day, as sure as day arose,
Would these three spirits meet me ere the close;
To hear and mark them daily was my doom,
And 'Come,' they said, with weak, sad voices, 'come.'
To row away with all my strength I tried,
But there were they, hard by me in the tide,

The three unbodied forms—and 'Come,' still 'come,' they cried.
  Fathers should pity—but this old man shook
His hoary locks, and froze me by a look.
Thrice, when I struck them, through the water came
A hollow groan, that weakened all my frame.
'Father!' said I, 'have mercy!'—He replied,
I know not what—the angry spirit lied—
'Didst thou not draw thy knife?' said he—'Twas true,
But I had pity and my arm withdrew:
He cried for mercy which I kindly gave,
But he has no compassion in his grave.
  There were three places, where they ever rose—
The whole long river has not such as those—
Places accursed, where, if a man remain,
He'll see the things which strike him to the brain;
And there they made me on my paddle lean,
And look at them for hours—accursed scene!
When they would glide to that smooth eddy-space,
Then bid me leap and join them in the place;
And at my groans each little villain sprite
Enjoyed my pains and vanished in delight.
  In one fierce summer day, when my poor brain
Was burning hot and cruel was my pain,
Then came this father-foe, and there he stood
With his two boys again upon the flood;
There was more mischief in their eyes, more glee
In their pale faces when they glared at me.
Still did they force me on the oar to rest,
And when they saw me fainting and oppressed,
He, with his hand, the old man, scooped the flood,
And there came flame about him mixed with blood;
He bade me stoop and look upon the place,
Then flung the hot-red liquor in my face;
Burning it blazed, and then I roared for pain;
I thought the demons would have turned my brain.
  Still there they stood, and forced me to behold
A place of horrors—they cannot be told—
Where the flood opened, there I heard the shriek
Of tortured guilt—no earthly tongue can speak:
'All days alike! forever!' did they say,
'And unremitted torments every day'—
Yes, so they said." But here he ceased and gazed

On all around, affrightened and amazed;
And still he tried to speak, and looked in dread
Of frightened females gathering round his bed;
Then dropped exhausted and appeared at rest,
Till the strong foe the vital powers possessed;
Then with an inward, broken voice he cried,
"Again they come," and muttered as he died.

WILLIAM BLAKE
(1757–1827)

TO THE EVENING STAR

Thou fair-haired angel of the evening,
Now, whilst the sun rests on the mountains, light
Thy bright torch of love: thy radiant crown
Put on, and smile upon our evening bed!
Smile on our loves: and, while thou drawest the
Blue curtains of the sky, scatter thy silver dew
On every flower that shuts its sweet eyes
In timely sleep. Let thy west wind sleep on
The lake: speak silence with thy glimmering eyes,
And wash the dusk with silver. Soon, full soon,
Dost thou withdraw; then the wolf rages wide,
And then the lion glares through the dun forest.
The fleeces of our flocks are covered with
Thy sacred dew: protect them with thine influence!

*

My silks and fine array,
    My smiles and languished air,
By love are driven away;
    And mournful lean Despair
Brings me yew to deck my grave:
Such end true lovers have.

His face is fair as heaven
    When springing buds unfold;
Oh why to him was't given,
    Whose heart is wintry cold?
His breast is love's all-worshipped tomb,
Where all love's pilgrims come.

Bring me an axe and spade,
    Bring me a winding-sheet;
When I my grave have made,
    Let winds and tempests beat:
Then down I'll lie, as cold as clay.
True love doth pass away!

MAD SONG

The wild winds weep,
    And the night is a-cold;
Come hither, Sleep,
    And my griefs enfold! . . .
But lo! the morning peeps
Over the eastern steeps,
And the rustling birds of dawn
The earth do scorn.

Lo! to the vault
    Of paved heaven,
With sorrow fraught,
    My notes are driven;
They strike the ear of Night,
Make weep the eyes of Day;
They make mad the roaring winds,
    And with tempests play.

Like a fiend in a cloud,
    With howling woe
After night I do crowd
    And with night will go;
I turn my back to the east
From whence comforts have increased:
For light doth seize my brain
With frantic pain.

from *SONGS OF INNOCENCE*

INTRODUCTION

Piping down the valleys wild,
    Piping songs of pleasant glee,
On a cloud I saw a child,
    And he laughing said to me:

"Pipe a song about a lamb!"
    So I piped with merry cheer.
"Piper, pipe that song again;"
    So I piped: he wept to hear.

"Drop thy pipe, thy happy pipe;
    Sing thy songs of happy cheer!"
So I sung the same again,
    While he wept with joy to hear.

"Piper, sit thee down and write
    In a book that all may read.
So he vanished from my sight;
    And I plucked a hollow reed,

And I made a rural pen,
    And I stained the water clear,
And I wrote my happy songs
    Every child may joy to hear.

THE LAMB

Little lamb, who made thee?
Dost thou know who made thee,
Gave thee life, and bid thee feed
By the stream and o'er the mead;
Gave thee clothing of delight,

Softest clothing, woolly, bright;
Gave thee such a tender voice,
Making all the vales rejoice?
   Little lamb, who made thee?
   Dost thou know who made thee?

   Little lamb, I'll tell thee;
   Little lamb, I'll tell thee:
He is called by thy name,
For He calls Himself a Lamb.
He is meek, and He is mild,
He became a little child.
I a child, and thou a lamb,
We are called by his name.
   Little lamb, God bless thee!
   Little lamb, God bless thee!

THE DIVINE IMAGE

To Mercy, Pity, Peace, and Love,
   All pray in their distress,
And to these virtues of delight
   Return their thankfulness.

For Mercy, Pity, Peace, and Love,
   Is God our Father dear;
And Mercy, Pity, Peace, and Love,
   Is man, His child and care.

For Mercy has a human heart;
   Pity, a human face;
And Love, the human form divine:
   And Peace, the human dress.

Then every man, of every clime,
   That prays in his distress,
Prays to the human form divine:
   Love, Mercy, Pity, Peace.

And all must love the human form,
        In heathen, Turk, or Jew.
Where Mercy, Love, and Pity dwell,
        There God is dwelling too.

THE CHIMNEY-SWEEPER

When my mother died I was very young,
And my father sold me while yet my tongue
Could scarcely cry "Weep! weep! weep! weep!"
So your chimneys I sweep, and in soot I sleep.

There's little Tom Dacre, who cried when his head,
That curled like a lamb's back, was shaved; so I said,
"Hush, Tom! never mind it, for, when your head's bare,
You know that the soot cannot spoil your white hair."

And so he was quiet, and that very night,
As Tom was asleeping, he had such a sight!—
That thousands of sweepers, Dick, Joe, Ned, and Jack,
Were all of them locked up in coffins of black.

And by came an angel, who had a bright key,
And he opened the coffins, and set them all free;
Then down a green plain, leaping, laughing, they run
And wash in a river, and shine in the sun.

Then naked and white, all their bags left behind,
They rise upon clouds, and sport in the wind;
And the angel told Tom, if he'd be a good boy,
He'd have God for his father, and never want joy.

And so Tom awoke, and we rose in the dark,
And got with our bags and our brushes to work.
Though the morning was cold, Tom was happy and warm:
So, if all do their duty, they need not fear harm.

INFANT JOY

"I have no name;
I am but two days old."
What shall I call thee?
"I happy am,
Joy is my name."
Sweet joy befall thee!

Pretty joy!
Sweet joy but two days old.
Sweet joy I call thee:
Thou dost smile,
I sing the while;
Sweet joy befall thee!

HOLY THURSDAY

'Twas on a holy Thursday, their innocent faces clean,
The children walking two and two, in red, and blue, and green:
Grey-headed beadles walked before, with wands as white as snow,
Till into the high dome of Paul's they like Thames waters flow.

Oh what a multitude they seemed, these flowers of London town!
Seated in companies they sit, with radiance all their own.
The hum of multitudes was there, but multitudes of lambs,
Thousands of little boys and girls raising their innocent hands.

Now like a mighty wind they raise to heaven the voice of song,
Or like harmonious thunderings the seats of heaven among:
Beneath them sit the aged men, wise guardians of the poor.
Then cherish pity, lest you drive an angel from your door.

from *SONGS OF EXPERIENCE*

INTRODUCTION

Hear the voice of the bard,
Who present, past, and future, sees;
Whose ears have heard
The Holy Word
That walked among the ancient trees;

Calling the lapsed soul,
And weeping in the evening dew;
That might control
The starry pole,
And fallen, fallen light renew!

"O Earth, O Earth, return!
Arise from out the dewy grass!
Night is worn,
And the morn
Rises from the slumbrous mass.

Turn away no more;
Why wilt thou turn away?
The starry floor,
The watery shore,
Is given thee till the break of day."

THE CLOD AND THE PEBBLE

"Love seeketh not itself to please,
    Nor for itself hath any care,
But for another gives its ease,
    And builds a heaven in hell's despair."

So sung a little clod of clay,
    Trodden with the cattle's feet,
But a pebble of the brook
    Warbled out these metres meet:

"Love seeketh only self to please,
　　To bind another to its delight,
Joys in another's loss of ease,
　　And builds a hell in heaven's despite."

HOLY THURSDAY

Is this a holy thing to see
　　In a rich and fruitful land—
Babes reduced to misery,
　　Fed with cold and usurous hand?

Is that trembling cry a song?
　　Can it be a song of joy?
And so many children poor?
　　It is a land of poverty!

And their sun does never shine,
　　And their fields are bleak and bare,
And their ways are filled with thorns,
　　It is eternal winter there.

For where'er the sun does shine,
　　And where'er the rain does fall,
Babe can never hunger there,
　　Nor poverty the mind appal.

THE CHIMNEY-SWEEPER

A little black thing among the snow,
Crying "weep! weep!" in notes of woe!
"Where are thy father and mother? Say!"
"They are both gone up to the church to pray.

Because I was happy upon the heath,
And smiled among the winter's snow,

They clothed me in the clothes of death,
And taught me to sing the notes of woe.

And because I am happy and dance and sing,
They think they have done me no injury,
And are gone to praise God and His priest and king,
Who make up a heaven of our misery."

THE TIGER

Tiger, tiger, burning bright
In the forests of the night,
What immortal hand or eye
Could frame thy fearful symmetry?

In what distant deeps or skies
Burnt the fire of thine eyes?
On what wings dare he aspire?
What the hand dare seize the fire?

And what shoulder and what art
Could twist the sinews of thy heart?
And, when thy heart began to beat,
What dread hand and what dread feet?

What the hammer? what the chain?
In what furnace was thy brain?
What the anvil? what dread grasp
Dare its deadly terrors clasp?

When the stars threw down their spears
And watered heaven with their tears,
Did He smile His work to see?
Did He who made the lamb make thee?

Tiger, tiger, burning bright
In the forests of the night,
What immortal hand or eye
Dare frame thy fearful symmetry?

AH, SUNFLOWER

Ah, sunflower, weary of time,
  Who countest the steps of the sun;
Seeking after that sweet golden clime
  Where the traveller's journey is done;

Where the youth pined away with desire,
  And the pale virgin shrouded in snow,
Arise from their graves, and aspire
  Where my sunflower wishes to go!

THE GARDEN OF LOVE

I went to the Garden of Love,
  And saw what I never had seen;
A chapel was built in the midst,
  Where I used to play on the green.

And the gates of this chapel were shut,
  And "Thou shalt not" writ over the door;
So I turned to the Garden of Love
  That so many sweet flowers bore.

And I saw it was filled with graves,
  And tombstones where flowers should be;
And priests in black gowns were walking their rounds,
  And binding with briars my joys and desires.

LONDON

I wander through each chartered street,
  Near where the chartered Thames does flow,
And mark in every face I meet,
  Marks of weakness, marks of woe.

In every cry of every man,
  In every infant's cry of fear,
In every voice, in every ban,
  The mind-forged manacles I hear:

How the chimney-sweeper's cry
  Every blackening church appals,
And the hapless soldier's sigh
  Runs in blood down palace-walls.

But most, through midnight streets I hear
  How the youthful harlot's curse
Blasts the new-born infant's tear,
  And blights with plagues the marriage-hearse.

A DIVINE IMAGE

Cruelty has a human heart,
  And Jealousy a human face;
Terror the human form divine,
  And Secrecy the human dress.

The human dress is forged iron,
  The human form a fiery forge,
The human face a furnace sealed,
  The human heart its hungry gorge.

THE BOOK OF THEL

THEL'S MOTTO

Does the Eagle know what is in the pit
  Or wilt thou go ask the Mole?
Can wisdom be put in a silver rod,
  Or love in a golden bowl?

1

The Daughters of the Seraphim led round their sunny flocks—
All but the youngest: she in paleness sought the secret air,
To fade away like morning beauty from her mortal day.
Down by the river of Adona her soft voice is heard,
And thus her gentle lamentation falls like morning dew.
"O life of this our Spring! why fades the lotus of the water?
Why fade these children of the Spring, born but to smile and fall?
Ah! Thel is like a watery bow, and like a parting cloud,
Like a reflection in a glass, like shadows in the water,
Like dreams of infants, like a smile upon an infant's face,
Like the dove's voice, like transient day, like music in the air.
Ah! gentle may I lay me down, and gentle rest my head,
And gentle sleep the sleep of death, and gentle hear the voice
Of Him that walketh in the garden in the evening time!"
The Lily of the Valley, breathing in the humble grass,
Answered the lovely maid, and said: "I am a watery weed,
And I am very small, and love to dwell in lowly vale;
So weak, the gilded butterfly scarce perches on my head.
Yet I am visited from heaven; and He that smiles on all
Walks in the valley, and each morn over me spreads His hand,
Saying, 'Rejoice, thou humble grass, thou new-born lily-flower,
Thou gentle maid of silent valleys and of modest brooks;
For thou shalt be clothed in light and fed with morning manna,
Till summer's heat melts thee beside the fountains and the springs,
To flourish in eternal vales.' Then why should Thel complain?
Why should the mistress of the vales of Har utter a sigh?"
She ceased, and smiled in tears, then sat down in her silver shrine.

Thel answered: "O thou little Virgin of the peaceful valley,
Giving to those that cannot crave, the voiceless, the o'ertired:
Thy breath doth nourish the innocent lamb; he smells thy milky garments,
He crops thy flowers, while thou sittest smiling in his face,
Wiping his mild and meekin mouth from all contagious taints.
Thy wine doth purify the golden honey; thy perfume,
Which thou dost scatter on every little blade of grass that springs,
Revives the milked cow, and tames the fire-breathing steed.
But Thel is like a faint cloud kindled at the rising sun:
I vanish from my pearly throne, and who shall find my place?"

"Queen of the vales," the Lily answered, "ask the tender Cloud,
And it shall tell thee why it glitters in the morning sky,
And why it scatters its bright beauty through the humid air.
Descend, O little Cloud, and hover before the eyes of Thel."
The Cloud descended; and the Lily bowed her modest head,
And went to mind her numerous charge among the verdant grass.

2.

"O little Cloud," the Virgin said, "I charge thee tell to me
Why thou complainest not, when in one hour thou fadest away:
Then we shall seek thee, but not find. Ah! Thel is like to thee—
I pass away; yet I complain, and no one hears my voice."
The Cloud then showed his golden head, and his bright form emerged
Hovering and glittering on the air, before the face of Thel.
"O Virgin, knowest thou not our steeds drink of the golden springs
Where Luvah doth renew his horses? Lookest thou on my youth,
And fearest thou because I vanish and am seen no more?
Nothing remains. O maid, I tell thee, when I pass away,
It is to tenfold life, to love, to peace, and raptures holy.
Unseen descending weigh my light wings upon balmy flowers,
And court the fair-eyed Dew to take me to her shining tent:
The weeping Virgin trembling kneels before the risen sun,
Till we arise, linked in a golden band, and never part,
But walk united, bearing food to all our tender flowers."

"Dost thou, O little Cloud? I fear that I am not like thee;
For I walk through the vales of Har, and smell the sweetest flowers,
But I feed not the little flowers: I hear the warbling birds,
But I feed not the warbling birds, they fly and seek their food.
But Thel delights in these no more! because I fade away,
And all shall say, 'Without a use this shining woman lived;
Or did she only live to be at death the food of worms?' "

The Cloud reclined upon his airy throne, and answered thus:
"Then if thou art the food of worms, O Virgin of the skies,
How great thy use, how great thy blessing! Every thing that lives
Lives not alone nor for itself. Fear not, and I will call
The weak Worm from its lowly bed, and thou shalt hear its voice.
Come forth, Worm of the silent valley, to thy pensive queen."

The helpless Worm arose, and sat upon the Lily's leaf,
And the bright Cloud sailed on to find his partner in the vale.

3.

Then Thel, astonished, viewed the Worm upon its dewy bed.
"Art thou a worm, image of weakness? art thou but a worm?
I see thee, like an infant, wrapped in the Lily's leaf.
Ah! weep not, little voice; thou canst not speak, but thou canst weep.
Is this a worm? I see thee lay helpless and naked, weeping,
And none to answer, none to cherish thee with mother's smiles."
The Clod of Clay heard the Worm's voice, and raised her pitying head:
She bowed over the weeping infant, and her life exhaled
In milky fondness: then on Thel she fixed her humble eyes.

"O beauty of the vales of Har! we live not for ourselves.
Thou seest me, the meanest thing, and so I am indeed.
My bosom of itself is cold, and of itself is dark;
But He that loves the lowly pours His oil upon my head,
And kisses me, and binds His nuptial bands around my breast,
And says: 'Thou mother of my children, I have loved thee,
And I have given thee a crown that none can take away.'
But how this is, sweet maid, I know not, and I cannot know:
I ponder, and I cannot ponder: yet I live and love!"

The Daughter of Beauty wiped her pitying tears with her white veil,
And said: "Alas! I knew not this, and therefore did I weep.
That God would love a worm I knew, and punish the evil foot
That wilful bruised its helpless form; but that He cherished it
With milk and oil I never knew, and therefore did I weep.
And I complained in the mild air, because I fade away,
And lay me down in thy cold bed, and leave my shining lot."

"Queen of the vales," the matron Clay answered, "I heard thy sighs,
And all thy moans flew o'er my roof, but I have called them down.
Wilt thou, O queen, enter my house? 'Tis given thee to enter,
And to return: fear nothing, enter with thy virgin feet."

4.

The eternal gates' terrific Porter lifted the northern bar;
Thel entered in, and saw the secrets of the land unknown.

338

She saw the couches of the dead, and where the fibrous root
Of every heart on earth infixes deep its restless twists:
A land of sorrows and of tears, where never smile was seen.

She wandered in the land of clouds, through valleys dark, listening
Dolours and lamentations: waiting oft beside a dewy grave,
She stood in silence, listening to the voices of the ground,
Till to her own grave-plot she came, and there she sat down,
And heard this voice of sorrow breathed from the hollow pit.

"Why cannot the ear be closed to its own destruction?
Or the glistening eye to the poison of a smile?
Why are eyelids stored with arrows ready drawn,
Where a thousand fighting-men in ambush lie,
Or an eye of gifts and graces showering fruits and coined gold?
Why a tongue impressed with honey from every wind?
Why an ear, a whirlpool fierce to draw creations in?
Why a nostril wide inhaling terror, trembling, and affright?
Why a tender curb upon the youthful burning boy?
Why a little curtain of flesh on the bed of our desire?"

The Virgin started from her seat, and with a shriek
Fled back unhindered till she came into the vales of Har.

*

There is a smile of love,
  And there is a smile of deceit,
And there is a smile of smiles
  In which these two smiles meet.

And there is a frown of hate,
  And there is a frown of disdain,
And there is a frown of frowns
  Which you strive to forget in vain.

For it sticks in the heart's deep core,
  And it sticks in the deep backbone.

339

And no smile ever was smiled
  But only one smile alone,

And betwixt the cradle and grave
  It only once smiled can be;
And when it once is smiled,
  There's an end to all misery.

*

I walked abroad on a snowy day,
I wooed the soft snow with me to play,
She played and she melted in all her prime;
And the winter called it a dreadful crime.

AN EPITAPH

Come knock your heads against this stone
For sorrow that poor John Thompson's gone.

ROBERT BURNS
(1759–96)

TO A MOUSE

Wee, sleekit, cow'rin', tim'rous beastie,
Oh, what a panic's in thy breastie!
Thou need na start awa sae hasty,
   Wi' bickering brattle!
I wad be laith to rin an' chase thee
   Wi' murd'ring pattle!

I'm truly sorry man's dominion
Has broken Nature's social union,
An' justifies that ill opinion
   Which makes thee startle
At me, thy poor, earth-born companion,
   An' fellow mortal!

I doubt na, whiles, but thou may thieve;
What then? poor beastie, thou maun live!
A daimen-icker in a thrave
   'S a sma' request!
I'll get a blessin' wi' the lave,
   And never miss 't!

Thy wee-bit housie, too, in ruin!
Its silly wa's the win's are strewin'!
An' naething, now, to big a new ane,
   O' foggage green!
An' bleak December's winds ensuin',
   Baith snell an' keen!

Thou saw the fields laid bare and waste,
An' weary winter comin' fast,
An' cozie here, beneath the blast,
   Thou thought to dwell,

Till crash! the cruel coulter passed
        Out-through thy cell.

That wee-bit heap o' leaves an' stibble
Has cost thee mony a weary nibble!
Now thou's turned out, for a' thy trouble,
        But house or hald,
To thole the winter's sleety dribble,
        An' cranreuch cauld!

But Mousie, thou art no thy lane,
In proving foresight may be vain:
The best-laid schemes o' mice an' men
        Gang aft agley,
An' lea'e us nought but grief an' pain,
        For promised joy.

Still thou art blest compared wi' me!
The present only toucheth thee:
But och! I backward cast me e'e
        On prospects drear!
An' forward though I canna see,
        I guess an' fear!

SCOTS, WHA HAE

Scots, wha hae wi' Wallace bled,
Scots, wham Bruce has aften led,
Welcome to your gory bed,
        Or to victory.

Now's the day, and now's the hour;
See the front o' battle lower;
See approach proud Edward's power—
        Chains and slavery!

Wha will be a traitor-knave?
Wha can fill a coward's grave?

Wha sae base as be a slave?
  Let him turn and flee!

Wha for Scotland's King and law
Freedom's sword will strongly draw,
Freeman stand, or freeman fa',
  Let him follow me!

By oppression's woes and pains!
By your sons in servile chains!
We will drain our dearest veins,
  But they shall be free!

Lay the proud usurpers low!
Tyrants fall in every foe!
Liberty's in every blow!
  Let us do, or die!

FOR A' THAT AND A' THAT

Is there, for honest poverty,
  That hangs his head, and a' that?
The coward slave, we pass him by,
  We dare be poor for a' that!
    For a' that, and a' that,
      Our toils obscure, and a' that;
    The rank is but the guinea's stamp,
      The man's the gowd for a' that.

What though on hamely fare we dine,
  Wear hodden-grey, and a' that?
Gie fools their silks, and knaves their wine,
  A man's a man for a' that;
    For a' that, and a' that,
      Their tinsel show, and a' that;
    The honest man, though e'er sae poor,
      Is king o' men for a' that.

Ye see yon birkie, ca'd a lord,
  Wha struts, and stares, and a' that!
Though hundreds worship at his word,
  He's but a coof for a' that:
    For a' that, and a' that,
      His riband, star, and a' that,
    The man of independent mind,
      He looks and laughs at a' that.

A prince can mak a belted knight,
  A marquis, duke, and a' that!
But an honest man's aboon his might,
  Guid faith he mauna fa' that!
    For a' that, and a' that,
      Their dignities, and a' that,
    The pith o' sense, and pride o' worth,
      Are higher rank than a' that.

Then let us pray that come it may,
  As come it will for a' that,
That sense and worth, o'er a' the earth,
  May bear the gree, and a' that.
    For a' that, and a' that,
      It's coming yet, for a' that,
    That man to man the warld o'er
      Shall brothers be for a' that.

A RED, RED ROSE

Oh my love's like a red, red rose,
  That's newly sprung in June;
Oh my love's like the melodie
  That's sweetly played in tune.

As fair art thou, my bonnie lass,
  So deep in love am I;
And I will love thee still, my dear,
  Till a' the seas gang dry.

344

Till a' the seas gang dry, my dear,
    And the rocks melt wi' the sun:
Oh I will love thee still, my dear,
    While the sands o' life shall run.

And fare thee weel, my only love,
    And fare thee weel awhile!
And I will come again, my love,
    Though it were ten thousand mile.

AULD LANG SYNE

Should auld acquaintance be forgot,
    And never brought to min'?
Should auld acquaintance be forgot,
    And days of auld lang syne?

For auld lang syne, my dear,
    For auld lang syne,
We'll take a cup o' kindness yet,
    For auld lang syne!

We twa hae run about the braes,
    And pu'd the gowans fine,
But we've wandered mony a weary foot,
    Sin' auld lang syne.

For auld lang syne, my dear,
    For auld lang syne,
We'll take a cup o' kindness yet,
    For auld lang syne!

We twa hae paidled i' the burn,
    From morning sun till dine,
But seas between us braid hae roared,
    Sin' auld lang syne.

For auld lang syne, my dear,
    For auld lang syne,

We'll take a cup o' kindness yet,
    For auld lang syne!

And there's a hand, my trusty fiere,
    And gie's a hand o' thine,
And we'll take a right gude-willie waught,
    For auld lang syne.

For auld lang syne, my dear,
    For auld lang syne,
We'll take a cup o' kindness yet,
    For auld lang syne!

And surely ye'll be your pint stowp,
    And surely I'll be mine,
And we'll take a cup o' kindness yet,
    For auld lang syne.

For auld lang syne, my dear,
    For auld lang syne,
We'll take a cup o' kindness yet,
    For auld lang syne!

WILLIAM WORDSWORTH
(1770–1850)

LONDON, 1802

Milton! Thou shouldst be living at this hour:
England hath need of thee: she is a fen
Of stagnant waters: altar, sword, and pen,
Fireside, the heroic wealth of hall and bower,
Have forefeited their ancient English dower
Of inward happiness. We are selfish men;
Oh! raise us up, return to us again;
And give us manners, virtue, freedom, power.
Thy soul was like a star, and dwelt apart;
Thou hadst a voice whose sound was like the sea:
Pure as the naked heavens, majestic, free,
So didst thou travel on life's common way,
In cheerful godliness; and yet thy heart
The lowliest duties on herself did lay.

THE WORLD IS TOO MUCH WITH US

The world is too much with us; late and soon,
Getting and spending, we lay waste our powers;
Little we see in nature that is ours;
We have given our hearts away, a sordid boon!
This sea that bares her bosom to the moon,
The winds that will be howling at all hours,
And are upgathered now like sleeping flowers,
For this, for everything, we are out of tune;
It moves us not. Great God! I'd rather be
A pagan suckled in a creed outworn;
So might I, standing on this pleasant lea,
Have glimpses that would make me less forlorn;

Have sight of Proteus rising from the sea;
Or hear old Triton blow his wreathed horn.

SURPRISED BY JOY

Surprised by joy—impatient as the wind
I turned to share the transport—oh! with whom
But thee, deep buried in the silent tomb,
That spot which no vicissitude can find?
Love, faithful love, recalled thee to my mind—
But how could I forget thee? Through what power,
Even for the least division of an hour,
Have I been so beguiled as to be blind
To my most grievous loss! That thought's return
Was the worst pang that sorrow ever bore,
Save one, one only, when I stood forlorn,
Knowing my heart's best treasure was no more;
That neither present time, nor years unborn
Could to my sight that heavenly face restore.

COMPOSED UPON WESTMINSTER BRIDGE, SEPTEMBER 3, 1802

Earth has not anything to show more fair:
Dull would he be of soul who could pass by
A sight so touching in its majesty:
This city now doth, like a garment, wear
The beauty of the morning; silent, bare,
Ships, towers, domes, theatres, and temples lie
Open unto the fields, and to the sky;
All bright and glittering in the smokeless air.
Never did sun more beautifully steep
In his first splendour, valley, rock, or hill;
Ne'er saw I, never felt, a calm so deep!
The river glideth at his own sweet will:
Dear God! the very houses seem asleep;
And all that mighty heart is lying still!

348

IT IS A BEAUTEOUS EVENING

It is a beauteous evening, calm and free,
The holy time is quiet as a nun
Breathless with adoration; the broad sun
Is sinking down in its tranquillity;
The gentleness of heaven broods o'er the sea:
Listen! the mighty being is awake,
And doth with his eternal motion make
A sound like thunder—everlastingly.
Dear child! dear girl! that walkest with me here,
If thou appear untouched by solemn thought,
Thy nature is not therefore less divine:
Thou liest in Abraham's bosom all the year,
And worshippest at the temple's inner shrine,
God being with thee when we know it not.

STRANGE FITS OF PASSION HAVE I KNOWN

Strange fits of passion have I known,
And I will dare to tell,
But in the lover's ear alone,
What once to me befell.

When she I loved looked every day
Fresh as a rose in June,
I to her cottage bent my way,
Beneath an evening-moon.

Upon the moon I fixed my eye,
All over the wide lea;
With quickening pace my horse drew nigh
Those paths so dear to me.

And now we reached the orchard-plot;
And, as we climbed the hill,

The sinking moon to Lucy's cot
Came near, and nearer still.

In one of those sweet dreams I slept,
Kind Nature's gentlest boon!
And all the while my eyes I kept
On the descending moon.

My horse moved on; hoof after hoof
He raised, and never stopped:
When down behind the cottage roof,
At once, the bright moon dropped.

What fond and wayward thoughts will slide
Into a lover's head!
"O mercy!" to myself I cried,
"If Lucy should be dead!"

SHE DWELT AMONG THE UNTRODDEN WAYS

She dwelt among the untrodden ways
    Beside the springs of Dove,
A maid whom there were none to praise
    And very few to love;

A violet by a mossy stone
    Half hidden from the eye!
—Fair as a star, when only one
    Is shining in the sky.

She lived unknown, and few could know
    When Lucy ceased to be;
But she is in her grave, and, oh,
    The difference to me!

A SLUMBER DID MY SPIRIT SEAL

A slumber did my spirit seal;
  I had no human fears:
She seemed a thing that could not feel
  The touch of earthly years.

No motion has she now, no force;
  She neither hears nor sees;
Rolled round in earth's diurnal course,
  With rocks, and stones, and trees.

LUCY GRAY

Oft I had heard of Lucy Gray,
And when I crossed the wild,
I chanced to see at break of day
The solitary child.

No mate, no comrade Lucy knew;
She dwelt on a wide moor,
—The sweetest thing that ever grew
Beside a human door!

You yet may spy the fawn at play,
The hare upon the green;
But the sweet face of Lucy Gray
Will never more be seen.

"To-night will be a stormy night—
You to the town must go;
And take a lantern, child, to light
Your mother through the snow."

"That, Father, will I gladly do:
'Tis scarcely afternoon—
The minster-clock has just struck two,
And yonder is the moon!"

351

At this the father raised his hook,
And snapped a faggot-band;
He plied his work—and Lucy took
The lantern in her hand.

Not blither is the mountain roe:
With many a wanton stroke
Her feet disperse the powdery snow,
That rises up like smoke.

The storm came on before its time:
She wandered up and down;
And many a hill did Lucy climb,
But never reached the town.

The wretched parents, all that night,
Went shouting far and wide;
But there was neither sound nor sight
To serve them for a guide.

At day-break on a hill they stood
That overlooked the moor;
And thence they saw the bridge of wood,
A furlong from their door.

They wept—and, turning homeward, cried,
"In heaven we all shall meet";
—When in the snow the mother spied
The print of Lucy's feet.

Then downwards from the steep hill's edge
They tracked the footmarks small;
And through the broken hawthorn hedge,
And by the long stone wall;

And then an open field they crossed:
The marks were still the same;
They tracked them on, nor ever lost;
And to the bridge they came.

They followed from the snowy bank
Those footmarks, one by one,

Into the middle of the plank;
And further there were none!

—Yet some maintain that to this day
She is a living child;
That you may see sweet Lucy Gray
Upon the lonesome wild.

O'er rough and smooth she trips along,
And never looks behind;
And sings a solitary song
That whistles in the wind.

I WANDERED LONELY AS A CLOUD

I wandered lonely as a cloud
That floats on high o'er vales and hills,
When all at once I saw a crowd,
A host, of golden daffodils,
Beside the lake, beneath the trees,
Fluttering and dancing in the breeze.

Continuous as the stars that shine
And twinkle on the milky way,
They stretched in never-ending line
Along the margin of a bay:
Ten thousand saw I at a glance,
Tossing their heads in sprightly dance.

The waves beside them danced; but they
Outdid the sparkling waves in glee;
A poet could not but be gay,
In such a jocund company:
I gazed—and gazed—but little thought
What wealth the show to me had brought:

For oft, when on my couch I lie
In vacant or in pensive mood,
They flash upon that inward eye

Which is the bliss of solitude;
And then my heart with pleasure fills,
And dances with the daffodils.

MY HEART LEAPS UP

My heart leaps up when I behold
 A rainbow in the sky:
So was it when my life began;
So is it now I am a man;
So be it when I shall grow old,
 Or let me die!
The child is father of the man;
And I could wish my days to be
Bound each to each by natural piety.

THE SOLITARY REAPER

Behold her, single in the field,
Yon solitary highland lass!
Reaping and singing by herself;
Stop here, or gently pass!
Alone she cuts and binds the grain,
And sings a melancholy strain;
Oh listen! for the vale profound
Is overflowing with the sound.

No nightingale did ever chaunt
More welcome notes to weary bands
Of travellers in some shady haunt,
Among Arabian sands;
A voice so thrilling ne'er was heard
In springtime from the cuckoo-bird,
Breaking the silence of the seas
Among the farthest Hebrides.

Will no one tell me what she sings?
Perhaps the plaintive numbers flow
For old, unhappy, far-off things,
And battles long ago:
Or is it some more humble lay,
Familiar matter of today?
Some natural sorrow, loss, or pain,
That has been, and may be again?

Whate'er the theme, the maiden sang
As if her song could have no ending;
I saw her singing at her work,
And o'er the sickle bending—
I listened, motionless and still;
And, as I mounted up the hill,
The music in my heart I bore,
Long after it was heard no more.

ODE:

INTIMATIONS OF IMMORTALITY FROM RECOLLECTIONS OF EARLY CHILDHOOD

There was a time when meadow, grove, and stream,
The earth, and every common sight,
To me did seem
Apparelled in celestial light,
The glory and the freshness of a dream.
It is not now as it hath been of yore—
Turn whereso'er I may,
By night or day,
The things which I have seen I now can see no more.

The rainbow comes and goes,
And lovely is the rose;
The moon doth with delight
Look round her when the heavens are bare;
Waters on a starry night
Are beautiful and fair;

The sunshine is a glorious birth;
But yet I know, where'er I go,
That there hath passed away a glory from the earth.

Now, while the birds thus sing a joyous song,
And while the young lambs bound
As to the tabor's sound,
To me alone there came a thought of grief:
A timely utterance gave that thought relief,
And I again am strong:
The cataracts blow their trumpets from the steep;
No more shall grief of mine the season wrong;
I hear the echoes through the mountains throng,
The winds come to me from the fields of sleep,
And all the earth is gay;
Land and sea
Give themselves up to jollity,
And with the heart of May
Doth every beast keep holiday—
Thou child of joy,
Shout round me, let me hear thy shouts, thou happy
Shepherd-boy!

Ye blessed creatures, I have heard the call
Ye to each other make; I see
The heavens laugh with you in your jubilee;
My heart is at your festival,
My head hath its coronal,
The fullness of your bliss, I feel—I feel it all.
Oh, evil day! If I were sullen
While Earth herself is adorning,
This sweet May morning,
And the children are culling
On every side,
In a thousand valleys far and wide,
Fresh flowers; while the sun shines warm,
And the babe leaps up on his mother's arm—
I hear, I hear, with joy I hear!
—But there's a tree, of many, one,
A single field which I have looked upon,
Both of them speak of something that is gone:
The pansy at my feet

Doth the same tale repeat:
Whither is fled the visionary gleam?
Where is it now, the glory and the dream?

Our birth is but a sleep and a forgetting:
The soul that rises with us, our life's star,
    Hath had elsewhere its setting,
      And cometh from afar:
    Not in entire forgetfulness,
    And not in utter nakedness,
But trailing clouds of glory do we come
    From God, who is our home:
Heaven lies about us in our infancy!
Shades of the prison-house begin to close
    Upon the growing boy,
      But he
Beholds the light, and whence it flows,
    He sees it in his joy;
The youth, who daily farther from the east
    Must travel, still is Nature's priest,
    And by the vision splendid
    Is on his way attended;
At length the man perceives it die away,
And fade into the light of common day.

Earth fills her lap with pleasures of her own;
Yearnings she hath in her own natural kind,
And, even with something of a mother's mind,
    And no unworthy aim,
    The homely nurse doth all she can
To make her foster child, her inmate man,
    Forget the glories he hath known,
And that imperial palace whence he came.

Behold the child among his newborn blisses,
A six-years' darling of a pygmy size!
See, where 'mid work of his own hand he lies,
Fretted by sallies of his mother's kisses,
With light upon him from his father's eyes!
See, at his feet, some little plan or chart,
Some fragment from his dream of human life,
Shaped by himself with newly-learned art;

A wedding or a festival,
A mourning or a funeral;
   And this hath now his heart,
And unto this he frames his song;
   Then will he fit his tongue
To dialogues of business, love, or strife;
   But it will not be long
   Ere this be thrown aside,
   And with new joy and pride
The little actor cons another part;
Filling from time to time his humorous stage
With all the persons, down to palsied Age,
That Life brings with her in her equipage;
   As if his whole vocation
   Were endless imitation.

Thou, whose exterior semblance doth belie
   Thy soul's immensity;
Thou best philosopher, who yet dost keep
Thy heritage, thou eye among the blind,
That, deaf and silent, readst the eternal deep,
Haunted forever by the eternal mind—
   Mighty prophet! Seer blest!
   On whom those truths do rest,
Which we are toiling all our lives to find,
In darkness lost, the darkness of the grave;
Thou, over whom thy immortality
Broods like the day, a master o'er a slave,
A presence which is not to be put by;
Thou little child, yet glorious in the might
Of heaven-born freedom on thy being's height;
Why with such earnest pains dost thou provoke
The years to bring the inevitable yoke,
Thus blindly with thy blessedness at strife?
Full soon thy soul shall have her earthly freight,
And custom lie upon thee with a weight
Heavy as frost, and deep almost as life!

   O joy! that in our embers
   Is something that doth live,
   That nature yet remembers
   What was so fugitive!

The thought of our past years in me doth breed
Perpetual benediction: not indeed
For that which is most worthy to be blest;
Delight and liberty, the simple creed
Of childhood, whether busy or at rest,
With new-fledged hope still fluttering in his breast—
   Not for these I raise
   The song of thanks and praise;
  But for those obstinate questionings
  Of sense and outward things,
  Fallings from us, vanishings;
  Blank misgivings of a creature
Moving about in worlds not realised,
High instincts before which our mortal nature
Did tremble like a guilty thing surprised;
   But, for those first affections,
   Those shadowy recollections,
  Which, be they what they may,
Are yet the fountain-light of all our day,
Are yet a master-light of all our seeing;
  Uphold us, cherish, and have power to make
Our noisy years seem moments in the being
Of the eternal silence: truths that wake,
   To perish never;
Which neither listlessness, nor mad endeavour,
   Nor man nor boy,
Nor all that is at enmity with joy,
Can utterly abolish or destroy!
  Hence in a season of calm weather,
  Though inland far we be,
Our souls have sight of that immortal sea
  Which brought us hither,
  Can in a moment travel thither,
And see the children sport upon the shore,
And hear the mighty waters rolling evermore.

Then sing, ye birds, sing, sing a joyous song!
  And let the young lambs bound
  As to the tabor's sound!
We in thought will join your throng,
  Ye that pipe and ye that play,
  Ye that through your hearts today

Feel the gladness of the May!
What though the radiance, which was once so bright,
Be now forever taken from my sight;
    Though nothing can bring back the hour
Of splendour in the grass, of glory in the flower;
        We will grieve not, rather find
        Strength in what remains behind;
        In the primal sympathy,
        Which having been must ever be;
        In the soothing thoughts that spring
        Out of human suffering;
        In the faith that looks through death,
In years that bring the philosophic mind.

And O ye fountains, meadows, hills, and groves,
Forebode not any severing of our loves!
Yet in my heart of hearts I feel your might;
I only have relinquished one delight
To live beneath your more habitual sway.
I love the brooks which down their channels fret,
Even more than when I tripped lightly as they;
The innocent brightness of a newborn day
        Is lovely yet;
The clouds that gather round the setting sun
Do take a sober colouring from an eye
That hath kept watch o'er man's mortality;
Another race hath been, and other palms are won.
Thanks to the human heart by which we live,
Thanks to its tenderness, its joys, and fears,
To me the meanest flower that blows can give
Thoughts that do often lie too deep for tears.

RESOLUTION AND INDEPENDENCE

There was a roaring in the wind all night;
The rain came heavily and fell in floods;
But now the sun is rising calm and bright;
The birds are singing in the distant woods;

Over his own sweet voice the stock dove broods;
The jay makes answer as the magpie chatters;
And all the air is filled with pleasant noise of waters.

All things that love the sun are out of doors;
The sky rejoices in the morning's birth;
The grass is bright with raindrops; on the moors
The hare is running races in her mirth;
And with her feet she from the plashy earth
Raises a mist that, glittering in the sun,
Runs with her all the way, wherever she doth run.

I was a traveller then upon the moor;
I saw the hare that raced about with joy;
I heard the woods and distant waters roar;
Or heard them not, as happy as a boy:
The pleasant season did my heart employ:
My old remembrances went from me wholly;
And all the ways of men, so vain and melancholy.

But, as it sometimes chanceth, from the might
Of joy in minds that can no further go,
As high as we have mounted in delight
In our dejection do we sink as low;
To me that morning did it happen so,
And fears and fancies thick upon me came;
Dim sadness—and blind thoughts, I knew not, nor could name.

I heard the skylark warbling in the sky;
And I bethought me of the playful hare:
Even such a happy child of earth am I;
Even as these blissful creatures do I fare;
Far from the world I walk, and from all care;
But there may come another day to me—
Solitude, pain of heart, distress, and poverty.

My whole life I have lived in pleasant thought,
As if life's business were a summer mood;
As if all needful things would come unsought
To genial faith, still rich in genial good;
But how can he expect that others should

361

Build for him, sow for him, and at his call
Love him, who for himself will take no heed at all?

I thought of Chatterton, the marvelous boy,
The sleepless soul that perished in his pride;
Of him who walked in glory and in joy
Following his plow, along the mountainside;
By our own spirits are we deified:
We poets in our youth begin in gladness,
But thereof come in the end despondency and madness.

Now, whether it were by peculiar grace,
A leading from above, a something given,
Yet it befell that, in this lonely place,
When I with these untoward thoughts had striven,
Beside a pool bare to the eye of heaven
I saw a man before me unawares:
The oldest man he seemed that ever wore grey hairs.

As a huge stone is sometimes seen to lie
Couched on the bald top of an eminence;
Wonder to all who do the same espy,
By what means it could thither come, and whence;
So that it seems a thing endued with sense:
Like a sea beast crawled forth, that on a shelf
Of rock or sand reposeth, there to sun itself;

Such seemed this man, not all alive nor dead,
Nor all asleep—in his extreme old age;
His body was bent double, feet and head
Coming together in life's pilgrimage;
As if some dire constraint of pain, or rage
Of sickness felt by him in times long past,
A more than human weight upon his frame had cast.

Himself he propped, limbs, body, and pale face,
Upon a long, grey staff of shaven wood;
And, still as I drew near with gentle pace,
Upon the margin of that moorish flood
Motionless as a cloud that old man stood,
That heareth not the loud winds when they call,
And moveth all together, if it move at all.

At length, himself unsettling, he the pond
Stirred with his staff, and fixedly did look
Upon the muddy water, which he conned,
As if he had been reading in a book;
And now a stranger's privilege I took,
And, drawing to his side, to him did say,
"This morning gives us promise of a glorious day."

A gentle answer did the old man make,
In courteous speech which forth he slowly drew;
And him with further words I thus bespake,
"What occupation do you there pursue?
This is a lonesome place for one like you."
Ere he replied, a flash of mild surprise
Broke from the sable orbs of his yet-vivid eyes.

His words came feebly, from a feeble chest,
But each in solemn order followed each,
With something of a lofty utterance dressed—
Choice word and measured phrase, above the reach
Of ordinary men; a stately speech;
Such as grave livers do in Scotland use,
Religious men, who give to God and man their dues.

He told, that to these waters he had come
To gather leeches, being old and poor:
Employment hazardous and wearisome!
And he had many hardships to endure:
From pond to pond he roamed, from moor to moor;
Housing, with God's good help, by choice or chance;
And in this way he gained an honest maintenance.

The old man still stood talking by my side;
But now his voice to me was like a stream
Scarce heard; nor word from word could I divide;
And the whole body of the man did seem
Like one whom I had met with in a dream;
Or like a man from some far region sent,
To give me human strength, by apt admonishment.

My former thoughts returned: the fear that kills;
And hope that is unwilling to be fed;
Cold, pain, and labour, and all fleshly ills;
And mighty poets in their misery dead.
—Perplexed, and longing to be comforted,
My question eagerly did I renew,
"How is it that you live, and what is it you do?"

He with a smile did then his words repeat;
And said that, gathering leeches, far and wide
He travelled, stirring thus about his feet
The waters of the pools where they abide.
"Once I could meet with them on every side,
But they have dwindled long by slow decay;
Yet still I persevere, and find them where I may."

While he was talking thus, the lonely place,
The old man's shape, and speech—all troubled me:
In my mind's eye I seemed to see him pace
About the weary moors continually,
Wandering about alone and silently.
While I these thoughts within myself pursued,
He, having made a pause, the same discourse renewed.

And soon with this he other matter blended,
Cheerfully uttered, with demeanour kind,
But stately in the main; and, when he ended,
I could have laughed myself to scorn to find
In that decrepit man so firm a mind.
"God," said I, "be my help and stay secure;
I'll think of the leech gatherer on the lonely moor!"

LINES COMPOSED A FEW MILES ABOVE TINTERN ABBEY ON REVISITING THE BANKS OF THE WYE DURING A TOUR. JULY 13, 1798

Five years have passed; five summers, with the length
Of five long winters! and again I hear
These waters, rolling from their mountain-springs
With a soft inland murmur—Once again
Do I behold these steep and lofty cliffs,
That on a wild secluded scene impress
Thoughts of more deep seclusion; and connect
The landscape with the quiet of the sky.
The day is come when I again repose
Here, under this dark sycamore, and view
These plots of cottage-ground, these orchard-tufts,
Which at this season, with their unripe fruits,
Are clad in one green hue, and lose themselves
'Mid groves and copses. Once again I see
These hedge-rows, hardly hedge-rows, little lines
Of sportive wood run wild; these pastoral farms,
Green to the very door; and wreaths of smoke
Sent up, in silence, from among the trees!
With some uncertain notice, as might seem
Of vagrant dwellers in the houseless woods,
Or of some hermit's cave, where by his fire
The hermit sits alone.

                These beauteous forms,
Through a long absence, have not been to me
As is a landscape to a blind man's eye:
But oft, in lonely rooms, and 'mid the din
Of towns and cities, I have owed to them,
In hours of weariness, sensations sweet,
Felt in the blood, and felt along the heart;
And passing even into my purer mind,
With tranquil restoration—feelings too
Of unremembered pleasure; such, perhaps,
As have no slight or trivial influence
On that best portion of a good man's life,
His little, nameless, unremembered acts
Of kindness and of love. Nor less, I trust,
To them I may have owed another gift

Of aspect more sublime; that blessed mood,
In which the burthen of the mystery,
In which the heavy and the weary weight
Of all this unintelligible world,
Is lightened—that serene and blessed mood
In which the affections gently lead us on—
Until, the breath of this corporeal frame
And even the motion of our human blood
Almost suspended, we are laid asleep
In body, and become a living soul;
While with an eye made quiet by the power
Of harmony, and the deep power of joy,
We see into the life of things.
                              If this
Be but a vain belief, yet, oh! how oft—
In darkness and amid the many shapes
Of joyless daylight; when the fretful stir
Unprofitable, and the fever of the world,
Have hung upon the beatings of my heart—
How oft, in spirit, have I turned to thee,
O sylvan Wye! thou wanderer through the woods,
How often has my spirit turned to thee!
     And now, with gleams of half-extinguished thought,
With many recognitions dim and faint,
And somewhat of a sad perplexity,
The picture of the mind revives again;
While here I stand, not only with the sense
Of present pleasure, but with pleasing thoughts
That in this moment there is life and food
For future years. And so I dare to hope,
Though changed, no doubt, from what I was when first
I came among these hills; when like a roe
I bounded o'er the mountains, by the sides
Of the deep rivers, and the lonely streams,
Wherever nature led—more like a man
Flying from something that he dreads than one
Who sought the thing he loved. For nature then
(The coarser pleasures of my boyish days,
And their glad animal movements all gone by)
To me was all in all—I cannot paint
What then I was. The sounding cataract
Haunted me like a passion; the tall rock,

The mountain, and the deep and gloomy wood,
Their colours and their forms, were then to me
An appetite; a feeling, and a love,
That had no need of a remoter charm,
By thought supplied, nor any interest
Unborrowed from the eye.—That time is past,
And all its aching joys are now no more,
And all its dizzy raptures. Not for this
Faint I, nor mourn nor murmur; other gifts
Have followed; for such loss, I would believe,
Abundant recompense. For I have learned
To look on nature, not as in the hour
Of thoughtless youth; but hearing oftentimes
The still, sad music of humanity,
Nor harsh nor grating, though of ample power
To chasten and subdue. And I have felt
A presence that disturbs me with the joy
Of elevated thoughts; a sense sublime
Of something far more deeply interfused,
Whose dwelling is the light of setting suns,
And the round ocean and the living air,
And the blue sky, and in the mind of man:
A motion and a spirit, that impels
All thinking things, all objects of all thought,
And rolls through all things. Therefore am I still
A lover of the meadows and the woods,
And mountains; and of all that we behold
From this green earth; of all the mighty world
Of eye, and ear—both what they half create,
And what perceive; well pleased to recognise
In nature and the language of the sense
The anchor of my purest thoughts, the nurse,
The guide, the guardian of my heart, and soul
Of all my moral being.
             Nor, perchance,
If I were not thus taught, should I the more
Suffer my genial spirits to decay:
For thou art with me here upon the banks
Of this fair river; thou my dearest friend,
My dear, dear friend; and in thy voice I catch
The language of my former heart, and read
My former pleasures in the shooting lights

Of thy wild eyes. Oh! yet a little while
May I behold in thee what I was once,
My dear, dear sister! and this prayer I make,
Knowing that Nature never did betray
The heart that loved her; 'tis her privilege,
Through all the years of this our life, to lead
From joy to joy: for she can so inform
The mind that is within us, so impress
With quietness and beauty, and so feed
With lofty thoughts, that neither evil tongues,
Rash judgments, nor the sneers of selfish men,
Nor greetings where no kindness is, nor all
The dreary intercourse of daily life,
Shall e'er prevail against us, or disturb
Our cheerful faith, that all which we behold
Is full of blessings. Therefore let the moon
Shine on thee in thy solitary walk;
And let the misty mountain winds be free
To blow against thee: and, in after years,
When these wild ecstasies shall be matured
Into a sober pleasure; when thy mind
Shall be a mansion for all lovely forms,
Thy memory be as a dwelling place
For all sweet sounds and harmonies; oh! then,
If solitude, or fear, or pain, or grief
Should be thy portion, with what healing thoughts
Of tender joy wilt thou remember me,
And these my exhortations! Nor, perchance—
If I should be where I no more can hear
Thy voice, nor catch from thy wild eyes these gleams
Of past existence—wilt thou then forget
That on the banks of this delightful stream
We stood together; and that I, so long
A worshipper of Nature, hither came
Unwearied in that service; rather say
With warmer love—oh! with far deeper zeal
Of holier love. Nor wilt thou then forget,
That after many wanderings, many years
Of absence, these steep woods and lofty cliffs,
And this green pastoral landscape, were to me
More dear, both for themselves and for thy sake!

WE ARE SEVEN

—A simple child,
That lightly draws its breath,
And feels its life in every limb,
What should it know of death?

I met a little cottage girl:
She was eight years old, she said;
Her hair was thick with many a curl
That clustered round her head.

She had a rustic, woodland air,
And she was wildly clad:
Her eyes were fair, and very fair;
—Her beauty made me glad.

"Sisters and brothers, little maid,
How many may you be?"
"How many? Seven in all," she said,
And wondering looked at me.

"And where are they? I pray you tell."
She answered, "Seven are we;
And two of us at Conway dwell,
And two are gone to sea.

"Two of us in the churchyard lie,
My sister and my brother;
And, in the churchyard cottage, I
Dwell near them with my mother."

"You say that two at Conway dwell,
And two are gone to sea,
Yet ye are seven! I pray you tell,
Sweet maid, how this may be."

Then did the little maid reply,
"Seven boys and girls are we;
Two of us in the churchyard lie,
Beneath the churchyard tree."

"You run about, my little maid,
Your limbs they are alive;
If two are in the churchyard laid,
Then ye are only five."

"Their graves are green, they may be seen,"
The little maid replied,
"Twelve steps or more from my mother's door,
And they are side by side.

"My stockings there I often knit,
My kerchief there I hem;
And there upon the ground I sit,
And sing a song to them.

"And often after sunset, sir,
When it is light and fair,
I take my little porringer,
And eat my supper there.

"The first that died was sister Jane;
In bed she moaning lay,
Till God released her of her pain;
And then she went away.

"So in the churchyard she was laid;
And, when the grass was dry,
Together round her grave we played,
My brother John and I.

"And when the ground was white with snow,
And I could run and slide,
My brother John was forced to go,
And he lies by her side."

"How many are you, then," said I,
"If they two are in heaven?"
Quick was the little maid's reply,
"O master! we are seven."

"But they are dead; those two are dead!
Their spirits are in heaven!"
'Twas throwing words away; for still
The little maid would have her will,
And said, "Nay, we are seven!"

SIR WALTER SCOTT
(1771–1832)

JOCK OF HAZELDEAN

"Why weep ye by the tide, lady?
  Why weep ye by the tide?
I'll wed ye to my youngest son,
  And ye sall be his bride;
And ye sall be his bride, lady,
  Sae comely to be seen"—
But ay she loot the tears down fa'
  For Jock of Hazeldean.

"Now let this wilfu' grief be done,
  And dry that cheek so pale;
Young Frank is chief of Errington
  And lord of Langley Dale;
His step is first in peaceful ha',
  His sword in battle keen"—
But ay she loot the tears down fa'
  For Jock of Hazeldean.

"A chain of gold ye sall not lack,
  Nor braid to bind your hair;
Nor mettled hound, nor managed hawk,
  Nor palfrey fresh and fair;
And you, the foremost o' them a',
  Shall ride our forest queen"—
But ay she loot the tears down fa'
  For Jock of Hazeldean.

The kirk was decked at morningtide,
  The tapers glimmered fair;
The priest and bridegroom wait the bride,
  And dame and knight are there.
They sought her baith by bower and ha';

The lady was not seen!
  She's o'er the Border and awa'
    Wi' Jock of Hazeldean.

PROUD MAISIE

Proud Maisie is in the wood
  Walking so early;
Sweet Robin sits on the bush,
  Singing so rarely.

"Tell me, thou bonny bird,
  When shall I marry me?"—
"When six braw gentlemen
  Kirkward shall carry ye."

"Who makes the bridal bed,
  Birdie, say truly?"—
"The grey-headed sexton
  That delves the grave duly."

"The glowworm o'er grave and stone
  Shall light thee steady,
The owl from the steeple sing,
  'Welcome, proud lady.' "

HELLVELLYN

I climbed the dark brow of the mighty Hellvellyn,
  Lakes and mountains beneath me gleamed misty and wide;
All was still, save by fits, when the eagle was yelling,
  And starting around me the echoes replied.
On the right, Striden-edge round the Red-tarn was bending,
And Catchedicam its left verge was defending,
One huge nameless rock in the front was ascending,
  When I marked the sad spot where the wanderer had died.

Dark green was that spot mid the brown mountain-heather,
　　Where the pilgrim of nature lay stretched in decay,
Like the corpse of an outcast abandoned to weather,
　　Till the mountain-winds wasted the tenantless clay.
Nor yet quite deserted, though lonely extended,
For, faithful in death, his mute favourite attended,
The much-loved remains of her master defended,
　　And chased the hill-fox and the raven away.

How long didst thou think that his silence was slumber?
　　When the wind waved his garment, how oft didst thou start?
How many long days and long weeks didst thou number,
　　Ere he faded before thee, the friend of thy heart?
And, oh, was it meet that—no requiem read o'er him,
No mother to weep, and no friend to deplore him,
And thou, little guardian, alone stretched before him—
　　Unhonoured the pilgrim from life should depart?

When a prince to the fate of the peasant has yielded,
　　The tapestry waves dark round the dim-lighted hall;
With scutcheons of silver the coffin is shielded,
　　And pages stand mute by the canopied pall:
Through the courts, at deep midnight, the torches are gleaming;
In the proudly-arched chapel the banners are beaming;
Far down the long aisle sacred music is streaming,
　　Lamenting a chief of the people should fall.

But meeter for thee, gentle lover of nature,
　　To lay down thy head like the meek mountain lamb,
When, wildered, he drops from some cliff huge in stature,
　　And draws his last sob by the side of his dam.
And more stately thy couch by this desert lake lying,
Thy obsequies sung by the gray plover flying,
With one faithful friend but to witness thy dying,
　　In the arms of Hellvellyn and Catchedicam.

SAMUEL TAYLOR COLERIDGE
(1772–1834)

THE RIME OF THE ANCIENT MARINER

Part I

It is an ancient mariner
And he stoppeth one of three.
—"By thy long grey beard and glittering eye,
Now wherefore stoppest thou me?

The bridegroom's doors are opened wide,
And I am next of kin;
The guests are met, the feast is set:
Mayst hear the merry din."

He holds him with his skinny hand,
"There was a ship," quoth he.
"Hold off! unhand me, grey-beard loon!"
Eftsoons his hand dropped he.

He holds him with his glittering eye—
The wedding-guest stood still,
And listens like a three-years' child:
The mariner hath his will.

The wedding-guest sat on a stone:
He cannot choose but hear;
And thus spake on that ancient man,
The bright-eyed mariner.

"The ship was cheered, the harbour cleared,
Merrily did we drop
Below the kirk, below the hill,
Below the lighthouse top.

The sun came up upon the left,
Out of the sea came he!
And he shone bright, and on the right
Went down into the sea.

Higher and higher every day,
Till over the mast at noon—"
The wedding-guest here beat his breast,
For he heard the loud bassoon.

The bride hath paced into the hall,
Red as a rose is she;
Nodding their heads before her goes
The merry minstrelsy.

The wedding-guest he beat his breast,
Yet he cannot choose but hear;
And thus spake on that ancient man,
The bright-eyed mariner.

"And now the storm-blast came, and he
Was tyrannous and strong;
He struck with his o'ertaking wings,
And chased us south along.

With sloping masts and dipping prow,
As who pursued with yell and blow
Still treads the shadow of his foe,
And forward bends his head,
The ship drove fast, loud roared the blast,
And southward aye we fled.

Listen, stranger! Mist and snow,
And it grew wondrous cold:
And ice mast-high came floating by,
As green as emerald.

And through the drifts the snowy clifts
Did send a dismal sheen:
Nor shapes of men nor beasts we ken—
The ice was all between.

The ice was here, the ice was there,
The ice was all around:
It cracked and growled, and roared and howled,
Like noises in a swound!

At length did cross an albatross,
Thorough the fog it came;
As if it had been a Christian soul,
We hailed it in God's name.

It ate the food it ne'er had eat,
And round and round it flew.
The ice did split with a thunder-fit;
The helmsman steered us through!

And a good south wind sprung up behind;
The albatross did follow,
And every day, for food or play,
Came to the mariners' hollo!

In mist or cloud, on mast or shroud,
It perched for vespers nine;
Whiles all the night, through fog-smoke white,
Glimmered the white moon-shine."

"God save thee, ancient mariner!
From the fiends, that plague thee thus!—
Why lookst thou so?" "With my crossbow
I shot the albatross.

Part II

The sun now rose upon the right:
Out of the sea came he,
Still hid in mist, and on the left
Went down into the sea.

And the good south wind still blew behind,
But no sweet bird did follow,
Nor any day for food or play
Came to the mariners' hollo!

And I had done an hellish thing,
And it would work 'em woe:
For all averred, I had killed the bird
That made the breeze to blow.
Ah wretch! said they, the bird to slay,
That made the breeze to blow!

Nor dim nor red, like an angel's head,
The glorious sun uprist:
Then all averred, I had killed the bird
That brought the fog and mist.
'Twas right, said they, such birds to slay,
That bring the fog and mist.

The fair breeze blew, the white foam flew,
The furrow followed free;
We were the first that ever burst
Into that silent sea.

Down dropped the breeze, the sails dropped down,
'Twas sad as sad could be;
And we did speak only to break
The silence of the sea!

All in a hot and copper sky,
The bloody sun, at noon,
Right up above the mast did stand,
No bigger than the moon.

Day after day, day after day,
We stuck, nor breath nor motion;
As idle as a painted ship
Upon a painted ocean.

Water, water, everywhere,
And all the boards did shrink;
Water, water, everywhere,
Nor any drop to drink.

The very deeps did rot: O Christ!
That ever this should be!

Yea, slimy things did crawl with legs
Upon the slimy sea.

About, about, in reel and rout
The death-fires danced at night;
The water, like a witch's oils,
Burnt green, and blue and white.

And some in dreams assured were
Of the spirit that plagued us so;
Nine fathom deep he had followed us
From the land of mist and snow.

And every tongue, through utter drought,
Was withered at the root;
We could not speak, no more than if
We had been choked with soot.

Ah! wel-a-day! what evil looks
Had I from old and young!
Instead of the cross, the albatross
About my neck was hung.

Part III

There passed a weary time. Each throat
Was parched, and glazed each eye.
A weary time! A weary time!
How glazed each weary eye,
When looking westward, I beheld
A something in the sky.

At first it seemed a little speck,
And then it seemed a mist;
It moved and moved, and took at last
A certain shape, I wist.

A speck, a mist, a shape, I wist!
And still it neared and neared:
As if it dodged a water sprite,
It plunged and tacked and veered.

With throats unslaked, with black lips baked,
We could nor laugh nor wail;
Through utter drouth all dumb we stood!
I bit my arm, I sucked the blood,
And cried, A sail! a sail!

With throats unslaked, with black lips baked,
Agape they heard me call:
Gramercy! they for joy did grin,
And all at once their breath drew in,
As they were drinking all.

See! see! (I cried) she tacks no more!
Hither to work us weal;
Without a breeze, without a tide,
She steadies with upright keel!

The western wave was all aflame.
The day was well nigh done!
Almost upon the western wave
Rested the broad bright sun;
When that strange shape drove suddenly
Betwixt us and the sun.

And straight the sun was flecked with bars,
(Heaven's mother send us grace!)
As if through a dungeon grate he peered
With broad and burning face.

Alas! (thought I, and my heart beat loud)
How fast she nears and nears!
Are those *her* sails that glance in the sun,
Like restless gossameres?

Are those *her* ribs through which the sun
Did peer, as through a grate?
And is that woman all her crew?
Is that a Death? and are there two?
Is Death that woman's mate?

Her lips were red, *her* looks were free,
Her locks were yellow as gold:
Her skin was as white as leprosy,
The nightmare Life-in-Death was she,
Who thicks man's blood with cold.

The naked hulk alongside came,
And the twain were casting dice;
'The game is done! I've won! I've won!'
Quoth she, and whistles thrice.

The sun's rim dips; the stars rush out:
At one stride comes the dark;
With far-heard whisper, o'er the sea,
Off shot the spectre bark.

We listened and looked sideways up!
Fear at my heart, as at a cup,
My lifeblood seemed to sip!
The stars were dim, and thick the night,
The steersman's face by his lamp gleamed white;
From the sails the dews did drip—
Till clomb above the eastern bar
The horned moon, with one bright star
Within the nether tip.

One after one, by the star-dogged moon,
Too quick for groan or sigh,
Each turned his face with ghastly pang,
And cursed me with his eye.

Four times fifty living men,
(And I heard nor sigh nor groan)
With heavy thump, a lifeless lump,
They dropped down one by one.

Their souls did from their bodies fly—
They fled to bliss or woe!
And every soul, it passed me by,
Like the whizz of my crossbow!"

Part IV

"I fear thee, ancient mariner!
I fear thy skinny hand!
And thou art long, and lank, and brown,
As is the ribbed sea-sand.

I fear thee and thy glittering eye,
And thy skinny hand, so brown."—
"Fear not, fear not, thou wedding-guest!
This body dropped not down.

Alone, alone, all, all alone,
Alone on a wide wide sea!
And never a saint took pity on
My soul in agony.

The many men, so beautiful!
And they all dead did lie:
And a thousand thousand slimy things
Lived on; and so did I.

I looked upon the rotting sea,
And drew my eyes away;
I looked upon the rotting deck,
And there the dead men lay.

I looked to heaven, and tried to pray;
But or ever a prayer had gushed,
A wicked whisper came, and made
My heart as dry as dust.

I closed my lids, and kept them close,
Till the balls like pulses beat;
For the sky and the sea, and the sea and the sky
Lay like a load on my weary eye,
And the dead were at my feet.

The cold sweat melted from their limbs,
Nor rot nor reek did they:
The look with which they looked on me
Had never passed away.

An orphan's curse would drag to hell
A spirit from on high;
But oh! more horrible than that
Is the curse in a dead man's eye!
Seven days, seven nights, I saw that curse,
And yet I could not die.

The moving moon went up the sky,
And nowhere did abide:
Softly she was going up,
And a star or two beside—

Her beams bemocked the sultry main,
Like April hoar-frost spread;
But where the ship's huge shadow lay,
The charmed water burnt alway
A still and awful red.

Beyond the shadow of the ship,
I watched the water snakes:
They moved in tracks of shining white,
And when they reared, the elfish light
Fell off in hoary flakes.

Within the shadow of the ship
I watched their rich attire:
Blue, glossy green, and velvet black,
They coiled and swam; and every track
Was a flash of golden fire.

O happy living things! No tongue
Their beauty might declare:
A spring of love gushed from my heart,
And I blessed them unaware:
Sure my kind saint took pity on me,
And I blessed them unaware.

The selfsame moment I could pray;
And from my neck so free
The albatross fell off, and sank
Like lead into the sea.

Part V

Oh sleep! it is a gentle thing,
Beloved from pole to pole!
To Mary-Queen the praise be given!
She sent the gentle sleep from heaven,
That slid into my soul.

The silly buckets on the deck,
That had so long remained,
I dreamt that they were filled with dew;
And when I awoke, it rained.

My lips were wet, my throat was cold,
My garments all were dank;
Sure I had drunken in my dreams,
And still my body drank.

I moved, and could not feel my limbs:
I was so light—almost
I thought that I had died in sleep,
And was a blessed ghost.

And soon I heard a roaring wind:
It did not come anear;
But with its sound it shook the sails,
That were so thin and sere.

The upper air bursts into life!
And a hundred fire-flags sheen,
To and fro they were hurried about!
And to and fro, and in and out,
The wan stars danced between.

And the coming wind did roar more loud,
And the sails did sigh like sedge;
And the rain poured down from one black cloud;
The moon was at its edge.

The thick black cloud was cleft, and still
The moon was at its side:
Like waters shot from some high crag,

The lightning fell with never a jag,
A river steep and wide.

The loud wind never reached the ship,
Yet now the ship moved on!
Beneath the lightning and the moon
The dead men gave a groan.

They groaned, they stirred, they all uprose,
Nor spake, nor moved their eyes;
It had been strange, even in a dream,
To have seen those dead men rise.

The helmsman steered, the ship moved on;
Yet never a breeze up-blew;
The mariners all 'gan work the ropes,
Where they were wont to do;
They raised their limbs like lifeless tools—
We were a ghastly crew.

The body of my brother's son
Stood by me, knee to knee:
The body and I pulled at one rope,
But he said nought to me."

"I fear thee, ancient mariner!"
"Be calm, thou wedding-guest!
'Twas not those souls that fled in pain,
Which to their corses came again,
But a troop of spirits blessed.

For when it dawned—they dropped their arms,
And clustered round the mast;
Sweet sounds rose slowly through their mouths,
And from their bodies passed.

Around, around, flew each sweet sound,
Then darted to the sun;

Slowly the sounds came back again,
Now mixed, now one by one.

Sometimes a-dropping from the sky
I heard the skylark sing;
Sometimes all little birds that are,
How they seemed to fill the sea and air
With their sweet jargoning!

And now 'twas like all instruments,
Now like a lonely flute;
And now it is an angel's song,
That makes the heavens be mute.

It ceased; yet still the sails made on
A pleasant noise till noon,
A noise like of a hidden brook
In the leafy month of June,
That to the sleeping woods all night
Singeth a quiet tune.

Till noon we silently sailed on,
Yet never a breeze did breathe:
Slowly and smoothly went the ship,
Moved onward from beneath.

Under the keel nine fathom deep,
From the land of mist and snow,
The spirit slid: and it was he
That made the ship to go.
The sails at noon left off their tune,
And the ship stood still also.

The sun, right up above the mast,
Had fixed her to the ocean:
But in a minute she 'gan stir,
With a short uneasy motion—
Backwards and forwards half her length
With a short uneasy motion.

Then like a pawing horse let go,
She made a sudden bound:

It flung the blood into my head,
And I fell down in a swound.

How long in that same fit I lay,
I have not to declare;
But ere my living life returned,
I heard and in my soul discerned
Two voices in the air.

'Is it he?' quoth one, 'Is this the man?
By him who died on cross,
With his cruel bow he laid full low
The harmless albatross.

The spirit who bideth by himself
In the land of mist and snow,
He loved the bird that loved the man
Who shot him with his bow.'

The other was a softer voice,
As soft as honeydew:
Quoth he, 'The man hath penance done,
And penance more will do.'

Part VI

FIRST VOICE

'But tell me, tell me! speak again,
Thy soft response renewing—
What makes that ship drive on so fast?
What is the ocean doing?'

SECOND VOICE

'Still as a slave before his lord,
The ocean hath no blast;
His great bright eye most silently
Up to the moon is cast—

If he may know which way to go;
For she guides him smooth or grim.

387

See, brother, see! how graciously
She looketh down on him.'

FIRST VOICE

'But why drives on that ship so fast,
Without or wave or wind?'

SECOND VOICE

'The air is cut away before,
And closes from behind.

Fly, brother, fly! more high, more high!
Or we shall be belated:
For slow and slow that ship will go,
When the mariner's trance is abated.'

I woke, and we were sailing on
As in a gentle weather:
'Twas night, calm night, the moon was high;
The dead men stood together.

All stood together on the deck,
For a charnel-dungeon fitter:
All fixed on me their stony eyes,
That in the moon did glitter.

The pang, the curse, with which they died,
Had never passed away:
I could not draw my eyes from theirs,
Nor turn them up to pray.

And now this spell was snapped: once more
I viewed the ocean green,
And looked far forth, yet little saw
Of what had else been seen—

Like one, that on a lonesome road
Doth walk in fear and dread,
And having once turned round walks on,
And turns no more his head;

388

Because he knows a frightful fiend
Doth close behind him tread.

But soon there breathed a wind on me,
Nor sound nor motion made:
Its path was not upon the sea,
In ripple or in shade.

It raised my hair, it fanned my cheek
Like a meadow-gale of spring—
It mingled strangely with my fears,
Yet it felt like a welcoming.

Swiftly, swiftly flew the ship,
Yet she sailed softly too:
Sweetly, sweetly blew the breeze—
On me alone it blew.

O dream of joy! is this indeed
The lighthouse top I see?
Is this the hill? is this the kirk?
Is this mine own country?

We drifted o'er the harbour bar,
And I with sobs did pray—
O let me be awake, my God!
Or let me sleep alway!

The harbour bay was clear as glass,
So smoothly it was strewn!
And on the bay the moonlight lay,
And the shadow of the moon.

The rock shone bright, the kirk no less,
That stands above the rock:
The moonlight steeped in silentness
The steady weathercock.

And the bay was white with silent light,
Till rising from the same,
Full many shapes, that shadows were,
In crimson colours came.

A little distance from the prow
Those crimson shadows were:
I turned my eyes upon the deck—
O Christ! what saw I there!

Each corse lay flat, lifeless and flat,
And, by the holy rood!
A man all light, a seraph man,
On every corse there stood.

This seraph band, each waved his hand:
It was a heavenly sight!
They stood as signals to the land,
Each one a lovely light;

This seraph band, each waved his hand,
No voice did they impart—
No voice; but oh! the silence sank
Like music on my heart.

But soon I heard the dash of oars,
I heard the pilot's cheer;
My head was turned perforce away
And I saw a boat appear.

The pilot and the pilot's boy,
I heard them coming fast:
Dear Lord in heaven! it was a joy
The dead men could not blast.

I saw a third—I heard his voice:
It is the hermit good!
He singeth loud his godly hymns
That he makes in the wood.
He'll shrieve my soul, he'll wash away
The albatross's blood.

Part VII

This hermit good lives in that wood
Which slopes down to the sea.
How loudly his sweet voice he rears!

He loves to talk with mariners
That come from a far country.

He kneels at morn, and noon, and eve—
He hath a cushion plump:
It is the moss that wholly hides
The rotted old oak stump.

The skiff boat neared: I heard them talk,
'Why, this is strange, I trow!
Where are those lights so many and fair,
That signal made but now?'

'Strange, by my faith!' the hermit said—
'And they answered not our cheer!
The planks look warped! and see those sails,
How thin they are and sere!
I never saw aught like to them,
Unless perchance it were

Brown skeletons of leaves that lag
My forest-brook along;
When the ivy tod is heavy with snow,
And the owlet whoops to the wolf below,
That eats the she-wolf's young.'

'Dear Lord! it hath a fiendish look,'
The pilot made reply,
'I am a-feared'—'Push on, push on!'
Said the hermit cheerily.

The boat came closer to the ship,
But I nor spake nor stirred;
The boat came close beneath the ship,
And straight a sound was heard.

Under the water it rumbled on,
Still louder and more dread:
It reached the ship, it split the bay;
The ship went down like lead.

Stunned by that loud and dreadful sound,
Which sky and ocean smote,
Like one that hath been seven days drowned
My body lay afloat;
But swift as dreams, myself I found
Within the pilot's boat.

Upon the whirl, where sank the ship,
The boat spun round and round;
And all was still, save that the hill
Was telling of the sound.

I moved my lips—the pilot shrieked
And fell down in a fit;
The holy hermit raised his eyes,
And prayed where he did sit.

I took the oars: the pilot's boy,
Who now doth crazy go,
Laughed loud and long, and all the while
His eyes went to and fro.
'Ha! ha!' quoth he, 'full plain I see,
The devil knows how to row.'

And now, all in my own country,
I stood on the firm land!
The hermit stepped forth from the boat,
And scarcely he could stand.

'Oh shrieve me, shrieve me, holy man!'
The hermit crossed his brow.
'Say quick,' quoth he, 'I bid thee say—
What manner of man art thou?'

Forthwith this frame of mine was wrenched
With a woeful agony,
Which forced me to begin my tale;
And then it left me free.

Since then, at an uncertain hour,
That agony returns:

And till my ghastly tale is told,
This heart within me burns.

I pass, like night, from land to land;
I have strange power of speech;
The moment that his face I see,
I know the man that must hear me:
To him my tale I teach.

What loud uproar bursts from that door!
The wedding-guests are there:
But in the garden-bower the bride
And bridemaids singing are:
And hark the little vesper bell,
Which biddeth me to prayer!

O wedding-guest! This soul hath been
Alone on a wide wide sea:
So lonely 'twas, that God himself
Scarce seemed there to be.

Oh sweeter than the marriage feast,
'Tis sweeter far to me,
To walk together to the kirk
With a goodly company!—

To walk together to the kirk,
And all together pray,
While each to his great Father bends,
Old men, and babes, and loving friends
And youths and maidens gay!

Farewell, farewell! but this I tell
To thee, thou wedding-guest!
He prayeth well, who loveth well
Both man and bird and beast.

He prayeth best, who loveth best
All things both great and small;
For the dear God who loveth us,
He made and loveth all."

The mariner, whose eye is bright,
Whose beard with age is hoar,
Is gone: and now the wedding-guest
Turned from the bridegroom's door.

He went like one that hath been stunned,
And is of sense forlorn:
A sadder and a wiser man,
He rose the morrow morn.

KUBLA KHAN

In Xanadu did Kubla Khan
A stately pleasure-dome decree:
Where Alph, the sacred river, ran
Through caverns measureless to man
   Down to a sunless sea.
So twice five miles of fertile ground
With walls and towers were girdled round:
And there were gardens bright with sinuous rills,
Where blossomed many an incense-bearing tree;
And here were forests ancient as the hills,
Enfolding sunny spots of greenery.

But, oh! that deep romantic chasm which slanted
Down the green hill athwart a cedarn cover!
A savage place! as holy and enchanted
As e'er beneath a waning moon was haunted
By woman wailing for her demon-lover!
And from this chasm, with ceaseless turmoil seething,
As if this earth in fast thick pants were breathing,
A mighty fountain momently was forced:
Amid whose swift half-intermitted burst
Huge fragments vaulted like rebounding hail,
Or chaffy grain beneath the thresher's flail:
And 'mid these dancing rocks at once and ever
It flung up momently the sacred river.
Five miles meandering with a mazy motion
Through wood and dale the sacred river ran,

Then reached the caverns measureless to man,
And sank in tumult to a lifeless ocean:
And 'mid this tumult Kubla heard from far
Ancestral voices prophesying war!
  The shadow of the dome of pleasure
    Floated midway on the waves;
  Where was heard the mingled measure
    From the fountain and the caves.
It was a miracle of rare device,
A sunny pleasure-dome with caves of ice!

    A damsel with a dulcimer
    In a vision once I saw;
    It was an Abyssinian maid,
    And on her dulcimer she played,
    Singing of Mount Abora.
    Could I revive within me
    Her symphony and song,
    To such a deep delight 'twould win me,
That with music loud and long,
I would build that dome in air,
That sunny dome! those caves of ice!
And all who heard should see them there,
And all should cry, Beware! Beware!
His flashing eyes, his floating hair!
Weave a circle round him thrice,
And close your eyes with holy dread,
For he on honey-dew hath fed,
And drunk the milk of Paradise.

WORK WITHOUT HOPE

All nature seems at work. Slugs leave their lair—
The bees are stirring—birds are on the wing—
And winter slumbering in the open air
Wears on his smiling face a dream of spring!
And I the while, the sole unbusy thing,
Nor honey make, nor pair, nor build, nor sing.

Yet well I ken the banks where amaranths blow,
Have traced the fount whence streams of nectar flow.
Bloom, O ye amaranths! Bloom for whom ye may,
For me ye bloom not! Glide, rich streams, away!
With lips unbrightened, wreathless brow, I stroll:
And would you learn the spells that drowse my soul?
Work without hope draws nectar in a sieve,
And hope without an object cannot live.

THE PAINS OF SLEEP

Ere on my bed my limbs I lay,
It hath not been my use to pray
With moving lips or bended knees;
But silently, by slow degrees,
My spirit I to love compose,
In humble trust mine eyelids close,
With reverential resignation,
No wish conceived, no thought expressed,
Only a sense of supplication;
A sense o'er all my soul impressed,
That I am weak, yet not unblessed,
Since in me, round me, everywhere
Eternal strength and wisdom are.

But yesternight I prayed aloud
In anguish and in agony,
Upstarting from the fiendish crowd
Of shapes and thoughts that tortured me:
A lurid light, a trampling throng,
Sense of intolerable wrong,
And whom I scorned, those only strong!

Thirst of revenge, the powerless will
Still baffled, and yet burning still!
Desire with loathing strangely mixed
On wild or hateful objects fixed.
Fantastic passions! Maddening brawl!
And shame and terror over all!

Deeds to be hid which were not hid,
Which all confused I could not know
Whether I suffered, or I did;
For all seemed guilt, remorse or woe,
My own or others still the same
Life-stifling fear, soul-stifling shame.

So two nights passed: the night's dismay
Saddened and stunned the coming day.
Sleep, the wide blessing, seemed to me
Distemper's worst calamity.
The third night, when my own loud scream
Had waked me from the fiendish dream,
O'ercome with sufferings strange and wild,
I wept as I had been a child;
And having thus by tears subdued
My anguish to a milder mood,
Such punishments, I said, were due
To natures deepliest stained with sin,
For aye entempesting anew
The unfathomable hell within,
The horror of their deeds to view,
To know and loathe, yet wish and do!
Such griefs with such men well agree,
But wherefore, wherefore fall on me?
To be beloved is all I need,
And whom I love, I love indeed.

ROBERT SOUTHEY
(1774–1843)

My days among the dead are past;
 Around me I behold,
Where'er these casual eyes are cast,
 The mighty minds of old;
My never-failing friends are they,
With whom I converse day by day.

With them I take delight in weal,
 And seek relief in woe;
And while I understand and feel
 How much to them I owe,
My cheeks have often been bedewed
With tears of thoughtful gratitude.

My thoughts are with the dead; with them
 I live in long-past years,
Their virtues love, their faults condemn,
 Partake their hopes and fears;
And from their lessons seek and find
Instruction with an humble mind.

My hopes are with the dead, anon
 My place with them will be,
And I with them shall travel on
 Through all futurity;
Yet leaving here a name, I trust,
That will not perish in the dust.

THE CATARACT OF LODORE

"How does the water
Come down at Lodore?"
My little boy asked me
Thus, once on a time.
And moreover he tasked me
To tell him in rhyme.
Anon at the word,
There first came one daughter
And then came another,
To second and third
The request of their brother,
And to hear how the water
Comes down at Lodore,
With its rush and its roar,
As many a time
They had seen it before.
So I told them in rhyme,
For of rhymes I had store:
And 'twas in my vocation
For their recreation
That so I should sing,
Because I was Laureate
To them and the King.

From its sources which well
In the tarn on the fell;
From its fountains
In the mountains,
Its rills and its gills;
Through moss and through brake,
It runs and it creeps
For awhile, till it sleeps
In its own little lake.
And thence at departing,
Awakening and starting,
It runs through the reeds
And away it proceeds,
Through meadow and glade,
In sun and in shade,
And through the wood-shelter,

399

Among crags in its flurry,
Helter-skelter,
Hurry-scurry.
Here it comes sparkling,
And there it lies darkling;
Now smoking and frothing
Its tumult and wrath in,
Till in this rapid race
On which it is bent,
It reaches the place
Of its steep descent.

The cataract strong
Then plunges along,
Striking and raging
As if a war waging
Its caverns and rocks among:
Rising and leaping,
Sinking and creeping,
Swelling and sweeping,
Showering and springing,
Flying and flinging,
Writhing and ringing,
Eddying and whisking,
Spouting and frisking,
Turning and twisting,
Around and around
With endless rebound!
Smiting and fighting,
A sight to delight in;
Confounding, astounding,
Dizzying and deafening the ear with its sound!

Collecting, projecting,
Receding and speeding,
And shocking and rocking,
And darting and parting,
And threading and spreading,
And whizzing and hissing,
And dripping and skipping,
And hitting and splitting,
And shining and twining,

And rattling and battling,
And shaking and quaking,
And pouring and roaring,
And waving and raving,
And tossing and crossing,
And flowing and going,
And running and stunning,
And foaming and roaming,
And dinning and spinning,
And dropping and hopping,
And working and jerking,
And guggling and struggling,
And heaving and cleaving,
And moaning and groaning,
And glittering and frittering,
And gathering and feathering,
And whitening and brightening,
And quivering and shivering,
And hurrying and scurrying,
And thundering and floundering;

Dividing and gliding and sliding,
And falling and brawling and sprawling,
And driving and riving and striving,
And sprinkling and twinkling and wrinkling,
And sounding and bounding and rounding,
And bubbling and troubling and doubling,
And grumbling and rumbling and tumbling,
And clattering and battering and shattering;

Retreating and beating and meeting and sheeting,
Delaying and straying and playing and spraying,
Advancing and prancing and glancing and dancing,
Recoiling, turmoiling and toiling and boiling,
And gleaming and streaming and steaming and beaming,
And rushing and flushing and brushing and gushing,
And flapping and rapping and clapping and slapping
And curling and whirling and purling and twirling,
And thumping and plumping and bumping and jumping,

And dashing and flashing and splashing and clashing;
And so never ending, but always descending,
Sounds and motions forever and ever are blending,
All at once and all o'er, with a mighty uproar,
And this way the water comes down at Lodore.

WALTER SAVAGE LANDOR
(1775–1864)

ROSE AYLMER

Ah what avails the sceptred race,
    Ah what the form divine!
What every virtue, every grace!
    Rose Aylmer, all were thine.

Rose Aylmer, whom these wakeful eyes
    May weep, but never see,
A night of memories and of sighs
    I consecrate to thee.

*

Mother, I cannot mind my wheel;
    My fingers ache, my lips are dry.
Oh! if you felt the pain I feel!
    But oh, who ever felt as I?

No longer could I doubt him true;
    All other men may use deceit.
He always said my eyes were blue,
    And often swore my lips were sweet.

*

Mild is the parting year, and sweet
    The odour of the falling spray;
Life passes on more rudely fleet,
    And balmless is its closing day.

I wait its close, I court its gloom,
  But mourn that never must there fall
Or on my breast or on my tomb
  The tear that would have soothed it all.

THOMAS MOORE
(1779–1852)

from *LALLA ROOKH*

THE LIGHT OF THE HAREM

Who has not heard of the Vale of Cashmere,
    With its roses, the brightest that earth ever gave,
Its temples and grottos, and fountains as clear
    As the love-lighted eyes that hang over their wave?
Oh! to see it at sunset—when warm o'er the lake
    Its splendour at parting a summer eve throws,
Like a bride full of blushes, when lingering to take
    A last look of her mirror at night ere she goes!—
When the shrines through the foliage are gleaming half shown,
And each hallows the hour by some rites of its own.
Here the music of prayer from a minaret swells,
    Here the magian his urn full of perfume is swinging,
And here at the altar, a zone of sweet bells
    Round the waist of some fair Indian dancer is ringing.
Or to see it by moonlight—when mellowly shines
The light o'er its palaces, gardens and shrines;
When the water-falls gleam like a quick fall of stars,
And the nightingales' hymn from the Isle of Chenars
Is broken by laughs and wild echoes of feet
From the cool, shining walks where the young people meet—
Or at morn when the magic of day-light awakes
A new wonder each minute, as slowly it breaks,
Hills, cupolas, fountains, called forth every one
Out of darkness, as they were just born of the sun.
When the spirit of Fragrance is up with the day,
From his harem of night-flowers stealing away;
And the wind full of wantonness, woos, like a lover,
The young aspen-trees till they tremble all over.
When the east is as warm as the light of first hopes,
    And day, with its banner of radiance unfurled,

Shines in through the mountainous portal that opes,
Sublime, from that valley of bliss to the world!

BELIEVE ME,
IF ALL THOSE ENDEARING YOUNG CHARMS

Believe me, if all those endearing young charms,
 Which I gaze on so fondly today,
Were to change by tomorrow, and fleet in my arms,
 Like fairy-gifts fading away,
Thou wouldst still be adored, as this moment thou art,
 Let thy loveliness fade as it will,
And around the dear ruin each wish of my heart
 Would entwine itself verdantly still.

It is not while beauty and youth are thine own,
 And thy cheeks unprofaned by a tear
That the fervour and faith of a soul can be known,
 To which time will but make thee more dear;
No, the heart that has truly loved never forgets,
 But as truly loves on to the close,
As the sunflower turns on her god, when he sets,
 The same look which she turned when he rose.

LEIGH HUNT
(1784–1859)

RONDEAU

Jenny kissed me when we met,
    Jumping from the chair she sat in;
Time, you thief, who love to get
    Sweets into your list, put that in:
Say I'm weary, say I'm sad,
    Say that health and wealth have missed me,
Say I'm growing old, but add:
    Jenny kissed me.

GEORGE GORDON, LORD BYRON
(1788–1824)

INSCRIPTION ON THE MONUMENT OF A
NEWFOUNDLAND DOG

When some proud son of man returns to earth,
Unknown to glory, but upheld by birth,
The sculptor's art exhausts the pomp of woe,
And storied urns record who rest below:
When all is done, upon the tomb is seen,
Not what he was, but what he should have been:
But the poor dog, in life the firmest friend,
The first to welcome, foremost to defend,
Whose honest heart is still his master's own,
Who labours, fights, lives, breathes for him alone,
Unhonoured falls, unnoticed all his worth,
Denied in heaven the soul he held on earth,
While man, vain insect! hopes to be forgiven,
And claims himself a sole exclusive heaven.
Oh man! thou feeble tenant of an hour,
Debased by slavery, or corrupt by power,
Who knows thee well must quit thee with disgust,
Degraded mass of animated dust!
Thy love is lust, thy friendship all a cheat,
Thy smiles hypocrisy, thy words deceit!
By nature vile, ennobled but by name,
Each kindred brute might bid thee blush for shame.
Ye! who perchance behold this simple urn,
Pass on—it honours none you wish to mourn:
To mark a friend's remains these stones arise;
I never knew but one—and here he lies.

THE DREAM

I

Our life is two-fold: sleep hath its own world,
A boundary between the things misnamed
Death and existence: sleep hath its own world,
And a wide realm of wild reality.
And dreams in their development have breath,
And tears, and tortures, and the touch of joy;
They leave a weight upon our waking thoughts,
They take a weight from off our waking toils,
They do divide our being; they become
A portion of ourselves as of our time,
And look like heralds of eternity;
They pass like spirits of the past, they speak
Like sibyls of the future: they have power—
The tyranny of pleasure and of pain;
They make us what we were not—what they will,
And shake us with the vision that's gone by,
The dread of vanished shadows—are they so?
Is not the past all shadow? What are they?
Creations of the mind? The mind can make
Substance, and people planets of its own
With beings brighter than have been, and give
A breath to forms which can outlive all flesh.
I would recall a vision which I dreamed
Perchance in sleep—for in itself a thought,
A slumbering thought, is capable of years,
And curdles a long life into one hour.

II

I saw two beings in the hues of youth
Standing upon a hill, a gentle hill,
Green and of mild declivity, the last
As 'twere the cape of a long ridge of such,
Save that there was no sea to lave its base,
But a most living landscape, and the wave
Of woods and corn-fields, and the abodes of men
Scattered at intervals, and wreathing smoke

Arising from such rustic roofs; the hill
Was crowned with a peculiar diadem
Of trees, in circular array, so fixed,
Not by the sport of nature, but of man:
These two, a maiden and a youth, were there
Gazing—the one on all that was beneath
Fair as herself—but the boy gazed on her;
And both were young, and one was beautiful:
And both were young—yet not alike in youth.
As the sweet moon on the horizon's verge,
The maid was on the eve of womanhood;
The boy had fewer summers, but his heart
Had far outgrown his years, and to his eye
There was but one beloved face on earth,
And that was shining on him: he had looked
Upon it till it could not pass away;
He had no breath, no being, but in hers;
She was his voice; he did not speak to her,
But trembled on her words; she was his sight,
For his eye followed hers, and saw with hers,
Which coloured all his objects—he had ceased
To live within himself; she was his life,
The ocean to the river of his thoughts,
Which terminated all: upon a tone,
A touch of hers, his blood would ebb and flow,
And his cheek change tempestuously—his heart
Unknowing of its cause of agony.
But she in these fond feelings had no share:
Her sighs were not for him; to her he was
Even as a brother—but no more; 'twas much,
For brotherless she was, save in the name
Her infant friendship had bestowed on him;
Herself the solitary scion left
Of a time-honoured race. It was a name
Which pleased him, and yet pleased him not—and why?
Time taught him a deep answer—when she loved
Another; even *now* she loved another,
And on the summit of that hill she stood
Looking afar if yet her lover's steed
Kept pace with her expectancy, and flew.

III

A change came o'er the spirit of my dream.
There was an ancient mansion, and before
Its walls there was a steed caparisoned;
Within an antique oratory stood
The boy of whom I spake; he was alone,
And pale, and pacing to and fro: anon
He sate him down, and seized a pen, and traced
Words which I could not guess of; then he leaned
His bowed head on his hands, and shook as 'twere
With a convulsion—then arose again,
And with his teeth and quivering hands did tear
What he had written, but he shed no tears,
And he did calm himself, and fix his brow
Into a kind of quiet: as he paused,
The lady of his love re-entered there;
She was serene and smiling then, and yet
She knew she was by him beloved—she knew,
For quickly comes such knowledge, that his heart
Was darkened with her shadow, and she saw
That he was wretched, but she saw not all.
He rose, and with a cold and gentle grasp
He took her hand; a moment o'er his face
A tablet of unutterable thoughts
Was traced, and then it faded, as it came;
He dropped the hand he held, and with slow steps
Retired, but not as bidding her adieu,
For they did part with mutual smiles; he passed
From out the massy gate of that old Hall,
And mounting on his steed he went his way;
And ne'er repassed that hoary threshold more.

IV

A change came o'er the spirit of my dream.
The boy was sprung to manhood: in the wilds
Of fiery climes he made himself a home,
And his soul drank their sunbeams: he was girt
With strange and dusky aspects; he was not
Himself like what he had been; on the sea
And on the shore he was a wanderer.

411

There was a mass of many images
Crowded like waves upon me, but he was
A part of all; and in the last he lay
Reposing from the noontide sultriness,
Couched among fallen columns, in the shade
Of ruined walls that had survived the names
Of those who reared them; by his sleeping side
Stood camels grazing, and some goodly steeds
Were fastened near a fountain; and a man
Clad in a flowing garb did watch the while,
While many of his tribe slumbered around:
And they were canopied by the blue sky,
So cloudless, clear, and purely beautiful,
That God alone was to be seen in heaven.

V

A change came o'er the spirit of my dream.
The lady of his love was wed with one
Who did not love her better: in her home,
A thousand leagues from his, her native home,
She dwelt, begirt with growing infancy,
Daughters and sons of beauty, but behold!
Upon her face there was the tint of grief,
The settled shadow of an inward strife,
And an unquiet drooping of the eye,
As if its lid were charged with unshed tears.
What could her grief be?—she had all she loved,
And he who had so loved her was not there
To trouble with bad hopes, or evil wish,
Or ill-repressed affliction, her pure thoughts.
What could her grief be?—she had loved him not,
Nor given him cause to deem himself beloved,
Nor could he be a part of that which preyed
Upon her mind—a spectre of the past.

VI

A change came o'er the spirit of my dream.
The wanderer was returned. I saw him stand
Before an altar—with a gentle bride;
Her face was fair, but was not that which made
The starlight of his boyhood; as he stood

412

Even at the altar, o'er his brow there came
The self-same aspect, and the quivering shock
That in the antique oratory shook
His bosom in its solitude; and then—
As in that hour—a moment o'er his face
The tablet of unutterable thoughts
Was traced, and then it faded as it came,
And he stood calm and quiet, and he spoke
The fitting vows, but heard not his own words,
And all things reeled around him; he could see
Not that which was, nor that which should have been—
But the old mansion, and the accustomed hall,
And the remembered chambers, and the place,
The day, the hour, the sunshine, and the shade,
All things pertaining to that place and hour,
And her who was his destiny—came back
And thrust themselves between him and the light:
What business had they there at such a time?

VII

A change came o'er the spirit of my dream.
The lady of his love: oh! she was changed
As by the sickness of the soul; her mind
Had wandered from its dwelling, and her eyes
They had not their own lustre, but the look
Which is not of the earth; she was become
The queen of a fantastic realm; her thoughts
Were combinations of disjointed things;
And forms impalpable and unperceived
Of others' sight familiar were to hers.
And this the world calls frenzy; but the wise
Have a far deeper madness, and the glance
Of melancholy is a fearful gift;
What is it but the telescope of truth?
Which strips the distance of its fantasies,
And brings life near in utter nakedness,
Making the cold reality too real!

VIII

A change came o'er the spirit of my dream.
The wanderer was alone as heretofore,

413

The beings which surrounded him were gone,
Or were at war with him; he was a mark
For blight and desolation, compassed round
With hatred and contention; pain was mixed
In all which was served up to him, until,
Like to the Pontic monarch of old days,
He fed on poisons, and they had no power,
But were a kind of nutriment; he lived
Through that which had been death to many men,
And made him friends of mountains: with the stars
And the quick spirit of the universe
He held his dialogues; and they did teach
To him the magic of their mysteries;
To him the book of night was opened wide,
And voices from the deep abyss revealed
A marvel and a secret—be it so.

IX

My dream was past; it had no further change.
It was of a strange order, that the doom
Of these two creatures should be thus traced out
Almost like a reality—the one
To end in madness—both in misery.

DARKNESS

I had a dream, which was not all a dream.
The bright sun was extinguished, and the stars
Did wander darkling in the eternal space,
Rayless, and pathless, and the icy earth
Swung blind and blackening in the moonless air;
Morn came and went—and came, and brought no day,
And men forgot their passions in the dread
Of this their desolation; and all hearts
Were chilled into a selfish prayer for light:
And they did live by watchfires—and the thrones,
The palaces of crowned kings—the huts,
The habitations of all things which dwell,
Were burnt for beacons; cities were consumed,

And men were gathered round their blazing homes
To look once more into each other's face;
Happy were those who dwelt within the eye
Of the volcanos, and their mountain-torch:
A fearful hope was all the world contained;
Forests were set on fire—but hour by hour
They fell and faded—and the crackling trunks
Extinguished with a crash—and all was black.
The brows of men by the despairing light
Wore an unearthly aspect, as by fits
The flashes fell upon them; some lay down
And hid their eyes and wept; and some did rest
Their chins upon their clenched hands, and smiled;
And others hurried to and fro, and fed
Their funeral piles with fuel, and looked up
With mad disquietude on the dull sky,
The pall of a past world; and then again
With curses cast them down upon the dust,
And gnashed their teeth and howled: the wild birds shrieked
And, terrified, did flutter on the ground,
And flap their useless wings; the wildest brutes
Came tame and tremulous; and vipers crawled
And twined themselves among the multitude,
Hissing, but stingless—they were slain for food.
And War, which for a moment was no more,
Did glut himself again: a meal was bought
With blood, and each sate sullenly apart
Gorging himself in gloom: no love was left;
All earth was but one thought—and that was death
Immediate and inglorious; and the pang
Of famine fed upon all entrails—men
Died, and their bones were tombless as their flesh;
The meagre by the meagre were devoured,
Even dogs assailed their masters, all save one,
And he was faithful to a corse, and kept
The birds and beasts and famished men at bay,
Till hunger clung them, or the dropping dead
Lured their lank jaws; himself sought out no food,
But with a piteous and perpetual moan,
And a quick desolate cry, licking the hand
Which answered not with a caress—he died.
The crowd was famished by degrees; but two

Of an enormous city did survive,
And they were enemies: they met beside
The dying embers of an altar-place
Where had been heaped a mass of holy things
For an unholy usage; they raked up,
And shivering scraped with their cold skeleton hands
The feeble ashes, and their feeble breath
Blew for a little life, and made a flame
Which was a mockery; then they lifted up
Their eyes as it grew lighter, and beheld
Each other's aspects—saw, and shrieked, and died—
Even of their mutual hideousness they died,
Unknowing who he was upon whose brow
Famine had written Fiend. The world was void,
The populous and the powerful was a lump,
Seasonless, herbless, treeless, manless, lifeless,
A lump of death—a chaos of hard clay.
The rivers, lakes, and ocean all stood still,
And nothing stirred within their silent depths;
Ships sailorless lay rotting on the sea,
And their masts fell down piecemeal: as they dropped
They slept on the abyss without a surge—
The waves were dead; the tides were in their grave,
The moon, their mistress, had expired before;
The winds were withered in the stagnant air,
And the clouds perished; Darkness had no need
Of aid from them—she was the universe.

THE VISION OF JUDGMENT

I

Saint Peter sat by the celestial gate:
    His keys were rusty, and the lock was dull,
So little trouble had been given of late;
    Not that the place by any means was full,
But since the Gallic era "eighty-eight"
    The devils had ta'en a longer, stronger pull,
And "a pull altogether," as they say
At sea—which drew most souls another way.

II

The angels all were singing out of tune,
　　And hoarse with having little else to do,
Excepting to wind up the sun and moon,
　　Or curb a runaway young star or two,
Or wild colt of a comet, which too soon
　　Broke out of bounds o'er the ethereal blue,
Splitting some planet with its playful tail,
As boats are sometimes by a wanton whale.

III

The guardian seraphs had retired on high,
　　Finding their charges past all care below;
Terrestrial business filled nought in the sky
　　Save the recording angel's black bureau;
Who found, indeed, the facts to multiply
　　With such rapidity of vice and woe,
That he had stripped off both his wings in quills,
And yet was in arrear of human ills.

IV

His business so augmented of late years,
　　That he was forced, against his will no doubt,
(Just like those cherubs, earthly ministers,)
　　For some resource to turn himself about,
And claim the help of his celestial peers,
　　To aid him ere he should be quite worn out
By the increased demand for his remarks:
Six angels and twelve saints were named his clerks.

V

This was a handsome board—at least for heaven;
　　And yet they had even then enough to do,
So many conquerors' cars were daily driven,
　　So many kingdoms fitted up anew;
Each day too slew its thousands six or seven,
　　Till at the crowning carnage, Waterloo,
They threw their pens down in divine disgust—
The page was so besmeared with blood and dust.

VI

This by the way; 'tis not mine to record
    What angels shrink from: even the very devil
On this occasion his own work abhorred,
    So surfeited with the infernal revel:
Though he himself had sharpened every sword,
    It almost quenched his innate thirst of evil.
(Here Satan's sole good work deserves insertion—
'Tis, that he has both generals in reversion.)

VII

Let's skip a few short years of hollow peace,
    Which peopled earth no better, hell as wont,
And heaven none—they form the tyrant's lease,
    With nothing but new names subscribed upon't;
'Twill one day finish: meantime they increase,
    "With seven heads and ten horns," and all in front,
Like Saint John's foretold beast; but ours are born
Less formidable in the head than horn.

VIII

In the first year of freedom's second dawn
    Died George the Third; although no tyrant, one
Who shielded tyrants, till each sense withdrawn
    Left him nor mental nor external sun:
A better farmer ne'er brushed dew from lawn,
    A worse king never left a realm undone!
He died—but left his subjects still behind,
One half as mad—and t'other no less blind.

IX

He died! his death made no great stir on earth:
    His burial made some pomp; there was profusion
Of velvet, gilding, brass, and no great dearth
    Of aught but tears—save those shed by collusion.
For these things may be bought at their true worth;
    Of elegy there was the due infusion—
Bought also; and the torches, cloaks, and banners,
Heralds, and relics of old Gothic manners,

X

Formed a sepulchral melodrame. Of all
  The fools who flocked to swell or see the show,
Who cared about the corpse? The funeral
  Made the attraction, and the black the woe.
There throbbed not there a thought which pierced the pall;
  And when the gorgeous coffin was laid low,
It seemed the mockery of hell to fold
The rottenness of eighty years in gold.

XI

So mix his body with the dust! It might
  Return to what it *must* far sooner, were
The natural compound left alone to fight
  Its way back into earth, and fire, and air;
But the unnatural balsams merely blight
  What nature made him at his birth, as bare
As the mere million's base unmummied clay—
Yet all his spices but prolong decay.

XII

He's dead—and upper earth with him has done;
  He's buried; save the undertaker's bill,
Or lapidary scrawl, the world is gone
  For him, unless he left a German will:
But where's the proctor who will ask his son?
  In whom his qualities are reigning still,
Except that household virtue, most uncommon,
Of constancy to a bad, ugly woman.

XIII

"God save the king!" It is a large economy
  In God to save the like; but if he will
Be saving, all the better; for not one am I
  Of those who think damnation better still:
I hardly know too if not quite alone am I
  In this small hope of bettering future ill
By circumscribing, with some slight restriction,
The eternity of hell's hot jurisdiction.

XIV

I know this is unpopular; I know
　'Tis blasphemous; I know one may be damned
For hoping no one else may e'er be so;
　I know my catechism; I know we're crammed
With the best doctrines till we quite o'erflow;
　I know that all save England's church have shammed,
And that the other twice two hundred churches
And synagogues have made a *damned* bad purchase.

XV

God help us all! God help me too! I am,
　God knows, as helpless as the devil can wish,
And not a whit more difficult to damn,
　Than is to bring to land a late-hooked fish,
Or to the butcher to purvey the lamb;
　Not that I'm fit for such a noble dish
As one day will be that immortal fry
Of almost everybody born to die.

XVI

Saint Peter sat by the celestial gate,
　And nodded o'er his keys; when, lo! there came
A wondrous noise he had not heard of late—
　A rushing sound of wind, and stream, and flame;
In short, a roar of things extremely great,
　Which would have made aught save a saint exclaim;
But he, with first a start and then a wink,
Said, "There's another star gone out, I think!"

XVII

But ere he could return to his repose,
　A cherub flapped his right wing o'er his eyes—
At which St. Peter yawned, and rubbed his nose:
　"Saint porter," said the angel, "prithee rise!"
Waving a goodly wing, which glowed, as glows
　An earthly peacock's tail, with heavenly dyes:
To which the saint replied, "Well, what's the matter?
Is Lucifer come back with all this clatter?"

XVIII

"No," quoth the cherub; "George the Third is dead."
   "And who *is* George the Third?" replied the apostle:
"What George? What Third?" "The king of England," said
  The angel. "Well! he won't find kings to jostle
Him on his way; but does he wear his head?
  Because the last we saw here had a tustle,
And ne'er would have got into heaven's good graces,
Had he not flung his head in all our faces.

XIX

He was, if I remember, king of France;
  That head of his, which could not keep a crown
On earth, yet ventured in my face to advance
  A claim to those of martyrs—like my own:
If I had had my sword, as I had once
  When I cut ears off, I had cut him down;
But having but my *keys,* and not my brand,
I only knocked his head from out his hand.

XX

And then he set up such a headless howl,
  That all the saints came out and took him in;
And there he sits by St. Paul, cheek by jowl;
  That fellow Paul—the parvenu! The skin
Of St. Bartholomew, which makes his cowl
  In heaven, and upon earth redeemed his sin,
So as to make a martyr, never sped
Better than did this weak and wooden head.

XXI

But had it come up here upon its shoulders,
  There would have been a different tale to tell:
The fellow-feeling in the saint's beholders
  Seems to have acted on them like a spell,
And so this very foolish head heaven solders
  Back on its trunk: it may be very well,
And seems the custom here to overthrow
Whatever has been wisely done below."

XXII

The angel answered, "Peter! do not pout:
    The king who comes has head and all entire,
And never knew much what it was about—
    He did as doth the puppet—by its wire,
And will be judged like all the rest, no doubt:
    My business and your own is not to inquire
Into such matters, but to mind our cue—
Which is to act as we are bid to do."

XXIII

While thus they spake, the angelic caravan,
    Arriving like a rush of mighty wind,
Cleaving the fields of space, as doth the swan
    Some silver stream (say Ganges, Nile, or Inde,
Or Thames, or Tweed), and 'midst them an old man
    With an old soul, and both extremely blind,
Halted before the gate, and in his shroud
Seated their fellow traveller on a cloud.

XXIV

But bringing up the rear of this bright host
    A spirit of a different aspect waved
His wings, like thunder-clouds above some coast
    Whose barren beach with frequent wrecks is paved;
His brow was like the deep when tempest-tossed;
    Fierce and unfathomable thoughts engraved
Eternal wrath on his immortal face,
And *where* he gazed a gloom pervaded space.

XXV

As he drew near, he gazed upon the gate
    Ne'er to be entered more by him or Sin,
With such a glance of supernatural hate,
    As made Saint Peter wish himself within;
He pattered with his keys at a great rate,
    And sweated through his apostolic skin:
Of course his perspiration was but ichor,
Or some such other spiritual liquor.

XXVI

The very cherubs huddled all together,
  Like birds when soars the falcon; and they felt
A tingling to the tip of every feather,
  And formed a circle like Orion's belt
Around their poor old charge; who scarce knew whither
  His guards had led him, though they gently dealt
With royal manes (for by many stories,
And true, we learn the angels all are Tories).

XXVII

As things were in this posture, the gate flew
  Asunder, and the flashing of its hinges
Flung over space an universal hue
  Of many-coloured flame, until its tinges
Reached even our speck of earth, and made a new
  Aurora borealis spread its fringes
O'er the North Pole; the same seen, when ice-bound,
By Captain Parry's crew, in "Melville's Sound."

XXVIII

And from the gate thrown open issued beaming
  A beautiful and mighty thing of light,
Radiant with glory, like a banner streaming
  Victorious from some world-o'erthrowing fight:
My poor comparisons must needs be teeming
  With earthly likenesses, for here the night
Of clay obscures our best conceptions, saving
Johanna Southcote, or Bob Southey raving.

XXIX

'Twas the archangel Michael; all men know
  The make of angels and archangels, since
There's scarce a scribbler has not one to show,
  From the fiends' leader to the angels' prince;
There also are some altar-pieces, though
  I really can't say that they much evince
One's inner notions of immortal spirits;
But let the connoisseurs explain *their* merits.

423

XXX

Michael flew forth in glory and in good;
    A goodly work of him from whom all glory
And good arise; the portal past—he stood;
    Before him the young cherubs and saints hoary—
(I say *young*, begging to be understood
    By looks, not years; and should be very sorry
To state, they were not older than St. Peter,
But merely that they seemed a little sweeter).

XXXI

The cherubs and the saints bowed down before
    That arch-angelic hierarch, the first
Of essences angelical, who wore
    The aspect of a god; but this ne'er nursed
Pride in his heavenly bosom, in whose core
    No thought, save for his master's service, durst
Intrude, however glorified and high;
He knew him but the viceroy of the sky.

XXXII

He and the sombre, silent spirit met—
    They knew each other both for good and ill;
Such was their power, that neither could forget
    His former friend and future foe; but still
There was a high, immortal, proud regret
    In either's eye, as if 'twere less their will
Than destiny to make the eternal years
Their date of war, and their "champ clos" the spheres.

XXXIII

But here they were in neutral space: we know
    From Job, that Satan hath the power to pay
A heavenly visit thrice a year or so:
    And that the "sons of God," like those of clay,
Must keep him company; and we might show
    From the same book, in how polite a way
The dialogue is held between the powers
Of good and evil—but 'twould take up hours.

XXXIV

And this is not a theologic tract,
  To prove with Hebrew and with Arabic,
If Job be allegory or a fact,
  But a true narrative; and thus I pick
From out the whole but such and such an act
  As sets aside the slightest thought of trick.
'Tis every tittle true, beyond suspicion,
And accurate as any other vision.

XXXV

The spirits were in neutral space, before
  The gate of heaven; like eastern thresholds is
The place where Death's grand cause is argued o'er,
  And souls despatched to that world or to this;
And therefore Michael and the other wore
  A civil aspect: though they did not kiss,
Yet still between his darkness and his brightness
There passed a mutual glance of great politeness.

XXXVI

The Archangel bowed, not like a modern beau,
  But with a graceful Oriental bend,
Pressing one radiant arm just where below
  The heart in good men is supposed to tend;
He turned as to an equal, not too low,
  But kindly; Satan met his ancient friend
With more hauteur, as might an old Castilian
Poor noble meet a mushroom rich civilian.

XXXVII

He merely bent his diabolic brow
  An instant; and then raising it, he stood
In act to assert his right or wrong, and show
  Cause why King George by no means could or should
Make out a case to be exempt from woe
  Eternal, more than other kings, endued
With better sense and hearts, whom history mentions,
Who long have "paved hell with their good intentions."

XXXVIII

Michael began: "What wouldst thou with this man,
   Now dead, and brought before the Lord? What ill
Hath he wrought since his mortal race began,
   That thou canst claim him? Speak! and do thy will,
If it be just: if in this earthly span
   He hath been greatly failing to fulfil
His duties as a king and mortal, say,
And he is thine; if not, let him have way."

"Michael!" replied the Prince of Air, "even here,
   Before the Gate of him thou servest, must
I claim my subject: and will make appear
   That as he was my worshipper in dust,
So shall he be in spirit, although dear
   To thee and thine, because nor wine nor lust
Were of his weaknesses; yet on the throne
He reigned o'er millions to serve me alone.

XL

Look to *our* earth, or rather *mine;* it was,
   Once, more thy master's: but I triumph not
In this poor planet's conquest; nor, alas!
   Need he thou servest envy me my lot:
With all the myriads of bright worlds which pass
   In worship round him, he may have forgot
Yon weak creation of such paltry things:
I think few worth damnation save their kings—

And these but as a kind of quit-rent, to
   Assert my right as lord: and even had
I such an inclination, 'twere (as you
   Well know) superfluous; they are grown so bad,
That hell has nothing better left to do
   Than leave them to themselves: so much more mad
And evil by their own internal curse,
Heaven cannot make them better, nor I worse.

Look to the earth, I said, and say again:
  When this old, blind, mad, helpless, weak, poor worm
Began in youth's first bloom and flush to reign,
  The world and he both wore a different form,
And much of earth and all the watery plain
  Of ocean called him king: through many a storm
His isles had floated on the abyss of time;
For the rough virtues chose them for their clime.

XLIII

He came to his sceptre young; he leaves it old:
  Look to the state in which he found his realm,
And left it; and his annals too behold,
  How to a minion first he gave the helm;
How grew upon his heart a thirst for gold,
  The beggar's vice, which can but overwhelm
The meanest hearts; and for the rest, but glance
Thine eye along America and France.

XLIV

'Tis true, he was a tool from first to last
  (I have the workmen safe); but as a tool
So let him be consumed. From out the past
  Of ages, since mankind have known the rule
Of monarchs—from the bloody rolls amassed
  Of sin and slaughter—from the Caesar's school,
Take the worst pupil; and produce a reign
More drenched with gore, more cumbered with the slain.

XLV

He ever warred with freedom and the free:
  Nations as men, home subjects, foreign foes,
So that they uttered the word 'Liberty!'
  Found George the Third their first opponent. Whose
History was ever stained as his will be
  With national and individual woes?
I grant his household abstinence; I grant
His neutral virtues, which most monarchs want;

XLVI

I know he was a constant consort; own
   He was a decent sire, and middling lord.
All this is much, and most upon a throne;
   As temperance, if at Apicius' board,
Is more than at an anchorite's supper shown.
   I grant him all the kindest can accord;
And this was well for him, but not for those
Millions who found him what oppression chose.

XLVII

The New World shook him off; the Old yet groans
   Beneath what he and his prepared, if not
Completed: he leaves heirs on many thrones
   To all his vices, without what begot
Compassion for him—his tame virtues; drones
   Who sleep, or despots who have now forgot
A lesson which shall be re-taught them, wake
Upon the thrones of earth; but let them quake!

XLVIII

Five millions of the primitive, who hold
   The faith which makes ye great on earth, implored
A *part* of that vast *all* they held of old—
   Freedom to worship—not alone your Lord,
Michael, but you, and you, Saint Peter! Cold
   Must be your souls, if you have not abhorred
The foe to Catholic participation
In all the license of a Christian nation.

XLIX

True! he allowed them to pray God; but as
   A consequence of prayer, refused the law
Which would have placed them upon the same base
   With those who did not hold the saints in awe."
But here Saint Peter started from his place,
   And cried, "You may the prisoner withdraw:
Ere heaven shall ope her portals to this Guelph,
While I am guard, may I be damned myself!

L

Sooner will I with Cerberus exchange
  My office (and *his* is no sinecure)
Than see this royal Bedlam bigot range
  The azure fields of heaven, of that be sure!"
"Saint!" replied Satan, "you do well to avenge
  The wrongs he made your satellites endure;
And if to this exchange you should be given,
I'll try to coax *our* Cerberus up to heaven!"

LI

Here Michael interposed: "Good saint! and devil!
  Pray, not so fast; you both outrun discretion.
Saint Peter! you were wont to be more civil!
  Satan! excuse this warmth of his expression,
And condescension to the vulgar's level:
  Even saints sometimes forget themselves in session.
Have you got more to say?"—"No."—"If you please,
I'll trouble you to call your witnesses."

LII

Then Satan turned and waved his swarthy hand,
  Which stirred with its electric qualities
Clouds farther off than we can understand,
  Although we find him sometimes in our skies;
Infernal thunder shook both sea and land
  In all the planets, and hell's batteries
Let off the artillery, which Milton mentions
As one of Satan's most sublime inventions.

LIII

This was a signal unto such damned souls
  As have the privilege of their damnation
Extended far beyond the mere controls
  Of worlds past, present, or to come; no station
Is theirs particularly in the rolls
  Of hell assigned; but where their inclination
Or business carries them in search of game,
They may range freely—being damned the same.

They're proud of this—as very well they may,
  It being a sort of knighthood, or gilt key
Stuck in their loins; or like to an "entré"
  Up the back stairs, or such freemasonry.
I borrow my comparisons from clay,
  Being clay myself. Let not those spirits be
Offended with such base low likenesses;
We know their posts are nobler far than these.

LV

When the great signal ran from heaven to hell—
  About ten million times the distance reckoned
From our sun to its earth, as we can tell
  How much time it takes up, even to a second,
For every ray that travels to dispel
  The fogs of London, through which, dimly beaconed,
The weathercocks are gilt some thrice a year,
If that the *summer* is not too severe:

LVI

I say that I can tell—'twas half a minute;
  I know the solar beams take up more time
Ere, packed up for their journey, they begin it;
  But then their telegraph is less sublime,
And if they ran a race, they would not win it
  'Gainst Satan's couriers bound for their own clime.
The sun takes up some years for every ray
To reach its goal—the devil not half a day.

LVII

Upon the verge of space, about the size
  Of half-a-crown, a little speck appeared
(I've seen a something like it in the skies
  In the Aegean, ere a squall); it neared,
And, growing bigger, took another guise;
  Like an aerial ship it tacked, and steered,
Or *was* steered (I am doubtful of the grammar
Of the last phrase, which makes the stanza stammer;

LVIII

But take your choice): and then it grew a cloud;
  And so it was—a cloud of witnesses.
But such a cloud! No land e'er saw a crowd
  Of locusts numerous as the heavens saw these;
They shadowed with their myriads space; their loud
  And varied cries were like those of wild geese
(If nations may be likened to a goose),
And realised the phrase of "hell broke loose."

LIX

Here crashed a sturdy oath of stout John Bull,
  Who damned away his eyes as heretofore:
There Paddy brogued "By Jasus!"—"What's your wull?"
  The temperate Scot exclaimed: the French ghost swore
In certain terms I shan't translate in full,
  As the first coachman will; and 'midst the war,
The voice of Jonathan was heard to express,
"*Our* president is going to war, I guess."

LX

Besides there were the Spaniard, Dutch, and Dane;
  In short, an universal shoal of shades,
From Otaheite's isle to Salisbury Plain,
  Of all climes and professions, years and trades,
Ready to swear against the good king's reign,
  Bitter as clubs in cards are against spades:
All summoned by this grand "subpoena," to
Try if kings mayn't be damned like me or you.

LXI

When Michael saw this host, he first grew pale,
  As angels can; next, like Italian twilight,
He turned all colours—as a peacock's tail,
  Or sunset streaming through a Gothic skylight
In some old abbey, or a trout not stale,
  Or distant lightning on the horizon *by* night,
Or a fresh rainbow, or a grand review
Of thirty regiments in red, green, and blue.

LXII

Then he addressed himself to Satan: "Why—
  My good old friend, for such I deem you, though
Our different parties make us fight so shy,
  I ne'er mistake you for a *personal* foe;
Our difference is *political*, and I
  Trust that, whatever may occur below,
You know my great respect for you: and this
Makes me regret whate'er you do amiss—

LXIII

Why, my dear Lucifer, would you abuse
  My call for witnesses? I did not mean
That you should half of earth and hell produce;
  'Tis even superfluous, since two honest, clean,
True testimonies are enough: we lose
  Our time, nay, our eternity, between
The accusation and defence: if we
Hear both, 'twill stretch our immortality."

LXIV

Satan replied, "To me the matter is
  Indifferent, in a personal point of view:
I can have fifty better souls than this
  With far less trouble than we have gone through
Already; and I merely argued his
  Late majesty of Britain's case with you
Upon a point of form: you may dispose
Of him; I've kings enough below, God knows!"

LXV

Thus spoke the demon (late called "multifaced"
  By multo-scribbling Southey). "Then we'll call
One or two persons of the myriads placed
  Around our congress, and dispense with all
The rest," quoth Michael. "Who may be so graced
  As to speak first? there's choice enough—who shall
It be?" Then Satan answered, "There are many;
But you may choose Jack Wilkes as well as any."

LXVI

A merry, cock-eyed, curious-looking sprite
　　Upon the instant started from the throng,
Dressed in a fashion now forgotten quite;
　　For all the fashions of the flesh stick long
By people in the next world; where unite
　　All the costumes since Adam's, right or wrong,
From Eve's fig-leaf down to the petticoat,
Almost as scanty, of days less remote.

The spirit looked around upon the crowds
　　Assembled, and exclaimed, "My friends of all
The spheres, we shall catch cold amongst these clouds;
　　So let's to business: why this general call?
If those are freeholders I see in shrouds,
　　And 'tis for an election that they bawl,
Behold a candidate with unturned coat!
Saint Peter, may I count upon your vote?"

LXVIII

"Sir," replied Michael, "you mistake; these things
　　Are of a former life, and what we do
Above is more august; to judge of kings
　　Is the tribunal met: so now you know."
"Then I presume those gentlemen with wings,"
　　Said Wilkes, "are cherubs; and that soul below
Looks much like George the Third, but to my mind
A good deal older. Bless me! Is he blind?"

"He is what you behold him, and his doom
　　Depends upon his deeds," the angel said;
"If you have aught to arraign in him, the tomb
　　Gives licence to the humblest beggar's head
To lift itself against the loftiest."—"Some,"
　　Said Wilkes, "don't wait to see them laid in lead,
For such a liberty—and I, for one,
Have told them what I thought beneath the sun."

LXX

"*Above* the sun repeat, then, what thou hast
　　To urge against him," said the archangel. "Why,"
Replied the spirit, "since old scores are past,
　　Must I turn evidence? In faith, not I.
Besides, I beat him hollow at the last,
　　With all his Lords and Commons: in the sky
I don't like ripping up old stories, since
His conduct was but natural in a prince.

LXXI

Foolish, no doubt, and wicked, to oppress
　　A poor unlucky devil without a shilling;
But then I blame the man himself much less
　　Than Bute and Grafton, and shall be unwilling
To see him punished here for their excess,
　　Since they were both damned long ago, and still in
Their place below: for me, I have forgiven,
And vote his *habeas corpus* into heaven."

LXXII

"Wilkes," said the Devil, "I understand all this;
　　You turned to half a courtier ere you died,
And seem to think it would not be amiss
　　To grow a whole one on the other side
Of Charon's ferry; you forget that *his*
　　Reign is concluded; whatsoe'er betide,
He won't be sovereign more: you've lost your labour,
For at the best he will but be your neighbour.

LXXIII

However, I knew what to think of it,
　　When I beheld you in your jesting way,
Flitting and whispering round about the spit
　　Where Belial, upon duty for the day,
With Fox's lard was basting William Pitt,
　　His pupil; I knew what to think, I say:
That fellow even in hell breeds farther ills;
I'll have him *gagged*—'twas one of his own bills.

LXXIV

Call Junius!" From the crowd a shadow stalked,
   And at the name there was a general squeeze,
So that the very ghosts no longer walked
   In comfort, at their own aerial ease,
But were all rammed, and jammed (but to be balked,
   As we shall see), and jostled hands and knees,
Like wind compressed and pent within a bladder,
Or like a human colic, which is sadder.

LXXV

The shadow came—a tall, thin, grey-haired figure,
   That looked as it had been a shade on earth;
Quick in its motions, with an air of vigour,
   But nought to mark its breeding or its birth;
Now it waxed little, then again grew bigger,
   With now an air of gloom, or savage mirth;
But as you gazed upon its features, they
Changed every instant—to *what*, none could say.

LXXVI

The more intently the ghosts gazed, the less
   Could they distinguish whose the features were;
The Devil himself seemed puzzled even to guess;
   They varied like a dream—now here, now there;
And several people swore from out the press,
   They knew him perfectly; and one could swear
He was his father: upon which another
Was sure he was his mother's cousin's brother:

LXXVII

Another, that he was a duke, or knight,
   An orator, a lawyer, or a priest,
A nabob, a man-midwife; but the wight
   Mysterious changed his countenance at least
As oft as they their minds; though in full sight
   He stood, the puzzle only was increased;
The man was a phantasmagoria in
Himself—he was so volatile and thin.

435

LXXVIII

The moment that you had pronounced him *one*,
　　Presto! his face changed, and he was another;
And when that change was hardly well put on,
　　It varied, till I don't think his own mother
(If that he had a mother) would her son
　　Have known, he shifted so from one to t'other;
Till guessing from a pleasure grew a task,
At this epistolary "Iron Mask."

LXXIX

For sometimes he like Cerberus would seem—
　　"Three gentlemen at once" (as sagely says
Good Mrs. Malaprop); then you might deem
　　That he was not even *one;* now many rays
Were flashing round him; and now a thick steam
　　Hid him from sight—like fogs on London days:
Now Burke, now Tooke, he grew to people's fancies,
And certes often like Sir Philip Francis.

LXXX

I've an hypothesis—'tis quite my own;
　　I never let it out till now, for fear
Of doing people harm about the throne,
　　And injuring some minister or peer,
On whom the stigma might perhaps be blown;
　　It is—my gentle public, lend thine ear!
'Tis, that what Junius we are wont to call
Was *really, truly,* nobody at all.

LXXXI

I don't see wherefore letters should not be
　　Written without hands, since we daily view
Them written without heads; and books, we see,
　　Are filled as well without the latter too:
And really till we fix on somebody
　　For certain sure to claim them as his due,
Their author, like the Niger's mouth, will bother
The world to say if *there* be mouth or author.

LXXXII

"And who and what art thou?" the Archangel said.
 "For *that* you may consult my title-page,"
Replied this mighty shadow of a shade:
 "If I have kept my secret half an age,
I scarce shall tell it now." "Canst thou upbraid,"
 Continued Michael, "George Rex, or allege
Aught further?" Junius answered, "You had better
First ask him for *his* answer to my letter:

LXXXIII

My charges upon record will outlast
 The brass of both his epitaph and tomb."
"Repentest thou not," said Michael, "of some past
 Exaggeration? something which may doom
Thyself if false, as him if true? Thou wast
 Too bitter—is it not so?—in thy gloom
Of passion?"—"Passion!" cried the phantom dim,
"I loved my country, and I hated him.

LXXXIV

What I have written, I have written: let
 The rest be on his head or mine!" So spoke
Old "Nominis Umbra"; and while speaking yet,
 Away he melted in celestial smoke.
Then Satan said to Michael, "Don't forget
 To call George Washington, and John Horne Tooke,
And Franklin"; but at this time there was heard
A cry for room, though not a phantom stirred.

LXXXV

At length with jostling, elbowing, and the aid
 Of cherubim appointed to that post,
The devil Asmodeus to the circle made
 His way, and looked as if his journey cost
Some trouble. When his burden down he laid,
 "What's this?" cried Michael; "why, 'tis not a ghost?"
"I know it," quoth the incubus; "but he
Shall be one, if you leave the affair to me.

LXXXVI

Confound the renegado! I have sprained
    My left wing, he's so heavy; one would think
Some of his works about his neck were chained.
    But to the point; while hovering o'er the brink
Of Skiddaw (where as usual it still rained),
    I saw a taper, far below me, wink,
And stooping, caught this fellow at a libel—
No less on history than the Holy Bible.

LXXXVII

The former is the devil's scripture, and
    The latter yours, good Michael: so the affair
Belongs to all of us, you understand.
    I snatched him up just as you see him there,
And brought him off for sentence out of hand:
    I've scarcely been ten minutes in the air—
At least a quarter it can hardly be:
I dare say that his wife is still at tea."

LXXXVIII

Here Satan said, "I know this man of old,
    And have expected him for some time here;
A sillier fellow you will scarce behold,
    Or more conceited in his petty sphere:
But surely it was not worth while to fold
    Such trash below your wing, Asmodeus dear:
We had the poor wretch safe (without being bored
With carriage) coming of his own accord.

LXXXIX

But since he's here, let's see what he has done."
    "Done!" cried Asmodeus, "he anticipates
The very business you are now upon,
    And scribbles as if head clerk to the Fates.
Who knows to what his ribaldry may run,
    When such an ass as this, like Balaam's, prates?"
"Let's hear," quoth Michael, "what he has to say:
You know we're bound to that in every way."

XC

Now the bard, glad to get an audience, which
   By no means often was his case below,
Began to cough, and hawk, and hem, and pitch
   His voice into that awful note of woe
To all unhappy hearers within reach
   Of poets when the tide of rhyme's in flow;
But stuck fast with his first hexameter,
Not one of all whose gouty feet would stir.

XCI

But ere the spavined dactyls could be spurred
   Into recitative, in great dismay
Both cherubim and seraphim were heard
   To murmur loudly through their long array;
And Michael rose ere he could get a word
   Of all his foundered verses under way,
And cried, "For God's sake stop, my friend! 'twere best—
Non Di, non homines—you know the rest."

XCII

A general bustle spread throughout the throng,
   Which seemed to hold all verse in detestation;
The angels had of course enough of song
   When upon service; and the generation
Of ghosts had heard too much in life, not long
   Before, to profit by a new occasion.
The monarch, mute till then, exclaimed, "What! what!
Pye come again? No more—no more of that!"

XCIII

The tumult grew; an universal cough
   Convulsed the skies, as during a debate,
When Castlereagh has been up long enough
   (Before he was first minister of state,
I mean—the *slaves hear now);* some cried "Off, off!"
   As at a farce; till, grown quite desperate,
The bard Saint Peter prayed to interpose
(Himself an author) only for his prose.

The varlet was not an ill-favoured knave;
   A good deal like a vulture in the face,
With a hook nose and a hawk's eye, which gave
   A smart and sharper-looking sort of grace
To his whole aspect, which, though rather grave,
   Was by no means so ugly as his case;
But that, indeed, was hopeless as can be,
Quite a poetic felony *"de se."*

XCV

Then Michael blew his trump, and stilled the noise
   With one still greater, as is yet the mode
On earth besides; except some grumbling voice,
   Which now and then will make a slight inroad
Upon decorous silence, few will twice
   Lift up their lungs when fairly overcrowed;
And now the bard could plead his own bad cause,
With all the attitudes of self-applause.

XCVI

He said—I only give the heads—he said,
   He meant no harm in scribbling; 'twas his way
Upon all topics; 'twas, besides, his bread,
   Of which he buttered both sides; 'twould delay
Too long the assembly (he was pleased to dread),
   And take up rather more time than a day,
To name his works—he would but cite a few—
"Wat Tyler"—"Rhymes on Blenheim"—"Waterloo."

XCVII

He had written praises of a regicide;
   He had written praises of all kings whatever;
He had written for republics far and wide,
   And then against them bitterer than ever;
For pantisocracy he once had cried
   Aloud, a scheme less moral than 'twas clever;
Then grew a hearty anti-jacobin—
Had turned his coat—and would have turned his skin.

He had sung against all battles, and again
   In their high praise and glory; he had called
Reviewing "the ungentle craft," and then
   Become as base a critic as e'er crawled—
Fed, paid, and pampered by the very men
   By whom his muse and morals had been mauled:
He had written much blank verse, and blanker prose,
And more of both than anybody knows.

XCIX

He had written Wesley's life:—here turning round
   To Satan, "Sir, I'm ready to write yours,
In two octavo volumes, nicely bound,
   With notes and preface, all that most allures
The pious purchaser; and there's no ground
   For fear, for I can choose my own reviewers:
So let me have the proper documents,
That I may add you to my other saints."

C

Satan bowed, and was silent. "Well, if you,
   With amiable modesty, decline
My offer, what says Michael? There are few
   Whose memoirs could be rendered more divine.
Mine is a pen of all work; not so new
   As it was once, but I would make you shine
Like your own trumpet. By the way, my own
Has more of brass in it, and is as well blown.

CI

But talking about trumpets, here's my Vision!
   Now you shall judge, all people; yes, you shall
Judge with my judgment, and by my decision
   Be guided who shall enter heaven or fall.
I settle all these things by intuition,
   Times present, past, to come, heaven, hell, and all,
Like King Alfonso. When I thus see double,
I save the Deity some worlds of trouble."

He ceased, and drew forth an MS; and no
    Persuasion on the part of devils, saints,
Or angels, now could stop the torrent; so
    He read the first three lines of the contents;
But at the fourth, the whole spiritual show
    Had vanished, with variety of scents,
Ambrosial and sulphureous, as they sprang,
Like lightning, off from his "melodious twang."

Those grand heroics acted as a spell:
    The angels stopped their ears and plied their pinions;
The devils ran howling, deafened, down to hell;
    The ghosts fled, gibbering, for their own dominions—
(For 'tis not yet decided where they dwell,
    And I leave every man to his opinions);
Michael took refuge in his trump—but, lo!
His teeth were set on edge, he could not blow!

Saint Peter, who has hitherto been known
    For an impetuous saint, upraised his keys,
And at the fifth line knocked the poet down;
    Who fell like Phaeton, but more at ease,
Into his lake, for there he did not drown;
    A different web being by the destinies
Woven for the laureate's final wreath, whene'er
Reform shall happen either here or there.

He first sank to the bottom—like his works,
    But soon rose to the surface—like himself;
For all corrupted things are buoyed like corks,
    By their own rottenness, light as an elf,
Or wisp that flits o'er a morass: he lurks,
    It may be, still, like dull books on a shelf,
In his own den, to scrawl some "Life" or "Vision,"
As Welborn says—"the devil turned precisian."

As for the rest, to come to the conclusion
    Of this true dream, the telescope is gone
Which kept my optics free from all delusion,
    And showed me what I in my turn have shown;
All I saw farther, in the last confusion,
    Was, that King George slipped into heaven for one;
And when the tumult dwindled to a calm,
I left him practising the hundredth psalm.

PERCY BYSSHE SHELLEY
(1792–1822)

MUTABILITY

We are as clouds that veil the midnight moon;
  How restlessly they speed, and gleam, and quiver,
Streaking the darkness radiantly! Yet soon
  Night closes round, and they are lost forever;

Or like forgotten lyres, whose dissonant strings
  Give various response to each varying blast,
To whose frail frame no second motion brings
  One mood or modulation like the last.

We rest. A dream has power to poison sleep;
  We rise. One wandering thought pollutes the day;
We feel, conceive, or reason, laugh or weep;
  Embrace fond woe, or cast our cares away:

It is the same! For be it joy or sorrow,
  The path of its departure still is free:
Man's yesterday may ne'er be like his morrow;
Nought may endure but mutability.

MONT BLANC

Lines Written in the Vale of Chamouni

I

The everlasting universe of things
Flows through the mind, and rolls its rapid waves,
Now dark—now glittering—now reflecting gloom—
Now lending splendour, where from secret springs

444

The source of human thought its tribute brings
Of waters—with a sound but half its own,
Such as a feeble brook will oft assume
In the wild woods, among the mountains lone,
Where waterfalls around it leap forever,
Where woods and winds contend, and a vast river
Over its rocks ceaselessly bursts and raves.

II

Thus thou, ravine of Arve—dark, deep ravine—
Thou many-coloured, many-voiced vale,
Over whose pines and crags and caverns sail
Fast clouds, shadows and sunbeams; awful scene!
Where power in likeness of the Arve comes down
From the ice-gulfs that gird his secret throne,
Bursting through these dark mountains like the flame
Of lightning through the tempest; thou dost lie,
The giant brood of pines around thee clinging,
Children of elder time, in whose devotion
The chainless winds still come and ever came
To drink their odours, and their mighty swinging
To hear—an old and solemn harmony:
Thine earthly rainbows stretched across the sweep
Of the ethereal waterfall, whose veil
Robes some unsculptured image; the strange sleep
Which, when the voices of the desert fail,
Wraps all in its own deep eternity;
Thy caverns echoing to the Arve's commotion
A loud, lone sound, no other sound can tame;
Thou art pervaded with that ceaseless motion,
Thou art the path of that unresting sound—
Dizzy ravine! And when I gaze on thee
I seem as in a trance sublime and strange
To muse on my own separate fantasy,
My own, my human mind, which passively
Now renders and receives fast influencings,
Holding an unremitting interchange
With the clear universe of things around;
One legion of wild thoughts, whose wandering wings
Now float above thy darkness, and now rest
Where that or thou art no unbidden guest,

In the still cave of the witch Poesy,
Seeking among the shadows that pass by
Ghosts of all things that are, some shade of thee,
Some phantom, some faint image; till the breast
From which they fled recalls them, thou art there!

III

Some say that gleams of a remoter world
Visit the soul in sleep—that death is slumber,
And that its shapes the busy thoughts outnumber
Of those who wake and live. I look on high:
Has some unknown omnipotence unfurled
The veil of life and death, or do I lie
In dream, and does the mightier world of sleep
Speed far around and inaccessibly
Its circles? For the very spirit fails,
Driven like a homeless cloud from steep to steep
That vanishes among the viewless gales!
Far, far above, piercing the infinite sky,
Mont Blanc appears—still, snowy and serene—
Its subject mountains their unearthly forms
Pile around it, ice and rock; broad vales between
Of frozen floods, unfathomable deeps,
Blue as the overhanging heaven, that spread
And wind among the accumulated steeps;
A desert peopled by the storms alone,
Save when the eagle brings some hunter's bone,
And the wolf tracks her there—how hideously
Its shapes are heaped around! rude, bare and high,
Ghastly and scarred and riven. Is this the scene
Where the old earthquake-demon taught her young
Ruin? Were these their toys? Or did a sea
Of fire envelop once this silent snow?
None can reply—all seems eternal now.
The wilderness has a mysterious tongue
Which teaches awful doubt, or faith so mild,
So solemn, so serene, that man may be
But for such faith with nature reconciled;
Thou hast a voice, great Mountain, to repeal
Large codes of fraud and woe; not understood

By all, but which the wise and great and good
Interpret, or make felt, or deeply feel.

IV

The fields, the lakes, the forests and the streams,
Ocean, and all the living things that dwell
Within the daedal earth—lightning and rain,
Earthquake and fiery flood and hurricane,
The torpor of the year when feeble dreams
Visit the hidden buds, or dreamless sleep
Holds every future leaf and flower—the bound
With which from that detested trance they leap;
The works and ways of man, their death and birth,
And that of him and all that his may be;
All things that move and breathe with toil and sound
Are born and die, revolve, subside and swell.
Power dwells apart in its tranquillity
Remote, serene and inaccessible:
And *this*, the naked countenance of earth,
On which I gaze, even these primeval mountains,
Teach the adverting mind. The glaciers creep
Like snakes that watch their prey, from their far fountains,
Slowly rolling on; there, many a precipice
Frost and the sun in scorn of mortal power
Have piled—dome, pyramid and pinnacle,
A city of death, distinct with many a tower
And wall impregnable of beaming ice.
Yet not a city, but a flood of ruin
Is there, that from the boundaries of the sky
Rolls its perpetual stream; vast pines are strewing
Its destined path, or in the mangled soil
Branchless and shattered stand; the rocks, drawn down
From yon remotest waste, have overthrown
The limits of the dead and living world,
Never to be reclaimed. The dwelling-place
Of insects, beasts and birds, becomes its spoil;
Their food and their retreat for ever gone,
So much of life and joy is lost. The race
Of man flies far in dread; his work and dwelling
Vanish, like smoke before the tempest's stream,
And their place is not known. Below, vast caves

447

Shine in the rushing torrent's restless gleam,
Which from those secret chasms in tumult welling
Meet in the vale, and one majestic river,
The breath and blood of distant lands, for ever
Rolls its loud waters to the ocean-waves,
Breathes its swift vapours to the circling air.

V

Mont Blanc yet gleams on high: the power is there,
The still and solemn power of many sights
And many sounds, and much of life and death.
In the calm darkness of the moonless nights,
In the lone glare of day, the snows descend
Upon that mountain; none beholds them there.
Nor when the flakes burn in the sinking sun,
Or the starbeams dart through them: winds contend
Silently there, and heap the snow with breath
Rapid and strong, but silently! Its home
The voiceless lightning in these solitudes
Keeps innocently, and like vapour broods
Over the snow. The secret strength of things
Which governs thought, and to the infinite dome
Of heaven is as a law, inhabits thee!
And what were thou and earth and stars and sea,
If to the human mind's imaginings
Silence and solitude were vacancy?

OZYMANDIAS

I met a traveller from an antique land
Who said: Two vast and trunkless legs of stone
Stand in the desert . . . Near them, on the sand,
Half sunk, a shattered visage lies, whose frown,
And wrinkled lip, and sneer of cold command,
Tell that its sculptor well those passions read
Which yet survive, stamped on these lifeless things,
The hand that mocked them, and the heart that fed:
And on the pedestal these words appear:
"My name is Ozymandias, king of kings:

Look on my works, ye mighty, and despair!"
Nothing beside remains. Round the decay
Of that colossal wreck, boundless and bare
The lone and level sands stretch far away.

ODE TO THE WEST WIND

I

O wild West Wind, thou breath of autumn's being,
Thou, from whose unseen presence the leaves dead
Are driven, like ghosts from an enchanter fleeing,

Yellow, and black, and pale, and hectic red,
Pestilence-stricken multitudes: O Thou,
Who chariotest to their dark wintry bed

The winged seeds, where they lie cold and low,
Each like a corpse within its grave, until
Thine azure sister of the spring shall blow

Her clarion o'er the dreaming earth, and fill
(Driving sweet buds like flocks to feed in air)
With living hues and odours plain and hill:

Wild Spirit, which art moving everywhere;
Destroyer and Preserver; hear, Oh hear!

II

Thou on whose stream, 'mid the steep sky's commotion,
Loose clouds like earth's decaying leaves are shed,
Shook from the tangled boughs of heaven and ocean,

Angels of rain and lightning: there are spread
On the blue surface of thine aery surge,
Like the bright hair uplifted from the head

Of some fierce maenad, even from the dim verge
Of the horizon to the zenith's height,
The locks of the approaching storm. Thou dirge

Of the dying year, to which this closing night
Will be the dome of a vast sepulchre,
Vaulted with all thy congregated might

Of vapours, from whose solid atmosphere
Black rain and fire and hail will burst: Oh hear!

III

Thou who didst waken from his summer dreams
The blue Mediterranean, where he lay,
Lulled by the coil of his chrystalline streams,

Beside a pumice isle in Baiae's bay,
And saw in sleep old palaces and towers
Quivering within the wave's intenser day,

All overgrown with azure moss and flowers
So sweet, the sense faints picturing them! Thou
For whose path the Atlantic's level powers

Cleave themselves into chasms, while far below
The sea-blooms and the oozy woods which wear
The sapless foliage of the ocean, know

Thy voice, and suddenly grow grey with fear,
And tremble and despoil themselves: Oh hear!

IV

If I were a dead leaf thou mightest bear;
If I were a swift cloud to fly with thee;
A wave to pant beneath thy power, and share

The impulse of thy strength, only less free
Than thou, O Uncontrollable! If even
I were as in my boyhood, and could be

The comrade of thy wanderings over heaven,
As then, when to outstrip thy skiey speed
Scarce seemed a vision; I would ne'er have striven

As thus with thee in prayer in my sore need.
Oh! lift me as a wave, a leaf, a cloud!
I fall upon the thorns of life! I bleed!

A heavy weight of hours has chained and bowed
One too like thee: tameless, and swift, and proud.

V

Make me thy lyre, even as the forest is:
What if my leaves are falling like its own!
The tumult of thy mighty harmonies

Will take from both a deep, autumnal tone,
Sweet though in sadness. Be thou, Spirit fierce,
My spirit! Be thou me, impetuous one!

Drive my dead thoughts over the universe
Like withered leaves to quicken a new birth!
And, by the incantation of this verse,

Scatter, as from an unextinguished hearth
Ashes and sparks, my words among mankind!
Be through my lips to unawakened earth

The trumpet of a prophecy! O Wind,
If winter comes, can spring be far behind?

451

TO A SKYLARK

Hail to thee, blithe spirit!
   Bird thou never wert,
That from heaven, or near it,
   Pourest thy full heart
In profuse strains of unpremeditated art.

Higher still and higher
   From the earth thou springest
Like a cloud of fire;
   The blue deep thou wingest,
And singing still dost soar, and soaring ever singest.

In the golden lightning
   Of the sunken sun,
O'er which clouds are brightening,
   Thou dost float and run;
Like an unbodied joy whose race is just begun.

The pale purple even
   Melts around thy flight;
Like a star of heaven,
   In the broad daylight
Thou art unseen, but yet I hear thy shrill delight,

Keen as are the arrows
   Of that silver sphere,
Whose intense lamp narrows
   In the white dawn clear
Until we hardly see; we feel that it is there.

All the earth and air
   With thy voice is loud,
As, when night is bare,
   From one lonely cloud
The moon rains out her beams, and heaven is overflowed.

What thou art we know not;
   What is most like thee?
From rainbow clouds there flow not

Drops so bright to see
As from thy presence showers a rain of melody.

Like a poet hidden
    In the light of thought,
Singing hymns unbidden,
    Till the world is wrought
To sympathy with hopes and fears it heeded not:

Like a high-born maiden
    In a palace-tower,
Soothing her love-laden
    Soul in secret hour
With music sweet as love, which overflows her bower:

Like a glow-worm golden
    In a dell of dew,
Scattering unbeholden
    Its aëreal hue
Among the flowers and grass, which screen it from the view!

Like a rose embowered
    In its own green leaves,
By warm winds deflowered,
    Till the scent it gives
Makes faint with too much sweet these heavy-winged thieves:

Sound of vernal showers
    On the twinkling grass,
Rain-awakened flowers,
    All that ever was
Joyous, and clear, and fresh, thy music doth surpass:

Teach us, sprite or bird,
    What sweet thoughts are thine:
I have never heard
    Praise of love or wine
That panted forth a flood of rapture so divine.

Chorus Hymeneal,
    Or triumphal chant,
Matched with thine would be all

But an empty vaunt,
A thing wherein we feel there is some hidden want.

What objects are the fountains
    Of thy happy strain?
What fields, or waves, or mountains?
    What shapes of sky or plain?
What love of thine own kind? What ignorance of pain?

With thy clear keen joyance
    Languor cannot be:
Shadow of annoyance
    Never came near thee:
Thou lovest—but ne'er knew love's sad satiety.

Waking or asleep,
    Thou of death must deem
Things more true and deep
    Than we mortals dream,
Or how could thy notes flow in such a crystal stream?

We look before and after,
    And pine for what is not:
Our sincerest laughter
    With some pain is fraught:
Our sweetest songs are those that tell of saddest thought.

Yet if we could scorn
    Hate, and pride, and fear;
If we were things born
    Not to shed a tear,
I know not how thy joy we ever should come near.

Better than all measures
    Of delightful sound,
Better than all treasures
    That in books are found,
Thy skill to poet were, thou scorner of the ground!

Teach me half the gladness
    That thy brain must know,
Such harmonious madness

From my lips would flow
The world should listen then—as I am listening now.

*

Worlds on worlds are rolling ever
  From creation to decay,
Like the bubbles on a river
  Sparkling, bursting, borne away!
    But they are still immortal
    Who, through birth's orient portal
And death's dark chasm hurrying to and fro,
    Clothe their unceasing flight
    In the brief dust and light
Gathered around their chariots as they go.
    New shapes they still may weave,
    New gods, new laws receive,
Bright or dim are they as the robes they last
  On Death's bare ribs had cast.

A power from the unknown God,
  A Promethean conqueror, came;
Like a triumphal path he trod
  The thorns of death and shame.
    A mortal shape to him
    Was like the vapour dim
Which the orient planet animates with light.
    Hell, Sin, and Slavery came,
    Like bloodhounds mild and tame,
Nor preyed, until their Lord had taken flight;
    The moon of Mahomet
    Arose, and it shall set:
While blazoned as on heaven's immortal noon
  The cross leads generations on.

Swift as the radiant shapes of sleep
  From one whose dreams are paradise
Fly, when the fond wretch wakes to weep,
  And Day peers forth with her blank eyes;
    So fleet, so faint, so fair,
    The powers of earth and air

Fled from the folding-star of Bethlehem:
    Apollo, Pan, and Love,
    And even Olympian Jove
Grew weak, for killing Truth had glared on them;
    Our hills and seas and streams,
    Dispeopled of their dreams,
Their waters turned to blood, their dew to tears,
    Wailed for the golden years.

*

The world's great age begins anew,
    The golden years return,
The earth doth like a snake renew
    Her winter weeds outworn;
Heaven smiles, and faiths and empires gleam,
Like wrecks of a dissolving dream.

A brighter Hellas rears its mountains
    From waves serener far;
A new Peneus rolls his fountains
    Against the morning star.
Where fairer Tempes bloom, there sleep
Young Cyclads on a sunnier deep.

A loftier Argo cleaves the main,
    Fraught with a later prize;
Another Orpheus sings again,
    And loves, and weeps, and dies.
A new Ulysses leaves once more
Calypso for his native shore.

Oh, write no more the tale of Troy,
    If earth Death's scroll must be!
Nor mix with Laian rage the joy
    Which dawns upon the free:
Although a subtler Sphinx renew
Riddles of death Thebes never knew.

Another Athens shall arise,
    And to remoter time

Bequeath, like sunset to the skies,
    The splendour of its prime;
And leave, if nought so bright may live,
All earth can take or heaven can give.

Saturn and Love their long repose
    Shall burst, more bright and good
Than all who fell, than One who rose,
    Than many unsubdued:
Not gold, not blood, their altar dowers,
But votive tears and symbol flowers.

Oh, cease! must hate and death return?
    Cease! must men kill and die?
Cease! drain not to its dregs the urn
    Of bitter prophecy.
The world is weary of the past,
Oh, might it die or rest at last!

STANZAS

Written In Dejection, Near Naples

I

The sun is warm, the sky is clear,
    The waves are dancing fast and bright;
Blue isles and snowy mountains wear
    The purple noon's transparent might,
    The breath of the moist earth is light,
Around its unexpanded buds;
    Like many a voice of one delight,
The winds, the birds, the ocean floods,
The city's voice itself, is soft like Solitude's.

II

I see the deep's untrampled floor
    With green and purple seaweeds strown;
I see the waves upon the shore,

Like light dissolved in star-showers, thrown:
  I sit upon the sands alone—
The lightning of the noontide ocean
  Is flashing round me, and a tone
  Arises from its measured motion;
How sweet! did any heart now share in my emotion.

III

Alas! I have nor hope nor health,
  Nor peace within nor calm around,
Nor that content surpassing wealth
  The sage in meditation found,
  And walked with inward glory crowned—
Nor fame, nor power, nor love, nor leisure.
  Others I see whom these surround—
  Smiling they live, and call life pleasure;
To me that cup has been dealt in another measure.

IV

Yet now despair itself is mild,
  Even as the winds and waters are;
I could lie down like a tired child,
  And weep away the life of care
  Which I have borne and yet must bear,
Till death like sleep might steal on me,
  And I might feel in the warm air
My cheek grow cold, and hear the sea
Breathe o'er my dying brain its last monotony.

V

Some might lament that I were cold,
  As I, when this sweet day is gone,
Which my lost heart, too soon grown old,
  Insults with this untimely moan;
  They might lament—for I am one
Whom men love not—and yet regret,
  Unlike this day, which, when the sun
Shall on its stainless glory set,
Will linger, though enjoyed, like joy in memory yet.

Rarely, rarely, comest thou,
  Spirit of delight!
Wherefore hast thou left me now
  Many a day and night?
Many a weary night and day
'Tis since thou art fled away.

How shall ever one like me
  Win thee back again?
With the joyous and the free
  Thou wilt scoff at pain.
Spirit false! thou hast forgot
All but those who need thee not.

As a lizard with the shade
  Of a trembling leaf,
Thou with sorrow art dismayed;
  Even the sighs of grief
Reproach thee, that thou art not near,
And reproach thou wilt not hear.

Let me set my mournful ditty
  To a merry measure;
Thou wilt never come for pity,
  Thou wilt come for pleasure;
Pity then will cut away
Those cruel wings, and thou wilt stay.

I love all that thou lovest,
  Spirit of delight!
The fresh earth in new leaves dressed,
  And the starry night;
Autumn evening, and the morn
When the golden mists are born.

I love snow, and all the forms
  Of the radiant frost;
I love waves, and winds, and storms,

Everything almost
Which is nature's, and may be
Untainted by man's misery.

I love tranquil solitude,
     And such society
As is quiet, wise, and good;
     Between thee and me
What difference? but thou dost possess
The things I seek, not love them less.

I love Love—though he has wings,
     And like light can flee,
But above all other things,
     Spirit, I love thee—
Thou art love and life! Oh, come,
Make once more my heart thy home.

TO NIGHT

Swiftly walk o'er the western wave,
     Spirit of night!
Out of the misty eastern cave,
Where, all the long and lone daylight,
Thou wovest dreams of joy and fear,
Which make thee terrible and dear,
     Swift be thy flight!

Wrap thy form in a mantle grey,
     Star-inwrought!
Blind with thine hair the eyes of day;
Kiss her until she be wearied out,
Then wander o'er city, and sea, and land,
Touching all with thine opiate wand—
     Come, long-sought!

When I arose and saw the dawn,
     I sighed for thee;
When light rode high, and the dew was gone,

And noon lay heavy on flower and tree,
And the weary day turned to his rest,
Lingering like an unloved guest,
    I sighed for thee.

Thy brother Death came, and cried,
    Wouldst thou me?
Thy sweet child Sleep, the filmy-eyed,
Murmured like a noontide bee,
Shall I nestle near thy side?
Wouldst thou me? And I replied,
    No, not thee!

Death will come when thou art dead,
    Soon, too soon—
Sleep will come when thou art fled;
Of neither would I ask the boon
I ask of thee, beloved night—
Swift be thine approaching flight,
    Come soon, soon!

A LAMENT

O world! O life! O time!
On whose last steps I climb,
  Trembling at that where I had stood before;
When will return the glory of your prime?
    No more—oh, never more!

Out of the day and night
A joy has taken flight;
  Fresh spring, and summer, and winter hoar,
Move my faint heart with grief, but with delight
    No more—oh, never more!

*

When the lamp is shattered
The light in the dust lies dead;

When the cloud is scattered
The rainbow's glory is shed.
When the lute is broken,
Sweet tones are remembered not;
When the lips have spoken,
Loved accents are soon forgot.

As music and splendour
Survive not the lamp and the lute,
The heart's echoes render
No song when the spirit is mute:
No song but sad dirges,
Like the wind through a ruined cell,
Or the mournful surges
That ring the dead seaman's knell.

When hearts have once mingled
Love first leaves the well-built nest;
The weak one is singled
To endure what it once possessed.
O Love! who bewailest
The frailty of all things here,
Why choose you the frailest
For your cradle, your home, and your bier?

Its passions will rock thee
As the storms rock the ravens on high;
Bright reason will mock thee,
Like the sun from a wintry sky.
From thy nest every rafter
Will rot, and thine eagle home
Leave thee naked to laughter,
When leaves fall and cold winds come.

A DIRGE

Rough wind, that moanest loud
Grief too sad for song;
Wild wind, when sullen cloud

Knells all the night long;
Sad storm, whose tears are vain,
Bare woods, whose branches strain,
Deep caves and dreary main,
    Wail, for the world's wrong!

JOHN CLARE
(1793–1864)

SAND MARTIN

Thou hermit haunter of the lonely glen
And common wild and heath—the desolate face
Of rude waste landscapes far away from men
Where frequent quarrys give thee dwelling place
With strangest taste and labour undeterred
Drilling small holes along the quarrys side
More like the haunts of vermin than a bird
And seldom by the nesting boy descried
Ive seen thee far away from all thy tribe
Flirting about the unfrequented sky
And felt a feeling that I cant describe
Of lone seclusion and a hermit joy
To see thee circle round nor go beyond
That lone heath and its melancholly pond

JOHN KEATS
(1795–1821)

TO MY BROTHERS

Small, busy flames play through the fresh-laid coals,
   And their faint cracklings o'er our silence creep
   Like whispers of the household gods that keep
A gentle empire o'er fraternal souls.
And while, for rhymes, I search around the poles,
   Your eyes are fixed, as in poetic sleep,
   Upon the lore so voluble and deep,
That aye at fall of night our care condoles.
This is your birthday, Tom, and I rejoice
   That thus it passes smoothly, quietly.
Many such eves of gently whispering noise
   May we together pass, and calmly try
What are this world's true joys, ere the great voice,
   From its fair face, shall bid our spirits fly.

*

Keen, fitful gusts are whispering here and there
   Among the bushes half leafless, and dry;
   The stars look very cold about the sky,
And I have many miles on foot to fare.
Yet feel I little of the cool bleak air,
   Or of the dead leaves rustling drearily,
   Or of those silver lamps that burn on high,
Or of the distance from home's pleasant lair.
For I am brimfull of the friendliness
   That in a little cottage I have found;
Of fair-haired Milton's eloquent distress,
   And all his love for gentle Lycid drowned;
Of lovely Laura in her light green dress,
   And faithful Petrarch gloriously crowned.

ON FIRST LOOKING INTO CHAPMAN'S HOMER

Much have I travelled in the realms of gold,
  And many goodly states and kingdoms seen;
  Round many western islands have I been
Which bards in fealty to Apollo hold.
Oft of one wide expanse had I been told
  That deep-browed Homer ruled as his demesne;
  Yet did I never breathe its pure serene
Till I heard Chapman speak out loud and bold.
Then felt I like some watcher of the skies
  When a new planet swims into his ken;
Or like stout Cortez when with eagle eyes
  He stared at the Pacific—and all his men
Looked at each other with a wild surmise—
  Silent, upon a peak in Darien.

*

After dark vapours have oppressed our plains
  For a long dreary season, comes a day
  Born of the gentle south, and clears away
From the sick heavens all unseemly stains.
The anxious month, relieved of its pains,
  Takes as a long-lost right the feel of May;
  The eyelids with the passing coolness play
Like rose leaves with the drip of summer rains.
The calmest thoughts come round us; as of leaves
  Budding—fruit ripening in stillness—autumn suns
Smiling at eve upon the quiet sheaves—
Sweet Sappho's cheek—a smiling infant's breath—
  The gradual sand that through an hour-glass runs—
A woodland rivulet—a poet's death.

ON THE SEA

It keeps eternal whisperings around
  Desolate shores, and with its mighty swell
  Gluts twice ten thousand caverns, till the spell
Of Hecate leaves them their old shadowy sound.
Often 'tis in such gentle temper found,
  That scarcely will the very smallest shell
  Be moved for days from where it sometime fell,
When last the winds of heaven were unbound.
Oh ye who have your eye-balls vexed and tired,
  Feast them upon the wideness of the sea;
    Oh ye whose ears are dinned with uproar rude,
  Or fed too much with cloying melody—
    Sit ye near some old cavern's mouth and brood,
Until ye start, as if the sea-nymphs quired!

*

When I have fears that I may cease to be
  Before my pen has gleaned my teeming brain,
Before high-piled books, in charactery,
  Hold like rich garners the full ripened grain;
When I behold, upon the night's starred face,
  Huge cloudy symbols of a high romance,
And think that I may never live to trace
  Their shadows, with the magic hand of chance;
And when I feel, fair creature of an hour,
  That I shall never look upon thee more,
Never have relish in the faery power
  Of unreflecting love; then on the shore
Of the wide world I stand alone, and think
Till love and fame to nothingness do sink.

TO SLEEP

O soft embalmer of the still midnight,
  Shutting, with careful fingers and benign,
Our gloom-pleased eyes, embowered from the light,

Enshaded in forgetfulness divine:
O soothest sleep! If so it please thee, close
   In midst of this thine hymn my willing eyes,
Or wait the amen, ere thy poppy throws
   Around my bed its lulling charities.
Then save me, or the passed day will shine
Upon my pillow, breeding many woes;
   Save me from curious conscience, that still lords
Its strength for darkness, burrowing like a mole;
   Turn the key deftly in the oiled wards,
And seal the hushed casket of my soul.

*

Why did I laugh tonight? No voice will tell;
   No god, no demon of severe response
Deigns to reply from heaven or from hell.
   Then to my human heart I turn at once.
Heart! Thou and I are here sad and alone;
   I say, why did I laugh! O mortal pain!
O darkness! darkness! ever must I moan,
   To question heaven and hell and heart in vain.
Why did I laugh? I know this being's lease,
   My fancy to its utmost blisses spreads;
Yet would I on this very midnight cease,
   And the world's gaudy ensigns see in shreds;
Verse, fame, and beauty are intense indeed,
But death intenser—death is life's high meed.

LA BELLE DAME SANS MERCI

Ah, what can ail thee, wretched wight,
   Alone and palely loitering;
The sedge is withered from the lake,
   And no birds sing.

Ah, what can ail thee, wretched wight,
   So haggard and so woe-begone?

The squirrel's granary is full,
　And the harvest's done.

I see a lilly on thy brow,
　With anguish moist and fever dew;
And on thy cheek a fading rose
　Fast withereth too.

I met a lady in the meads
　Full beautiful, a faery's child;
Her hair was long, her foot was light,
　And her eyes were wild.

I set her on my pacing steed,
　And nothing else saw all day long;
For sideways would she lean, and sing
　A faery's song.

I made a garland for her head,
　And bracelets too, and fragrant zone;
She looked at me as she did love,
　And made sweet moan.

She found me roots of relish sweet,
　And honey wild, and manna dew;
And sure in language strange she said,
　I love thee true.

She took me to her elfin grot,
　And there she gazed and sighed deep,
And there I shut her wild sad eyes—
　So kissed to sleep.

And there we slumbered on the moss,
　And there I dreamed, ah woe betide,
The latest dream I ever dreamed
　On the cold hill side.

I saw pale kings, and princes too,
　Pale warriors, death-pale were they all;
Who cried—"La belle Dame sans merci
　Hath thee in thrall!"

I saw their starved lips in the gloam
  With horrid warning gaped wide,
And I awoke, and found me here
  On the cold hill side.

And this is why I sojourn here
  Alone and palely loitering,
Though the sedge is withered from the lake,
  And no birds sing.

MEG MERRILIES

Old Meg she was a gypsy,
  And lived upon the moors:
Her bed it was the brown heath turf,
  And her house was out of doors.

Her apples were swart blackberries,
  Her currants pods o' broom;
Her wine was dew of the wild white rose,
  Her book a churchyard tomb.

Her brothers were the craggy hills,
  Her sisters larchen trees—
Alone with her great family
  She lived as she did please.

No breakfast had she many a morn,
  No dinner many a noon,
And 'stead of supper she would stare
  Full hard against the moon.

But every morn of woodbine fresh
  She made her garlanding,
And every night the dark glen yew
  She wove, and she would sing.

And with her fingers old and brown
  She plaited mats o' rushes,

And gave them to the cottagers
　　She met among the bushes.

Old Meg was brave as Margaret Queen
　　And tall as Amazon:
And old red blanket cloak she wore;
　　A chip hat had she on.
God rest her aged bones somewhere—
　　She died full long agone!

　　　　　　　　　*

'Tis the witching hour of night,
Orbed is the moon and bright,
And the stars they glisten, glisten,
Seeming with bright eyes to listen—
　　For what listen they?
For a song and for a charm,
See they glisten in alarm,
And the moon is waxing warm
　　To hear what I shall say.
Moon! keep wide thy golden ears—
Hearken, stars! and hearken, spheres!
Hearken, thou eternal sky!
I sing an infant's lullaby,
　　A pretty lullaby.
Listen, listen, listen, listen,
Glisten, glisten, glisten, glisten,
　　And hear my lullaby!
Though the rushes that will make
Its cradle still are in the lake;
Though the linen that will be
Its swathe, is on the cotton tree;
Though the woollen that will keep
It warm, is on the silly sheep;
Listen, starlight, listen, listen,
Glisten, glisten, glisten, glisten,
　　And hear my lullaby!
Child, I see thee! Child, I've found thee
Midst of the quiet all around thee!
Child, I see thee! Child, I spy thee!

And thy mother sweet is nigh thee!
Child, I know thee! Child no more,
But a poet evermore!
See, see, the lyre, the lyre,
In a flame of fire,
Upon the little cradle's top
Flaring, flaring, flaring,
Past the eyesight's bearing.
Awake it from its sleep,
And see if it can keep
Its eyes upon the blaze—
    Amaze, amaze!
It stares, it stares, it stares,
It dares what no one dares!
It lifts its little hand into the flame
Unharmed, and on the strings
Paddles a little tune, and sings,
With dumb endeavour sweetly—
Bard art thou completely!
    Little child
      O' the western wild,
Bard art thou completely!
Sweetly with dumb endeavour,
A poet now or never,
    Little child
      O' the western wild,
A poet now or never!

*

In a drear-nighted December,
    Too happy, happy tree,
Thy branches ne'er remember
    Their green felicity.
The north cannot undo them,
With a sleety whistle through them;
Nor frozen thawings glue them
    From budding at the prime.

In a drear-nighted December,
    Too happy, happy brook,

Thy bubblings ne'er remember
    Apollo's summer look;
But with a sweet forgetting,
They stay their crystal fretting,
Never, never petting
    About the frozen time.

Ah! would 'twere so with many
    A gentle girl and boy!
But were there ever any
    Writhed not of passed joy?
To know the change and feel it,
When there is none to heal it,
Nor numbed sense to steel it,
    Was never said in rhyme.

ODE TO A NIGHTINGALE

My heart aches, and a drowsy numbness pains
    My sense, as though of hemlock I had drunk,
Or emptied some dull opiate to the drains
    One minute past, and Lethe-wards had sunk.
'Tis not through envy of thy happy lot,
    But being too happy in thine happiness—
        That thou, light-winged dryad of the trees,
            In some melodious plot
Of beechen green, and shadows numberless,
    Singest of summer in full-throated ease.

O, for a draught of vintage! that hath been
    Cooled a long age in the deep-delved earth,
Tasting of Flora and the country green,
    Dance, and Provençal song, and sunburnt mirth!
O for a beaker full of the warm south,
    Full of the true, the blushful Hippocrene,
        With beaded bubbles winking at the brim,
            And purple-stained mouth;
That I might drink, and leave the world unseen,
    And with thee fade away into the forest dim!

473

Fade far away, dissolve, and quite forget
    What thou among the leaves hast never known,
The weariness, the fever, and the fret
    Here, where men sit and hear each other groan;
Where palsy shakes a few, sad, last grey hairs,
    Where youth grows pale, and spectre-thin, and dies;
        Where but to think is to be full of sorrow
            And leaden-eyed despairs,
        Where beauty cannot keep her lustrous eyes,
            Or new love pine at them beyond tomorrow.

Away! away! for I will fly to thee,
    Not charioted by Bacchus and his pards,
But on the viewless wings of poesy,
    Though the dull brain perplexes and retards.
Already with thee! tender is the night,
    And haply the Queen-Moon is on her throne,
        Clustered around by all her starry fays;
            But here there is no light,
        Save what from heaven is with the breezes blown
            Through verdurous glooms and winding mossy ways.

I cannot see what flowers are at my feet,
    Nor what soft incense hangs upon the boughs,
But, in embalmed darkness, guess each sweet
    Wherewith the seasonable month endows
The grass, the thicket, and the fruit-tree wild;
    White hawthorn, and the pastoral eglantine;
        Fast fading violets covered up in leaves;
            And mid-May's eldest child,
    The coming musk-rose, full of dewy wine,
        The murmurous haunt of flies on summer eves.

Darkling I listen; and, for many a time
    I have been half in love with easeful Death,
Called him soft names in many a mused rhyme,
    To take into the air my quiet breath;
Now more than ever seems it rich to die,
    To cease upon the midnight with no pain,
        While thou art pouring forth thy soul abroad
            In such an ecstasy!

Still wouldst thou sing, and I have ears in vain—
    To thy high requiem become a sod.

Thou wast not born for death, immortal bird!
    No hungry generations tread thee down;
The voice I hear this passing night was heard
    In ancient days by emperor and clown:
Perhaps the self-same song that found a path
    Through the sad heart of Ruth, when, sick for home,
        She stood in tears amid the alien corn;
            The same that oft-times hath
    Charmed magic casements, opening on the foam
    Of perilous seas, in faery lands forlorn.

Forlorn! the very word is like a bell
    To toll me back from thee to my sole self!
Adieu! the fancy cannot cheat so well
    As she is famed to do, deceiving elf.
Adieu! adieu! thy plaintive anthem fades
    Past the near meadows, over the still stream,
        Up the hill side; and now 'tis buried deep
            In the next valley-glades:
    Was it a vision, or a waking dream?
    Fled is that music. Do I wake or sleep?

ODE ON A GRECIAN URN

Thou still unravished bride of quietness,
    Thou foster-child of silence and slow time;
Sylvan historian, who canst thus express
    A flowery tale more sweetly than our rhyme:
What leaf-fringed legend haunts about thy shape
    Of deities or mortals, or of both,
        In Tempe or the dales of Arcady?
    What men or gods are these? What maidens loth?
What mad pursuit? What struggle to escape?
    What pipes and timbrels? What wild ecstasy?

Heard melodies are sweet, but those unheard
　　Are sweeter; therefore, ye soft pipes, play on;
Not to the sensual ear, but, more endeared,
　　Pipe to the spirit ditties of no tone.
Fair youth, beneath the trees, thou canst not leave
　　Thy song, nor ever can those trees be bare;
　　　Bold lover, never, never canst thou kiss,
Though winning near the goal—yet, do not grieve;
　　She cannot fade, though thou hast not thy bliss,
　　　Forever wilt thou love, and she be fair!

Ah, happy, happy boughs! that cannot shed
　　Your leaves, nor ever bid the spring adieu;
And, happy melodist, unwearied,
　　Forever piping songs forever new;
More happy love! more happy, happy love!
　　Forever warm and still to be enjoyed,
　　　Forever panting, and forever young;
All breathing human passion far above,
　　That leaves a heart high-sorrowful and cloyed,
　　　A burning forehead, and a parching tongue.

Who are these coming to the sacrifice?
　　To what green altar, O mysterious priest,
Leadest thou that heifer lowing at the skies,
　　And all her silken flanks with garlands dressed?
What little town by river or sea shore,
　　Or mountain-built with peaceful citadel,
　　　Is emptied of this folk, this pious morn?
And, little town, thy streets forevermore
　　Will silent be; and not a soul to tell
　　　Why thou art desolate, can e'er return.

O Attic shape! Fair attitude! with brede
　　Of marble men and maidens overwrought,
With forest branches and the trodden weed;
　　Thou, silent form, dost tease us out of thought
As doth eternity: Cold pastoral!
　　When old age shall this generation waste,
　　　Thou shalt remain, in midst of other woe
Than ours, a friend to man, to whom thou sayest,

"Beauty is truth, truth beauty—that is all
Ye know on earth, and all ye need to know."

TO AUTUMN

Season of mists and mellow fruitfulness,
    Close bosom-friend of the maturing sun;
Conspiring with him how to load and bless
    With fruit the vines that round the thatch-eves run;
To bend with apples the mossed cottage-trees,
    And fill all fruit with ripeness to the core;
        To swell the gourd, and plump the hazel shells
    With a sweet kernel; to set budding more,
And still more, later flowers for the bees,
Until they think warm days will never cease,
        For summer has o'er-brimmed their clammy cells.

Who hath not seen thee oft amid thy store?
    Sometimes whoever seeks abroad may find
Thee sitting careless on a granary floor,
    Thy hair soft-lifted by the winnowing wind;
Or on a half-reaped furrow sound asleep,
    Drowsed with the fume of poppies, while thy hook
        Spares the next swath and all its twined flowers:
And sometimes like a gleaner thou dost keep
    Steady thy laden head across a brook;
    Or by a cyder-press, with patient look,
        Thou watchest the last oozings hours by hours.

Where are the songs of spring? Ay, where are they?
    Think not of them, thou hast thy music too;
While barred clouds bloom the soft-dying day,
    And touch the stubble-plains with rosy hue;
Then in a wailful choir the small gnats mourn
    Among the river sallows, borne aloft
        Or sinking as the light wind lives or dies;
And full-grown lambs loud bleat from hilly bourn;
    Hedge-crickets sing; and now with treble soft

The red-breast whistles from a garden-croft;
And gathering swallows twitter in the skies.

ODE ON MELANCHOLY

No, no, go not to Lethe, neither twist
   Wolf's-bane, tight-rooted, for its poisonous wine;
Nor suffer thy pale forehead to be kissed
   By nightshade, ruby grape of Proserpine;
Make not your rosary of yew-berries,
   Nor let the beetle, nor the death-moth be
     Your mournful Psyche, nor the downy owl
A partner in your sorrow's mysteries;
   For shade to shade will come too drowsily,
     And drown the wakeful anguish of the soul.

But when the melancholy fit shall fall
   Sudden from heaven like a weeping cloud,
That fosters the droop-headed flowers all,
   And hides the green hill in an April shroud;
Then glut thy sorrow on a morning rose,
   Or on the rainbow of the salt sand-wave,
     Or on the wealth of globed peonies;
Or if thy mistress some rich anger shows,
   Emprison her soft hand, and let her rave,
     And feed deep, deep upon her peerless eyes.

She dwells with Beauty—Beauty that must die;
   And Joy, whose hand is ever at his lips
Bidding adieu; and aching Pleasure nigh,
   Turning to poison while the bee-mouth sips:
Ay, in the very temple of delight
   Veiled Melancholy has her sovran shrine,
     Though seen of none save him whose strenuous tongue
Can burst Joy's grape against his palate fine;
His soul shall taste the sadness of her might,
     And be among her cloudy trophies hung.

THE EVE OF ST. AGNES

St. Agnes' Eve—ah, bitter chill it was!
The owl, for all his feathers, was a-cold;
The hare limped trembling through the frozen grass,
And silent was the flock in woolly fold.
Numb were the beadsman's fingers, while he told
His rosary, and while his frosted breath,
Like pious incense from a censer old,
Seemed taking flight for heaven, without a death,
Past the sweet Virgin's picture, while his prayer he saith.

His prayer he saith, this patient, holy man;
Then takes his lamp, and riseth from his knees,
And back returneth, meagre, barefoot, wan,
Along the chapel aisle by slow degrees.
The sculptured dead, on each side, seem to freeze,
Emprisoned in black, purgatorial rails:
Knights, ladies, praying in dumb oratories,
He passeth by; and his weak spirit fails
To think how they may ache in icy hoods and mails.

Northward he turneth through a little door,
And scarce three steps, ere music's golden tongue
Flattered to tears this aged man and poor;
But no—already had his deathbell rung.
The joys of all his life were said and sung;
His was harsh penance on St. Agnes' Eve.
Another way he went, and soon among
Rough ashes sat he for his soul's reprieve,
And all night kept awake, for sinners' sake to grieve.

That ancient beadsman heard the prelude soft;
And so it chanced, for many a door was wide,
From hurry to and fro. Soon, up aloft,
The silver, snarling trumpets 'gan to chide.
The level chambers, ready with their pride,
Were glowing to receive a thousand guests;

The carved angels, ever eager-eyed,
Stared, where upon their heads the cornice rests,
With hair blown back, and wings put cross-wise on their breasts.

At length burst in the argent revelry,
With plume, tiara, and all rich array,
Numerous as shadows haunting fairily
The brain, new stuffed, in youth, with triumphs gay
Of old romance. These let us wish away,
And turn, sole-thoughted, to one lady there,
Whose heart had brooded, all that wintry day,
On love, and winged St. Agnes' saintly care,
As she had heard old dames full many times declare.

They told her how, upon St. Agnes' Eve,
Young virgins might have visions of delight,
And soft adorings from their loves receive
Upon the honeyed middle of the night,
If ceremonies due they did aright;
As, supperless to bed they must retire,
And couch supine their beauties, lily white;
Nor look behind, nor sideways, but require
Of heaven with upward eyes for all that they desire.

Full of this whim was thoughtful Madeline;
The music, yearning like a god in pain,
She scarcely heard; her maiden eyes divine,
Fixed on the floor, saw many a sweeping train
Pass by—she heeded not at all. In vain
Came many a tiptoe, amorous cavalier,
And back retired; not cooled by high disdain,
But she saw not: her heart was otherwhere:
She sighed for Agnes' dreams, the sweetest of the year.

She danced along with vague, regardless eyes,
Anxious her lips, her breathing quick and short;
The hallowed hour was near at hand: she sighs
Amid the timbrels, and the thronged resort
Of whisperers in anger, or in sport;
'Mid looks of love, defiance, hate, and scorn,
Hoodwinked with fairy fancy; all amort,

480

Save to St. Agnes and her lambs unshorn,
And all the bliss to be before tomorrow morn.

So, purposing each moment to retire,
She lingered still. Meantime, across the moors,
Had come young Porphyro, with heart on fire
For Madeline. Beside the portal doors,
Buttressed from moonlight, stands he, and implores
All saints to give him sight of Madeline,
But for one moment in the tedious hours,
That he might gaze and worship all unseen;
Perchance speak, kneel, touch, kiss—in sooth such things have been.

He ventures in; let no buzzed whisper tell;
All eyes be muffled, or a hundred swords
Will storm his heart, Love's feverous citadel.
For him, those chambers held barbarian hordes,
Hyena foemen, and hot-blooded lords,
Whose very dogs would execrations howl
Against his lineage; not one breast affords
Him any mercy, in that mansion foul,
Save one old beldame, weak in body and in soul.

Ah, happy chance! The aged creature came,
Shuffling along with ivory-headed wand,
To where he stood, hid from the torch's flame,
Behind a broad hall-pillar, far beyond
The sound of merriment and chorus bland;
He startled her; but soon she knew his face,
And grasped his fingers in her palsied hand,
Saying, "Mercy, Porphyro! Hie thee from this place:
They are all here tonight, the whole blood-thirsty race!

Get hence! get hence! there's dwarfish Hildebrand;
He had a fever late, and in the fit
He cursed thee and thine, both house and land:
Then there's that old Lord Maurice, not a whit
More tame for his grey hairs—Alas me! flit!
Flit like a ghost away."—"Ah, Gossip dear,
We're safe enough; here in this arm-chair sit,
And tell me how"—"Good Saints! not here, not here;
Follow me, child, or else these stones will be thy bier."

He followed through a lowly arched way,
Brushing the cobwebs with his lofty plume,
And as she muttered "Well-a—well-a-day!"
He found him in a little moonlight room,
Pale, latticed, chill, and silent as a tomb.
"Now tell me where is Madeline," said he,
"Oh tell me, Angela, by the holy loom
Which none but secret sisterhood may see,
When they St. Agnes' wool are weaving piously."

"St. Agnes! Ah! it is St. Agnes' Eve—
Yet men will murder upon holy days;
Thou must hold water in a witch's sieve,
And be liege-lord of all the elves and fays,
To venture so: it fills me with amaze
To see thee, Porphyro!—St. Agnes' Eve!
God's help! my lady fair the conjuror plays
This very night: good angels her deceive!
But let me laugh awhile, I've mickle time to grieve."

Feebly she laugheth in the languid moon,
While Porphyro upon her face doth look,
Like puzzled urchin on an aged crone
Who keepeth closed a wondrous riddle-book,
As spectacled she sits in chimney nook.
But soon his eyes grew brilliant, when she told
His lady's purpose; and he scarce could brook
Tears, at the thought of those enchantments cold,
And Madeline asleep in lap of legends old.

Sudden a thought came like a full-blown rose,
Flushing his brow, and in his pained heart
Made purple riot: then doth he propose
A stratagem, that makes the beldame start:
"A cruel man and impious thou art:
Sweet lady, let her pray, and sleep, and dream
Alone with her good angels, far apart
From wicked men like thee. Go, go!—I deem
Thou canst not surely be the same that thou didst seem."

"I will not harm her, by all saints I swear,"
Quoth Porphyro: "Oh, may I ne'er find grace

When my weak voice shall whisper its last prayer,
If one of her soft ringlets I displace,
Or look with ruffian passion in her face:
Good Angela, believe me by these tears;
Or I will, even in a moment's space,
Awake, with horrid shout, my foemen's ears,
And beard them, though they be more fanged than wolves and bears."

"Ah! why wilt thou affright a feeble soul?
A poor, weak, palsy-stricken, churchyard thing,
Whose passing-bell may ere the midnight toll;
Whose prayers for thee, each morn and evening,
Were never missed." Thus plaining, doth she bring
A gentler speech from burning Porphyro;
So woful, and of such deep sorrowing,
That Angela gives promise she will do
Whatever he shall wish, betide her weal or woe.

Which was, to lead him, in close secrecy,
Even to Madeline's chamber, and there hide
Him in a closet, of such privacy
That he might see her beauty unespied,
And win perhaps that night a peerless bride,
While legioned fairies paced the coverlet,
And pale enchantment held her sleepy-eyed.
Never on such a night have lovers met,
Since Merlin paid his demon all the monstrous debt.

"It shall be as thou wishest," said the dame;
"All cates and dainties shall be stored there
Quickly on this feast-night: by the tambour frame
Her own lute thou wilt see: no time to spare,
For I am slow and feeble, and scarce dare
On such a catering trust my dizzy head.
Wait here, my child, with patience; kneel in prayer
The while: Ah! thou must needs the lady wed,
Or may I never leave my grave among the dead."

So saying, she hobbled off with busy fear.
The lover's endless minutes slowly passed;
The dame returned, and whispered in his ear
To follow her; with aged eyes aghast

483

From fright of dim espial. Safe at last,
Through many a dusky gallery, they gain
The maiden's chamber, silken, hushed, and chaste;
Where Porphyro took covert, pleased amain.
His poor guide hurried back with agues in her brain.

Her faltering hand upon the balustrade,
Old Angela was feeling for the stair,
When Madeline, St. Agnes' charmed maid,
Rose, like a missioned spirit, unaware:
With silver taper's light, and pious care,
She turned, and down the aged gossip led
To a safe level matting. Now prepare,
Young Porphyro, for gazing on that bed;
She comes, she comes again, like ring-dove frayed and fled.

Out went the taper as she hurried in;
Its little smoke, in pallid moonshine, died.
She closed the door, she panted, all akin
To spirits of the air, and visions wide:
No uttered syllable, or, woe betide!
But to her heart, her heart was voluble,
Paining with eloquence her balmy side;
As though a tongueless nightingale should swell
Her throat in vain, and die, heart-stifled, in her dell.

A casement high and triple-arched there was,
All garlanded with carven imageries
Of fruits, and flowers, and bunches of knot-grass,
And diamonded with panes of quaint device,
Innumerable of stains and splendid dyes,
As are the tiger-moth's deep-damasked wings;
And in the midst, 'mong thousand heraldries,
And twilight saints, and dim emblazonings,
A shielded scutcheon blushed with blood of queens and kings.

Full on this casement shone the wintry moon,
And threw warm gules on Madeline's fair breast,
As down she knelt for heaven's grace and boon;
Rose-bloom fell on her hands, together pressed,
And on her silver cross soft amethyst,
And on her hair a glory, like a saint.

She seemed a splendid angel, newly dressed,
  Save wings, for heaven. Porphyro grew faint,
She knelt, so pure a thing, so free from mortal taint.

Anon his heart revives; her vespers done,
  Of all its wreathed pearls her hair she frees;
Unclasps her warmed jewels one by one;
  Loosens her fragrant bodice; by degrees
Her rich attire creeps rustling to her knees:
  Half-hidden, like a mermaid in sea-weed,
Pensive awhile she dreams awake, and sees,
  In fancy, fair St. Agnes in her bed,
But dares not look behind, or all the charm is fled.

Soon, trembling in her soft and chilly nest,
  In sort of wakeful swoon, perplexed she lay,
Until the poppied warmth of sleep oppressed
  Her soothed limbs, and soul fatigued away;
Flown, like a thought, until the morrow-day;
  Blissfully havened both from joy and pain;
Clasped like a missal where swart paynims pray;
  Blinded alike from sunshine and from rain,
As though a rose should shut, and be a bud again.

Stolen to this paradise, and so entranced,
  Porphyro gazed upon her empty dress,
And listened to her breathing, if it chanced
  To wake into a slumberous tenderness;
Which when he heard, that minute did he bless,
  And breathed himself: then from the closet crept,
Noiseless as fear in a wide wilderness,
  And over the hushed carpet, silent, stepped,
And 'tween the curtains peeped, where, lo!—how fast she slept.

Then by the bedside, where the faded moon
  Made a dim, silver twilight, soft he set
A table, and, half anguished, threw thereon
  A cloth of woven crimson, gold, and jet;
Oh for some drowsy Morphean amulet!
  The boisterous, midnight, festive clarion,
The kettle-drum, and far-heard clarinet,

Affray his ears, though but in dying tone.
The hall door shuts again, and all the noise is gone.

And still she slept an azure-lidded sleep,
In blanched linen, smooth, and lavendered,
While he from forth the closet brought a heap
Of candied apple, quince, and plum, and gourd;
With jellies soother than the creamy curd,
And lucent syrups, tinct with cinnamon;
Manna and dates, in argosy transferred
From Fez; and spiced dainties, every one,
From silken Samarcand to cedared Lebanon.

These delicates he heaped with glowing hand
On golden dishes and in baskets bright
Of wreathed silver: sumptuous they stand
In the retired quiet of the night,
Filling the chilly room with perfume light.
"And now, my love, my seraph fair, awake!
Thou art my heaven, and I thine eremite:
Open thine eyes, for meek St. Agnes' sake,
Or I shall drowse beside thee, so my soul doth ache."

Thus whispering, his warm, unnerved arm
Sank in her pillow. Shaded was her dream
By the dusk curtains; 'twas a midnight charm
Impossible to melt as iced stream:
The lustrous salvers in the moonlight gleam;
Broad golden fringe upon the carpet lies.
It seemed he never, never could redeem
From such a steadfast spell his lady's eyes;
So mused awhile, entoiled in woofed phantasies.

Awakening up, he took her hollow lute—
Tumultuous—and, in chords that tenderest be,
He played an ancient ditty, long since mute,
In Provence called, "La belle Dame sans merci,"
Close to her ear touching the melody,
Wherewith disturbed, she uttered a soft moan.
He ceased—she panted quick—and suddenly
Her blue affrayed eyes wide open shone.
Upon his knees he sank, pale as smooth-sculptured stone.

Her eyes were open, but she still beheld,
Now wide awake, the vision of her sleep:
There was a painful change, that nigh expelled
The blisses of her dream so pure and deep
At which fair Madeline began to weep,
And moan forth witless words with many a sigh;
While still her gaze on Porphyro would keep;
Who knelt, with joined hands and piteous eye,
Fearing to move or speak, she looked so dreamingly.

"Ah, Porphyro!" said she, "but even now
Thy voice was at sweet tremble in mine ear,
Made tuneable with every sweetest vow;
And those sad eyes were spiritual and clear:
How changed thou art! how pallid, chill, and drear!
Give me that voice again, my Porphyro,
Those looks immortal, those complainings dear!
Oh leave me not in this eternal woe,
For if thou diest, my love, I know not where to go."

Beyond a mortal man impassioned far
At these voluptuous accents, he arose,
Ethereal, flushed, and like a throbbing star
Seen mid the sapphire heaven's deep repose;
Into her dream he melted, as the rose
Blendeth its odour with the violet,
Solution sweet: meantime the frost-wind blows
Like Love's alarum pattering the sharp sleet
Against the window-panes; St. Agnes' moon hath set.

'Tis dark: quick pattereth the flaw-blown sleet:
"This is no dream, my bride, my Madeline!"
'Tis dark: the iced gusts still rave and beat.
"No dream, alas! alas! and woe is mine!
Porphyro will leave me here to fade and pine.
Cruel! what traitor could thee hither bring?
I curse not, for my heart is lost in thine,
Though thou forsakest a deceived thing;
A dove forlorn and lost with sick unpruned wing."

"My Madeline! sweet dreamer! lovely bride!
Say, may I be for aye thy vassal blessed?

487

Thy beauty's shield, heart-shaped and vermeil dyed?
Ah, silver shrine, here will I take my rest
After so many hours of toil and quest,
A famished pilgrim, saved by miracle.
Though I have found, I will not rob thy nest
Saving of thy sweet self; if thou thinkest well
To trust, fair Madeline, to no rude infidel.

Hark! 'tis an elfin-storm from fairy land,
Of haggard seeming, but a boon indeed:
Arise—arise! the morning is at hand;
The bloated wassaillers will never heed!
Let us away, my love, with happy speed;
There are no ears to hear, or eyes to see,
Drowned all in Rhenish and the sleepy mead.
Awake! arise! my love, and fearless be,
For o'er the southern moors I have a home for thee."

She hurried at his words, beset with fears,
For there were sleeping dragons all around,
At glaring watch, perhaps, with ready spears—
Down the wide stairs a darkling way they found.
In all the house was heard no human sound.
A chain-drooped lamp was flickering by each door;
The arras, rich with horseman, hawk, and hound,
Fluttered in the besieging wind's uproar;
And the long carpets rose along the gusty floor.

They glide, like phantoms, into the wide hall;
Like phantoms, to the iron porch, they glide;
Where lay the porter, in uneasy sprawl,
With a huge empty flaggon by his side.
The wakeful bloodhound rose, and shook his hide,
But his sagacious eye an inmate owns.
By one, and one, the bolts full easy slide;
The chains lie silent on the footworn stones;
The key turns, and the door upon its hinges groans.

And they are gone: aye, ages long ago
These lovers fled away into the storm.
That night the baron dreamt of many a woe,
And all his warrior-guests, with shade and form

Of witch, and demon, and large coffin-worm,
    Were long be-nightmared. Angela the old
Died palsy-twitched, with meagre face deform;
    The beadsman, after thousand aves told,
For aye unsought for slept among his ashes cold.

THOMAS HOOD
(1799–1845)

THE SONG OF THE SHIRT

With fingers weary and worn,
  With eyelids heavy and red,
A woman sat, in unwomanly rags,
  Plying her needle and thread—
    Stitch! stitch! stitch!
In poverty, hunger, and dirt,
And still with a voice of dolorous pitch
She sang "The Song of the Shirt!"

"Work! work! work!
While the cock is crowing aloof!
  And work—work—work,
Till the stars shine through the roof!
It's oh! to be a slave
  Along with the barbarous Turk,
Where woman has never a soul to save,
  If this is Christian work!

Work—work—work
Till the brain begins to swim;
  Work—work—work
Till the eyes are heavy and dim!
Seam, and gusset, and band,
  Band, and gusset, and seam,
Till over the buttons I fall asleep,
  And sew them on in a dream!

"O! Men with sisters dear!
  O! Men! With mothers and wives!
It is not linen you're wearing out,
  But human creatures' lives!
    Stitch—stitch—stitch,

In poverty, hunger, and dirt,
Sewing at once, with a double thread,
 A shroud as well as a shirt.

But why do I talk of Death?
 That phantom of grisly bone,
I hardly fear his terrible shape,
 It seems so like my own—
 It seems so like my own,
 Because of the fasts I keep,
Oh! God! that bread should be so dear,
 And flesh and blood so cheap!

Work—work—work!
 My labour never flags;
And what are its wages? A bed of straw,
 A crust of bread—and rags.
That shattered roof—and this naked floor—
 A table—a broken chair—
And a wall so blank, my shadow I thank
 For sometimes falling there!

Work—work—work!
From weary chime to chime,
 Work—work—work—
As prisoners work for crime!
 Band, and gusset, and seam,
 Seam, and gusset, and band,
Till the heart is sick, and the brain benumbed,
 As well as the weary hand.

Work—work—work,
In the dull December light,
 And work—work—work,
When the weather is warm and bright—
While underneath the eaves
 The brooding swallows cling
As if to show me their sunny backs
 And twit me with the spring.

Oh! but to breathe the breath
Of the cowslip and primrose sweet—

491

With the sky above my head,
And the grass beneath my feet,
For only one short hour
    To feel as I used to feel,
Before I knew the woes of want
    And the walk that costs a meal!

Oh but for one short hour!
    A respite however brief!
No blessed leisure for love or hope,
    But only time for grief!
A little weeping would ease my heart,
    But in their briny bed
My tears must stop, for every drop
    Hinders needle and thread!"

With fingers weary and worn,
    With eyelids heavy and red,
A woman sate in unwomanly rags,
    Plying her needle and thread—
        Stitch! stitch! stitch!
    In poverty, hunger, and dirt,
And still with a voice of dolorous pitch—
Would that its tone could reach the rich!—
    She sang this "Song of the Shirt!"

HENRY TAYLOR
(1800–86)

SONNET IN THE MAIL COACH

What means at this unusual hour the light
  In yonder casement? Doth it hint a tale
  Of trouble, where some maiden mourner pale
Confides her sorrows to the secret night?
Or doth it speak of youth uprising bright
  With glad alacrity ere morning break
To chase a hope new-started; or—but lo!
The wan light creeps with stealthy motion slow
  Across the chamber: shall we token take
From this, that o'er sick bed or mortal throe
  Sad watch is kept? Small answer can I make,
Nor more can of that dim-seen watcher know,
  Than that some object, passion, throb, or ache,
  Has kept some solitary heart awake.

ELIZABETH BARRETT BROWNING
(1806–61)

I learnt the collects and the catechism,
The creeds, from Athanasius back to Nice,
The articles . . . the tracts *against* the times,
(By no means Buonaventure's "Prick of Love")
And various popular synopses of
Inhuman doctrines never taught by John,
Because she liked instructed piety.
I learnt my complement of classic French
(Kept pure of Balzac and neologism)
And German also, since she liked a range
Of liberal education—tongues, not books.
I learnt a little algebra, a little
Of the mathematics—brushed with extreme flounce
The circle of the sciences, because
She misliked women who are frivolous.
I learnt the royal genealogies
Of Oviedo, the internal laws
Of the Burmese Empire . . . by how many feet
Mount Chimborazo outsoars Himmeleh,
What navigable river joins itself
To Lara, and what census of the year five
Was taken at Klagenfurt—because she liked
A general insight into useful facts.
I learnt much music—such as would have been
As quite impossible in Johnson's day
As still it might be wished—fine sleights of hand
And unimagined fingering, shuffling off
The hearer's soul through hurricanes of notes
To a noisy Tophet; and I drew . . . costumes
From French engravings, nereids neatly draped,
With smirks of simmering godship—I washed in
From nature, landscapes (rather say, washed out).

494

I danced the polka and Cellarius,
Spun glass, stuffed birds, and modelled flowers in wax,
Because she liked accomplishments in girls.
I read a score of books on womanhood
To prove, if women do not think at all,
They may teach thinking (to a maiden aunt
Or else the author)—books demonstrating
Their right of comprehending husband's talk
When not too deep, and even of answering
With pretty "may it please you," or "so it is"—
Their rapid insight and fine aptitude,
Particular worth and general missionariness,
As long as they keep quiet by the fire
And never say "no" when the world says "ay,"
For that is fatal—their angelic reach
Of virtue, chiefly used to sit and darn,
And fatten household sinners—their, in brief,
Potential faculty in everything
Of abdicating power in it: she owned
She liked a woman to be womanly,
And English women, she thanked God and sighed
(Some people always sigh in thanking God)
Were models to the universe. And last
I learnt cross-stitch, because she did not like
To see me wear the night with empty hands,
A-doing nothing. So, my shepherdess
Was something after all (the pastoral saints
Be praised for't) leaning lovelorn with pink eyes
To match her shoes, when I mistook the silks;
Her head uncrushed by that round weight of hat
So strangely similar to the tortoise-shell
Which slew the tragic poet.

                        By the way,
The works of women are symbolical.
We sew, sew, prick our fingers, dull our sight,
Producing what? A pair of slippers, sir,
To put on when you're weary—or a stool
To tumble over and vex you . . . "curse that stool!"
Or else at best, a cushion where you lean
And sleep, and dream of something we are not,
But would be for your sake. Alas, alas!

This hurts most, this . . . that, after all, we are paid
The worth of our work, perhaps.

TO GEORGE SAND

A DESIRE

Thou large-brained woman and large-hearted man,
Self-called George Sand! whose soul, amid the lions
Of thy tumultuous senses, moans defiance
And answers roar for roar, as spirits can:
I would some mild miraculous thunder ran
Above the applauded circus, in appliance
Of thine own nobler nature's strength and science,
Drawing two pinions, white as wings of swan,
From thy strong shoulders, to amaze the place
With holier light! that thou to woman's claim
And man's, mightst join beside the angel's grace
Of a pure genius sanctified from blame,
Till child and maiden pressed to thine embrace
To kiss upon thy lips a stainless fame.

TO GEORGE SAND

A RECOGNITION

True genius, but true woman! dost deny
The woman's nature with a manly scorn,
And break away the gauds and armlets worn
By weaker women in captivity?
Ah, vain denial! That revolted cry
Is sobbed in by a woman's voice forlorn—
Thy woman's hair, my sister, all unshorn
Floats back dishevelled strength in agony,
Disproving thy man's name: and while before
The world thou burnest in a poet-fire,
We see thy woman-heart beat evermore

Through the large flame. Beat purer, heart, and higher,
Till God unsex thee on the heavenly shore
Where unincarnate spirits purely aspire!

*

How do I love thee? Let me count the ways.
I love thee to the depth and breadth and height
My soul can reach, when feeling out of sight
For the ends of being and ideal grace.
I love thee to the level of everyday's
Most quiet need, by sun and candle-light.
I love thee freely, as men strive for right;
I love thee purely, as they turn from praise.
I love thee with the passion put to use
In my old griefs, and with my childhood's faith.
I love thee with a love I seemed to lose
With my lost saints—I love with the breath,
Smiles, tears, of all my life!—and, if God choose,
I shall but love thee better after death.

EDWARD FITZGERALD
(1809–83)

from THE RUBÁIYÁT OF OMAR KHÁYYÁM

Come, fill the cup, and in the fire of spring
Your winter-garment of repentance fling;
   The bird of time has but a little way
To flutter—and the bird is on the wing.

Whether at Naishápur or Babylon,
Whether the cup with sweet or bitter run,
   The wine of life keeps oozing drop by drop,
The leaves of life keep falling one by one.

Each morn a thousand roses brings, you say;
Yes, but where leaves the rose of yesterday?
   And this first summer month that brings the rose
Shall take Jamshyd and Kaikobád away.

Well, let it take them! What have we to do
With Kaikobád the Great, or Kaikhosrú?
   Let Zál and Rustum bluster as they will,
Or Hátim call to supper—heed not you.

With me along the strip of herbage strown
That just divides the desert from the sown,
   Where name of slave and sultán is forgot—
And peace to Mahmúd on his golden throne!

A book of verses underneath the bough,
A jug of wine, a loaf of bread—and thou
   Beside me singing in the wilderness—
Oh, wilderness were paradise enow!

ALFRED, LORD TENNYSON
(1809–92)

THE LADY OF SHALOTT

PART I

On either side the river lie
Long fields of barley and of rye,
That clothe the wold and meet the sky;
And through the field the road runs by
      To many-towered Camelot;
And up and down the people go,
Gazing where the lilies blow
Round an island there below,
      The island of Shalott.

Willows whiten, aspens quiver,
Little breezes dusk and shiver
Through the wave that runs forever
By the island in the river
      Flowing down to Camelot.
Four grey walls, and four grey towers,
Overlook a space of flowers,
And the silent isle imbowers
      The Lady of Shalott.

By the margin, willow-veiled,
Slide the heavy barges trailed
By slow horses; and unhailed
The shallop flitteth silken-sailed
      Skimming down to Camelot:
But who hath seen her wave her hand?
Or at the casement seen her stand?
Or is she known in all the land,
      The Lady of Shalott?

Only reapers, reaping early
In among the bearded barley,
Hear a song that echoes cheerly
From the river winding clearly,
   Down to towered Camelot:
And by the moon the reaper weary,
Piling sheaves in uplands airy,
Listening, whispers " 'Tis the fairy
   Lady of Shalott."

PART II

There she weaves by night and day
A magic web with colours gay.
She has heard a whisper say,
A curse is on her if she stay
   To look down to Camelot.
She knows not what the curse may be,
And so she weaveth steadily,
And little other care hath she,
   The Lady of Shalott.

And moving through a mirror clear
That hangs before her all the year,
Shadows of the world appear.
There she sees the highway near
   Winding down to Camelot:
There the river eddy whirls,
And there the surly village-churls,
And the red cloaks of market girls,
   Pass onward from Shalott.

Sometimes a troop of damsels glad,
An abbot on an ambling pad,
Sometimes a curly shepherd-lad,
Or long-haired page in crimson clad,
   Goes by to towered Camelot;
And sometimes through the mirror blue
The knights come riding two and two:

She hath no loyal knight and true,
        The Lady of Shalott.

But in her web she still delights
To weave the mirror's magic sights,
For often through the silent nights
A funeral, with plumes and lights
        And music, went to Camelot:
Or when the moon was overhead,
Came two young lovers lately wed;
"I am half sick of shadows," said
        The Lady of Shalott.

PART III

A bow-shot from her bower-eaves,
He rode between the barley-sheaves,
The sun came dazzling through the leaves,
And flamed upon the brazen greaves
        Of bold Sir Lancelot.
A red-cross knight forever kneeled
To a lady in his shield,
That sparkled on the yellow field,
        Beside remote Shalott.

The gemmy bridle glittered free,
Like to some branch of stars we see
Hung in the golden galaxy.
The bridle bells rang merrily
        As he rode down to Camelot:
And from his blazoned baldric slung
A mighty silver bugle hung,
And as he rode his armour rung,
        Beside remote Shalott.

All in the blue unclouded weather
Thick-jewelled shone the saddle-leather,
The helmet and the helmet-feather
Burned like one burning flame together,
        As he rode down to Camelot.
As often through the purple night,

Below the starry clusters bright,
Some bearded meteor, trailing light,
      Moves over still Shalott.

His broad clear brow in sunlight glowed;
On burnished hooves his war-horse trode;
From underneath his helmet flowed
His coal-black curls as on he rode,
      As he rode down to Camelot.
From the bank and from the river
He flashed into the crystal mirror,
"Tirra lirra," by the river
      Sang Sir Lancelot.

She left the web, she left the loom,
She made three paces through the room,
She saw the water-lily bloom,
She saw the helmet and the plume,
      She looked down to Camelot.
Out flew the web and floated wide;
The mirror cracked from side to side;
"The curse is come upon me," cried
      The Lady of Shalott.

PART IV

In the stormy east-wind straining,
The pale yellow woods were waning,
The broad stream in his banks complaining,
Heavily the low sky raining
      Over towered Camelot;
Down she came and found a boat
Beneath a willow left afloat,
And round about the prow she wrote
      The Lady of Shalott.

And down the river's dim expanse
Like some bold seer in a trance,
Seeing all his own mischance—
With a glassy countenance
      Did she look to Camelot.

And at the closing of the day
She loosed the chain, and down she lay;
The broad stream bore her far away,
        The Lady of Shalott.

Lying, robed in snowy white
That loosely flew to left and right—
The leaves upon her falling light—
Through the noises of the night
        She floated down to Camelot:
And as the boat-head wound along
The willowy hills and fields among,
They heard her singing her last song,
        The Lady of Shalott.

Heard a carol, mournful, holy,
Chanted loudly, chanted lowly,
Till her blood was frozen slowly,
And her eyes were darkened wholly,
        Turned to towered Camelot.
For ere she reached upon the tide
The first house by the water-side,
Singing in her song she died,
        The Lady of Shalott.

Under tower and balcony,
By garden-wall and gallery,
A gleaming shape she floated by,
Dead-pale between the houses high,
        Silent into Camelot.
Out upon the wharfs they came,
Knight and burgher, lord and dame,
And round the prow they read her name,
        The Lady of Shalott.

Who is this? and what is here?
And in the lighted palace near
Died the sound of royal cheer;
And they crossed themselves for fear,
        All the knights at Camelot:
But Lancelot mused a little space;
He said, "She has a lovely face;

God in his mercy lend her grace,
         The Lady of Shalott."

MARIANA

With blackest moss the flower-plots
    Were thickly crusted, one and all:
The rusted nails fell from the knots
    That held the pear to the gable-wall.
The broken sheds looked sad and strange:
    Unlifted was the clinking latch;
    Weeded and worn the ancient thatch
Upon the lonely moated grange.
    She only said, "My life is dreary,
        He cometh not," she said;
    She said, "I am aweary, aweary,
        I would that I were dead!"

Her tears fell with the dews at even;
    Her tears fell ere the dews were dried;
She could not look on the sweet heaven,
    Either at morn or eventide.
After the flitting of the bats,
    When thickest dark did trance the sky,
    She drew her casement-curtain by,
And glanced athwart the glooming flats.
    She only said, "The night is dreary,
        He cometh not," she said;
    She said, "I am aweary, aweary,
        I would that I were dead!"

Upon the middle of the night,
    Waking she heard the night-fowl crow:
The cock sung out an hour ere light:
    From the dark fen the oxen's low
Came to her: without hope of change,
    In sleep she seemed to walk forlorn,
    Till cold winds woke the grey-eyed morn
About the lonely moated grange.

She only said, "The day is dreary,
  He cometh not," she said;
She said, "I am aweary, aweary,
  I would that I were dead!"

About a stone-cast from the wall
  A sluice with blackened waters slept,
And o'er it many, round and small,
  The clustered marish-mosses crept.
Hard by a poplar shook alway,
  All silver-green with gnarled bark:
For leagues no other tree did mark
The level waste, the rounding gray.
  She only said, "My life is dreary,
    He cometh not," she said;
  She said, "I am aweary, aweary,
    I would that I were dead!"

And ever when the moon was low,
  And the shrill winds were up and away,
In the white curtain, to and fro,
  She saw the gusty shadow sway.
But when the moon was very low,
  And wild winds bound within their cell,
  The shadow of the poplar fell
Upon her bed, across her brow.
  She only said, "The night is dreary,
    He cometh not," she said;
  She said, "I am aweary, aweary,
    I would that I were dead!"

All day within the dreamy house,
  The doors upon their hinges creaked;
The blue fly sung in the pane; the mouse
  Behind the mouldering wainscot shrieked,
Or from the crevice peered about.
  Old faces glimmered through the doors,
  Old footsteps trod the upper floors,
Old voices called her from without.
  She only said, "My life is dreary,
    He cometh not," she said;

She said, "I am aweary, aweary,
　　I would that I were dead!"

The sparrow's chirrup on the roof,
　　The slow clock ticking, and the sound
Which to the wooing wind aloof
　　The poplar made, did all confound
Her sense; but most she loathed the hour
　　When the thick-moted sunbeam lay
Athwart the chambers, and the day
Was sloping toward his western bower.
　　Then, said she, "I am very dreary,
　　　　He will not come," she said;
　　She wept, "I am aweary, aweary,
　　　　Oh God, that I were dead!"

THE LOTOS-EATERS

"Courage!" he said, and pointed toward the land,
"This mounting wave will roll us shoreward soon."
In the afternoon they came unto a land
In which it seemed always afternoon.
All round the coast the languid air did swoon,
Breathing like one that hath a weary dream.
Full-faced above the valley stood the moon;
And, like a downward smoke, the slender stream
Along the cliff to fall and pause and fall did seem.

A land of streams! Some, like a downward smoke,
Slow-dropping veils of thinnest lawn, did go;
And some through wavering lights and shadows broke,
Rolling a slumbrous sheet of foam below.
They saw the gleaming river's seaward flow
From the inner land; far off, three mountaintops
Three silent pinnacles of aged snow,
Stood sunset-flushed; and, dewed with showery drops,
Up-clomb the shadowy pine above the woven copse.

The charmed sunset lingered low adown
In the red west; through mountain clefts, the dale
Was seen far inland, and the yellow down
Bordered with palm, and many a winding vale
And meadow, set with slender galingale;
A land where all things always seemed the same!
And round about the keel with faces pale,
Dark faces pale against that rosy flame,
The mild-eyed melancholy lotos-eaters came.

Branches they bore of that enchanted stem,
Laden with flower and fruit, whereof they gave
To each, but whoso did receive of them
And taste, to him the gushing of the wave
Far far away did seem to mourn and rave
On alien shores; and if his fellow spake,
His voice was thin, as voices from the grave;
And deep-asleep he seemed, yet all awake,
And music in his ears his beating heart did make.

They sat them down upon the yellow sand,
Between the sun and moon upon the shore;
And sweet it was to dream of fatherland,
Of child, and wife, and slave; but evermore
Most weary seemed the sea, weary the oar,
Weary the wandering fields of barren foam.
Then some one said, "We will return no more";
And all at once they sang, "Our island home
Is far beyond the wave; we will no longer roam."

Choric Song

There is sweet music here that softer falls
Than petals from blown roses on the grass,
Or night-dews on still waters between walls
Of shadowy granite, in a gleaming pass;
Music that gentlier on the spirit lies,
Than tired eyelids upon tired eyes;
Music that brings sweet sleep down from the blissful skies.
Here are cool mosses deep,
And through the moss the ivies creep,

And in the stream the long-leaved flowers weep,
And from the craggy ledge the poppy hangs in sleep.

Why are we weighed upon with heaviness,
And utterly consumed with sharp distress,
While all things else have rest from weariness?
All things have rest: why should we toil alone,
We only toil, who are the first of things,
And make perpetual moan,
Still from one sorrow to another thrown;
Nor ever fold our wings,
And cease from wanderings,
Nor steep our brows in slumber's holy balm;
Nor harken what the inner spirit sings,
"There is no joy but calm!"
Why should we only toil, the roof and crown of things?

Lo! In the middle of the wood,
The folded leaf is woo'd from out the bud
With winds upon the branch, and there
Grows green and broad, and takes no care,
Sun-steeped at noon, and in the moon
Nightly dew-fed; and turning yellow
Falls, and floats adown the air.
Lo! Sweetened with the summer light,
The full-juiced apple, waxing over-mellow,
Drops in a silent autumn night.
All its allotted length of days
The flower ripens in its place,
Ripens and fades, and falls, and hath no toil,
Fast-rooted in the fruitful soil.

Hateful is the dark blue sky,
Vaulted o'er the dark blue sea.
Death is the end of life; ah, why
Should life all labour be?
Let us alone. Time driveth onward fast,
And in a little while our lips are dumb.
Let us alone. What is it that will last?
All things are taken from us, and become
Portions and parcels of the dreadful past.
Let us alone. What pleasure can we have

To war with evil? Is there any peace
In ever climbing up the climbing wave?
All things have rest, and ripen toward the grave
In silence—ripen, fall, and cease;
Give us long rest or death, dark death, or dreamful ease.

How sweet it were, hearing the downward stream,
With half-shut eyes ever to seem
Falling asleep in a half-dream!
To dream and dream, like yonder amber light,
Which will not leave the myrrh-bush on the height;
To hear each other's whispered speech;
Eating the lotos day by day,
To watch the crisping ripples on the beach,
And tender curving lines of creamy spray;
To lend our hearts and spirits wholly
To the influence of mild-minded melancholy;
To muse and brood and live again in memory,
With the old faces of our infancy
Heaped over with a mound of grass,
Two handfuls of white dust, shut in an urn of brass!

Dear is the memory of our wedded lives,
And dear the last embraces of our wives
And their warm tears; but all hath suffered change:
For surely now our household hearths are cold,
Our sons inherit us, our looks are strange,
And we should come like ghosts to trouble joy.
Or else the island princes overbold
Have eat our substance, and the minstrel sings
Before them of the ten years' war in Troy,
And our great deeds, as half-forgotten things.
Is there confusion in the little isle?
Let what is broken so remain.
The gods are hard to reconcile;
'Tis hard to settle order once again.
There is confusion worse than death,
Trouble on trouble, pain on pain,
Long labour unto aged breath,
Sore tasks to hearts worn out by many wars
And eyes grown dim with gazing on the pilot-stars.

But, propped on beds of amaranth and moly,
How sweet—while warm airs lull us, blowing lowly—
With half-dropped eyelids still,
Beneath a heaven dark and holy,
To watch the long, bright river drawing slowly
His waters from the purple hill—
To hear the dewy echoes calling
From cave to cave through the thick-twined vine—
To watch the emerald-coloured water falling
Through many a woven acanthus-wreath divine!
Only to hear and see the far-off sparkling brine,
Only to hear were sweet, stretched out beneath the pine.

The lotos blooms below the barren peak,
The lotos blows by every winding creek;
All day the wind breathes low with mellower tone;
Through every hollow cave and alley lone
Round and round the spicy downs the yellow lotos dust is blown.
We have had enough of action, and of motion we,
Rolled to starboard, rolled to larboard, when the surge was seething free,
Where the wallowing monster spouted his foam-fountains in the sea.
Let us swear an oath, and keep it with an equal mind,
In the hollow lotos land to live and lie reclined
On the hills like gods together, careless of mankind.
For they lie beside their nectar, and the bolts are hurled
Far below them in the valleys, and the clouds are lightly curled
Round their golden houses, girdled with the gleaming world;
Where they smile in secret, looking over wasted lands,
Blight and famine, plague and earthquake, roaring deeps and fiery sands,
Clanging fights, and flaming towns, and sinking ships, and praying hands.
But they smile; they find a music centred in a doleful song
Steaming up, a lamentation and an ancient tale of wrong,
Like a tale of little meaning though the words are strong;
Chanted from an ill-used race of men that cleave the soil,
Sow the seed, and reap the harvest with enduring toil,
Storing yearly little dues of wheat, and wine and oil;
Till they perish and they suffer—some, 'tis whispered—down in hell,
Suffer endless anguish, others in Elysian valleys dwell,
Resting weary limbs at last on beds of asphodel.
Surely, surely, slumber is more sweet than toil, the shore

Than labour in the deep mid-ocean, wind and wave and oar;
Oh rest ye, brother mariners, we will not wander more.

ULYSSES

It little profits that an idle king,
By this still hearth, among these barren crags,
Matched with an aged wife, I mete and dole
Unequal laws unto a savage race,
That hoard, and sleep, and feed, and know not me.

I cannot rest from travel; I will drink
Life to the lees. All times I have enjoyed
Greatly, have suffered greatly, both with those
That loved me, and alone; on shore, and when
Through scudding drifts the rainy Hyades
Vexed the dim sea. I am become a name;
For always roaming with a hungry heart
Much have I seen and known—cities of men
And manners, climates, councils, governments,
Myself not least, but honoured of them all—
And drunk delight of battle with my peers,
Far on the ringing plains of windy Troy.
I am a part of all that I have met;
Yet all experience is an arch wherethrough
Gleams that untravelled world whose margin fades
Forever and forever when I move.
How dull it is to pause, to make an end,
To rust unburnished, not to shine in use!
As though to breathe were life! Life piled on life
Were all too little, and of one to me
Little remains; but every hour is saved
From that eternal silence, something more,
A bringer of new things; and vile it were
For some three suns to store and hoard myself,
And this grey spirit yearning in desire
To follow knowledge like a sinking star,
Beyond the utmost bound of human thought.

This is my son, mine own Telemachus,
To whom I leave the sceptre and the isle—
Well-loved of me, discerning to fulfill
This labour, by slow prudence to make mild
A rugged people, and through soft degrees
Subdue them to the useful and the good.
Most blameless is he, centred in the sphere
Of common duties, decent not to fail
In offices of tenderness, and pay
Meet adoration to my household gods,
When I am gone. He works his work, I mine.

There lies the port; the vessel puffs her sail;
There gloom the dark, broad seas. My mariners,
Souls that have toiled, and wrought, and thought with me—
That ever with a frolic welcome took
The thunder and the sunshine, and opposed
Free hearts, free foreheads—you and I are old;
Old age hath yet his honour and his toil.
Death closes all; but something ere the end,
Some work of noble note, may yet be done,
Not unbecoming men that strove with gods.
The lights begin to twinkle from the rocks;
The long day wanes; the slow moon climbs; the deep
Moans round with many voices. Come, my friends,
'Tis not too late to seek a newer world.
Push off, and sitting well in order smite
The sounding furrows; for my purpose holds
To sail beyond the sunset, and the baths
Of all the western stars, until I die.
It may be that the gulfs will wash us down;
It may be we shall touch the happy isles,
And see the great Achilles, whom we knew.
Though much is taken, much abides; and though
We are not now that strength which in old days
Moved earth and heaven, that which we are, we are—
One equal temper of heroic hearts,
Made weak by time and fate, but strong in will
To strive, to seek, to find, and not to yield.

TITHONUS

The woods decay, the woods decay and fall,
The vapours weep their burthen to the ground,
Man comes and tills the field and lies beneath,
And after many a summer dies the swan.
Me only cruel immortality
Consumes: I wither slowly in thine arms,
Here at the quiet limit of the world,
A white-haired shadow roaming like a dream
The ever-silent spaces of the east,
Far-folded mists, and gleaming halls of morn.

Alas! for this grey shadow, once a man—
So glorious in his beauty and thy choice,
Who madest him thy chosen, that he seemed
To his great heart none other than a god!
I asked thee, "Give me immortality."
Then didst thou grant mine asking with a smile,
Like wealthy men who care not how they give.
But thy strong hours indignant worked their wills,
And beat me down and marred and wasted me,
And though they could not end me, left me maimed
To dwell in presence of immortal youth,
Immortal age beside immortal youth,
And all I was, in ashes. Can thy love,
Thy beauty, make amends, though even now,
Close over us, the silver star, thy guide,
Shines in those tremulous eyes that fill with tears
To hear me? Let me go: take back thy gift:
Why should a man desire in any way
To vary from the kindly race of men,
Or pass beyond the goal of ordinance
Where all should pause, as is most meet for all?

A soft air fans the cloud apart; there comes
A glimpse of that dark world where I was born.
Once more the old mysterious glimmer steals
From thy pure brows, and from thy shoulders pure,
And bosom beating with a heart renewed.
Thy cheek begins to redden through the gloom,

Thy sweet eyes brighten slowly close to mine,
Ere yet they blind the stars, and the wild team
Which love thee, yearning for thy yoke, arise,
And shake the darkness from their loosened manes,
And beat the twilight into flakes of fire.

Lo! Ever thus thou growest beautiful
In silence, then before thine answer given
Departest, and thy tears are on my cheek.

Why wilt thou ever scare me with thy tears,
And make me tremble lest a saying learnt,
In days far-off, on that dark earth, be true?
"The gods themselves cannot recall their gifts."

Ay me! ay me! with what another heart
In days far-off, and with what other eyes
I used to watch—if I be he that watched—
The lucid outline forming round thee; saw
The dim curls kindle into sunny rings;
Changed with thy mystic change, and felt my blood
Glow with the glow that slowly crimsoned all
Thy presence and thy portals, while I lay,
Mouth, forehead, eyelids, growing dewy-warm
With kisses balmier than half-opening buds
Of April, and could hear the lips that kissed
Whispering I knew not what of wild and sweet,
Like that strange song I heard Apollo sing,
While Ilion like a mist rose into towers.

Yet hold me not forever in thine east:
How can my nature longer mix with thine?
Coldly thy rosy shadows bathe me, cold
Are all thy lights, and cold my wrinkled feet
Upon thy glimmering thresholds, when the steam
Floats up from those dim fields about the homes
Of happy men that have the power to die,
And grassy barrows of the happier dead.
Release me, and restore me to the ground;
Thou seest all things, thou wilt see my grave:
Thou wilt renew thy beauty morn by morn;

I earth in earth forget these empty courts,
And thee returning on thy silver wheels.

TEARS, IDLE TEARS

Tears, idle tears, I know not what they mean,
Tears from the depth of some divine despair
Rise in the heart, and gather to the eyes,
In looking on the happy autumn-fields,
And thinking of the days that are no more.

Fresh as the first beam glittering on a sail,
That brings our friends up from the underworld,
Sad as the last which reddens over one
That sinks with all we love below the verge;
So sad, so fresh, the days that are no more.

Ah, sad and strange as in dark summer dawns
The earliest pipe of half-awakened birds
To dying ears, when unto dying eyes
The casement slowly grows a glimmering square;
So sad, so strange, the days that are no more.

Dear as remembered kisses after death,
And sweet as those by hopeless fancy feigned
On lips that are for others; deep as love,
Deep as first love, and wild with all regret;
O death in life, the days that are no more.

BREAK, BREAK, BREAK

Break, break, break,
    On thy cold grey stones, O sea!

515

And I would that my tongue could utter
The thoughts that arise in me.

Oh well for the fisherman's boy,
That he shouts with his sister at play!
Oh well for the sailor lad,
That he sings in his boat on the bay!

And the stately ships go on
To their haven under the hill;
But oh for the touch of a vanished hand,
And the sound of a voice that is still!

Break, break, break,
At the foot of thy crags, O sea!
But the tender grace of a day that is dead
Will never come back to me.

THE CHARGE OF THE LIGHT BRIGADE

Half a league, half a league,
Half a league onward,
All in the valley of death
Rode the six hundred.
"Forward the Light Brigade!
Charge for the guns!" he said;
Into the valley of death
Rode the six hundred.

"Forward, the Light Brigade!"
Was there a man dismayed?
Not though the soldier knew
Someone had blundered.
Theirs not to make reply,
Theirs not to reason why,
Theirs but to do and die.
Into the valley of death
Rode the six hundred.

Cannon to right of them,
Cannon to left of them,
Cannon in front of them
  Volleyed and thundered;
Stormed at with shot and shell,
Boldly they rode and well,
Into the jaws of death,
Into the mouth of hell
  Rode the six hundred.

Flashed all their sabres bare,
Flashed all at once in air
Sabering the gunners there,
Charging an army, while
  All the world wondered.
Plunged in the battery smoke
Right through the line they broke;
Cossack and Russian
Reeled from the sabre stroke
  Shattered and sundered.
Then they rode back, but not,
  Not the six hundred.

Cannon to right of them,
Cannon to left of them,
Cannon behind them
  Volleyed and thundered;
Stormed at with shot and shell,
While horse and hero fell,
They that had fought so well
Came through the jaws of death,
Back from the mouth of hell,
All that was left of them,
  Left of six hundred.

When can their glory fade?
Oh, the wild charge they made!
  All the world wondered.
Honour the charge they made!
Honour the Light Brigade,
  Noble six hundred!

FLOWER IN THE CRANNIED WALL

Flower in the crannied wall,
I pluck you out of the crannies,
I hold you here, root and all, in my hand,
Little flower—but *if* I could understand
What you are, root and all, and all in all,
I should know what God and man is.

CROSSING THE BAR

Sunset and evening star,
  And one clear call for me!
And may there be no moaning of the bar,
  When I put out to sea,

But such a tide as moving seems asleep,
  Too full for sound and foam,
When that which drew from out the boundless deep
  Turns again home.

Twilight and evening bell,
  And after that the dark!
And may there be no sadness of farewell,
  When I embark;

For though from out our bourne of time and place
  The flood may bear me far,
I hope to see my pilot face to face
  When I have crossed the bar.

ROBERT BROWNING
(1812–89)

PORPHYRIA'S LOVER

The rain set early in tonight,
    The sullen wind was soon awake,
It tore the elm-tops down for spite,
    And did its worst to vex the lake:
    I listened with heart fit to break.
When glided in Porphyria; straight
    She shut the cold out and the storm,
And kneeled and made the cheerless grate
    Blaze up, and all the cottage warm;
    Which done, she rose, and from her form
Withdrew the dripping cloak and shawl,
    And laid her soiled gloves by, untied
Her hat and let the damp hair fall,
    And, last, she sat down by my side
    And called me. When no voice replied,
She put my arm about her waist,
    And made her smooth white shoulder bare,
And all her yellow hair displaced,
    And, stooping, made my cheek lie there,
    And spread, o'er all, her yellow hair,
Murmuring how she loved me—she
    Too weak, for all her heart's endeavour,
To set its struggling passion free
    From pride, and vainer ties dissever,
    And give herself to me forever.
But passion sometimes would prevail,
    Nor could tonight's gay feast restrain
A sudden thought of one so pale
    For love of her, and all in vain:
    So, she was come through wind and rain.
Be sure I looked up at her eyes
    Happy and proud; at last I knew

Porphyria worshiped me; surprise
    Made my heart swell, and still it grew
    While I debated what to do.
That moment she was mine, mine, fair,
    Perfectly pure and good; I found
A thing to do, and all her hair
    In one long yellow string I wound
    Three times her little throat around,
And strangled her. No pain felt she;
    I am quite sure she felt no pain.
As a shut bud that holds a bee,
    I warily oped her lids; again
    Laughed the blue eyes without a stain.
And I untightened next the tress
    About her neck; her cheek once more
Blushed bright beneath my burning kiss;
    I propped her head up as before,
    Only, this time my shoulder bore
Her head, which droops upon it still:
    The smiling rosy little head,
So glad it has its utmost will,
    That all it scorned at once is fled,
    And I, its love, am gained instead!
Porphyria's love; she guessed not how
    Her darling one wish would be heard.
And thus we sit together now,
    And all night long we have not stirred,
    And yet God has not said a word!

SOLILOQUY OF THE SPANISH CLOISTER

    Gr-r-r—there go, my heart's abhorrence!
        Water your damned flowerpots, do!
    If hate killed men, Brother Lawrence,
        God's blood, would not mine kill you!
    What? Your myrtle bush wants trimming?
        Oh, that rose has prior claims—
    Needs its leaden vase filled brimming?
        Hell dry you up with its flames!

At the meal we sit together:
    Salve tibi! I must hear
Wise talk of the kind of weather,
    Sort of season, time of year:
Not a plenteous cork crop: scarcely
    Dare we hope oak-galls, I doubt:
What's the Latin name for "parsley"?
    What's the Greek name for swine's snout?

Whew! We'll have our platter burnished,
    Laid with care on our own shelf!
With a fire-new spoon we're furnished,
    And a goblet for ourself,
Rinsed like something sacrificial
    Ere 'tis fit to touch our chaps—
Marked with L. for our initial!
    (He-he! There his lily snaps!)

Saint, forsooth! While brown Dolores
    Squats outside the convent bank
With Sanchicha, telling stories,
    Steeping tresses in the tank,
Blue-black, lustrous, thick like horsehairs,
    —Can't I see his dead eye glow,
Bright as 'twere a Barbary corsair's
    (That is, if he'd let it show!)

When he finishes refection,
    Knife and fork he never lays
Cross-wise, to my recollection,
    As do I, in Jesu's praise.
I the trinity illustrate,
    Drinking watered orange pulp—
In three sips the Arian frustrate;
    While he drains his at one gulp.

Oh, those melons? If he's able
    We're to have a feast! so nice!
One goes to the abbot's table,
    All of us get each a slice.
How go on your flowers? None double?

Not one fruit-sort can you spy?
   Strange!—And I, too, at such trouble,
   Keep them close-nipped on the sly!

There's a great text in Galatians,
   Once you trip on it, entails
Twenty-nine distinct damnations,
   One sure, if another fails:
If I trip him just a-dying,
   Sure of heaven as sure can be,
Spin him round and send him flying
   Off to hell, a Manichee?

Or my scrofulous French novel
   On grey paper with blunt type!
Simply glance at it, you grovel
   Hand and foot in Belial's gripe:
If I double down its pages
   At the woeful sixteenth print,
When he gathers his greengages,
   Ope a sieve and slip it in't?

Or, there's Satan!—one might venture
   Pledge one's soul to him, yet leave
Such a flaw in the indenture
   As he'd miss till, past retrieve,
Blasted lay that rose-acacia
   We're so proud of! *Hy, Zy, Hine* . . .
'St, there's Vespers! *Plena gratia*
   Ave, Virgo! Gr-r-r—you swine!

MY LAST DUCHESS

That's my last duchess painted on the wall,
Looking as if she were alive. I call
That piece a wonder, now: Fra Pandolf's hands
Worked busily a day, and there she stands.
Will't please you sit and look at her? I said
"Fra Pandolf" by design, for never read

Strangers like you that pictured countenance,
The depth and passion of its earnest glance,
But to myself they turned (since none puts by
The curtain I have drawn for you, but I)
And seemed as they would ask me, if they durst,
How such a glance came there; so, not the first
Are you to turn and ask thus. Sir, 'twas not
Her husband's presence only, called that spot
Of joy into the duchess' cheek: perhaps
Fra Pandolf chanced to say "Her mantle laps
Over my lady's wrist too much," or "Paint
Must never hope to reproduce the faint
Half-flush that dies along her throat": such stuff
Was courtesy, she thought, and cause enough
For calling up that spot of joy. She had
A heart—how shall I say?—too soon made glad,
Too easily impressed; she liked whate'er
She looked on, and her looks went everywhere.
Sir, 'twas all one! My favour at her breast,
The dropping of the daylight in the west,
The bough of cherries some officious fool
Broke in the orchard for her, the white mule
She rode with round the terrace—all and each
Would draw from her alike the approving speech,
Or blush, at least. She thanked men—good! but thanked
Somehow—I know not how—as if she ranked
My gift of a nine-hundred-years-old name
With anybody's gift. Who'd stoop to blame
This sort of trifling? Even had you skill
In speech (which I have not) to make your will
Quite clear to such an one, and say, "Just this
Or that in you disgusts me; here you miss,
Or there exceed the mark"—and if she let
Herself be lessoned so, nor plainly set
Her wits to yours, forsooth, and made excuse
—E'en then would be some stooping; and I choose
Never to stoop. Oh sir, she smiled, no doubt,
Whene'er I passed her; but who passed without
Much the same smile? This grew; I gave commands;
Then all smiles stopped together. There she stands
As if alive. Will't please you rise? We'll meet
The company below, then. I repeat,

The Count your master's known munificence
Is ample warrant that no just pretence
Of mine for dowry will be disallowed;
Though his fair daughter's self, as I avowed
At starting, is my object. Nay, we'll go
Together down, sir. Notice Neptune, though,
Taming a sea horse, thought a rarity,
Which Claus of Innsbruck cast in bronze for me!

SIBRANDUS SCHAFNABURGENSIS

Plague take all your pedants, say I!
    He who wrote what I hold in my hand,
Centuries back was so good as to die,
    Leaving this rubbish to cumber the land;
This, that was a book in its time,
    Printed on paper and bound in leather,
Last month in the white of a matin-prime,
    Just when the birds sang all together,

Into the garden I brought it to read,
    And under the arbute and laurustine
Read it, so help me grace in my need,
    From title-page to closing line.
Chapter on chapter did I count,
    As a curious traveller counts Stonehenge;
Added up the mortal amount;
    And then proceeded to my revenge.

Yonder's a plum-tree with a crevice
    An owl would build in, were he but sage;
For a lap of moss, like a fine pont-levis
    In a castle of the middle age,
Joins to a lip of gum, pure amber;
    When he'd be private, there might he spend
Hours alone in his lady's chamber:
    Into this crevice I dropped our friend.

Splash, went he, as under he ducked,
  —At the bottom, I knew, rain-drippings stagnate;
Next, a handful of blossoms I plucked
  To bury him with, my bookshelf's magnate;
Then I went in-doors, brought out a loaf,
  Half a cheese, and a bottle of Chablis;
Lay on the grass and forgot the oaf
  Over a jolly chapter of Rabelais.

Now, this morning, betwixt the moss
  And gum that locked our friend in limbo,
A spider had spun his web across,
  And sat in the midst with arms akimbo:
So, I took pity, for learning's sake,
  And, *de profundis, accentibus loetis.*
Cantate! quoth I, as I got a rake;
  And up I fished his delectable treatise.

Here you have it, dry in the sun,
  With all the binding all of a blister,
And great blue spots where the ink has run,
  And reddish streaks that wink and glister
O'er the page so beautifully yellow:
  Oh, well have the droppings played their tricks!
Did he guess how toadstools grow, this fellow?
  Here's one stuck in his chapter six!

How did he like it when the live creatures
  Tickled and toused and browsed him all over,
And worm, slug, eft, with serious features,
  Came in, each one, for his right of trover?
—When the water-beetle with great blind deaf face
  Made of her eggs the stately deposit,
And the newt borrowed just so much of the preface
  As tiled in the top of his black wife's closet?

All that life and fun and romping,
  All that frisking and twisting and coupling,
While slowly our poor friend's leaves were swamping,
  And clasps were cracking and covers suppling!
As if you had carried sour John Knox
  To the play-house at Paris, Vienna or Munich,

525

Fastened him into a front-row box,
  And danced off the ballet with trousers and tunic.

Come, old martyr! What, torment enough is it?
  Back to my room shall you take your sweet self.
Good-bye, mother-beetle; husband-eft, *sufficit!*
  See the snug niche I have made on my shelf!
A's book shall prop you up, B's shall cover you,
  Here's C to be grave with, or D to be gay,
And with E on each side, and F right over you,
  Dry-rot at ease till the Judgment-day!

HOME-THOUGHTS, FROM ABROAD

Oh, to be in England,
Now that April's there,
And whoever wakes in England
Sees, some morning, unaware,
That the lowest boughs and the brushwood sheaf
Round the elm-tree bole are in tiny leaf,
While the chaffinch sings on the orchard bough
In England—now!

And after April, when May follows,
And the whitethroat builds, and all the swallows!
Hark, where my blossomed pear-tree in the hedge
Leans to the field and scatters on the clover
Blossoms and dewdrops—at the bent spray's edge—
That's the wise thrush; he sings each song twice over,
Lest you should think he never could recapture
The first fine careless rapture!
And though the fields look rough with hoary dew,
All will be gay when noontide wakes anew
The buttercups, the little children's dower
—Far brighter than this gaudy melon-flower!

THE BISHOP ORDERS HIS TOMB AT
SAINT PRAXED'S CHURCH

Vanity, saith the preacher, vanity!
Draw round my bed: is Anselm keeping back?
Nephews—sons mine . . . Ah God, I know not! Well—
She, men would have to be your mother once,
Old Gandolf envied me, so fair she was!
What's done is done, and she is dead beside,
Dead long ago, and I am Bishop since,
And as she died so must we die ourselves,
And thence ye may perceive the world's a dream.
Life, how and what is it? As here I lie
In this state chamber, dying by degrees,
Hours and long hours in the dead night, I ask
"Do I live, am I dead?" Peace, peace seems all.
Saint Praxed's ever was the church for peace;
And so, about this tomb of mine. I fought
With tooth and nail to save my niche, ye know:
—Old Gandolf cozened me, despite my care;
Shrewd was that snatch from out the corner south
He graced his carrion with, God curse the same!
Yet still my niche is not so cramped but thence
One sees the pulpit o' the epistle side,
And somewhat of the choir, those silent seats,
And up into the airy dome where live
The angels, and a sunbeam's sure to lurk:
And I shall fill my slab of basalt there,
And 'neath my tabernacle take my rest,
With those nine columns round me, two and two,
The odd one at my feet where Anselm stands:
Peach-blossom marble all, the rare, the ripe,
As fresh-poured red wine of a mighty pulse.
—Old Gandolf with his paltry onion-stone,
Put me where I may look at him! True peach,
Rosy and flawless: how I earned the prize!
Draw close: that conflagration of my church
—What then? So much was saved if aught were missed!
My sons, ye would not be my death? Go dig
The white-grape vineyard where the oil-press stood,
Drop water gently till the surface sink,

And if ye find . . . Ah God, I know not, I! . . .
Bedded in store of rotten fig leaves soft,
And corded up in a tight olive-frail,
Some lump, ah God, of lapis lazuli,
Big as a Jew's head cut off at the nape,
Blue as a vein o'er the Madonna's breast . . .
Sons, all have I bequeathed you, villas, all,
That brave Frascati villa with its bath,
So, let the blue lump poise between my knees,
Like God the Father's globe on both his hands
Ye worship in the Jesu Church so gay,
For Gandolf shall not choose but see and burst!
Swift as a weaver's shuttle fleet our years:
Man goeth to the grave, and where is he?
Did I say basalt for my slab, sons? Black—
'Twas ever antique-black I meant! How else
Shall ye contrast my frieze to come beneath?
The bas-relief in bronze ye promised me,
Those Pans and nymphs ye wot of, and perchance
Some tripod, thyrsus, with a vase or so,
The Saviour at his sermon on the mount,
Saint Praxed in a glory, and one Pan
Ready to twitch the nymph's last garment off,
And Moses with the tables . . . but I know
Ye mark me not! What do they whisper thee,
Child of my bowels, Anselm? Ah, ye hope
To revel down my villas while I gasp
Bricked o'er with beggar's moldy travertine
Which Gandolf from his tomb-top chuckles at!
Nay, boys, ye love me—all of jasper, then!
'Tis jasper ye stand pledged to, lest I grieve
My bath must needs be left behind, alas!
One block, pure green as a pistachio nut,
There's plenty jasper somewhere in the world—
And have I not Saint Praxed's ear to pray
Horses for ye, and brown Greek manuscripts,
And mistresses with great smooth marbly limbs?
—That's if ye carve my epitaph aright,
Choice Latin, picked phrase, Tully's every word,
No gaudy ware like Gandolf's second line—
Tully, my masters? Ulpian serves his need!
And then how I shall lie through centuries,

And hear the blessed mutter of the mass,
And see God made and eaten all day long,
And feel the steady candle flame, and taste
Good strong thick stupefying incense-smoke!
For as I lie here, hours of the dead night,
Dying in state and by such slow degrees,
I fold my arms as if they clasped a crook,
And stretch my feet forth straight as stone can point,
And let the bedclothes, for a mortcloth, drop
Into great laps and folds of sculptor's work:
And as yon tapers dwindle, and strange thoughts
Grow, with a certain humming in my ears,
About the life before I lived this life,
And this life too, popes, cardinals, and priests,
Saint Praxed at his sermon on the mount,
Your tall pale mother with her talking eyes,
And new-found agate urns as fresh as day,
And marble's language, Latin pure, discreet
—Aha, *elucescebat* quoth our friend?
No Tully, said I, Ulpian at the best!
Evil and brief hath been my pilgrimage.
All lapis, all, sons! Else I give the Pope
My villas! Will ye ever eat my heart?
Ever your eyes were as a lizard's quick,
They glitter like your mother's for my soul,
Or ye would heighten my impoverished frieze,
Pierce out its starved design, and fill my vase
With grapes, and add a vizor and a Term,
And to the tripod ye would tie a lynx
That in his struggle throws the thyrsus down,
To comfort me on my entablature
Whereon I am to lie till I must ask
"Do I live, am I dead?" There, leave me, there!
For ye have stabbed me with ingratitude
To death—ye wish it—God, ye wish it! Stone—
Gritstone, a-crumble! Clammy squares which sweat
As if the corpse they keep were oozing through—
And no more lapis to delight the world!
Well go! I bless ye. Fewer tapers there,
But in a row: and, going, turn your backs
—Aye, like departing altar-ministrants,
And leave me in my church, the church for peace,

That I may watch at leisure if he leers—
Old Gandolf, at me, from his onion-stone,
As still he envied me, so fair she was!

A TOCCATA OF GALUPPI'S

Oh, Galuppi, Baldassaro, this is very sad to find!
I can hardly misconceive you; it would prove me deaf and blind;
But although I take your meaning, 'tis with such a heavy mind!

Here you come with your old music, and here's all the good it brings.
What, they lived once thus at Venice where the merchants were the
     kings,
Where Saint Mark's is, where the Doges used to wed the sea with rings?

Aye, because the sea's the street there; and 'tis arched by . . . what you
     call
. . . Shylock's bridge with houses on it, where they kept the carnival:
I was never out of England—it's as if I saw it all.

Did young people take their pleasure when the sea was warm in May?
Balls and masks begun at midnight, burning ever to midday,
When they made up fresh adventures for the morrow, do you say?

Was a lady such a lady, cheeks so round and lips so red—
On her neck the small face buoyant, like a bellflower on its bed,
O'er the breast's superb abundance where a man might base his head?

Well, and it was graceful of them—they'd break talk off and afford
—She, to bite her mask's black velvet—he, to finger on his sword,
While you sat and played toccatas, stately at the clavichord?

What? Those lesser thirds so plaintive, sixths diminished, sigh on sigh,
Told them something? Those suspensions, those solutions—"Must we
     die?"
Those commiserating sevenths—"Life might last! We can but try!"

"Were you happy?"—"Yes."—"And are you still as happy?"—"Yes. And
     you?"

—"Then, more kisses!"—"Did I stop them, when a million seemed so
few?"
Hark, the dominant's persistence till it must be answered to!

So, an octave struck the answer. Oh, they praised you, I dare say!
"Brave Galuppi! That was music; good alike at grave and gay!
I can always leave off talking when I hear a master play!"

Then they left you for their pleasure: till in due time, one by one,
Some with lives that came to nothing, some with deeds as well undone,
Death stepped tacitly and took them where they never see the sun.

But when I sit down to reason, think to take my stand nor swerve,
While I triumph o'er a secret wrung from nature's close reserve,
In you come with your cold music till I creep through every nerve.

Yes, you, like a ghostly cricket, creaking where a house was burned:
"Dust and ashes, dead and done with, Venice spent what Venice earned.
The soul, doubtless, is immortal—where a soul can be discerned.

Yours for instance: you know physics, something of geology,
Mathematics are your pastime; souls shall rise in their degree;
Butterflies may dread extinction—you'll not die, it cannot be!

As for Venice and her people, merely born to bloom and drop,
Here on earth they bore their fruitage, mirth and folly were the crop:
What of soul was left, I wonder, when the kissing had to stop?

Dust and ashes!" So you creak it, and I want the heart to scold.
Dear dead women, with such hair, too—what's become of all the gold
Used to hang and brush their bosoms? I feel chilly and grown old.

PICTOR IGNOTUS

I could have painted pictures like that youth's
    Ye praise so. How my soul springs up! No bar
Stayed me—ah, thought which saddens while it soothes—
    Never did fate forbid me, star by star,
To outburst on your night with all my gift

Of fires from God: nor would my flesh have shrunk
From seconding my soul, with eyes uplift
    And wide to heaven, or, straight like thunder, sunk
To the centre, of an instant; or around
    Turned calmly and inquisitive, to scan
The license and the limit, space and bound,
    Allowed to truth made visible in man.
And, like that youth ye praise so, all I saw,
    Over the canvas could my hand have flung,
Each face obedient to its passion's law,
    Each passion clear proclaimed without a tongue;
Whether hope rose at once in all the blood,
    A-tiptoe for the blessing of embrace,
Or rapture drooped the eyes, as when her brood
    Pull down the nesting dove's heart to its place;
Or confidence lit swift the forehead up,
    And locked the mouth fast, like a castle braved—
O human faces, hath it spilt, my cup?
    What did ye give me that I have not saved?
Nor will I say I have not dreamed (how well!)
    Of going—I, in each new picture—forth,
As, making new hearts beat and bosoms swell,
    To Pope or Kaiser, east, west, south, or north,
Bound for the calmly satisfied great state,
    Or glad aspiring little burgh, it went,
Flowers cast upon the car which bore the freight,
    Through old streets named afresh from the event,
Till it reached home, where learned age should greet
    My face, and youth, the star not yet distinct
Above his hair, lie learning at my feet!—
    Oh, thus to live, I and my picture, linked
With love about, and praise, till life should end,
    And then not go to heaven, but linger here,
Here on my earth, earth's every man my friend—
    The thought grew frightful, 'twas so wildly dear!
But a voice changed it. Glimpses of such sights
    Have scared me, like the revels through a door
Of some strange house of idols at its rites!
    This world seemed not the world it was before:
Mixed with my loving trusting ones, there trooped
    . . . Who summoned those cold faces that begun
To press on me and judge me? Though I stooped

Shrinking, as from the soldiery a nun,
They drew me forth, and spite of me . . . enough!
  These buy and sell our pictures, take and give,
Count them for garniture and household-stuff,
  And where they live needs must our pictures live
And see their faces, listen to their prate,
  Partakers of their daily pettiness,
Discussed of—"This I love, or this I hate,
  This likes me more, and this affects me less!"
Wherefore I chose my portion. If at whiles
  My heart sinks, as monotonous I paint
These endless cloisters and eternal aisles
  With the same series, virgin, babe and saint,
With the same cold calm beautiful regard—
  At least no merchant traffics in my heart;
The sanctuary's gloom at least shall ward
  Vain tongues from where my pictures stand apart:
Only prayer breaks the silence of the shrine
  While, blackening in the daily candle-smoke,
They moulder on the damp wall's travertine,
  'Mid echoes the light footstep never woke.
So, die my pictures! surely, gently die!
  O youth, men praise so—holds their praise its worth?
Blown harshly, keeps the trump its golden cry?
  Tastes sweet the water with such specks of earth?

FRA LIPPO LIPPI

I am poor brother Lippo, by your leave!
You need not clap your torches to my face.
Zooks, what's to blame? You think you see a monk!
What, 'tis past midnight, and you go the rounds,
And here you catch me at an alley's end
Where sportive ladies leave their doors ajar?
The Carmine's my cloister: hunt it up,
Do—harry out, if you must show your zeal,
Whatever rat, there, haps on his wrong hole,
And nip each softling of a wee white mouse,
Weke, weke, that's crept to keep him company!
Aha, you know your betters! Then, you'll take

Your hand away that's fiddling on my throat,
And please to know me likewise. Who am I?
Why, one, sir, who is lodging with a friend
Three streets off—he's a certain . . . how d'ye call?
Master—a . . . Cosimo of the Medici,
I' the house that caps the corner. Boh! You were best!
Remember and tell me, the day you're hanged,
How you affected such a gullet's gripe!
But you, sir, it concerns you that your knaves
Pick up a manner nor discredit you:
Zooks, are we pilchards, that they sweep the streets
And count fair prize what comes into their net?
He's Judas to a tittle, that man is!
Just such a face! Why, sir, you make amends.
Lord, I'm not angry! Bid your hangdogs go
Drink out this quarter-florin to the health
Of the munificent house that harbours me
(And many more beside, lads! more beside!)
And all's come square again. I'd like his face—
His, elbowing on his comrade in the door
With the pike and lantern—for the slave that holds
John Baptist's head a-dangle by the hair
With one hand ("Look you, now," as who should say)
And his weapon in the other, yet unwiped!
It's not your chance to have a bit of chalk,
A wood-coal or the like? Or you should see!
Yes, I'm the painter, since you style me so.
What, brother Lippo's doings, up and down,
You know them and they take you? Like enough!
I saw the proper twinkle in your eye—
'Tell you, I liked your looks at very first.
Let's sit and set things straight now, hip to haunch.
Here's spring come, and the nights one makes up bands
To roam the town and sing out carnival,
And I've been three weeks shut within my mew,
A-painting for the great man, saints and saints
And saints again. I could not paint all night—
Ouf! I leaned out of window for fresh air.
There came a hurry of feet and little feet,
A sweep of lute-strings, laughs, and whiffs of song—
Flower o' the broom,
Take away love, and our earth is a tomb!

Flower o' the quince,
I let Lisa go, and what good in life since?
Flower o' the thyme—and so on. Round they went.
Scarce had they turned the corner when a titter
Like the skipping of rabbits by moonlight—three slim shapes,
And a face that looked up . . . zooks, sir, flesh and blood,
That's all I'm made of! Into shreds it went,
Curtain and counterpane and coverlet,
All the bed-furniture—a dozen knots,
There was a ladder! Down I let myself,
Hands and feet, scrambling somehow, and so dropped,
And after them. I came up with the fun
Hard by Saint Laurence, hail fellow, well met—
Flower o' the rose,
If I've been merry, what matter who knows?
And so as I was stealing back again
To get to bed and have a bit of sleep,
Ere I rise up tomorrow and go work
On Jerome knocking at his poor old breast
With his great round stone to subdue the flesh,
You snap me of the sudden. Ah, I see!
Though your eye twinkles still, you shake your head—
Mine's shaved—a monk, you say—the sting's in that!
If Master Cosimo announced himself,
Mum's the word naturally; but a monk!
Come, what am I a beast for? Tell us, now!
I was a baby when my mother died
And father died and left me in the street.
I starved there, God knows how, a year or two
On fig skins, melon parings, rinds and shucks,
Refuse and rubbish. One fine, frosty day,
My stomach being empty as your hat,
The wind doubled me up and down I went.
Old Aunt Lapaccia trussed me with one hand
(Its fellow was a stinger as I knew),
And so along the wall, over the bridge,
By the straight cut to the convent. Six words there,
While I stood munching my first bread that month:
"So, boy, you're minded," quoth the good fat father,
Wiping his own mouth, 'twas refection time—
"To quit this very miserable world?
Will you renounce" . . . "the mouthful of bread?" thought I;

535

By no means! Brief, they made a monk of me;
I did renounce the world, its pride and greed,
Palace, farm, villa, shop, and banking house,
Trash, such as these poor devils of Medici
Have given their hearts to—all at eight years old.
Well, sir, I found in time, you may be sure,
'Twas not for nothing—the good bellyful,
The warm serge and the rope that goes all round,
And day-long blessed idleness beside!
"Let's see what the urchin's fit for"—that came next.
Not overmuch their way, I must confess.
Such a to-do! They tried me with their books:
Lord, they'd have taught me Latin in pure waste!
Flower o' the clove,
All the Latin I construe is "amo," I love!
But, mind you, when a boy starves in the streets
Eight years together, as my fortune was,
Watching folk's faces to know who will fling
The bit of half-stripped grape bunch he desires,
And who will curse or kick him for his pains—
Which gentleman processional and fine,
Holding a candle to the sacrament,
Will wink and let him lift a plate and catch
The droppings of the wax to sell again,
Or holla for the eight and have him whipped—
How say I?—nay, which dog bites, which lets drop
His bone from the heap of offal in the street—
Why, soul and sense of him grow sharp alike,
He learns the look of things, and none the less
For admonition from the hunger-pinch.
I had a store of such remarks, be sure,
Which, after I found leisure, turned to use.
I drew men's faces on my copybooks,
Scrawled them within the antiphonary's marge,
Joined legs and arms to the long music-notes,
Found eyes and nose and chin for A's and B's,
And made a string of pictures of the world
Betwixt the ins and outs of verb and noun,
On the wall, the bench, the door. The monks looked black.
"Nay," quoth the prior, "turn him out, d' ye say?
In no wise. Lose a crow and catch a lark.
What if at last we get our man of parts,

We Carmelites, like those Camaldolese
And preaching friars, to do our church up fine
And put the front on it that ought to be!"
And hereupon he bade me daub away.
Thank you! my head being crammed, the walls a blank,
Never was such prompt disemburdening.
First, every sort of monk, the black and white,
I drew them, fat and lean: then, folk at church,
From good old gossips waiting to confess
Their cribs of barrel droppings, candle ends—
To the breathless fellow at the altar-foot,
Fresh from his murder, safe and sitting there
With the little children round him in a row
Of admiration, half for his beard and half
For that white anger of his victim's son
Shaking a fist at him with one fierce arm,
Signing himself with the other because of Christ
(Whose sad face on the cross sees only this
After the passion of a thousand years)
Till some poor girl, her apron o'er her head
(Which the intense eyes looked through), came at eve
On tiptoe, said a word, dropped in a loaf,
Her pair of earrings and a bunch of flowers
(The brute took growling), prayed, and so was gone.
I painted all, then cried, " 'Tis ask and have;
Choose, for more's ready!"—laid the ladder flat,
And showed my covered bit of cloister wall.
The monks closed in a circle and praised loud
Till checked, taught what to see and not to see,
Being simple bodies—"That's the very man!
Look at the boy who stoops to pat the dog!
That woman's like the prior's niece who comes
To care about his asthma: it's the life!"
But there my triumph's straw-fire flared and funked;
Their betters took their turn to see and say:
The prior and the learned pulled a face
And stopped all that in no time. "How? What's here?
Quite from the mark of painting, bless us all!
Faces, arms, legs and bodies like the true
As much as pea and pea! It's devil's game!
Your business is not to catch men with show,
With homage to the perishable clay,

537

But lift them over it, ignore it all,
Make them forget there's such a thing as flesh.
Your business is to paint the souls of men—
Man's soul, and it's a fire, smoke . . . no, it's not . . .
It's vapour done up like a newborn babe—
(In that shape when you die it leaves your mouth)
It's . . . well, what matters talking, it's the soul!
Give us no more of body than shows soul!
Here's Giotto, with his saint a-praising God,
That sets us praising—why not stop with him?
Why put all thoughts of praise out of our head
With wonder at lines, colours, and what not?
Paint the soul, never mind the legs and arms!
Rub all out, try at it a second time.
Oh, that white, smallish female with the breasts,
She's just my niece . . . Herodias, I would say—
Who went and danced and got men's heads cut off!
Have it all out!" Now, is this sense, I ask?
A fine way to paint soul, by painting body
So ill, the eye can't stop there, must go further
And can't fare worse! Thus, yellow does for white
When what you put for yellow's simply black,
And any sort of meaning looks intense
When all beside itself means and looks nought.
Why can't a painter lift each foot in turn,
Left foot and right foot, go a double step,
Make his flesh liker and his soul more like,
Both in their order? Take the prettiest face,
The prior's niece . . . patron-saint—is it so pretty
You can't discover if it means hope, fear,
Sorrow or joy? Won't beauty go with these?
Suppose I've made her eyes all right and blue,
Can't I take breath and try to add life's flash,
And then add soul and heighten them threefold?
Or say there's beauty with no soul at all—
(I never saw it—put the case the same)
If you get simple beauty and nought else,
You get about the best thing God invents:
That's somewhat: and you'll find the soul you have missed,
Within yourself, when you return him thanks.
"Rub all out!" Well, well, there's my life, in short,
And so the thing has gone on ever since.

I'm grown a man no doubt, I've broken bounds:
You should not take a fellow eight years old
And make him swear to never kiss the girls.
I'm my own master, paint now as I please—
Having a friend, you see, in the corner-house!
Lord, it's fast holding by the rings in front—
Those great rings serve more purposes than just
To plant a flag in, or tie up a horse!
And yet the old schooling sticks, the old grave eyes
Are peeping o'er my shoulder as I work,
The heads shake still—"It's art's decline, my son!
You're not of the true painters, great and old;
Brother Angelico's the man, you'll find;
Brother Lorenzo stands his single peer:
Fag on at flesh, you'll never make the third!"
Flower o' the pine,
You keep your mistr . . . manners, and I'll stick to mine!
I'm not the third, then: bless us, they must know!
Don't you think they're the likeliest to know,
They with their Latin? So, I swallow my rage,
Clench my teeth, suck my lips in tight, and paint
To please them—sometimes do and sometimes don't;
For, doing most, there's pretty sure to come
A turn, some warm eve finds me at my saints—
A laugh, a cry, the business of the world—
(Flower o' the peach,
Death for us all, and his own life for each!)
And my whole soul revolves, the cup runs over,
The world and life's too big to pass for a dream,
And I do these wild things in sheer despite,
And play the fooleries you catch me at,
In pure rage! The old mill-horse, out at grass
After hard years, throws up his stiff heels so,
Although the miller does not preach to him
The only good of grass is to make chaff.
What would men have? Do they like grass or no—
May they or mayn't they? All I want's the thing
Settled forever one way. As it is,
You tell too many lies and hurt yourself:
You don't like what you only like too much,
You do like what, if given you at your word,
You find abundantly detestable.

For me, I think I speak as I was taught;
I always see the garden and God there
A-making man's wife: and, my lesson learned,
The value and significance of flesh,
I can't unlearn ten minutes afterwards.

You understand me: I'm a beast, I know.
But see, now—why, I see as certainly
As that the morning star's about to shine,
What will hap some day. We've a youngster here
Comes to our convent, studies what I do,
Slouches and stares and lets no atom drop:
His name is Guidi—he'll not mind the monks—
They call him Hulking Tom, he lets them talk—
He picks my practice up—he'll paint apace,
I hope so—though I never live so long,
I know what's sure to follow. You be judge!
You speak no Latin more than I, belike;
However, you're my man, you've seen the world
—The beauty and the wonder and the power,
The shapes of things, their colours, lights and shades,
Changes, surprises—and God made it all!
—For what? Do you feel thankful, aye or no,
For this fair town's face, yonder river's line,
The mountains round it and the sky above,
Much more the figures of man, woman, child,
These are the frame to? What's it all about?
To be passed over, despised? Or dwelt upon,
Wondered at? Oh, this last, of course!—you say.
But why not do as well as say—paint these
Just as they are, careless what comes of it?
God's works—paint any one, and count it crime
To let a truth slip. Don't object, "His works
Are here already; nature is complete:
Suppose you reproduce her (which you can't)
There's no advantage! You must beat her, then."
For, don't you mark? We're made so that we love
First when we see them painted, things we have passed
Perhaps a hundred times nor cared to see;
And so they are better, painted—better to us,
Which is the same thing. Art was given for that;
God uses us to help each other so,

540

Lending our minds out. Have you noticed, now,
Your cullion's hanging face? A bit of chalk,
And trust me but you should, though! How much more,
If I drew higher things with the same truth!
That were to take the prior's pulpit-place,
Interpret God to all of you! Oh, oh,
It makes me mad to see what men shall do
And we in our graves! This world's no blot for us,
Nor blank; it means intensely, and means good:
To find its meaning is my meat and drink.
"Aye, but you don't so instigate to prayer!"
Strikes in the prior: "When your meaning's plain
It does not say to folk—remember matins,
Or, mind you fast next Friday!" Why, for this
What need of art at all? A skull and bones,
Two bits of stick nailed crosswise, or, what's best,
A bell to chime the hour with, does as well.
I painted a Saint Laurence six months since
At Prato, splashed the fresco in fine style:
"How looks my painting, now the scaffold's down?"
I ask a brother: "Hugely," he returns—
"Already not one phiz of your three slaves
Who turn the deacon off his toasted side,
But it's scratched and prodded to our heart's content,
The pious people have so eased their own
With coming to say prayers there in a rage:
We get on fast to see the bricks beneath.
Expect another job this time next year,
For pity and religion grow i' the crowd—
Your painting serves its purpose!" Hang the fools!

—That is, you'll not mistake an idle word
Spoke in a huff by a poor monk, God wot,
Tasting the air this spicy night which turns
The unaccustomed head like Chianti wine!
Oh, the church knows! Don't misreport me, now!
It's natural a poor monk out of bounds
Should have his apt word to excuse himself:
And hearken how I plot to make amends.
I have bethought me: I shall paint a piece
. . . There's for you! Give me six months, then go, see
Something in Sant' Ambrogio's! Bless the nuns!

541

They want a cast o' my office. I shall paint
God in the midst, Madonna and her babe,
Ringed by a bowery flowery angel brood,
Lilies and vestments and white faces, sweet
As puff on puff of grated orris-root
When ladies crowd to church at midsummer.
And then i' the front, of course, a saint or two—
Saint John, because he saves the Florentines,
Saint Ambrose, who puts down in black and white
The convent's friends and gives them a long day,
And Job, I must have him there past mistake,
The man of Uz (and Us without the z,
Painters who need his patience). Well, all these
Secured at their devotion, up shall come
Out of a corner when you least expect,
As one by a dark stair into a great light,
Music and talking, who but Lippo! I!—
Mazed, motionless and moonstruck—I'm the man!
Back I shrink—what is this I see and hear?
I, caught up with my monk's things by mistake,
My old serge gown and rope that goes all round,
I, in this presence, this pure company!
Where's a hole, where's a corner for escape?
Then steps a sweet, angelic slip of a thing
Forward, puts out a soft palm—"Not so fast!"
—Addresses the celestial presence, "Nay—
He made you and devised you, after all,
Though he's none of you! Could Saint John there draw—
His camel-hair make up a painting-brush?
We come to brother Lippo for all that,
Iste perfecit opus!" So, all smile—
I shuffle sideways with my blushing face
Under the cover of a hundred wings
Thrown like a spread of kirtles when you're gay
And play hot cockles, all the doors being shut,
Till, wholly unexpected, in there pops
The hothead husband! Thus I scuttle off
To some safe bench behind, not letting go
The palm of her, the little lily-thing
That spoke the good word for me in the nick,
Like the prior's niece . . . Saint Lucy, I would say.
And so all's saved for me, and for the church

A pretty picture gained. Go, six months hence!
Your hand, sir, and good-by: no lights, no lights!
The street's hushed, and I know my own way back,
Don't fear me! There's the grey beginning. Zooks!

RABBI BEN EZRA

Grow old along with me!
The best is yet to be,
The last of life, for which the first was made:
Our times are in His hand
Who saith, "A whole I planned,
Youth shows but half; trust God: see all nor be afraid!"

Not that, amassing flowers,
Youth sighed, "Which rose make ours,
Which lily leave and then as best recall?"
Not that, admiring stars,
It yearned, "Nor Jove, nor Mars;
Mine be some figured flame which blends, transcends them all!"

Not for such hopes and fears
Annulling youth's brief years,
Do I remonstrate: folly wide the mark!
Rather I prize the doubt
Low kinds exist without,
Finished and finite clods, untroubled by a spark.

Poor vaunt of life indeed,
Were man but formed to feed
On joy, to solely seek and find and feast:
Such feasting ended, then
As sure an end to men;
Irks care the crop-full bird? Frets doubt the maw-crammed beast!

Rejoice we are allied
To That which doth provide
And not partake, effect and not receive!
A spark disturbs our clod;

Nearer we hold of God
Who gives, than of His tribes that take, I must believe.

Then, welcome each rebuff
That turns earth's smoothness rough,
Each sting that bids nor sit nor stand but go!
Be our joys three parts pain!
Strive, and hold cheap the strain;
Learn, nor account the pang; dare, never grudge the throe!

For thence—a paradox
Which comforts while it mocks—
Shall life succeed in that it seems to fail:
What I aspired to be,
And was not, comforts me:
A brute I might have been, but would not sink i' the scale.

What is he but a brute
Whose flesh has soul to suit,
Whose spirit works lest arms and legs want play?
To man, propose this test—
Thy body at its best,
How far can that project thy soul on its lone way?

Yet gifts should prove their use:
I own the past profuse
Of power each side, perfection every turn:
Eyes, ears took in their dole,
Brain treasured up the whole;
Should not the heart beat once, "How good to live and learn"?

Not once beat, "Praise be Thine!
I see the whole design,
I, who saw power, see now love perfect too:
Perfect I call Thy plan:
Thanks that I was a man!
Maker, remake, complete—I trust what Thou shalt do!"

For pleasant is this flesh;
Our soul, in its rose-mesh
Pulled over to the earth, still yearns for rest;
Would we some prize might hold

544

To match those manifold
Possessions of the brute—gain most, as we did best!

Let us not always say,
"Spite of this flesh today
I strove, made head, gained ground upon the whole!"
As the bird wings and sings,
Let us cry, "All good things
Are ours, nor soul helps flesh more, now, than flesh helps soul!"

Therefore I summon age
To grant youth's heritage,
Life's struggle having so far reached its term:
Thence shall I pass, approved
A man, for aye removed
From the developed brute; a god though in the germ.

And I shall thereupon
Take rest, ere I be gone
Once more on my adventure brave and new:
Fearless and unperplexed,
When I wage battle next,
What weapons to select, what armour to indue.

Youth ended, I shall try
My gain or loss thereby;
Leave the fire ashes, what survives is gold:
And I shall weigh the same,
Give life its praise or blame:
Young, all lay in dispute; I shall know, being old.

For note, when evening shuts,
A certain moment cuts
The deed off, calls the glory from the grey:
A whisper from the west
Shoots—"Add this to the rest,
Take it and try its worth: here dies another day."

So, still within this life,
Though lifted o'er its strife,
Let me discern, compare, pronounce at last,
"This rage was right i' the main,

That acquiescence vain:
The future I may face now I have proved the past."

For more is not reserved
To man, with soul just nerved
To act tomorrow what he learns today:
Here, work enough to watch
The master work, and catch
Hints of the proper craft, tricks of the tool's true play.

As it was better, youth
Should strive, through acts uncouth,
Toward making, than repose on aught found made:
So, better, age, exempt
From strife, should know, than tempt
Further. Thou waitedst age; wait death nor be afraid!

Enough now, if the right
And good and infinite
Be named here, as thou callest thy hand thine own,
With knowledge absolute,
Subject to no dispute
From fools that crowded youth, nor let thee feel alone.

Be there, for once and all,
Severed great minds from small,
Announced to each his station in the past!
Was I, the world arraigned,
Were they, my soul disdained,
Right? Let age speak the truth and give us peace at last!

Now, who shall arbitrate?
Ten men love what I hate,
Shun what I follow, slight what I receive;
Ten, who in ears and eyes
Match me: we all surmise,
They this thing, and I that: whom shall my soul believe?

Not on the vulgar mass
Called work must sentence pass,
Things done, that took the eye and had the price;
O'er which, from level stand,

The low world laid its hand,
Found straightway to its mind, could value in a trice:

But all, the world's coarse thumb
And finger failed to plumb,
So passed in making up the main account;
All instincts immature,
All purposes unsure,
That weighed not as his work, yet swelled the man's amount:

Thoughts hardly to be packed
Into a narrow act,
Fancies that broke through language and escaped;
All I could never be,
All, men ignored in me,
This, I was worth to God, whose wheel the pitcher shaped.

Aye, note that potter's wheel,
That metaphor! and feel
Why time spins fast, why passive lies our clay—
Thou, to whom fools propound,
When the wine makes its round,
"Since life fleets, all is change; the past gone, seize today!"

Fool! All that is, at all,
Lasts ever, past recall;
Earth changes, but thy soul and God stand sure:
What entered into thee,
That was, is, and shall be:
Time's wheel runs back or stops: potter and clay endure.

He fixed thee 'mid this dance
Of plastic circumstance,
This present, thou, forsooth, wouldst fain arrest:
Machinery just meant
To give thy soul its bent,
Try thee and turn thee forth, sufficiently impressed.

What though the earlier grooves
Which ran the laughing loves
Around thy base, no longer pause and press?
What though, about thy rim,

547

Skull-things in order grim
Grow out, in graver mood, obey the sterner stress?

Look not thou down but up!
To uses of a cup,
The festal board, lamp's flash, and trumpet's peal,
The new wine's foaming flow,
The master's lips a-glow!
Thou, heaven's consummate cup, what needst thou with earth's
wheel?

But I need, now as then,
Thee, God, who moldest men;
And since, not even while the whirl was worst,
Did I—to the wheel of life
With shapes and colours rife,
Bound dizzily—mistake my end, to slake Thy thirst:

So, take and use Thy work:
Amend what flaws may lurk,
What strain o' the stuff, what warpings past the aim!
My times be in Thy hand!
Perfect the cup as planned!
Let age approve of youth, and death complete the same!

PIPPA'S SONG

The year's at the spring
And day's at the morn;
Morning's at seven;
The hillside's dew-pearled;
The lark's on the wing;
The snail's on the thorn:
God's in his heaven—
All's right with the world!

EPILOGUE TO *ASOLANDO*

At the midnight in the silence of the sleep-time,
    When you set your fancies free,
Will they pass to where—by death, fools think, imprisoned—
Low he lies who once so loved you, whom you loved so,
        —Pity me?

Oh to love so, be so loved, yet so mistaken!
    What had I on earth to do
With the slothful, with the mawkish, the unmanly?
Like the aimless, helpless, hopeless, did I drivel
        —Being—who?

One who never turned his back but marched breast forward,
    Never doubted clouds would break,
Never dreamed, though right were worsted, wrong would triumph,
Held we fall to rise, are baffled to fight better,
        Sleep to wake.

No, at noonday in the bustle of man's work-time
    Greet the unseen with a cheer!
Bid him forward, breast and back as either should be,
"Strive and thrive!" cry, "Speed—fight on, fare ever
        There as here!"

EDWARD LEAR
(1812–88)

THE JUMBLIES

They went to sea in a sieve, they did;
  In a sieve they went to sea;
In spite of all their friends could say,
On a winter's morn, on a stormy day,
  In a sieve they went to sea.
And when the sieve turned round and round,
And everyone cried, "You'll be drowned!"
They called aloud, "Our sieve ain't big,
But we don't care a button; we don't care a fig—
  In a sieve we'll go to sea!"
    Far and few, far and few,
      Are the lands where the Jumblies live.
      Their heads are green, and their hands are blue;
      And they went to sea in a sieve.

They sailed away in a sieve, they did,
  In a sieve they sailed so fast,
With only a beautiful pea-green veil
Tied with a ribbon, by way of a sail,
  To a small tobacco-pipe mast.
And everyone said who saw them go,
"Oh! won't they be soon upset, you know,
For the sky is dark, and the voyage is long;
And, happen what may, it's extremely wrong
  In a sieve to sail so fast."

The water it soon came in, it did;
  The water it soon came in.
So, to keep them dry, they wrapped their feet
In a pinky paper all folded neat;
  And they fastened it down with a pin.
And they passed the night in a crockery jar;

And each of them said, "How wise we are!
Though the sky be dark, and the voyage be long,
Yet we never can think we were rash or wrong,
    While round in our sieve we spin."

And all night long they sailed away;
    And, when the sun went down,
They whistled and warbled a moony song
To the echoing sound of a coppery gong,
    In the shade of the mountains brown,
"O Timballoo! how happy we are
When we live in a sieve and a crockery jar!
And all night long, in the moonlight pale,
We sail away with a pea-green sail
    In the shade of the mountains brown."

They sailed to the Western Sea, they did—
    To a land all covered with trees;
And they bought an owl, and a useful cart,
And a pound of rice, and a cranberry tart,
    And a hive of silvery bees;
And they bought a pig, and some green jackdaws,
And a lovely monkey with lollipop paws,
And seventeen bags of edelweiss tea,
And forty bottles of ring-bo-ree,
    And no end of Stilton cheese.

And in twenty years they all came back—
    In twenty years or more;
And everyone said, "How tall they've grown!
For they've been to the Lakes, and the Torrible Zone,
    And the hills of the Chankly Bore."
And they drank their health, and gave them a feast
Of dumplings made of beautiful yeast;
And everyone said, "If we only live,
We, too, will go to sea in a sieve,
    To the hills of the Chankly Bore."
        Far and few, far and few,
            Are the lands where the Jumblies live.
        Their heads are green, and their hands are blue;
            And they went to sea in a sieve.

LIMERICKS

There was an old man with a beard, who said, "It is just as I feared!—
Two owls and a hen, four larks and a wren,
Have all built their nests in my beard!"

There was an old man in a tree, who was horribly bored by a bee;
When they said, "Does it buzz?" he replied, "Yes, it does!
It's a regular brute of a bee!"

There was an old man who said, "Hush! I perceive a young bird in this
bush!"
When they said, "Is it small?" he replied, "Not at all!
It is four times as big as the bush!"

There was a young person of Smyrna, whose grandmother threatened to
burn her;
But she seized on the cat, and said, "Granny, burn that!
You incongruous old woman of Smyrna!"

EMILY BRONTË
(1818–48)

REMEMBRANCE

Cold in the earth and the deep snow piled above thee!
Far, far removed, cold in the dreary grave!
Have I forgot, my only love, to love thee,
Severed at last by time's all-wearing wave?

Now, when alone, do my thoughts no longer hover
Over the mountains on Angora's shore;
Resting their wings where heath and fern-leaves cover
That noble heart for ever, ever more?

Cold in the earth, and fifteen wild Decembers
From those brown hills have melted into spring—
Faithful indeed is the spirit that remembers
After such years of change and suffering!

Sweet love of youth, forgive if I forget thee
While the world's tide is bearing me along:
Sterner desires and darker hopes beset me,
Hopes which obscure but cannot do thee wrong.

No other sun has lightened up my heaven;
No other star has ever shone for me:
All my life's bliss from thy dear life was given—
All my life's bliss is in the grave with thee.

But when the days of golden dreams had perished
And even despair was powerless to destroy,
Then did I learn how existence could be cherished,
Strengthened and fed without the aid of joy.

Then did I check the tears of useless passion,
Weaned my young soul from yearning after thine;

Sternly denied its burning wish to hasten
Down to that tomb already more than mine!

And even yet, I dare not let it languish,
Dare not indulge in memory's rapturous pain;
Once drinking deep of that divinest anguish,
How could I seek the empty world again?

*

Tell me, tell me, smiling child,
What the past is like to thee?
"An autumn evening soft and mild
With a wind that sighs mournfully."

Tell me, what is the present hour?
"A green and flowery spray
Where a young bird sits gathering its power
To mount and fly away."

And what is the future, happy one?
"A sea beneath a cloudless sun;
A mighty, glorious, dazzling sea
Stretching into infinity."

*

I die; but when the grave shall press
The heart so long endeared to thee,
When earthly cares no more distress
And earthly joys are nought to me,

Weep not, but think that I have past
Before thee o'er a sea of gloom,
Have anchored safe, and rest at last
Where tears and mourning cannot come.

'Tis I should weep to leave thee here,
On that dark ocean, sailing drear,
With storms around and fears before
And no kind light to point the shore.

554

But long or short though life may be
'Tis nothing to eternity;
We part below to meet on high
Where blissful ages never die.

THE NIGHT WIND

In summer's mellow midnight
A cloudless moon shone through
Our open parlour window
And rosetrees wet with dew.

I sat in silent musing—
The soft wind waved my hair;
It told me heaven was glorious
And sleeping earth was fair.

I needed not its breathing
To bring such thoughts to me
But still it whispered lowly
"How dark the woods will be!

The thick leaves in my murmur
Are rustling like a dream,
And all their myriad voices
Instinct with spirit seem."

I said: "Go gentle singer,
Thy wooing voice is kind,
But do not think its music
Has power to reach my mind.

Play with the scented flower,
The young tree's supple bough—
And leave my human feelings
In their own course to flow."

The wanderer would not leave me;
Its kiss grew warmer still—

"Oh come," it sighed so sweetly,
"I'll win thee 'gainst thy will.

Have we not been from childhood friends?
Have I not loved thee long?
As long as thou hast loved the night
Whose silence wakes my song.

And when thy heart is laid at rest
Beneath the church-yard stone
I shall have time enough to mourn
And thou to be alone."

ARTHUR HUGH CLOUGH
(1819–61)

SAY NOT THE STRUGGLE NOUGHT AVAILETH

Say not the struggle nought availeth,
  The labour and the wounds are vain,
The enemy faints not, nor faileth,
  And as things have been they remain.

If hopes were dupes, fears may be liars;
  It may be, in yon smoke concealed,
Your comrades chase e'en now the fliers,
  And, but for you, possess the field.

For while the tired waves, vainly breaking,
  Seem here no painful inch to gain,
Far back, through creeks and inlets making,
  Comes silent, flooding in, the main.

And not by eastern windows only,
  When daylight comes, comes in the light,
In front, the sun climbs slow, how slowly,
  But westward, look, the land is bright!

MATTHEW ARNOLD
(1822–88)

ISOLATION. TO MARGUERITE

We were apart; yet, day by day,
I bade my heart more constant be.
I bade it keep the world away,
And grow a home for only thee;
Nor feared but thy love likewise grew,
Like mine, each day, more tried, more true.

The fault was grave! I might have known,
What far too soon, alas! I learned—
The heart can bind itself alone,
And faith may well be unreturned.
Self-swayed our feelings ebb and swell—
Thou lov'st no more—Farewell! Farewell!

Farewell!—and thou, thou lonely heart,
Which never yet without remorse
Even for a moment didst depart
From thy remote and sphered course
To haunt the place where passions reign—
Back to thy solitude again!

Back! with the conscious thrill of shame
Which Luna felt, that summer night,
Flash through her pure immortal frame,
When she forsook the starry height
To hang over Endymion's sleep
Upon the pine-grown Latmian steep.

Yet she, chaste queen, had never proved
How vain a thing is mortal love,
Wandering in heaven, far removed.
But thou hast long had place to prove

This truth—to prove, and make thine own:
"Thou hast been, shalt be, art, alone."

Or, if not quite alone, yet they
Which touch thee are unmating things—
Ocean and clouds and night and day;
Lorn autumns and triumphant springs;
And life, and others' joy and pain,
And love, if love, of happier men.

Of happier men—for they, at least,
Have *dreamed* two human hearts might blend
In one, and were through faith released
From isolation without end
Prolonged; nor knew, although not less
Alone than thou, their loneliness.

TO MARGUERITE—CONTINUED

Yes! in the sea of life enisled,
With echoing straits between us thrown,
Dotting the shoreless watery wild,
We mortal millions live *alone*.
The islands feel the enclasping flow,
And then their endless bounds they know.

But when the moon their hollows lights,
And they are swept by balms of spring,
And in their glens, on starry nights,
The nightingales divinely sing;
And lovely notes, from shore to shore,
Across the sounds and channels pour—

Oh! then a longing like despair
Is to their farthest caverns sent;
For surely once, they feel, we were
Parts of a single continent!

Now round us spreads the watery plain—
Oh might our marges meet again!

Who ordered that their longing's fire
Should be, as soon as kindled, cooled?
Who renders vain their deep desire?
A God, a God their severance ruled!
And bade betwixt their shores to be
The unplumbed, salt, estranging sea.

THE SCHOLAR-GYPSY

Go, for they call you, shepherd, from the hill;
  Go, shepherd, and untie the wattled cotes!
    No longer leave thy wistful flock unfed,
  Nor let thy bawling fellows rack their throats,
    Nor the cropped grasses shoot another head.
      But when the fields are still,
  And the tired men and dogs all gone to rest,
    And only the white sheep are sometimes seen
    Cross and recross the strips of moon-blanched green,
  Come, shepherd, and again begin the quest!

Here, where the reaper was at work of late—
  In this high field's dark corner, where he leaves
    His coat, his basket, and his earthen cruse,
  And in the sun all morning binds the sheaves,
    Then here, at noon, comes back his stores to use—
      Here will I sit and wait,
  While to my ear, from uplands far away,
    The bleating of the folded flocks is borne,
    With distant cries of reapers in the corn—
  All the live murmur of a summer's day.

Screened is this nook o'er the high, half-reaped field,
  And here till sundown, shepherd will I be.
    Through the thick corn the scarlet poppies peep,
  And round green roots and yellowing stalks I see
    Pale blue convolvulus in tendrils creep;

And air-swept lindens yield
Their scent, and rustle down their perfumed showers
Of bloom on the bent grass where I am laid,
And bower me from the August sun with shade;
And the eye travels down to Oxford's towers.

And near me on the grass lies Glanvill's book—
Come, let me read the oft-read tale again!
The story of the Oxford scholar poor,
Of pregnant parts and quick, inventive brain,
Who, tired of knocking at preferment's door,
One summer morn forsook
His friends, and went to learn the gypsy lore,
And roamed the world with that wild brotherhood,
And came, as most men deemed, to little good,
But came to Oxford and his friends no more.

But once, years after, in the country lanes,
Two scholars, whom at college erst he knew,
Met him, and of his way of life inquired;
Whereat he answered that the gypsy-crew,
His mates, had arts to rule as they desired
The workings of men's brains,
And they can bind them to what thoughts they will.
"And I," he said, "the secret of their art,
When fully learned, will to the world impart;
But it needs heaven-sent moments for this skill."

This said, he left them, and returned no more.
But rumours hung about the countryside,
That the lost scholar long was seen to stray,
Seen by rare glimpses, pensive and tonguetied,
In hat of antique shape, and cloak of grey,
The same the gypsies wore.
Shepherds had met him on the Hurst in spring;
At some lone alehouse in the Berkshire moors,
On the warm ingle-bench, the smock-frocked boors
Had found him seated at their entering,

But, 'mid their drink and clatter, he would fly.
And I myself seem half to know thy looks,
And put the shepherds, wanderer, on thy trace;

And boys who in lone wheatfields scare the rooks
 I ask if thou hast passed their quiet place;
  Or in my boat I lie,
Moored to the cool bank in the summer heats,
 'Mid wide grass meadows which the sunshine fills,
 And watch the warm, green-muffled Cumnor hills,
And wonder if thou haunt'st their shy retreats.

For most, I know, thou lov'st retired ground!
 Thee at the ferry Oxford riders blithe,
  Returning home on summer nights, have met
Crossing the stripling Thames at Bab-lock-hithe,
 Trailing in the cool stream thy fingers wet,
  As the punt's rope chops round;
 And leaning backward in a pensive dream,
  And fostering in thy lap a heap of flowers
  Plucked in shy fields and distant Wychwood bowers,
And thine eyes resting on the moonlit stream.

And then they land, and thou art seen no more!
 Maidens, who from the distant hamlets come
  To dance around the Fyfield elm in May,
Oft through the darkening fields have seen thee roam,
 Or cross a stile into the public way.
  Oft thou hast given them store
 Of flowers—the frail-leafed, white anemone,
  Dark bluebells drenched with dews of summer eves,
  And purple orchises with spotted leaves—
But none hath words she can report of thee.

And, above Godstow Bridge, when hay time's here,
 In June, and many a scythe in sunshine flames,
  Men who through those wide fields of breezy grass
Where black-winged swallows haunt the glittering Thames,
 To bathe in the abandoned lasher pass,
  Have often passed thee near
Sitting upon the river bank o'ergrown;
 Marked thine outlandish garb, thy figure spare,
  Thy dark, vague eyes, and soft, abstracted air—
But, when they came from bathing, thou wast gone!

At some lone homestead in the Cumnor hills,
  Where at her open door the housewife darns,
    Thou hast been seen, or hanging on a gate,
  To watch the threshers in the mossy barns.
      Children, who early range these slopes and late
        For cresses from the rills,
  Have known thee eying, all an April day,
    The springing pastures and the feeding kine;
    And marked thee, when the stars come out and shine,
  Through the long, dewy grass move slow away.

In autumn, on the skirts of Bagley Wood—
  Where most the gypsies by the turf-edged way
    Pitch their smoked tents, and every bush you see
  With scarlet patches tagged and shreds of grey,
      Above the forest ground called Thessaly—
        The blackbird, picking food,
  Sees thee, nor stops his meal, nor fears at all;
    So often has he known thee past him stray,
    Rapt, twirling in thy hand a withered spray,
  And waiting for the spark from heaven to fall.

And once, in winter, on the causeway chill
  Where home through flooded fields foot-travellers go,
    Have I not passed thee on the wooden bridge,
  Wrapped in thy cloak and battling with the snow,
      Thy face toward Hinksey and its wintry ridge?
        And thou hast climbed the hill,
  And gained the white brow of the Cumnor range;
    Turned once to watch, while thick the snowflakes fall,
    The line of festal light in Christ Church hall—
  Then sought thy straw in some sequestered grange.

But what—I dream! Two hundred years are flown,
  Since first thy story ran through Oxford halls,
    And the grave Glanvill did the tale inscribe,
  That thou wert wandered from the studious walls
      To learn strange arts, and join a gypsy tribe;
        And thou from earth art gone
  Long since, and in some quiet churchyard laid—
    Some country nook, where o'er thy unknown grave

563

Tall grasses and white-flowering nettles wave,
Under a dark, red-fruited yew tree's shade.

—No, no, thou hast not felt the lapse of hours!
For what wears out the life of mortal men?
   'Tis that from change to change their being rolls;
'Tis that repeated shocks, again, again,
   Exhaust the energy of strongest souls
     And numb the elastic powers.
Till, having used our nerves with bliss and teen,
   And tired upon a thousand schemes our wit,
   To the just-pausing genius we remit
Our worn-out life, and are—what we have been.

Thou hast not lived, why shouldst thou perish, so?
   Thou hadst *one* aim, *one* business, *one* desire;
     Else wert thou long since numbered with the dead!
Else hadst thou spent, like other men, thy fire!
     The generations of thy peers are fled,
       And we ourselves shall go;
But thou possessest an immortal lot,
     And we imagine thee exempt from age,
     And living as thou liv'st on Glanvill's page,
Because thou hadst—what we, alas, have not.

For early didst thou leave the world, with powers
   Fresh, undiverted to the world without,
     Firm to their mark, not spent on other things;
Free from the sick fatigue, the languid doubt,
     Which much to have tried, in much been baffled, brings.
       O life unlike to ours!
Who fluctuate idly without term or scope,
     Of whom each strives, nor knows for what he strives,
     And each half-lives a hundred different lives;
Who wait like thee, but not, like thee, in hope.

Thou waitest for the spark from heaven, and we,
   Light half-believers of our casual creeds.
     Who never deeply felt, nor clearly willed,
Whose insight never has borne fruit in deeds,
     Whose vague resolves never have been fulfilled;
       For whom each year we see

Breeds new beginnings, disappointments new;
   Who hesitate and falter life away,
   And lose tomorrow the ground won today—
Ah! do not we, wanderer, await it too?

Yes, we await it!—But it still delays,
   And then we suffer, and amongst us one,
    Who most has suffered, takes dejectedly
His seat upon the intellectual throne;
     And all his store of sad experience he
      Lays bare of wretched days;
Tells us his misery's birth and growth and signs,
   And how the dying spark of hope was fed,
   And how the breast was soothed, and how the head,
And all his hourly varied anodynes.

This for our wisest, and we others pine,
   And wish the long, unhappy dream would end,
   And waive all claim to bliss, and try to bear;
With close-lipped patience for our only friend,
    Sad patience, too-near neighbour to despair—
     But none has hope like thine!
Thou through the fields and through the woods dost stray,
   Roaming the countryside, a truant boy,
   Nursing thy project in unclouded joy,
And every doubt long blown by time away.

Oh, born in days when wits were fresh and clear,
   And life ran gaily as the sparkling Thames;
    Before this strange disease of modern life,
With its sick hurry, its divided aims,
    Its heads o'ertaxed, its palsied hearts, was rife—
     Fly hence, our contact fear!
Still fly, plunge deeper in the bowering wood!
   Averse, as Dido did with gesture stern
   From her false friend's approach in Hades turn,
Wave us away, and keep thy solitude!

Still nursing the unconquerable hope,
   Still clutching the inviolable shade,
    With a free, onward impulse brushing through,
    By night, the silvered branches of the glade—

Far on the forest skirts, where none pursue.
On some mild pastoral slope
Emerge, and resting on the moonlit pales,
Freshen thy flowers as in former years
With dew, or listen with enchanted ears,
From the dark dingles, to the nightingales!

But fly our paths, our feverish contact fly!
For strong the infection of our mental strife,
Which, though it gives no bliss, yet spoils for rest;
And we should win thee from thy own fair life,
Like us distracted, and like us unblessed.
Soon, soon thy cheer would die,
Thy hopes grow timorous, and unfixed thy powers,
And thy clear aims be cross and shifting made;
And then thy glad, perennial youth would fade,
Fade, and grow old at last, and die like ours.

Then fly our greetings, fly our speech and smiles!
—As some grave Tyrian trader, from the sea,
Descried at sunrise an emerging prow
Lifting the cool-haired creepers stealthily,
The fringes of a southward-facing brow
Among the Aegean isles;
And saw the merry Grecian coaster come,
Freighted with amber grapes, and Chian wine,
Green, bursting figs, and tunnies steeped in brine—
And knew the intruders on his ancient home,

The young, lighthearted masters of the waves—
And snatched his rudder, and shook out more sail;
And day and night held on indignantly
O'er the blue midland waters with the gale,
Betwixt the Syrtes and soft Sicily,
To where the Atlantic raves
Outside the western straits; and unbent sails
There, where down cloudy cliffs, through sheets of foam,
Shy traffickers, the dark Iberians come;
And on the beach undid his corded bales.

Through Alpine meadows soft-suffused
With rain, where thick the crocus blows,
Past the dark forges long disused,
The mule-track from Saint Laurent goes.
The bridge is crossed, and slow we ride,
Through forest, up the mountainside.

The autumnal evening darkens round,
The wind is up, and drives the rain;
While, hark, far down, with strangled sound,
Doth the Dead Guier's stream complain,
Where that wet smoke, among the woods,
Over his boiling cauldron broods.

Swift rush the spectral vapours white
Past limestone scars with ragged pines,
Showing—then blotting from our sight!—
Halt—through the cloud-drift something shines!
High in the valley, wet and drear,
The huts of Courrerie appear.

Strike leftward! cries our guide; and higher
Mounts up the stony forest way.
At last the encircling trees retire;
Look! Through the showery twilight grey
What pointed roofs are these advance?—
A palace of the kings of France?

Approach, for what we seek is here!
Alight, and sparely sup, and wait
For rest in this outbuilding near;
Then cross the sward and reach that gate.
Knock; pass the wicket! Thou art come
To the Carthusians' world-famed home.

The silent courts, where night and day
Into their stone-carved basins cold,
The splashing, icy fountains play—
The humid corridors behold!

Where, ghostlike in the deepening night,
Cowled forms brush by in gleaming white.

The chapel, where no organ's peal
Invests the stern and naked prayer—
With penitential cries they kneel
And wrestle; rising then, with bare
And white uplifted faces, stand,
Passing the host from hand to hand;

Each takes, and then his visage wan
Is buried in his cowl once more.
The cells!—the suffering son of man
Upon the wall—the knee-worn floor—
And where they sleep, that wooden bed,
Which shall their coffin be, when dead!

The library, where tract and tome
Not to feed priestly pride are there,
To hymn the conquering march of Rome,
Nor yet to amuse, as ours are!
They paint of souls the inner strife,
Their drops of blood, their death in life.

The garden, overgrown—yet mild,
See, fragrant herbs are flowering there!
Strong children of the Alpine wild,
Whose culture is the brethren's care;
Of human tasks their only one,
And cheerful works beneath the sun.

Those halls, too, destined to contain
Each its own pilgrim-host of old,
From England, Germany, or Spain—
All are before me! I behold
The house, the brotherhood austere!
—And what am I, that I am here?

For rigorous teachers seized my youth,
And purged its faith, and trimmed its fire,
Showed me the high, white star of truth,
There bade me gaze, and there aspire.

568

Even now their whispers pierce the gloom:
What dost thou in this living tomb?

Forgive me, masters of the mind!
At whose behest I long ago
So much unlearnt, so much resigned—
I come not here to be your foe!
I seek these anchorites, not in ruth,
To curse and to deny your truth;

Not as their friend or child I speak!
But as, on some far northern strand,
Thinking of his own gods, a Greek
In pity and mournful awe might stand
Before some fallen runic stone—
For both were faiths, and both are gone.

Wandering between two worlds, one dead,
The other powerless to be born,
With nowhere yet to rest my head,
Like these, on earth I wait forlorn.
Their faith, my tears, the world deride—
I come to shed them at their side.

Oh, hide me in your gloom profound,
Ye solemn seats of holy pain!
Take me, cowled forms, and fence me round,
Till I possess my soul again;
Till free my thoughts before me roll,
Not chafed by hourly false control!

For the world cries your faith is now
But a dead time's exploded dream;
My melancholy, sciolists say,
Is a passed mode, an outworn theme—
As if the world had ever had
A faith, or sciolists been sad!

Ah, if it be passed, take away,
At least, the restlessness, the pain;
Be man henceforth no more a prey
To these out-dated stings again!

The nobleness of grief is gone—
Ah, leave us not the fret alone!

But—if you cannot give us ease—
Last of the race of them who grieve,
Here leave us to die out with these
Last of the people who believe!
Silent, while years engrave the brow;
Silent—the best are silent now.

Achilles ponders in his tent,
The kings of modern thought are dumb;
Silent they are, though not content,
And wait to see the future come.
They have the grief men had of yore,
But they contend and cry no more.

Our fathers watered with their tears
This sea of time whereon we sail,
Their voices were in all men's ears
Who passed within their puissant hail.
Still the same ocean round us raves,
But we stand mute, and watch the waves.

For what availed it, all the noise
And outcry of the former men?
Say, have their sons achieved more joys;
Say, is life lighter now than then?
The sufferers died, they left their pain—
The pangs which tortured them remain.

What helps it now, that Byron bore,
With haughty scorn which mocked the smart,
Through Europe to the Aetolian shore
The pageant of his bleeding heart?
That thousands counted every groan,
And Europe made his woe her own?

What boots it, Shelley, that the breeze
Carried thy lovely wail away,
Musical through Italian trees,
Which fringe thy soft blue Spezzian bay?

570

Inheritors of thy distress
Have restless hearts one throb the less?

Or are we easier, to have read,
O Obermann, the sad, stern page,
Which tells us how thou hiddest thy head
From the fierce tempest of thine age
In the lone brakes of Fontainebleau,
Or chalets near the Alpine snow?

Ye slumber in your silent grave!—
The world, which for an idle day
Grace to your mood of sadness gave,
Long since hath flung her weeds away.
The eternal trifler breaks your spell;
But we—we learnt your lore too well!

Years hence, perhaps, may dawn an age,
More fortunate, alas, than we,
Which, without hardness, will be sage,
And gay without frivolity.
Sons of the world, oh, speed those years;
But, while we wait, allow our tears!

Allow them! We admire with awe
The exulting thunder of your race;
You give the universe your law,
You triumph over time and space!
Your pride of life, your tireless powers,
We praise them, but they are not ours.

We are like children reared in shade
Beneath some old-world abbey wall,
Forgotten in a forest glade,
And secret from the eyes of all.
Deep, deep the greenwood round them waves,
Their abbey, and its close of graves!

But, where the road runs near the stream,
Oft through the trees they catch a glance
Of passing troops in the sun's beam—
Pennon, and plume, and flashing lance!

Forth to the world those soldiers fare,
To life, to cities, and to war!

And, through the wood, another way,
Faint bugle-notes from far are borne,
Where hunters gather, staghounds bay,
Round some fair forest-lodge at morn.
Gay dames are there, in sylvan green;
Laughter and cries—those notes between!

The banners flashing through the trees
Make their blood dance and chain their eyes;
That bugle music, on the breeze,
Arrests them with a charmed surprise.
Banner by turns and bugle woo:
Ye shy recluses, follow, too!

O children, what do ye reply?—
"Action and pleasure, will ye roam
Through these secluded dells to cry
And call us?—but too late ye come!
Too late for us your call ye blow,
Whose bent was taken long ago.

Long since we pace this shadowed nave;
We watch those yellow tapers shine,
Emblems of hope over the grave,
In the high altar's depth divine;
The organ carries to our ear
Its accents of another sphere.

Fenced early in this cloistral round
Of reverie, of shade, of prayer,
How should we grow in other ground?
How can we flower in foreign air?
—Pass, banners, pass, and bugles, cease;
And leave our desert to its peace!"

DOVER BEACH

The sea is calm tonight.
The tide is full, the moon lies fair
Upon the straits—on the French coast the light
Gleams and is gone; the cliffs of England stand,
Glimmering and vast, out in the tranquil bay.
Come to the window; sweet is the night air!
Only, from the long line of spray
Where the sea meets the moon-blanched land,
Listen! You hear the grating roar
Of pebbles which the waves draw back, and fling,
At their return, up the high strand,
Begin, and cease, and then again begin,
With tremulous cadence slow, and bring
The eternal note of sadness in.

Sophocles long ago
Heard it on the Aegean, and it brought
Into his mind the turbid ebb and flow
Of human misery; we
Find also in the sound a thought,
Hearing it by this distant northern sea.

The sea of faith
Was once, too, at the full, and round earth's shore
Lay like the folds of a bright girdle furled.
But now I only hear
Its melancholy, long, withdrawing roar,
Retreating, to the breath
Of the night wind, down the vast edges drear
And naked shingles of the world.

Ah, love, let us be true
To one another! for the world, which seems
To lie before us like a land of dreams,
So various, so beautiful, so new,
Hath really neither joy, nor love, nor light,
Nor certitude, nor peace, nor help for pain;
And we are here as on a darkling plain
Swept with confused alarms of struggle and flight,
Where ignorant armies clash by night.

GEIST'S GRAVE

Four years!—and didst thou stay above
The ground, which hides thee now, but four?
And all that life, and all that love,
Were crowded, Geist! into no more?

Only four years those winning ways,
Which make me for thy presence yearn,
Called us to pet thee or to praise,
Dear little friend! at every turn?

That loving heart, that patient soul,
Had they indeed no longer span,
To run their course, and reach their goal,
And read their homily to man?

That liquid, melancholy eye,
From whose pathetic, soul-fed springs
Seemed surging the Virgilian cry,
The sense of tears in mortal things—

That steadfast, mournful strain, consoled
By spirits gloriously gay,
And temper of heroic mould—
What, was four years their whole short day?

Yes, only four!—and not the course
Of all the centuries yet to come,
And not the infinite resource
Of nature, with her countless sum

Of figures, with her fulness vast
Of new creation evermore,
Can ever quite repeat the past,
Or just thy little self restore.

Stern law of every mortal lot!
Which man, proud man, finds hard to bear,
And builds himself I know not what
Of second life I know not where.

But thou, when struck thine hour to go,
On us, who stood despondent by,
A meek last glance of love didst throw,
And humbly lay thee down to die.

Yet would we keep thee in our heart—
Would fix our favourite on the scene,
Nor let thee utterly depart
And be as if thou ne'er hadst been.

And so there rise these lines of verse
On lips that rarely form them now;
While to each other we rehearse:
Such ways, such arts, such looks hadst thou!

We stroke thy broad brown paws again,
We bid thee to thy vacant chair,
We greet thee by the window-pane,
We hear thy scuffle on the stair.

We see the flaps of thy large ears
Quick raised to ask which way we go;
Crossing the frozen lake, appears
Thy small black figure on the snow!

Nor to us only art thou dear
Who mourn thee in thine English home.
Thou hast thine absent master's tear,
Dropped by the far Australian foam;

Thy memory lasts both here and there,
And thou shalt live as long as we.
And after that—thou dost not care!
In us was all the world to thee.

Yet, fondly zealous for thy fame,
Even to a date beyond our own

We strive to carry down thy name,
By mounded turf, and graven stone.

We lay thee, close within our reach,
Here, where the grass is smooth and warm,
Between the holly and the beech,
Where oft we watched thy couchant form,

Asleep, yet lending half an ear
To travellers on the Portsmouth road—
There build we thee, O guardian dear,
Marked with a stone, thy last abode!

Then some, who through this garden pass,
When we too, like thyself, are clay,
Shall see thy grave upon the grass,
And stop before the stone, and say:

People who lived here long ago
Did by this stone, it seems, intend
To name for future times to know
The dachs-hound, Geist, their little friend.

GEORGE MEREDITH
(1828–1909)

from MODERN LOVE

Not solely that the future she destroys,
And the fair life which in the distance lies
For all men, beckoning out from dim rich skies:
Nor that the passing hour's supporting joys
Have lost the keen-edged flavour, which begat
Distinction in old times, and still should breed
Sweet memory, and hope—earth's modest seed,
And heaven's high-prompting: not that the world is flat
Since that soft-luring creature I embraced
Among the children of illusion went:
Methinks with all this loss I were content,
If the mad past, on which my foot is based,
Were firm, or might be blotted: but the whole
Of life is mixed: the mocking past will stay:
And if I drink oblivion of a day,
So shorten I the stature of my soul.

Mark where the pressing wind shoots javelinlike
Its skeleton shadow on broad-backed wave!
Here is a fitting spot to dig love's grave;
Here where the ponderous breakers plunge and strike,
And dart their hissing tongues high up the sand:
In hearing of the ocean, and in sight
Of those ribbed wind-streaks running into white.
If I the death of love had deeply planned,
I never could have made it half so sure,
As by the unblessed kisses which upbraid
The full-waked sense: or failing that, degrade!
'Tis morning: but no morning can restore
What we have forfeited. I see no sin:
The wrong is mixed. In tragic life, God wot,

No villain need be! Passions spin the plot:
We are betrayed by what is false within.

ODE TO THE SPIRIT OF EARTH
IN AUTUMN

Fair Mother Earth lay on her back last night,
To gaze her fill on autumn's sunset skies,
When at a waving of the fallen light
Sprang realms of rosy fruitage o'er her eyes.
A lustrous heavenly orchard hung the west,
Wherein the blood of Eden bloomed again:
Red were the myriad cherub-mouths that pressed,
Among the clusters, rich with song, full fain,
But dumb, because that overmastering spell
Of rapture held them dumb: then, here and there,
A golden harp lost strings; a crimson shell
Burnt grey; and sheaves of lustre fell to air.
The illimitable eagerness of hue
Bronzed, and the beamy winged bloom that flew
'Mid those bunched fruits and thronging figures failed.
A green-edged lake of saffron touched the blue,
With isles of fireless purple lying through:
And fancy on that lake to seek lost treasures sailed.

Not long the silence followed:
The voice that issues from thy breast,
O glorious south-west,
Along the gloom-horizon holloa'd;
Warning the valleys with a mellow roar
Through flapping wings; then sharp the woodland bore
A shudder and a noise of hands:
A thousand horns from some far vale
In ambush sounding on the gale.
Forth from the cloven sky came bands
Of revel-gathering spirits; trooping down,
Some rode the tree-tops; some on torn cloud-strips
Burst screaming through the lighted town:
And scudding seaward, some fell on big ships:
Or mounting the sea-horses blew

Bright foam-flakes on the black review
Of heaving hulls and burying beaks.

Still on the farthest line, with outpuffed cheeks,
'Twixt dark and utter dark, the great wind drew
From heaven that disenchanted harmony
To join earth's laughter in the midnight blind:
Booming a distant chorus to the shrieks
                    Preluding him: then he,
His mantle streaming thunderingly behind,
Across the yellow realm of stiffened day,
Shot through the woodland alleys signals three;
          And with the pressure of a sea
Plunged broad upon the vale that under lay.

          Night on the rolling foliage fell:
          But I, who love old hymning night,
          And know the dryad voices well,
          Discerned them as their leaves took flight,
          Like souls to wander after death:
          Great armies in imperial dyes,
          And mad to tread the air and rise,
          The savage freedom of the skies
          To taste before they rot. And here,
          Like frail white-bodied girls in fear,
          The birches swung from shrieks to sighs;
          The aspens, laughers at a breath,
          In showering spray-falls mixed their cries,
          Or raked a savage ocean-strand
          With one incessant drowning screech.
          Here stood a solitary beech,
          That gave its gold with open hand,
          And all its branches, toning chill,
          Did seem to shut their teeth right fast,
          To shriek more mercilessly shrill,
          And match the fierceness of the blast.

          But heard I a low swell that noised
          Of far-off ocean, I was 'ware
          Of pines upon their wide roots poised,
          Whom never madness in the air
          Can draw to more than loftier stress

Of mournfulness, not mournfulness
For melancholy, but joy's excess,
That singing on the lap of sorrow faints:
And peace, as in the hearts of saints
Who chant unto the Lord their God;
Deep peace below upon the muffled sod,
The stillness of the sea's unswaying floor.
Could I be sole there not to see
The life within the life awake;
The spirit bursting from the tree,
And rising from the troubled lake?
Pour, let the wines of heaven pour!
The golden harp is struck once more,
And all its music is for me!
Pour, let the wines of heaven pour!
And, ho, for a night of pagan glee!

There is a curtain o'er us.
For once, good souls, we'll not pretend
To be aught better than her who bore us,
And is our only visible friend.
Hark to her laughter! who laughs like this,
Can she be dead, or rooted in pain?
She has been slain by the narrow brain,
But for us who love her she lives again.
Can she die? Oh, take her kiss!
The crimson-footed nymph is panting up the glade,
With the wine-jar at her arm-pit, and the drunken ivy-braid
Round her forehead, breasts, and thighs: starts a satyr, and they speed:
Hear the crushing of the leaves: hear the cracking of the bough!
And the whistling of the bramble, the piping of the weed!

But the bull-voiced oak is battling now:
The storm has seized him half-asleep,
And round him the wild woodland throngs
To hear the fury of his songs,
The uproar of an outraged deep.
He wakes to find a wrestling giant
Trunk to trunk and limb to limb,
And on his rooted force reliant
He laughs and grasps the broadened giant,
And twist and roll the Anakim;

580

And multitudes acclaiming to the cloud,
    Cry which is breaking, which is bowed.

        Away, for the cymbals clash aloft
        In the circles of pine, on the moss-floor soft.
        The nymphs of the woodland are gathering there.
        They huddle the leaves, and trample, and toss;
        They swing in the branches, they roll in the moss,
            They blow the seed on the air.
        Back to back they stand and blow
        The winged seed on the cradling air,
        A fountain of leaves over bosom and back.
        The pipe of the faun comes on their track,
        And the weltering alleys overflow
        With musical shrieks and wind-wedded hair.
        The riotous companies melt to a pair.
            Bless them, mother of kindness!

        A star has nodded through
        The depths of the flying blue.
        Time only to plant the light
        Of a memory in the blindness.
        But time to show me the sight
        Of my life through the curtain of night;
        Shining a moment, and mixed
        With the onward-hurrying stream,
        Whose pressure is darkness to me;
        Behind the curtain, fixed,
        Beams with endless beam
        That star on the changing sea.

Great Mother Nature! teach me, like thee,
To kiss the season and shun regrets.
And am I more than the mother who bore,
Mock me not with thy harmony!
        Teach me to blot regrets,
        Great Mother! Me inspire
        With faith that forward sets
        But feeds the living fire,
        Faith that never frets
        For vagueness in the form.
        In life, oh keep me warm!

For, what is human grief?
And what do men desire?
Teach me to feel myself the tree,
And not the withered leaf.
Fixed am I and await the dark to-be.
And O green bounteous Earth!
Bacchante Mother! stern to those
Who live not in thy heart of mirth;
Death shall I shrink from, loving thee?
Into the breast that gives the rose,
Shall I with shuddering fall?
Earth, the mother of all,
Moves on her stedfast way,
Gathering, flinging, sowing.
Mortals, we live in her day,
She in her children is growing.

She can lead us, only she,
Unto God's footstool, whither she reaches:
Loved, enjoyed, her gifts must be,
Reverenced the truths she teaches,
Ere a man may hope that he
Ever can attain the glee
Of things without a destiny!

She knows not loss:
She feels but her need,
Who the winged seed
With the leaf doth toss.

And may not men to this attain?
That the joy of motion, the rapture of being,
Shall throw strong light when our season is fleeing,
Nor quicken aged blood in vain,
At the gates of the vault, on the verge of the plain?
Life thoroughly lived is a fact in the brain,
While eyes are left for seeing.
Behold, in yon stripped autumn, shivering grey,
Earth knows no desolation.
She smells regeneration
In the moist breath of decay.

Prophetic of the coming joy and strife,
  Like the wild western war-chief sinking
  Calm to the end he eyes unblinking,
Her voice is jubilant in ebbing life.
  He for his happy hunting-fields
  Forgets the droning chant, and yields
  His numbered breaths to exultation
  In the proud anticipation:
  Shouting the glories of his nation,
  Shouting the grandeur of his race,
  Shouting his own great deeds of daring;
  And when at last death grasps his face,
  And stiffened on the ground in peace
He lies with all his painted terrors glaring;
Hushed are the tribe to hear a threading cry:
  Not from the dead man;
  Not from the standers-by:
  The spirit of the red man
Is welcomed by his fathers up on high.

DANTE GABRIEL ROSSETTI
(1828–82)

THE BLESSED DAMOZEL

The blessed damozel leaned out
  From the gold bar of heaven;
Her eyes were deeper than the depth
  Of waters stilled at even;
She had three lilies in her hand,
  And the stars in her hair were seven.

Her robe, ungirt from clasp to hem,
  No wrought flowers did adorn,
But a white rose of Mary's gift,
  For service meetly worn;
Her hair that lay along her back
  Was yellow like ripe corn.

Herseemed she scarce had been a day
  One of God's choristers;
The wonder was not yet quite gone
  From that still look of hers;
Albeit, to them she left, her day
  Had counted as ten years.

(To one it is ten years of years.
  . . . Yet now, and in this place,
Surely she leaned o'er me—her hair
  Fell all about my face. . . .
Nothing: the autumn-fall of leaves.
  The whole year sets apace.)

It was the rampart of God's house
  That she was standing on;
By God built over the sheer depth
  The which is space begun;

So high, that looking downward thence
   She scarce could see the sun.

It lies in heaven, across the flood
   Of aether, as a bridge.
Beneath the tides of day and night
   With flame and darkness ridge
The void, as low as where this earth
   Spins like a fretful midge.

Around her, lovers, newly met
   'Mid deathless love's acclaims,
Spoke evermore among themselves
   Their heart-remembered names;
And the souls mounting up to God
   Went by her like thin flames.

And still she bowed herself and stooped
   Out of the circling charm;
Until her bosom must have made
   The bar she leaned on warm,
And the lilies lay as if asleep
   Along her bended arm.

From the fixed place of heaven she saw
   Time like a pulse shake fierce
Through all the worlds. Her gaze still strove
   Within the gulf to pierce
Its path; and now she spoke as when
   The stars sang in their spheres.

The sun was gone now; the curled moon
   Was like a little feather
Fluttering far down the gulf; and now
   She spoke through the still weather.
Her voice was like the voice the stars
   Had when they sang together.

(Ah, sweet! Even now, in that bird's song,
   Strove not her accents there,
Fain to be harkened? When those bells
   Possessed the midday air,

Strove not her steps to reach my side
    Down all the echoing stair?)

"I wish that he were come to me,
    For he will come," she said.
"Have I not prayed in heaven?—on earth,
    Lord, Lord, has he not prayed?
Are not two prayers a perfect strength?
    And shall I feel afraid?

When round his head the aureole clings,
    And he is clothed in white,
I'll take his hand and go with him
    To the deep wells of light;
As unto a stream we will step down,
    And bathe there in God's sight.

We two will stand beside that shrine,
    Occult, withheld, untrod,
Whose lamps are stirred continually
    With prayer sent up to God;
And see our old prayers, granted, melt
    Each like a little cloud.

We two will lie in the shadow of
    That living mystic tree
Within whose secret growth the Dove
    Is sometimes felt to be,
While every leaf that His plumes touch
    Saith His Name audibly.

And I myself will teach to him,
    I myself, lying so,
The songs I sing here; which his voice
    Shall pause in, hushed and slow,
And find some knowledge at each pause,
    Or some new thing to know."

(Alas! We two, we two, thou sayest!
    Yea, one wast thou with me
That once of old. But shall God lift
    To endless unity

The soul whose likeness with thy soul
Was but its love for thee?)

"We two," she said, "will seek the groves
Where the lady Mary is,
With her five handmaidens, whose names
Are five sweet symphonies,
Cecily, Gertrude, Magdalen,
Margaret, and Rosalys.

Circlewise sit they, with bound locks
And foreheads garlanded;
Into the fine cloth white like flame
Weaving the golden thread,
To fashion the birth-robes for them
Who are just born, being dead.

He shall fear, haply, and be dumb;
Then will I lay my cheek
To his, and tell about our love,
Not once abashed or weak;
And the dear Mother will approve
My pride, and let me speak.

Herself shall bring us, hand in hand,
To Him round whom all souls
Kneel, the clear-ranged unnumbered heads
Bowed with their aureoles;
And angels meeting us shall sing
To their citherns and citoles.

There will I ask of Christ the Lord
Thus much for him and me—
Only to live as once on earth
With love—only to be,
As then awhile, forever now,
Together, I and he."

She gazed and listened and then said,
Less sad of speech than mild—
"All this is when he comes." She ceased.
The light thrilled toward her, filled

With angels in strong, level flight.
   Her eyes prayed, and she smiled.

(I saw her smile.) But soon their path
   Was vague in distant spheres;
And then she cast her arms along
   The golden barriers,
And laid her face between her hands,
   And wept (I heard her tears).

CHRISTINA ROSSETTI
(1830–94)

AFTER DEATH

The curtains were half drawn, the floor was swept
  And strewn with rushes, rosemary and may
  Lay thick upon the bed on which I lay,
Where through the lattice ivy-shadows crept.
He leaned above me, thinking that I slept
  And could not hear him; but I heard him say,
  "Poor child, poor child": and as he turned away
Came a deep silence, and I knew he wept.
He did not touch the shroud, or raise the fold
  That hid my face, or take my hand in his,
    Or ruffle the smooth pillows for my head:
    He did not love me living; but once dead
  He pitied me; and very sweet it is
To know he still is warm though I am cold.

WINTER: MY SECRET

  I tell my secret? No indeed, not I:
  Perhaps some day, who knows?
  But not to-day; it froze, and blows, and snows,
  And you're too curious: fie!
  You want to hear it? well:
  Only, my secret's mine, and I won't tell.

  Or, after all, perhaps there's none:
  Suppose there is no secret after all,
  But only just my fun.
  To-day's a nipping day, a biting day;
  In which one wants a shawl,

A veil, a cloak, and other wraps:
I cannot ope to every one who taps,
And let the draughts come whistling through my hall;
Come bounding and surrounding me,
Come buffeting, astounding me,
Nipping and clipping through my wraps and all.
I wear my mask for warmth: who ever shows
His nose to Russian snows
To be pecked at by every wind that blows?
You would not peck? I thank you for good will,
Believe, but leave that truth untested still.

Spring's an expansive time: yet I don't trust
March with its peck of dust,
Nor April with its rainbow-crowned brief showers,
Nor even May, whose flowers
One frost may wither through the sunless hours.

Perhaps some languid summer day,
When drowsy birds sing less and less,
And golden fruit is ripening to excess,
If there's not too much sun nor too much cloud,
And the warm wind is neither still nor loud,
Perhaps my secret I may say,
Or you may guess.

"NO, THANK YOU, JOHN"

I never said I loved you, John;
    Why will you tease me day by day,
And wax a weariness to think upon
    With always "do" and "pray"?

You know I never loved you, John;
    No fault of mine made me your toast:
Why will you haunt me with a face as wan
    As shows an hour-old ghost?

I dare say Meg or Moll would take
   Pity upon you, if you'd ask:
And pray don't remain single for my sake
   Who can't perform that task.

I have no heart?—Perhaps I have not;
   But then you're mad to take offence
That I don't give you what I have not got:
   Use your own common sense.

Let bygones be bygones:
   Don't call me false, who owed not to be true:
I'd rather answer "No" to fifty Johns
   Than answer "Yes" to you.

Let's mar our pleasant days no more,
   Song-birds of passage, days of youth:
Catch at to-day, forget the days before;
   I'll wink at your untruth.

Let us strike hands as hearty friends;
   No more, no less; and friendship's good:
Only don't keep in view ulterior ends,
   And points not understood

In open treaty. Rise above
   Quibbles and shuffling off and on.
Here's friendship for you if you like; but love—
   No, thank you, John.

ENRICA, 1865

She came among us from the south,
   And made the north her home awhile;
   Our dimness brightened in her smile,
Our tongue grew sweeter in her mouth.

We chilled beside her liberal glow,
   She dwarfed us by her ampler scale,

591

Her full-blown blossom made us pale—
She summer-like and we like snow.

We Englishwomen, trim, correct,
    All minted in the selfsame mould,
    Warm-hearted but of semblance cold,
All-courteous out of self-respect.

She, woman in her natural grace,
    Less trammelled she by lore of school,
    Courteous by nature not by rule,
Warm-hearted and of cordial face.

So for awhile she made her home
    Among us in the rigid north,
    She who from Italy came forth
And scaled the Alps and crossed the foam.

But, if she found us like our sea,
    Of aspect colourless and chill,
    Rock-girt—like it she found us still
Deep at our deepest, strong and free.

LEWIS CARROLL
(1832–98)

JABBERWOCKY

'Twas brillig, and the slithy toves
　　Did gyre and gimble in the wabe;
All mimsy were the borogoves,
　　And the mome raths outgrabe.

"Beware the Jabberwock, my son!
　　The jaws that bite, the claws that catch!
Beware the Jubjub bird, and shun
　　The frumious Bandersnatch!"

He took his vorpal sword in hand;
　　Long time the manxome foe he sought—
So rested he by the Tumtum tree,
　　And stood awhile in thought.

And, as in uffish thought he stood,
　　The Jabberwock, with eyes of flame,
Came whiffling through the tulgey wood,
　　And burbled as it came!

One, two! One, two! And through and through
　　The vorpal blade went snicker-snack!
He left it dead, and with its head
　　He went galumphing back.

"And hast thou slain the Jabberwock?
　　Come to my arms, my beamish boy!
O frabjous day! Callooh! Callay!"
　　He chortled in his joy.

'Twas brillig, and the slithy toves
　　Did gyre and gimble in the wabe;
All mimsy were the borogoves,
　　And the mome raths outgrabe.

THE WALRUS AND THE CARPENTER

The sun was shining on the sea,
  Shining with all his might;
He did his very best to make
  The billows smooth and bright—
And this was odd, because it was
  The middle of the night.

The moon was shining sulkily,
  Because she thought the sun
Had got no business to be there
  After the day was done—
"It's very rude of him," she said,
  "To come and spoil the fun!"

The sea was wet as wet could be,
  The sands were dry as dry.
You could not see a cloud, because
  No cloud was in the sky;
No birds were flying overhead—
  There were no birds to fly.

The walrus and the carpenter
  Were walking close at hand;
They wept like anything to see
  Such quantities of sand.
"If this were only cleared away,"
  They said, "it *would* be grand!"

"If seven maids with seven mops
  Swept it for half a year,
Do you suppose," the walrus said,
  "That they could get it clear?"
"I doubt it," said the carpenter,
  And shed a bitter tear.

594

"O oysters, come and walk with us!"
    The walrus did beseech.
"A pleasant walk, a pleasant talk,
    Along the briny beach;
We cannot do with more than four,
    To give a hand to each."

The eldest oyster looked at him,
    But never a word he said;
The eldest oyster winked his eye,
    And shook his heavy head—
Meaning to say he did not choose
    To leave the oyster-bed.

But four young oysters hurried up,
    All eager for the treat;
Their coats were brushed, their faces washed,
    Their shoes were clean and neat—
And this was odd, because, you know,
    They hadn't any feet.

Four other oysters followed them,
    And yet another four;
And thick and fast they came at last,
    And more, and more, and more—
All hopping through the frothy waves,
    And scrambling to the shore.

The walrus and the carpenter
    Walked on a mile or so,
And then they rested on a rock
    Conveniently low;
And all the little oysters stood
    And waited in a row.

"The time has come," the walrus said,
    "To talk of many things:
Of shoes—and ships—and sealing-wax—
    Of cabbages—and kings—
And why the sea is boiling hot—
    And whether pigs have wings."

"But wait a bit," the oysters cried,
    "Before we have our chat;
For some of us are out of breath,
    And all of us are fat!"
"No hurry!" said the carpenter.
    They thanked him much for that.

"A loaf of bread," the walrus said,
    "Is what we chiefly need;
Pepper and vinegar besides
    Are very good indeed—
Now, if you're ready, oysters dear,
    We can begin to feed."

"But not on us!" the oysters cried,
    Turning a little blue.
"After such kindness, that would be
    A dismal thing to do!"
"The night is fine," the walrus said,
    "Do you admire the view?

It was so kind of you to come!
    And you are very nice!"
The carpenter said nothing but
    "Cut us another slice.
I wish you were not quite so deaf—
    I've had to ask you twice!"

"It seems a shame," the walrus said,
    "To play them such a trick,
After we've brought them out so far,
    And made them trot so quick!"
The carpenter said nothing but
    "The butter's spread too thick!"

"I weep for you," the walrus said;
    "I deeply sympathise."
With sobs and tears he sorted out
    Those of the largest size,
Holding his pocket-handkerchief
    Before his streaming eyes.

"O oysters," said the carpenter,
  "You've had a pleasant run!
Shall we be trotting home again?"
    But answer came there none—
And this was scarcely odd, because
  They'd eaten every one.

WILLIAM MORRIS
(1834–96)

THE DEFENCE OF GUENEVERE

But, knowing now that they would have her speak,
She threw her wet hair backward from her brow,
Her hand close to her mouth touching her cheek,

As though she had had there a shameful blow,
And feeling it shameful to feel ought but shame
All through her heart, yet felt her cheek burned so,

She must a little touch it; like one lame
She walked away from Gauwaine, with her head
Still lifted up; and on her cheek of flame

The tears dried quick; she stopped at last and said:
"O knights and lords, it seems but little skill
To talk of well-known things past now and dead.

"God wot I ought to say, I have done ill,
And pray you all forgiveness heartily!
Because you might be right such great lords—still,

"Listen, suppose your time were come to die,
And you were quite alone and very weak;
Yea, laid a-dying while very mightily

"The wind was ruffling up the narrow streak
Of river through your broad lands running well;
Suppose a hush should come, then someone speak:

" 'One of these cloths is heaven, and one is hell,
Now choose one cloth forever, which they be,
I will not tell you, you must somehow tell

" 'Of your own strength and mightiness; here, see!'
Yea, yea, my lord, and you to ope your eyes,
At foot of your familiar bed to see

"A great God's angel standing, with such dyes,
Not known on earth, on his great wings, and hands,
Held out two ways, light from the inner skies

"Showing him well, and making his commands
Seem to be God's commands, moreover, too,
Holding within his hands the cloths on wands;

"And one of these strange choosing cloths was blue,
Wavy and long, and one cut short and red;
No man could tell the better of the two.

"After a shivering half hour you said,
'God help! heaven's colour, the blue'; and he said, 'Hell.'
Perhaps you then would roll upon your bed,

"And cry to all good men that loved you well,
'Ah, Christ! If only I had known, known, known';
Launcelot went away, then I could tell,

"Like wisest man how all things would be, moan,
And roll and hurt myself, and long to die,
And yet fear much to die for what was sown.

"Nevertheless, you, O Sir Gauwaine, lie,
Whatever may have happened through these years,
God knows I speak truth, saying that you lie."

Her voice was low at first, being full of tears,
But, as it cleared, it grew full loud and shrill,
Growing a windy shriek in all men's ears,

A ringing in their startled brains, until
She said that Gauwaine lied; then her voice sunk,
And her great eyes began again to fill,

Though still she stood right up, and never shrunk,
But spoke on bravely, glorious lady fair!
Whatever tears her full lips may have drunk,

She stood, and seemed to think, and wrung her hair,
Spoke out at last with no more trace of shame,
With passionate twisting of her body there:

"It chanced upon a day that Launcelot came
To dwell at Arthur's court: at Christmas time
This happened; when the heralds sang his name,

" 'Son of King Ban of Benwick,' seemed to chime
Along with all the bells that rang that day,
O'er the white roofs, with little change of rhyme.

"Christmas and whitened winter passed away,
And over me the April sunshine came,
Made very awful with black hailclouds, yea.

"And in summer I grew white with flame,
And bowed my head down—autumn, and the sick,
Sure knowledge things would never be the same,

"However often spring might be most thick
Of blossoms and buds, smote on me, and I grew
Careless of most things, let the clock tick, tick,

"To my unhappy pulse, that beat right through
My eager body; while I laughed out loud,
And let my lips curl up at false or true,

"Seemed cold and shallow without any cloud.
Behold, my judges, then the cloths were brought:
While I was dizzied thus, old thoughts would crowd,

"Belonging to the time ere I was bought
By Arthur's great name and his little love;
Must I give up forever then, I thought,

"That which I deemed would ever round me move
Glorifying all things; for a little word,
Scarce ever meant at all, must I now prove

"Stone-cold for ever? Pray you, does the Lord
Will that all folks should be quite happy and good?
I love God now a little, if this cord

"Were broken, once for all, what striving could
Make me love anything in earth or heaven?
So day by day it grew, as if one should

"Slip slowly down some path worn smooth and even,
Down to a cool sea on a summer day;
Yet still in slipping there was some small leaven

"Of stretched hands catching small stones by the way,
Until one surely reached the sea at last,
And felt strange new joy as the worn head lay

"Back, with the hair like seaweed; yea, all past
Sweat of the forehead, dryness of the lips,
Washed utterly out by the dear waves o'ercast,

"In the lone sea, far off from any ships!
Do I not know now of a day in spring?
No minute of that wild day ever slips

"From out my memory; I hear thrushes sing,
And wheresoever I may be, straightway
Thoughts of it all come up with most fresh sting;

"I was half mad with beauty on that day,
And went without my ladies all alone,
In a quiet garden walled round every way;

"I was right joyful of that wall of stone
That shut the flowers and trees up with the sky,
And trebled all the beauty; to the bone,

"Yea right through to my heart, grown very shy
With weary thoughts, it pierced, and made me glad;
Exceedingly glad, and I knew, verily,

"A little thing just then had made me mad;
I dared not think, as I was wont to do,
Sometimes, upon my beauty. If I had

"Held out my long hand up against the blue,
And, looking on the tenderly darkened fingers,
Thought that by rights one ought to see quite through,

"There, see you, where the soft, still light yet lingers,
Round by the edges; what should I have done,
If this had joined with yellow-spotted singers,

"And startling green drawn upward by the sun?
But shouting, loosed out, see now! All my hair,
And trancedly stood watching the west wind run

"With faintest, half-heard breathing sound—why, there
I lose my head e'en now in doing this;
But shortly listen—In that garden fair

"Came Launcelot walking; this is true, the kiss
Wherewith we kissed in meeting, that spring day,
I scarce dare talk of the remembered bliss,

"When both our mouths went wandering in one way,
And aching sorely, met among the leaves;
Our hands being left behind strained far away.

"Never within a yard of my bright sleeves
Had Launcelot come before—and now, so nigh!
After that day why is it Guenevere grieves?

"Nevertheless you, O Sir Gauwaine, lie;
Whatever happened on through all those years,
God knows I speak truth, saying that you lie.

"Being such a lady, could I weep these tears
If this were true? A great queen such as I,
Having sinned this way, straight her conscience sears;

"And afterwards she liveth hatefully,
Slaying and poisoning, certes never weeps—
Gauwaine, be friends now, speak me lovingly.

"Do I not see how God's dear pity creeps
All through your frame, and trembles in your mouth?
Remember in what grave your mother sleeps,

"Buried in some place far down in the south,
Men are forgetting as I speak to you;
By her head severed in that awful drouth

"Of pity that drew Agravaine's fell blow.
I pray your pity! Let me not scream out
Forever after, when the shrill winds blow

"Through half your castle-locks! Let me not shout
Forever after in the winter night
When you ride out alone! In battle rout

"Let not my rusting tears make your sword light!
Ah! God of mercy, how he turns away!
So ever must I dress me to the fight,

"So—let God's justice work! Gauwaine, I say,
See me hew down your proofs; yea, all men know
Even as you said how Mellyagraunce one day,

"One bitter day in *la Fausse Garde*, for so
All good knights held it after, saw—
Yea, sirs, by cursed, unknightly outrage; though

"You, Gauwaine, held his word without a flaw,
This Mellyagraunce saw blood upon my bed—
Whose blood then pray you? Is there any law

"To make a queen say why some spots of red
Lie on her coverlet? Or will you say,
'Your hands are white, lady, as when you wed,

" 'Where did you bleed?' And must I stammer out—'Nay,
I blush indeed, fair lord, only to rend
My sleeve up to my shoulder, where there lay

" 'A knife-point last night': so must I defend
The honour of the lady Guenevere?
Not so, fair lords, even if the world should end

"This very day, and you were judges here
Instead of God. Did you see Mellyagraunce,
When Launcelot stood by him? What white fear

"Curdled his blood, and how his teeth did dance,
His side sink in, as my knight cried and said,
'Slayer of unarmed men, here is a chance!

" 'Setter of traps, I pray you guard your head!
By God, I am so glad to fight with you,
Stripper of ladies, that my hand feels lead

" 'For driving weight; hurrah now! Draw and do,
For all my wounds are moving in my breast,
And I am getting mad with waiting so.'

"He struck his hands together o'er the beast,
Who fell down flat, and grovelled at his feet,
And groaned at being slain so young—'at least.'

"My knight said, 'Rise you, sir, who are so fleet
At catching ladies, half-armed will I fight,
My left side all uncovered!' Then I weet,

"Up sprang Sir Mellyagraunce with great delight
Upon his knave's face; not until just then
Did I quite hate him, as I saw my knight

"Along the lists look to my stake and pen
With such a joyous smile, it made me sigh
From agony beneath my waist-chain, when

"The fight began, and to me they drew nigh;
Ever Sir Launcelot kept him on the right,
And traversed warily, and ever high

"And fast leaped caitiff's sword, until my knight
Sudden threw up his sword to his left hand,
Caught it, and swung it; that was all the fight.

"Except a spout of blood on the hot land;
For it was hottest summer; and I know
I wondered how the fire, while I should stand,

"And burn, against the heat, would quiver so,
Yards above my head; thus these matters went;
Which things were only warnings of the woe

"That fell on me. Yet Mellyagraunce was shent,
For Mellyagraunce had fought against the Lord;
Therefore, my lords, take heed lest you be blent

"With all this wickedness; say no rash word
Against me, being so beautiful; my eyes,
Wept all away the grey, may bring some sword

"To drown you in your blood; see my breast rise,
Like waves of purple sea, as here I stand;
And how my arms are moved in wonderful wise,

"Yea also at my full heart's strong command,
See through my long throat how the words go up
In ripples to my mouth; how in my hand

"The shadow lies like wine within a cup
Of marvellously coloured gold; yea now
This little wind is rising, look you up,

"And wonder how the light is falling so
Within my moving tresses; will you dare,
When you have looked a little on my brow,

"To say this thing is vile? or will you care
For any plausible lies of cunning woof,
When you can see my face with no lie there

"Forever? Am I not a gracious proof—
'But in your chamber Launcelot was found'—
Is there a good knight then would stand aloof,

"When a queen says, with gentle queenly sound:
'O true as steel, come now and talk with me,
I love to see your step upon the ground

" 'Unwavering; also well I love to see
That gracious smile light up your face, and hear
Your wonderful words, that all mean verily

" 'The thing they seem to mean; good friend, so dear
To me in everything, come here tonight,
Or else the hours will pass most dull and drear;

" 'If you come not, I fear this time I might
Get thinking overmuch of times gone by,
When I was young, and green hope was in sight:

" 'For no man cares now to know why I sigh;
And no man comes to sing me pleasant songs,
Nor any brings me the sweet flowers that lie

" 'So thick in the gardens; therefore one so longs
To see you, Launcelot, that we may be
Like children once again, free from all wrongs

" 'Just for one night.' Did he not come to me?
What thing could keep true Launcelot away
If I said 'Come?' There was one less than three

"In my quiet room that night, and we were gay;
Till sudden I rose up, weak, pale, and sick,
Because a bawling broke our dream up, yea,

"I looked at Launcelot's face and could not speak,
For he looked helpless too, for a little while;
Then I remember how I tried to shriek,

"And could not, but fell down; from tile to tile
The stones they threw up rattled o'er my head
And made me dizzier; till within a while

"My maids were all about me, and my head
On Launcelot's breast was being soothed away
From its white chattering, until Launcelot said—

"By God! I will not tell you more today,
Judge any way you will—what matters it?
You know quite well the story of that fray,

"How Launcelot stilled their bawling, the mad fit
That caught up Gauwaine—all, all, verily,
But just that which would save me; these things flit.

"Nevertheless, you, O Sir Gauwaine, lie;
Whatever may have happened these long years,
God knows I speak truth, saying that you lie!

"All I have said is truth, by Christ's dear tears."
She would not speak another word, but stood,
Turned sideways, listening, like a man who hears

His brother's trumpet sounding through the wood
Of his foes' lances. She leaned eagerly,
And gave a slight spring sometimes, as she could

At last hear something really; joyfully
Her cheek grew crimson, as the headlong speed
Of the roan charger drew all men to see,
The knight who came was Launcelot at good need.

ALFRED AUSTIN
(1835–1913)

THE THRUSH

Hark to the thrush gurgling in yonder tree!
He hath inhaled the liquid air whilst flying,
And, now he chooses him another perch,
Gives it back in notes intangible;
Which is the very music that we want,
Did we but know it. For your spoken song,
Too full of meaning, lacks significance.
Hark how again he sings celestially,
The very heaven of music meaningless!
He is a better poet than us all.

THE MAIDEN OF THE SMILE

In that fair land where slope and plain
    Shine back to sun and sky,
And olives shield the sprouting grain
    When wintry arrows fly,
Where snow-fed streams seek sun-warmed vale
    Through vineyard-scarped defile,
The world we enter with a wail
    She greeted with a smile.

Slumbering she smiled, and smiling woke,
    And, when she felt the smart
Of grave sad life, smile still bespoke
    Her tenderness of heart.
And nightly when she knelt and prayed
    Beside her snow-white bed,

608

Her face was one pure smile that made
   A heaven about her head.

When love first trembled in her ear
   The heart-throbs that beguile,
She listened with assenting tear,
   Then chased it with a smile.
Anguish and loss with smiles she bore
   Unto her latest breath;
But the sweetest smile she ever wore
   Was the smile she wore in death.

ALGERNON
CHARLES SWINBURNE
(1837–1909)

from ATALANTA IN CALYDON

When the hounds of spring are on winter's traces,
    The mother of months in meadow or plain
Fills the shadows and windy places
    With lisp of leaves and ripple of rain;
And the brown bright nightingale amorous
Is half assuaged for Itylus,
For the Thracian ships and the foreign faces,
    The tongueless vigil, and all the pain.

Come with bows bent and with emptying of quivers,
    Maiden most perfect, lady of light,
With a noise of winds and many rivers,
    With a clamour of waters, and with might;
Bind on thy sandals, O thou most fleet,
Over the splendour and speed of thy feet;
For the faint east quickens, the wan west shivers,
    Round the feet of the day and the feet of the night.

Where shall we find her, how shall we sing to her,
    Fold our hands round her knees, and cling?
Oh that man's heart were as fire and could spring to her,
    Fire, or the strength of the streams that spring!
For the stars and the winds are unto her
As raiment, as songs of the harp-player;
For the risen stars and the fallen cling to her,
    And the southwest-wind and the west-wind sing.

For winter's rains and ruins are over,
   And all the season of snows and sins;
The days dividing lover and lover,
   The light that loses, the night that wins;
And time remembered is grief forgotten,
And frosts are slain and flowers begotten,
And in green underwood and cover
   Blossom by blossom the spring begins.

The full streams feed on flower of rushes,
   Ripe grasses trammel a travelling foot,
The faint fresh flame of the young year flushes
   From leaf to flower and flower to fruit;
And fruit and leaf are as gold and fire,
And the oat is heard above the lyre,
And the hoofed heel of a satyr crushes
   The chestnut-husk at the chestnut-root.

And Pan by noon and Bacchus by night,
   Fleeter of foot than the fleet-foot kid,
Follows with dancing and fills with delight
   The Maenad and the Bassarid;
And soft as lips that laugh and hide
The laughing leaves of the trees divide,
And screen from seeing and leave in sight
   The god pursuing, the maiden hid.

The ivy falls with the Bacchanal's hair
   Over her eyebrows hiding her eyes;
The wild vine slipping down leaves bare
   Her bright breast shortening into sighs;
The wild vine slips with the weight of its leaves,
But the berried ivy catches and cleaves
To the limbs that glitter, the feet that scare
   The wolf that follows, the fawn that flies.

HYMN TO PROSERPINE

I have lived long enough, having seen one thing, that love
    hath an end;
Goddess and maiden and queen, be near me now and befriend.
Thou art more than the day or the morrow, the seasons that laugh
    or that weep;
For these give joy and sorrow; but thou, Proserpine, sleep.
Sweet is the treading of wine, and sweet the feet of the dove;
But a goodlier gift is thine than foam of the grapes or love.
Yea, is not even Apollo, with hair and harpstring of gold,
A bitter god to follow, a beautiful god to behold?
I am sick of singing: the bays burn deep and chafe: I am fain
To rest a little from praise and grievous pleasure and pain.
For the gods we know not of, who give us our daily breath,
We know they are cruel as love or life, and lovely as death.
O gods dethroned and deceased, cast forth, wiped out in a day!
From your wrath is the world released, redeemed from your chains,
    men say.
New gods are crowned in the city; their flowers have broken
    your rods;
They are merciful, clothed with pity, the young compassionate
    gods.
But for me their new device is barren, the days are bare;
Things long past over suffice, and men forgotten that were.
Time and the gods are at strife; ye dwell in the midst thereof,
Draining a little life from the barren breasts of love.
I say to you, cease, take rest; yea, I say to you all, be at peace,
Till the bitter milk of her breast and the barren bosom shall cease.
Wilt thou yet take all, Galilean? But these thou shalt not take,
The laurel, the palms and the paean, the breasts of the nymphs in
    the brake;
Breasts more soft than a dove's, that tremble with tenderer breath;
And all the wings of the loves, and all the joy before death;
All the feet of the hours that sound as a single lyre,
Dropped and deep in the flowers, with strings that flicker like fire.
More than these wilt thou give, things fairer than all these things?

Nay, for a little we live, and life hath mutable wings.
A little while and we die; shall life not thrive as it may?
For no man under the sky lives twice, outliving his day.
And grief is a grievous thing, and a man hath enough of his tears:
Why should he labour, and bring fresh grief to blacken his years?
Thou hast conquered, O pale Galilean; the world has grown grey
    from thy breath;
We have drunken of things Lethean, and fed on the fullness of
    death.
Laurel is green for a season, and love is sweet for a day;
But love grows bitter with treason, and laurel outlives not May.
Sleep, shall we sleep after all? For the world is not sweet in the
    end;
For the old faiths loosen and fall, the new years ruin and rend.
Fate is a sea without shore, and the soul is a rock that abides;
But her ears are vexed with the roar and her face with the foam of
    the tides.
O lips that the live blood faints in, the leavings of racks and rods!
O ghastly glories of saints, dead limbs of gibbeted gods!
Though all men abase them before you in spirit, and all knees
    bend,
I kneel not, neither adore you, but standing, look to the end.
All delicate days and pleasant, all spirits and sorrows are cast
Far out with the foam of the present that sweeps to the surf of
    the past:
Where beyond the extreme sea-wall, and between the remote sea-
    gates,
Waste water washes, and tall ships founder, and deep death waits:
Where, mighty with deepening sides, clad about with the seas as
    with wings,
And impelled of invisible tides, and fulfilled of unspeakable things,
White-eyed and poisonous-finned, shark-toothed and serpentine-
    curled,
Rolls, under the whitening wind of the future, the wave of the
    world.
The depths stand naked in sunder behind it, the storms flee away;
In the hollow before it the thunder is taken and snared as a prey;
In its sides is the north-wind bound; and its salt is of all men's
    tears;
With light of ruin, and sound of changes, and pulse of years:

With travail of day after day, and with trouble of hour upon hour;
And bitter as blood is the spray; and the crests are as fangs that
    devour:
And its vapour and storm of its steam as the sighing of spirits to be;
And its noise as the noise in a dream; and its depth as the roots of
    the sea:
And the height of its heads as the height of the utmost stars of the
    air:
And the ends of the earth at the might thereof tremble, and time
    is made bare.
Will ye bridle the deep sea with reins, will ye chasten the high sea
    with rods?
Will ye take her to chain her with chains, who is older than all ye gods?
All ye as a wind shall go by, as a fire shall ye pass and be past;
Ye are gods, and behold, ye shall die, and the waves be upon you at last.
In the darkness of time, in the deeps of the years, in the changes
    of things,
Ye shall sleep as a slain man sleeps, and the world shall forget you
    for kings.
Though the feet of thine high priests tread where thy lords and our
    forefathers trod,
Though these that were gods are dead, and thou being dead art a god,
Though before thee the throned Cytherean be fallen, and hidden
    her head,
Yet thy kingdom shall pass, Galilean, thy dead shall go down to
    thee dead.
Of the maiden thy mother men sing as a goddess with grace clad around;
Thou art throned where another was king; where another was queen
    she is crowned.
Yea, once we had sight of another: but now she is queen, say these.
Not as thine, not as thine was our mother, a blossom of flowering seas,
Clothed round with the world's desire as with raiment, and fair as
    the foam,
And fleeter than kindled fire, and a goddess, and mother of Rome.
For thine came pale and a maiden, and sister to sorrow; but ours,
Her deep hair heavily laden with odour and colour of flowers,
White rose of the rose-white water, a silver splendour, a flame,
Bent down unto us that besought her, and earth grew sweet with
    her name.
For thine came weeping, a slave among slaves, and rejected; but she

Came flushed from the full-flushed wave, and imperial, her foot on
  the sea.
And the wonderful waters knew her, the winds and the viewless ways,
And the roses grew rosier, and bluer the sea-blue stream of the bays.
Ye are fallen, our lords, by what token? We wist that ye should not fall.
Ye were all so fair that are broken; and one more fair than ye all.
But I turn to her still, having seen she shall surely abide in the end;
Goddess and maiden and queen, be near me now and befriend.
O daughter of earth, of my mother, her crown and blossom of birth,
I am also, I also, thy brother; I go as I came unto earth.
In the night where thine eyes are as moons are in heaven, the
  night where thou art,
Where the silence is more than all tunes, where sleep overflows
  from the heart,
Where the poppies are sweet as the rose in our world, and the red
  rose is white,
And the wind falls faint as it blows with the fume of the flowers of
  the night,
And the murmur of spirits that sleep in the shadow of gods from afar
Grows dim in thine ears and deep as the deep dim soul of a star,
In the sweet low light of thy face, under heavens untrod by the sun,
Let my soul with their souls find place, and forget what is done
  and undone.
Thou art more than the gods who number the days of our temporal
  breath;
For these give labour and slumber; but thou, Proserpine, death.
Therefore now at thy feet I abide for a season in silence. I know
I shall die as my fathers died, and sleep as they sleep; even so.
For the glass of the years is brittle wherein we gaze for a span;
A little soul for a little bears up this corpse which is man.
So long I endure, no longer; and laugh not again, neither weep.
For there is no god found stronger than death; and death is a sleep.

Lift up thy lips, turn round, look back for love,
   Blind love that comes by night and casts out rest;
   Of all things tired thy lips look weariest,
Save the long smile that they are wearied of.
Ah sweet, albeit no love be sweet enough,
   Choose of two loves and cleave unto the best;
   Two loves at either blossom of thy breast
Strive until one be under and one above.
Their breath is fire upon the amorous air,
   Fire in thine eyes and where thy lips suspire:
And whosoever hath seen thee, being so fair;
   Two things turn all his life and blood to fire;
A strong desire begot on great despair,
   A great despair cast out by strong desire.

Where between sleep and life some brief space is,
   With love like gold bound round about the head,
   Sex to sweet sex with lips and limbs is wed,
Turning the fruitful feud of hers and his
To the waste wedlock of a sterile kiss;
   Yet from them something like as fire is shed
   That shall not be assuaged till death be dead,
Though neither life nor sleep can find out this.
Love made himself of flesh that perisheth
   A pleasure-house for all the loves his kin;
But on the one side sat a man like death,
   And on the other a woman sat like sin.
So with veiled eyes and sobs between his breath
   Love turned himself and would not enter in.

Love, is it love or sleep or shadow or light
   That lies between thine eyelids and thine eyes?
   Like a flower laid upon a flower it lies,
Or like the night's dew laid upon the night.
Love stands upon thy left hand and thy right,
   Yet by no sunset and by no moonrise
   Shall make thee man and ease a woman's sighs,
Or make thee woman for a man's delight.
To what strange end hath some strange god made fair
   The double blossom of two fruitless flowers?

Hid love in all the folds of all thy hair,
    Fed thee on summers, watered thee with showers,
Given all the gold that all the seasons wear
    To thee that art a thing of barren hours?

Yea, love, I see; it is not love but fear.
    Nay, sweet, it is not fear but love, I know;
    Or wherefore should thy body's blossom blow
So sweetly, or thine eyelids leave so clear
Thy gracious eyes that never made a tear—
    Though for their love our tears like blood should flow,
    Though love and life and death should come and go,
So dreadful, so desirable, so dear?
Yea, sweet, I know; I saw in what swift wise
    Beneath the woman's and the water's kiss
    Thy moist limbs melted into Salmacis,
And the large light turned tender in thine eyes,
And all thy boy's breath softened into sighs;
    But Love being blind, how should he know of this?

EVENING ON THE BROADS

Over two shadowless waters, adrift as a pinnace in peril,
    Hangs as in heavy suspense, charged with irresolute light,
Softly the soul of the sunset upholden awhile on the sterile
    Waves and wastes of the land, half repossessed by the night.
Inland glimmer the shallows asleep and afar in the breathless
    Twilight: yonder the depths darken afar and asleep.
Slowly the semblance of death out of heaven descends on the
    deathless
    Waters: hardly the light lives on the face of the deep—
Hardly, but here for awhile. All over the grey soft shallow
    Hover the colours and clouds of the twilight, void of a star.
As a bird unfledged is the broad-winged night, whose winglets
    are callow
    Yet, but soon with their plumes will she cover her brood from
    afar,
Cover the brood of her worlds that cumber the skies with
    their blossom

Thick as the darkness of leaf-shadowed spring is encumbered
　with flowers.
World upon world is enwound in the bountiful girth of her bosom,
　Warm and lustrous with life lovely to look on as ours.
Still is the sunset adrift as a spirit in doubt that dissembles
　Still with itself, being sick of division and dimmed by dismay—
Nay, not so; but with love and delight beyond passion it trembles,
　Fearful and fain of the night, lovely with love of the day:
Fain and fearful of rest that is like unto death, and begotten
　Out of the womb of the tomb, born of the seed of the grave:
Lovely with shadows of loves that are only not wholly forgotten,
　Only not wholly suppressed by the dark as a wreck by the wave.
Still there linger the loves of the morning and noon, in a vision
　Blindly beheld, but in vain: ghosts that are tired, and would rest.
But the glories beloved of the night rise all too dense for division,
　Deep in the depth of her breast sheltered as doves in a nest.
Fainter the beams of the loves of the daylight season enkindled
　Wane, and the memories of hours that were fair with the love of
　　them fade:
Loftier, aloft of the lights of the sunset stricken and dwindled,
　Gather the signs of the love at the heart of the night new-made.
New-made night, new-born of the sunset, immeasurable, endless,
　Opens the secret of love hid from of old in her heart,
In the deep sweet heart full-charged with faultless love of
　　the friendless
　Spirits of men that are eased when the wheels of the sun depart.
Still is the sunset afloat as a ship on the waters upholden
　Full-sailed, wide-winged, poised softly forever asway—
Nay, not so, but at least for a little, awhile at the golden
　Limit of arching air fain for an hour to delay.
Here on the bar of the sand-bank, steep yet aslope to the gleaming
　Waste of the water without, waste of the water within,
Lights overhead and lights underneath seem doubtfully dreaming
　Whether the day be done, whether the night may begin.
Far and afar and farther again they falter and hover,
　Warm on the water and deep in the sky and pale on the cloud:
Colder again and slowly remoter, afraid to recover
　Breath, yet fain to revive, as it seems, from the skirt of
　　the shroud.
Faintly the heartbeats shorten and pause of the light in the
　　westward
　Heaven, as eastward quicken the paces of star upon star

Hurried and eager of life as a child that strains to the breast-ward
   Eagerly, yearning forth of the deeps where the ways of them are,
Glad of the glory of the gift of their life and the wealth of
   its wonder,
   Fain of the night and the sea and the sweet wan face of the
    earth.
Over them air grows deeper, intense with delight in them: under
   Things are thrilled in their sleep as with sense of a sure
    new birth.
But here by the sand-bank watching, with eyes on the sea-
    line, stranger
   Grows to me also the weight of the sea-ridge gazed on of me,
Heavily heaped up, changefully changeless, void though of danger
   Void not of menace, but full of the might of the dense dull sea.
Like as the wave is before me, behind is the bank deep-drifted;
   Yellow and thick as the bank is behind me in front is the wave.
As the wall of a prison imprisoning the mere is the girth of it
    lifted:
   But the rampire of water in front is erect as the wall of a grave.
And the crests of it crumble and topple and change, but the wall is
    not broken:
   Standing still dry-shod, I see it as higher than my head,
Moving inland alway again, reared up as in token
   Still of impending wrath still in the foam of it shed.
And even in the pauses between them, dividing the rollers in
    sunder,
   High overhead seems ever the sea-line fixed as a mark,
And the shore where I stand as a valley beholden of hills whence
    thunder
   Cloud and torrent and storm, darkening the depths of the dark.
Up to the sea, not upon it or over it, upward from under
   Seems he to gaze, whose eyes yearn after it here from the shore:
A wall of turbid water, aslope to the wide sky's wonder
   Of colour and cloud, it climbs, or spreads as a slanted floor.
And the large lights change on the face of the mere like things
    that were living,
   Winged and wonderful, beams like as birds are that pass and
    are free:
But the light is dense as darkness, a gift withheld in the giving,
   That lies as dead on the fierce dull face of the landward sea.

Stained and stifled and soiled, made earthier than earth is
    and duller,
  Grimly she puts back light as rejected, a thing put away:
No transparent rapture, a molten music of colour;
  No translucent love taken and given of the day.
Fettered and marred and begrimed is the light's live self on
    her falling,
  As the light of a man's life lighted the fume of a dungeon mars:
Only she knows of the wind, when her wrath gives ear to him
    calling;
  The delight of the light she knows not, nor answers the sun or
    the stars.
Love she hath none to return for the luminous love of their giving:
  None to reflect from the bitter and shallow response of her
    heart.
Yearly she feeds on her dead, yet herself seems dead and not living,
  Or confused as a soul heavy-laden with trouble that will
    not depart.
In the sound of her speech to the darkness the moan of her evil
    remorse is,
  Haply, for strong ships gnawed by the dog-toothed sea-bank's
    fang
And trampled to death by the rage of the feet of her foam-lipped
    horses
  Whose manes are yellow as plague, and as ensigns of pestilence
    hang,
That wave in the foul faint air of the breath of a death-stricken
    city;
  So menacing heaves she the manes of her rollers knotted
    with sand,
Discoloured, opaque, suspended in sign as of strength without pity,
  That shake with flameless thunder the low long length of
    the strand.
Here, far off in the farther extreme of the shore as it lengthens
  Northward, lonely for miles, ere ever a village begin,
On the lapsing land that recedes as the growth of the strong sea
    strengthens
  Shoreward, thrusting further and further its outworks in,
Here in Shakespeare's vision, a flower of her kin forsaken,
  Lay in her golden raiment alone on the wild wave's edge,
Surely by no shore else, but here on the bank storm-shaken,
  Perdita, bright as a dew-drop engilt of the sun on the sedge.

Here on a shore unbeheld of his eyes in a dream he beheld her
  Outcast, fair as a fairy, the child of a far-off king:
And over the babe-flower gently the head of a pastoral elder
  Bowed, compassionate, hoar as the hawthorn-blossom in spring,
And kind as harvest in autumn: a shelter of shade on the lonely
  Shelterless unknown shore scourged of implacable waves:
Here, where the wind walks royal, alone in his kingdom, and only
  Sounds to the sedges a wail as of triumph that conquers
    and craves.
All these waters and wastes are his empire of old, and awaken
  From barren and stagnant slumber at only the sound of his
    breath:
Yet the hunger is eased not that aches in his heart, nor the
    goal overtaken
  That his wide wings yearn for and labour as hearts that yearn
    after death.
All the solitude sighs and expects with a blind expectation
  Somewhat unknown of its own sad heart, grown heartsick
    of strife:
Till sometime its wild heart maddens, and moans, and the vast
    ululation
  Takes wings with the clouds on the waters, and wails to be quit
    of its life.
For the spirit and soul of the waste is the wind, and his wings
    with their waving
  Darken and lighten the darkness and light of it thickened or
    thinned;
But the heart that impels them is even as a conqueror's insatiably
    craving
  That victory can fill not, as power cannot satiate the want of
    the wind.
All these moorlands and marshes are full of his might, and oppose
    not
  Aught of defence nor of barrier, of forest or precipice piled:
But the will of the wind works ever as his that desires what he
    knows not,
  And the wail of his want unfulfilled is as one making moan for
    her child.
And the cry of his triumph is even as the crying of hunger that
    maddens
  The heart of a strong man aching in vain as the wind's heart
    aches

And the sadness itself of the land for its infinite solitude saddens
   More for the sound than the silence athirst for the sound that
      slakes.
And the sunset at last and the twilight are dead: and the darkness
      is breathless
   With fear of the wind's breath rising that seems and seems not
      to sleep:
But a sense of the sound of it alway, a spirit unsleeping and
      deathless,
   Ghost or God, evermore moves on the face of the deep.

A FORSAKEN GARDEN

In a coign of the cliff between lowland and highland,
   At the sea-down's edge between windward and lee,
Walled round with rocks as an inland island,
   The ghost of a garden fronts the sea.
A girdle of brushwood and thorn encloses
   The steep square slope of the blossomless bed
Where the weeds that grew green from the graves of its roses
         Now lie dead.

The fields fall southward, abrupt and broken,
   To the low last edge of the long lone land.
If a step should sound or a word be spoken,
   Would a ghost not rise at the strange guest's hand?
So long have the grey bare walks lain guestless,
   Through branches and briars if a man make way,
He shall find no life but the sea-wind's, restless
         Night and day.

The dense, hard passage is blind and stifled
   That crawls by a track none turn to climb
To the strait waste place that the years have rifled
   Of all but the thorns that are touched not of time.
The thorns he spares when the rose is taken;
   The rocks are left when he wastes the plain.
The wind that wanders, the weeds wind-shaken,
         These remain.

Not a flower to be pressed of the foot that falls not;
    As the heart of a dead man the seed-plots are dry;
From the thicket of thorns whence the nightingale calls not,
    Could she call, there were never a rose to reply.
Over the meadows that blossom and wither
    Rings but the note of a sea-bird's song;
Only the sun and the rain come hither
        All year long.

The sun burns sere and the rain dishevels
    One gaunt bleak blossom of scentless breath.
Only the wind here hovers and revels
    In a round where life seems barren as death.
Here there was laughing of old, there was weeping,
    Haply, of lovers none ever will know,
Whose eyes went seaward a hundred sleeping
        Years ago.

Heart handfast in heart as they stood, "Look thither,"
    Did he whisper? "Look forth from the flowers to the sea;
For the foam-flowers endure when the rose-blossoms wither,
    And men that love lightly may die—but we?"
And the same wind sang and the same waves whitened,
    And or ever the garden's last petals were shed,
In the lips that had whispered, the eyes that had lightened,
        Love was dead.

Or they loved their life through, and then went whither?
    And were one to the end—but what end who knows?
Love deep as the sea as a rose must wither,
    As the rose-red seaweed that mocks the rose.
Shall the dead take thought for the dead to love them?
    What love was ever as deep as a grave?
They are loveless now as the grass above them
        Or the wave.

All are at one now, roses and lovers,
    Not known of the cliffs and the fields and the sea.
Not a breath of the time that has been hovers
    In the air now soft with a summer to be.
Not a breath shall there sweeten the seasons hereafter
    Of the flowers or the lovers that laugh now or weep,

When as they that are free now of weeping and laughter
        We shall sleep.

Here death may deal not again forever;
    Here change may come not till all change end.
From the graves they have made they shall rise up never,
    Who have left nought living to ravage and rend.
Earth, stones, and thorns of the wild ground growing,
    While the sun and the rain live, these shall be;
Till a last wind's breath upon all these blowing
        Roll the sea.

Till the slow sea rise and the sheer cliff crumble,
    Till terrace and meadow the deep gulfs drink,
Till the strength of the waves of the high tides humble
    The fields that lessen, the rocks that shrink,
Here now in his triumph where all things falter,
    Stretched out on the spoils that his own hand spread,
As a god self-slain on his own strange altar,
        Death lies dead.

THOMAS HARDY
(1840–1928)

HAP

If but some vengeful god would call to me
From up the sky, and laugh: "Thou suffering thing,
Know that thy sorrow is my ecstasy,
That thy love's loss is my hate's profiting!"

Then would I bear it, clench myself, and die,
Steeled by the sense of ire unmerited;
Half-eased in that a Powerfuller than I
Had willed and meted me the tears I shed.

But not so. How arrives it joy lies slain,
And why unblooms the best hope ever sown?
—Crass Casualty obstructs the sun and rain,
And dicing Time for gladness casts a moan. . . .
These purblind Doomsters had as readily strown
Blisses about my pilgrimage as pain.

NEUTRAL TONES

We stood by a pond that winter day,
And the sun was white, as though chidden of God,
And a few leaves lay on the starving sod;
    —They had fallen from an ash, and were gray.

Your eyes on me were as eyes that rove
Over tedious riddles of years ago;
And some words played between us to and fro
    On which lost the more by our love.

The smile on your mouth was the deadest thing
Alive enough to have strength to die;
And a grin of bitterness swept thereby
      Like an ominous bird a-wing. . . .

Since then, keen lessons that love deceives,
And wrings with wrong, have shaped to me
Your face, and the God-curst sun, and a tree,
      And a pond edged with grayish leaves.

NATURE'S QUESTIONING

When I look forth at dawning, pool,
      Field, flock, and lonely tree,
      All seem to gaze at me
Like chastened children sitting silent in a school;

Their faces dulled, constrained, and worn,
      As though the master's ways
      Through the long teaching days
Had cowed them till their early zest was overborne.

Upon them stirs in lippings mere
      (As if once clear in call,
      But now scarce breathed at all)—
"We wonder, ever wonder, why we find us here!

"Has some Vast Imbecility,
      Mighty to build and blend,
      But impotent to tend,
Framed us in jest, and left us now to hazardry?

"Or come we of an Automaton
      Unconscious of our pains? . . .
      Or are we live remains
Of Godhead dying downwards, brain and eye now gone?

"Or is it that some high Plan betides,
　　　As yet not understood,
　　　Of Evil stormed by Good,
We the Forlorn Hope over which Achievement strides?"

Thus things around. No answerer I. . . .
　　　Meanwhile the winds, and rains,
　　　And Earth's old glooms and pains
Are still the same, and Life and Death are neighbours nigh.

THE SUBALTERNS

I

"Poor wanderer," said the leaden sky,
　　　"I fain would lighten thee,
But there are laws in force on high
　　　Which say it must not be."

II

—"I would not freeze thee, shorn one," cried
　　　The North, "knew I but how
To warm my breath, to slack my stride;
　　　But I am ruled as thou."

III

—"To-morrow I attack thee, wight,"
　　　Said Sickness. "Yet I swear
I bear thy little ark no spite,
　　　But am bid enter there."

IV

—"Come hither, Son," I heard Death say;
　　　"I did not will a grave
Should end thy pilgrimage to-day,
　　　But I, too, am a slave!"

We smiled upon each other then,
  And life to me had less
Of that fell look it wore ere when
  They owned their passiveness.

THE DARKLING THRUSH

I leant upon a coppice gate
  When Frost was spectre-gray,
And Winter's dregs made desolate
  The weakening eye of day.
The tangled bine-stems scored the sky
  Like strings of broken lyres,
And all mankind that haunted nigh
  Had sought their household fires.

The land's sharp features seemed to be
  The Century's corpse outleant,
His crypt the cloudy canopy,
  The wind his death-lament.
The ancient pulse of germ and birth
  Was shrunken hard and dry,
And every spirit upon earth
  Seemed fervourless as I.

At once a voice arose among
  The bleak twigs overhead
In a full-hearted evensong
  Of joy illimited;
An aged thrush, frail, gaunt, and small,
  In blast-beruffled plume,
Had chosen thus to fling his soul
  Upon the growing gloom.

So little cause for carolings
  Of such ecstatic sound
Was written on terrestrial things

Afar or nigh around,
That I could think there trembled through
    His happy good-night air
Some blessed hope, whereof he knew
    And I was unaware.

31 December 1900

THE RUINED MAID

"O 'Melia, my dear, this does everything crown!
Who could have supposed I should meet you in town?
And whence such fair garments, such prosperi-ty?"—
"O didn't you know I'd been ruined?" said she.

—"You left us in tatters, without shoes or socks,
Tired of digging potatoes, and spudding up docks;
And now you've gay bracelets and bright feathers three!"—
"Yes: that's how we dress when we're ruined," said she.

—"At home in the barton you said 'thee' and 'thou,'
And 'thik oon,' and 'theäs oon,' and 't'other'; but now
Your talking quite fits 'ee for high compa-ny!"—
"Some polish is gained with one's ruin," said she.

—"Your hands were like paws then, your face blue and bleak
But now I'm bewitched by your delicate cheek,
And your little gloves fit as on any la-dy!"—
"We never do work when we're ruined," said she.

—"You used to call home-life a hag-ridden dream,
And you'd sigh, and you'd sock; but at present you seem
To know not of megrims or melancho-ly!"—
"True. One's pretty lively when ruined," said she.

—"I wish I had feathers, a fine sweeping gown,
And a delicate face, and could strut about town!"—
"My dear—a raw country girl, such as you be,
Cannot quite expect that. You ain't ruined," said she.

TESS'S LAMENT

I

I would that folk forgot me quite,
           Forgot me quite!
I would that I could shrink from sight,
    And no more see the sun.
Would it were time to say farewell,
To claim my nook, to need my knell,
Time for them all to stand and tell
    Of my day's work as done.

II

Ah! dairy where I lived so long,
           I lived so long;
Where I would rise up staunch and strong,
    And lie down hopefully.
'Twas there within the chimney-seat
He watched me to the clock's slow beat—
Loved me, and learnt to call me Sweet,
    And whispered words to me.

III

And now he's gone; and now he's gone; . . .
           And now he's gone!
The flowers we potted perhaps are thrown
    To rot upon the farm.
And where we had our supper-fire
May now grow nettle, dock, and briar,
And all the place be mould and mire
    So cozy once and warm.

IV

And it was I who did it all,
           Who did it all;
'Twas I who made the blow to fall

On him who thought no guile.
Well, it is finished—past, and he
Has left me to my misery,
And I must take my Cross on me
For wronging him awhile.

V

How gay we looked that day we wed,
That day we wed!
"May joy be with ye!" they all said
A-standing by the durn.
I wonder what they say o'us now,
And if they know my lot; and how
She feels who milks my favourite cow,
And takes my place at churn!

VI

It wears me out to think of it,
To think of it;
I cannot bear my fate as writ,
I'd have my life unbe;
Would turn my memory to a blot,
Make every relic of me rot,
My doings be as they were not,
And gone all trace of me!

THE CONVERGENCE OF THE TWAIN

(Lines on the loss of the Titanic)

I

In a solitude of the sea
Deep from human vanity,
And the Pride of Life that planned her, stilly couches she.

II

Steel chambers, late the pyres
Of her salamandrine fires,
Cold currents thrid, and turn to rhythmic tidal lyres.

Over the mirrors meant
To glass the opulent
The sea-worm crawls—grotesque, slimed, dumb, indifferent.

IV

Jewels in joy designed
To ravish the sensuous mind
Lie lightless, all their sparkles bleared and black and blind.

V

Dim moon-eyed fishes near
Gaze at the gilded gear
And query: "What does this vaingloriousness down here?" . . .

VI

Well: while was fashioning
This creature of cleaving wing,
The Immanent Will that stirs and urges everything

VII

Prepared a sinister mate
For her—so gaily great—
A Shape of Ice, for the time far and dissociate.

VIII

And as the smart ship grew
In stature, grace, and hue,
In shadowy silent distance grew the Iceberg too.

IX

Alien they seemed to be:
No mortal eye could see
The intimate welding of their later history,

Or sign that they were bent
By paths coincident
On being anon twin halves of one august event,

Till the Spinner of the Years
Said "Now!" And each one hears,
And consummation comes, and jars two hemispheres.

AH, ARE YOU DIGGING ON MY GRAVE?

"Ah, are you digging on my grave,
  My loved one?—planting rue?"
—"No: yesterday he went to wed
One of the brightest wealth has bred.
'It cannot hurt her now,' he said,
  'That I should not be true.' "

"Then who is digging on my grave?
  My nearest dearest kin?"
—"Ah, no: they sit and think, 'What use!
What good will planting flowers produce?
No tendance of her mound can loose
  Her spirit from Death's gin.' "

"But some one digs upon my grave?
  My enemy? prodding sly?"
—"Nay: when she heard you had passed the Gate
That shuts on all flesh soon or late,
She thought you no more worth her hate,
  And cares not where you lie."

"Then, who is digging on my grave?
  Say—since I have not guessed!"
—"O it is I, my mistress dear,
Your little dog, who still lives near,

And much I hope my movements here
　　Have not disturbed your rest?"

"Ah, yes! *You* dig upon my grave. . . .
　　Why flashed it not on me
That one true heart was left behind!
What feeling do we ever find
To equal among human kind
　　A dog's fidelity!"

"Mistress, I dug upon your grave
　　To bury a bone, in case
I should be hungry near this spot
When passing on my daily trot.
I am sorry, but I quite forgot
　　It was your resting-place."

TRANSFORMATIONS

Portion of this yew
Is a man my grandsire knew,
Bosomed here at its foot:
This branch may be his wife,
A ruddy human life
Now turned to a green shoot.

These grasses must be made
Of her who often prayed,
Last century, for repose;
And the fair girl long ago
Whom I often tried to know
May be entering this rose.

So, they are not underground,
But as nerves and veins abound
In the growths of upper air,
And they feel the sun and rain,
And the energy again
That made them what they were!

DURING WIND AND RAIN

They sing their dearest songs—
He, she, all of them—yea,
Treble and tenor and bass,
    And one to play;
With the candles mooning each face. . . .
    Ah, no; the years O!
How the sick leaves reel down in throngs!

They clear the creeping moss—
Elders and juniors—aye,
Making the pathways neat
    And the garden gay;
And they build a shady seat. . . .
    Ah, no; the years, the years;
See, the white storm-birds wing across!

They are blithely breakfasting all—
Men and maidens—yea,
Under the summer tree,
    With a glimpse of the bay,
While pet fowl come to the knee. . . .
    Ah, no; the years O!
And the rotten rose is ript from the wall.

They change to a high new house,
He, she, all of them—aye,
Clocks and carpets and chairs
    On the lawn all day,
And brightest things that are theirs. . . .
    Ah, no; the years, the years;
Down their carved names the rain-drop ploughs.

HE RESOLVES TO SAY NO MORE

O my soul, keep the rest unknown!
It is too like a sound of moan
    When the charnel-eyed
    Pale Horse has nighed:
Yea, none shall gather what I hide!

Why load men's minds with more to bear
That bear already ails to spare?
    From now alway
    Till my last day
What I discern I will not say.

Let Time roll backward if it will;
(Magians who drive the midnight quill
    With brain aglow
    Can see it so,)
What I have learnt no man shall know.

And if my vision range beyond
The blinkered sight of souls in bond,
    —By truth made free—
    I'll let all be,
And show to no man what I see.

AUSTIN DOBSON
(1840–1921)

A CITY FLOWER

To and fro in the city I go,
Tired of the ceaseless ebb and flow,
  Sick of the crowded mart;
Tired of the din and rattle of wheels,
Sick of the dust as one who feels
  The dust is over his heart.

And again and again, as the sunlight wanes,
I think of the lights in the leafy lanes,
  With the bits of blue between;
And when about Rimmel's the perfumes play,
I smell no vapours of "Ess Bouquet,"
  But violets hid in the green;
And I love—how I love—the plants that fill
The pots on my dust-dry window-sill—
  A sensitive sickly crop—
But a flower that charms me more, I think,
Than cowslip, or crocus, or rose, or pink,
  Blooms—in a milliner's shop.

Hazel eyes that wickedly peep,
Flash, abash, and suddenly sleep
  Under the lids drawn in;
Ripple of hair that rioteth out,
Mouth with a half-born smile and a pout,
  And a baby breadth of chin;
Hands that light as the lighting bird,
On the bloom-bent bough, and the bough is stirred
  With a delicate ecstasy;
Fingers tipped with a roseate flush,
Flicking and flirting a feathery brush
  Over the papery bonnetry—

Till the gauzy rose begins to glow,
And the gauzy hyacinths break and blow,
  And the dusty grape grows red;
And the flaunting grasses seem to say,
"Do we look like ornaments—tell us, we pray—
  Fit for a lady's head?"
And the butterfly wakes to a wiry life,
Like an elderly gentleman taking a wife,
  Knowing he must be gay,
And all the bonnets nid-noddle about,
Like chattering chaperons set at a rout,
  Quarrelling over their play.

How can I otherwise choose than look
At the beautiful face like a beautiful book,
  And learn a tiny part?
So I feel somehow that every day
Some flake of the dust is brushed away
  That had settled over my heart.

GERARD MANLEY HOPKINS
(1844–89)

GOD'S GRANDEUR

The world is charged with the grandeur of God.
  It will flame out, like shining from shook foil;
  It gathers to a greatness, like the ooze of oil
Crushed. Why do men then now not reck his rod?
Generations have trod, have trod, have trod;
  And all is seared with trade; bleared, smeared with toil;
  And wears man's smudge and shares man's smell: the soil
Is bare now, nor can foot feel, being shod.

And for all this, nature is never spent;
  There lives the dearest freshness deep down things;
And though the last lights off the black West went
  Oh, morning, at the brown brink eastward, springs—
Because the Holy Ghost over the bent
  World broods with warm breast and with ah! bright wings.

THE WINDHOVER

TO CHRIST OUR LORD

I caught this morning morning's minion, king-
  dom of daylight's dauphin, dapple-dawn-drawn Falcon, in his riding
  Of the rolling level underneath him steady air, and striding
High there, how he rung upon the rein of a wimpling wing
In his ecstasy! then off, off forth on swing,
  As a skate's heel sweeps smooth on a bow-bend: the hurl and gliding
  Rebuffed the big wind. My heart in hiding
Stirred for a bird,—the achieve of, the mastery of the thing!

Brute beauty and valour and act, oh, air, pride, plume, here
  Buckle! AND the fire that breaks from thee then, a billion
Times told lovelier, more dangerous, O my chevalier!

No wonder of it: shéer plód makes plough down sillion
Shine, and blue-bleak embers, ah my dear,
  Fall, gall themselves, and gash gold-vermilion.

PIED BEAUTY

Glory be to God for dappled things—
  For skies of couple-colour as a brinded cow;
    For rose-moles all in stipple upon trout that swim;
Fresh-firecoal chestnut-falls; finches' wings;
  Landscape plotted and pieced—fold, fallow, and plough;
    And áll trádes, their gear and tackle and trim.
All things counter, original, spare, strange;
  Whatever is fickle, freckled (who knows how?)
    With swift, slow; sweet, sour; adazzle, dim;
He fathers-forth whose beauty is past change:
                    Praise him.

HENRY PURCELL

The poet wishes well to the divine genius of Purcell and praises him that, whereas other musicians have given utterance to the moods of man's mind, he has, beyond that, uttered in notes the very make and species of man as created both in him and in all men generally.

Have fair fallen, O fair, fair have fallen, so dear
To me, so arch-especial a spirit as heaves in Henry Purcell,
An age is now since passed, since parted; with the reversal
Of the outward sentence low lays him, listed to a heresy, here.

Not mood in him nor meaning, proud fire or sacred fear,
Or love or pity or all that sweet notes not his might nursle:

It is the forgèd feature finds me; it is the rehearsal
Of own, of abrúpt sélf there so thrusts on, so throngs the ear.

Let him oh! with his air of angels then lift me, lay me! only I'll
Have an eye to the sakes of him, quaint moonmarks, to his pelted
    plumage under
Wings: so some great stormfowl, whenever he has walked his while

The thunder-purple seabeach plumèd purple-of-thunder,
If a wuthering of his palmy snow-pinions scatter a colossal smile
Off him, but meaning motion fans fresh our wits with wonder.

SPRING AND FALL:

TO A YOUNG CHILD

Márgarét, áre you gríeving
Over Goldengrove unleaving?
Leáves, líke the things of man, you
With your fresh thoughts care for, can you?
Áh! ás the heart grows older
It will come to such sights colder
By and by, nor spare a sigh
Though worlds of wanwood leafmeal lie;
And yet you *will* weep and know why.
Now no matter, child, the name:
Sórrow's spríngs áre the same.
Nor mouth had, no nor mind, expressed
What heart heard of, ghost guessed:
It ís the blight man was born for,
It is Margaret you mourn for.

CARRION COMFORT

Not, I'll not, carrion comfort, Despair, not feast on thee;
Not untwist—slack they may be—these last strands of man

In me ór, most weary, cry *I can no more*. I can;
Can something, hope, wish day come, not choose not to be.

But ah, but O thou terrible, why wouldst thou rude on me
Thy wring-world right foot rock? lay a lionlimb against me? scan
With darksome devouring eyes my bruisèd bones? and fan,
O in turns of tempest, me heaped there; me frantic to avoid thee and
    flee?
Why? That my chaff might fly; my grain lie, sheer and clear.
Nay in all that toil, that coil, since (seems) I kissed the rod,
Hand rather, my heart lo! lapped strength, stole joy, would laugh, chéer.
Cheer whom though? The hero whose heaven-handling flung me, fóot
    tród
Me? or me that fought him? O which one? is it each one? That night,
    that year
Of now done darkness I wretch lay wrestling with (my God!) my God.

THAT NATURE IS A HERACLITEAN FIRE AND OF THE COMFORT OF THE RESURRECTION

Cloud-puffball, torn tufts, tossed pillows [|] flaunt forth, then chevy on an air-
built thoroughfare: heaven-roysterers, in gay-gangs [|] they throng; they glitter
    in marches.
Down roughcast, down dazzling whitewash, [|] wherever an elm arches,
Shivelights and shadowtackle in long [|] lashes lace, lance, and pair.
Delightfully the bright wind boisterous [|] ropes, wrestles, beats earth bare
Of yestertempest's creases; [|] in pool and rutpeel parches
Squandering ooze to squeezed [|] dough, crust, dust; stanches, starches
Squadroned masks and manmarks [|] treadmire toil there
Footfretted in it. Million-fuelèd, [|] nature's bonfire burns on.
But quench her bonniest, dearest [|] to her, her clearest-selvèd spark
Man, how fast his firedint, [|] his mark on mind, is gone!
Both are in an unfathomable, all is in an enormous dark
Drowned. O pity and indig [|] nation! Manshape, that shone
Sheer off, disseveral, a star, [|] death blots black out; nor mark
          Is any of him at all so stark
But vastness blurs and time [|] beats level. Enough! the Resurrection,
A heart's-clarion! Away grief's gasping, [|] joyless days, dejection.
          Across my foundering deck shone

642

A beacon, an eternal beam. |Flesh fade, and mortal trash
Fall to the residuary worm; |world's wildfire, leave but ash:
      In a flash, at a trumpet crash,
I am all at once what Christ is, |since he was what I am, and
This Jack, joke, poor potsherd, |patch, matchwood, immortal diamond,
      Is immortal diamond.

THE WRECK OF THE DEUTSCHLAND

To the
happy memory of five Franciscan nuns
exiles by the Falck Laws
drowned between midnight and morning of
Dec. 7th, 1875

PART THE FIRST

      Thou mastering me
    God! giver of breath and bread;
  World's strand, sway of the sea;
    Lord of living and dead;
Thou hast bound bones and veins in me, fastened me flesh,
And after it almost unmade, what with dread,
    Thy doing: and dost thou touch me afresh?
Over again I feel thy finger and find thee.

      I did say yes
    O at lightning and lashed rod;
Thou heardst me truer than tongue confess
    Thy terror, O Christ, O God;
Thou knowest the walls, altar and hour and night:
The swoon of a heart that the sweep and the hurl of thee trod
    Hard down with a horror of height:
And the midriff astrain with leaning of, laced with fire of stress.

      The frown of his face
    Before me, the hurtle of hell
Behind, where, where was a, where was a place?
    I whirled out wings that spell
And fled with a fling of the heart to the heart of the Host.
My heart, but you were dovewinged, I can tell,

Carrier-witted, I am bold to boast,
To flash from the flame to the flame then, tower from the grace to the
    grace.

                    I am soft sift
                In an hourglass—at the wall
            Fast, but mined with a motion, a drift,
                And it crowds and it combs to the fall;
        I steady as a water in a well, to a poise, to a pane,
        But roped with, always, all the way down from the tall
            Fells or flanks of the voel, a vein
Of the gospel proffer, a pressure, a principle, Christ's gift.

                    I kiss my hand
                To the stars, lovely-asunder
            Starlight, wafting him out of it; and
                Glow, glory in thunder;
        Kiss my hand to the dappled-with-damson west:
        Since, tho' he is under the world's splendour and wonder,
            His mystery must be instressed, stressed;
For I greet him the days I meet him, and bless when I understand.

                    Not out of his bliss
                Springs the stress felt
            Nor first from heaven (and few know this)
                Swings the stroke dealt—
        Stroke and a stress that stars and storms deliver,
        That guilt is hushed by, hearts are flushed by and melt—
            But it rides time like riding a river
(And here the faithful waver, the faithless fable and miss).

                    It dates from day
                Of his going in Galilee;
            Warm-laid grave of a womb-life grey;
                Manger, maiden's knee;
        The dense and the driven Passion, and frightful sweat:
        Thence the discharge of it, there its swelling to be,
            Though felt before, though in high flood yet—
What none would have known of it, only the heart, being hard at bay,

                    Is out with it! Oh,
                We lash with the best or worst

Word last! How a lush-kept plush-capped sloe
　　Will, mouthed to flesh-burst,
Gush!—flush the man, the being with it, sour or sweet,
　　Brim, in a flash, full!—Hither then, last or first,
　　　To hero of Calvary, Christ,'s feet—
Never ask if meaning it, wanting it, warned of it—men go.

　　　Be adored among men,
　　God, three-numberèd form;
　　Wring thy rebel, dogged in den,
　　　Man's malice, with wrecking and storm.
Beyond saying sweet, past telling of tongue,
　　Thou art lightning and love, I found it, a winter and warm;
　　Father and fondler of heart thou hast wrung:
Hast thy dark descending and most art merciful then.

　　　With an anvil-ding
　　And with fire in him forge thy will
　　Or rather, rather then, stealing as Spring
　　　Through him, melt him but master him still:
Whether at once, as once at a crash Paul,
　　Or as Austin, a lingering-out swéet skíll,
　　Make mercy in all of us, out of us all
Mastery, but be adored, but be adored King.

PART THE SECOND

　　　'Some find me a sword; some
　　The flange and the rail; flame,
　　Fang, or flood' goes Death on drum,
　　　And storms bugle his fame.
But wé dream we are rooted in earth—Dust!
　　Flesh falls within sight of us, we, though our flower the same,
　　Wave with the meadow, forget that there must
The sour scythe cringe, and the blear share come.

　　　On Saturday sailed from Bremen,
　　American-outward-bound,
　　Take settler and seamen, tell men with women,
　　　Two hundred souls in the round—
O Father, not under thy feathers nor ever as guessing
The goal was a shoal, of a fourth the doom to be drowned;

645

Yet did the dark side of the bay of thy blessing
Not vault them, the million of rounds of thy mercy not reeve even them
 in?

Into the snows she sweeps,
Hurling the haven behind,
The Deutschland, on Sunday; and so the sky keeps,
For the infinite air is unkind,
And the sea flint-flake, black-backed in the regular blow,
Sitting Eastnortheast, in cursed quarter, the wind;
Wiry and white-fiery and whirlwind-swivellèd snow
Spins to the widow-making unchilding unfathering deeps.

She drove in the dark to leeward,
She struck—not a reef or a rock
But the combs of a smother of sand: night drew her
Dead to the Kentish Knock;
And she beat the bank down with her bows and the ride of her
 keel;
The breakers rolled on her beam with ruinous shock;
And canvas and compass, the whorl and the wheel
Idle for ever to waft her or wind her with, these she endured.

Hope had grown grey hairs,
Hope had mourning on,
Trenched with tears, carved with cares,
Hope was twelve hours gone;
And frightful a nightfall folded rueful a day
Nor rescue, only rocket and lightship, shone,
And lives at last were washing away:
To the shrouds they took,—they shook in the hurling and horrible airs.

One stirred from the rigging to save
The wild woman-kind below,
With a rope's end round the man, handy and brave—
He was pitched to his death at a blow,
For all his dreadnought breast and braids of thew:
They could tell him for hours, dandled the to and fro
Through the cobbled foam-fleece. What could he do
With the burl of the fountains of air, buck and the flood of the wave?

646

They fought with God's cold—
And they could not and fell to the deck
(Crushed them) or water (and drowned them) or rolled
With the sea-romp over the wreck.
Night roared, with the heart-break hearing a heart-broke rabble,
The woman's wailing, the crying of child without check—
Till a lioness arose breasting the babble,
A prophetess towered in the tumult, a virginal tongue told.

Ah, touched in your bower of bone,
Are you! turned for an exquisite smart,
Have you! make words break from me here all alone,
Do you!—mother of being in me, heart.
O unteachably after evil, but uttering truth,
Why, tears! is it? tears; such a melting, a madrigal start!
Never-eldering revel and river of youth,
What can it be, this glee? the good you have there of your own?

Sister, a sister calling
A master, her master and mine!—
And the inboard seas run swirling and hawling;
The rash smart sloggering brine
Blinds her; but she that weather sees one thing, one;
Has one fetch in her: she rears herself to divine
Ears, and the call of the tall nun
To the men in the tops and the tackle rode over the storm's brawling.

She was first of a five and came
Of a coifèd sisterhood.
(O Deutschland, double a desperate name!
O world wide of its good!
But Gertrude, lily, and Luther, are two of a town,
Christ's lily and beast of the waste wood:
From life's dawn it is drawn down,
Abel is Cain's brother and breasts they have sucked the same.)

Loathed for a love men knew in them,
Banned by the land of their birth,
Rhine refused them, Thames would ruin them;
Surf, snow, river and earth
Gnashed: but thou art above, thou Orion of light;
Thy unchancelling poising palms were weighing the worth,

> Thou martyr-master: in thy sight
> Storm flakes were scroll-leaved flowers, lily showers—sweet heaven was
>   astrew in them.

> Five! the finding and sake
> And cipher of suffering Christ.
> Mark, the mark is of man's make
> And the word of it Sacrificed.
> But he scores it in scarlet himself on his own bespoken,
> Before-time-taken, dearest prizèd and priced—
> Stigma, signal, cinquefoil token
> For lettering of the lamb's fleece, ruddying of the rose-flake.

> Joy fall to thee, father Francis,
> Drawn to the Life that died;
> With the gnarls of the nails in thee, niche of the lance, his
> Lovescape crucified
> And seal of his seraph-arrival! and these thy daughters
> And five-livèd and leavèd favour and pride,
> Are sisterly sealed in wild waters,
> To bathe in his fall-gold mercies, to breathe in his all-fire glances.

> Away in the loveable west,
> On a pastoral forehead of Wales,
> I was under a roof here, I was at rest,
> And they the prey of the gales;
> She to the black-about air, to the breaker, the thickly
> Falling flakes, to the throng that catches and quails
> Was calling 'O Christ, Christ, come quickly':
> The cross to her she calls Christ to her, christens her wild-worst Best.

> The majesty! what did she mean?
> Breathe, arch and original Breath.
> Is it love in her of the being as her lover had been?
> Breathe, body of lovely Death.
> They were else-minded then, altogether, the men
> Woke thee with a *We are perishing* in the weather of Gennesareth.
> Or is it that she cried for the crown then,
> The keener to come at the comfort for feeling the combating keen?

> For how to the heart's cheering
> The down-dugged ground-hugged grey

Hovers off, the jay-blue heavens appearing
          Of pied and peeled May!
Blue-beating and hoary-glow height; or night, still higher,
     With belled fire and the moth-soft Milky Way,
          What by your measure is the heaven of desire,
The treasure never eyesight got, nor was ever guessed what for the
     hearing?

          No, but it was not these.
          The jading and jar of the cart,
     Time's tasking, it is fathers that asking for ease
          Of the sodden-with-its-sorrowing heart,
Not danger, electrical horror; then further it finds
     The appealing of the Passion is tenderer in prayer apart:
          Other, I gather, in measure her mind's
Burden, in wind's burly and beat of endragonèd seas.

          But how shall I . . . make me room there:
          Reach me a . . . Fancy, come faster—
     Strike you the sight of it? look at it loom there,
          Thing that she . . . There then! the Master,
Ipse, the only one, Christ, King, Head:
     He was to cure the extremity where he had cast her;
          Do, deal, lord it with living and dead;
Let him ride, her pride, in his triumph, despatch and have done with his
     doom there.

          Ah! there was a heart right!
          There was single eye!
     Read the unshapeable shock night
          And knew the who and the why;
Wording it how but by him that present and past,
Heaven and earth are word of, worded by?—
     The Simon Peter of a soul! to the blast
Tarpeïan-fast, but a blown beacon of light.

          Jesu, heart's light,
          Jesu, maid's son,
     What was the feast followed the night
          Thou hadst glory of this nun?—
Feast of the one woman without stain.
For so conceivèd, so to conceive thee is done;

But here was heart-throe, birth of a brain,
Word, that heard and kept thee and uttered thee outright.

　　　Well, she has thee for the pain, for the
　　　　Patience; but pity of the rest of them!
　　　Heart, go and bleed at a bitterer vein for the
　　　　Comfortless unconfessed of them—
No not uncomforted: lovely-felicitous Providence
Finger of a tender of, O of a feathery delicacy, the breast of the
　　Maiden could obey so, be a bell to, ring of it, and
Startle the poor sheep back! is the shipwrack then a harvest, does tempest
　　carry the grain for thee?

　　　I admire thee, master of the tides,
　　　　Of the Yore-flood, of the year's fall;
　　　The recurb and the recovery of the gulf's sides,
　　　　The girth of it and the wharf of it and the wall;
　　Stanching, quenching ocean of a motionable mind;
　　Ground of being, and granite of it: past all
　　　Grasp God, throned behind
Death with a sovereignty that heeds but hides, bodes but abides;

　　　With a mercy that outrides
　　　　The all of water, an ark
　　　For the listener; for the lingerer with a love glides
　　　　Lower than death and the dark;
　　A vein for the visiting of the past-prayer, pent in prison,
　　The-last-breath penitent spirits—the uttermost mark
　　　Our passion-plungèd giant risen,
The Christ of the Father compassionate, fetched in the storm of his
　　strides.

　　　Now burn, new born to the world,
　　　　Double-naturèd name,
　　　The heaven-flung, heart-fleshed, maiden-furled
　　　　Miracle-in-Mary-of-flame,
　　Mid-numberèd he in three of the thunder-throne!
　　Not a dooms-day dazzle in his coming nor dark as he came;
　　　Kind, but royally reclaiming his own;
A released shower, let flash to the shire, not a lightning of fire hard-hurled.

650

Dame, at our door
Drowned, and among our shoals,
Remember us in the roads, the heaven-haven of the reward:
Our King back, Oh, upon English souls!
Let him easter in us, be a dayspring to the dimness of us, be
a crimson-cresseted east,
More brightening her, rare-dear Britain, as his reign rolls,
Pride, rose, prince, hero of us, high-priest,
Our hearts' charity's hearth's fire, our thoughts' chivalry's throng's Lord.

WILLIAM ERNEST HENLEY
(1849–1903)

INVICTUS

Out of the night that covers me,
　　Black as the pit from pole to pole,
I thank whatever gods may be
　　For my unconquerable soul.

In the fell clutch of circumstance
　　I have not winced nor cried aloud.
Under the bludgeonings of chance
　　My head is bloody, but unbowed.

Beyond this place of wrath and tears
　　Looms but the horror of the shade,
And yet the menace of the years
　　Finds, and shall find, me unafraid.

It matters not how strait the gate,
　　How charged with punishments the scroll,
I am the master of my fate;
　　I am the captain of my soul.

ROBERT LOUIS STEVENSON
(1850–94)

MY SHADOW

I have a little shadow that goes in and out with me,
And what can be the use of him is more than I can see.
He is very, very like me from the heels up to the head;
And I see him jump before me, when I jump into my bed.

The funniest thing about him is the way he likes to grow—
Not at all like proper children, which is always very slow;
For he sometimes shoots up taller like an india-rubber ball,
And he sometimes gets so little that there's none of him at all.

He hasn't got a notion of how children ought to play,
And can only make a fool of me in every sort of way.
He stays so close beside me, he's a coward you can see;
I'd think shame to stick to nursie as that shadow sticks to me!

One morning, very early, before the sun was up,
I rose and found the shining dew on every buttercup;
But my lazy little shadow, like an arrant sleepy-head,
Had stayed at home behind me and was fast asleep in bed.

SYSTEM

Every night my prayers I say,
And get my dinner every day;
And every day that I've been good,
I get an orange after food.

The child that is not clean and neat,
With lots of toys and things to eat,

He is a naughty child, I'm sure—
Or else his dear papa is poor.

THE SWING

How do you like to go up in a swing,
    Up in the air so blue?
Oh, I do think it the pleasantest thing
    Ever a child can do!

Up in the air and over the wall,
    Till I can see so wide,
Rivers and trees and cattle and all
    Over the countryside—

Till I look down on the garden green,
    Down on the roof so brown—
Up in the air I go flying again,
    Up in the air and down!

OSCAR WILDE
(1856–1900)

HÉLAS!

To drift with every passion till my soul
Is a stringed lute on which all winds can play,
Is it for this that I have given away
Mine ancient wisdom, and austere control?
Methinks my life is a twice-written scroll
Scrawled over on some boyish holiday
With idle songs for pipe and virelay,
Which do but mar the secret of the whole.
Surely there was a time I might have trod
The sunlit heights, and from life's dissonance
Struck one clear chord to reach the ears of God:
Is that time dead? Lo! With a little rod
I did but touch the honey of romance—
And must I lose a soul's inheritance?

from THE BALLAD OF READING GAOL

Yet each man kills the thing he loves,
   By each let this be heard,
Some do it with a bitter look,
   Some with a flattering word.
The coward does it with a kiss,
   The brave man with a sword!

Some kill their love when they are young,
   And some when they are old;
Some strangle with the hands of lust,
   Some with the hands of gold:

655

The kindest use a knife, because
  The dead so soon grow cold.

Some love too little, some too long,
  Some sell, and others buy;
Some do the deed with many tears,
  And some without a sigh:
For each man kills the thing he loves,
  Yet each man does not die.

He does not die a death of shame
  On a day of dark disgrace,
Nor have a noose about his neck,
  Nor a cloth upon his face,
Nor drop feet foremost through the floor
  Into an empty space.

He does not sit with silent men
  Who watch him night and day;
Who watch him when he tries to weep,
  And when he tries to pray;
Who watch him lest himself should rob
  The prison of its prey.

He does not wake at dawn to see
  Dread figures throng his room,
The shivering chaplain robed in white,
  The sheriff stern with gloom,
And the governor all in shiny black,
  With the yellow face of doom.

He does not rise in piteous haste
  To put on convict-clothes,
While some coarse-mouthed doctor gloats, and notes
  Each new and nerve-twitched pose,
Fingering a watch whose little ticks
  Are like horrible hammer-blows.

He does not feel that sickening thirst
  That sands one's throat, before
The hangman with his gardener's gloves
  Comes through the padded door,

And binds one with three leathern thongs,
  That the throat may thirst no more.

He does not bend his head to hear
  The Burial Office read,
Nor, while the anguish of his soul
  Tells him he is not dead,
Cross his own coffin, as he moves
  Into the hideous shed.

He does not stare upon the air
  Through a little roof of glass:
He does not pray with lips of clay
  For his agony to pass;
Nor feel upon his shuddering cheek
  The kiss of Caiaphas.

A. E. HOUSMAN
(1859–1936)

Loveliest of trees, the cherry now
Is hung with bloom along the bough,
And stands about the woodland ride
Wearing white for Eastertide.

Now, of my threescore years and ten,
Twenty will not come again,
And take from seventy springs a score,
It only leaves me fifty more.

And since to look at things in bloom
Fifty springs are little room,
About the woodlands I will go
To see the cherry hung with snow.

TO AN ATHLETE DYING YOUNG

The time you won your town the race
We chaired you through the market-place;
Man and boy stood cheering by,
And home we brought you shoulder-high.

To-day, the road all runners come,
Shoulder-high we bring you home,
And set you at your threshold down,
Townsman of a stiller town.

Smart lad, to slip betimes away
From fields where glory does not stay
And early though the laurel grows
It withers quicker than the rose.

Eyes the shady night has shut
Cannot see the record cut,
And silence sounds no worse than cheers
After earth has stopped the ears:

Now you will not swell the rout
Of lads that wore their honours out,
Runners whom renown outran
And the name died before the man.

So set, before its echoes fade,
The fleet foot on the sill of shade,
And hold to the low lintel up
The still-defended challenge-cup.

And round that early-laurelled head
Will flock to gaze the strengthless dead,
And find unwithered on its curls
The garland briefer than a girl's.

PARTA QUIES

Good-night; ensured release,
Imperishable peace,
    Have these for yours,
While sea abides, and land,
And earth's foundations stand,
    And heaven endures.

When earth's foundations flee,
Nor sky nor land nor sea
    At all is found,
Content you, let them burn:
It is not your concern;
    Sleep on, sleep sound.

ERNEST DOWSON
(1867–1900)

NON SUM QUALIS ERAM BONAE
SUB REGNO CYNARAE

Last night, ah, yesternight, betwixt her lips and mine
There fell thy shadow, Cynara! Thy breath was shed
Upon my soul between the kisses and the wine;
And I was desolate and sick of an old passion,
    Yea, I was desolate and bowed my head:
I have been faithful to thee, Cynara! in my fashion.

All night upon mine heart I felt her warm heart beat,
Night-long within mine arms in love and sleep she lay;
Surely the kisses of her bought red mouth were sweet;
But I was desolate and sick of an old passion,
    When I awoke and found the dawn was gray:
I have been faithful to thee, Cynara! in my fashion.

I have forgot much, Cynara! Gone with the wind,
Flung roses, roses riotously with the throng,
Dancing, to put thy pale, lost lilies out of mind;
But I was desolate and sick of an old passion,
    Yea, all the time, because the dance was long:
I have been faithful to thee, Cynara! in my fashion.

I cried for madder music and for stronger wine,
But when the feast is finished and the lamps expire,
Then falls thy shadow, Cynara! The night is thine;
And I am desolate and sick of an old passion,
    Yea hungry for the lips of my desire:
I have been faithful to thee, Cynara! in my fashion.

RUDYARD KIPLING
(1865–1936)

DANNY DEEVER

"What are the bugles blowin' for?" said Files-on-Parade.
"To turn you out, to turn you out," the Colour-Sergeant said.
"What makes you look so white, so white?" said Files-on-Parade.
"I'm dreadin' what I've got to watch," the Colour-Sergeant said.
   For they're hangin' Danny Deever, you can hear the Dead March play,
   The regiment's in 'ollow square—they're hangin' him today;
   They've taken of his buttons off an' cut his stripes away,
   An' they're hangin' Danny Deever in the mornin'.

"What makes the rear rank breathe so 'ard?" said Files-on-Parade.
"It's bitter cold, it's bitter cold," the Colour-Sergeant said.
"What makes that front-rank man fall down?" said Files-on-Parade.
"A touch o' sun, a touch o' sun," the Colour-Sergeant said.
   They are hangin' Danny Deever, they are marchin' of 'im round,
   They'ave 'alted Danny Deever by 'is coffin on the ground;
   An' 'e'll swing in 'arf a minute for a sneakin' shootin' hound—
   O they're hangin' Danny Deever in the mornin'!

" 'Is cot was right-'and cot to mine," said Files-on-Parade.
" 'E's sleepin' out an' far tonight," the Colour-Sergeant said.
"I've drunk 'is beer a score o' times," said Files-on-Parade.
" 'E's drinkin bitter beer alone," the Colour-Sergeant said.
   They are hangin' Danny Deever, you must mark 'im to 'is place,
   For 'e shot a comrade sleepin'—you must look 'im in the face;
   Nine 'undred of 'is county an' the Regiment's disgrace,
   While they're hangin' Danny Deever in the mornin'.

"What's that so black agin the sun?" said Files-on-Parade.
"It's Danny fightin' 'ard for life," the Colour-Sergeant said.
"What's that that whimpers over'ead?" said Files-on-Parade.
"It's Danny's soul that's passin' now," the Colour-Sergeant said.

For they're done with Danny Deever, you can 'ear the quickstep play,
The regiment's in column, an' they're marchin' us away;
Ho! the young recruits are shakin', an' they'll want their beer today,
After hangin' Danny Deever in the mornin'.

WILLIAM BUTLER YEATS
(1865–1939)

TO THE ROSE UPON THE ROOD OF TIME

Red Rose, proud Rose, sad Rose of all my days!
Come near me, while I sing the ancient ways:
Cuchulain battling with the bitter tide;
The Druid, grey, wood-nurtured, quiet-eyed,
Who cast round Fergus dreams, and ruin untold;
And thine own sadness, whereof stars, grown old
In dancing silver-sandalled on the sea,
Sing in their high and lonely melody.
Come near, that no more blinded by man's fate,
I find under the boughs of love and hate,
In all poor foolish things that live a day,
Eternal beauty wandering on her way.

Come near, come near, come near—Ah, leave me still
A little space for the rose-breath to fill!
Lest I no more hear common things that crave;
The weak worm hiding down in its small cave,
The field-mouse running by me in the grass,
And heavy mortal hopes that toil and pass;
But seek alone to hear the strange things said
By God to the bright hearts of those long dead,
And learn to chaunt a tongue men do not know.
Come near; I would, before my time to go,
Sing of old Eire and the ancient ways:
Red Rose, proud Rose, sad Rose of all my days.

THE LAKE ISLE OF INNISFREE

I will arise and go now, and go to Innisfree,
And a small cabin build there, of clay and wattles made:
Nine bean-rows will I have there, a hive for the honeybee,
And live alone in the bee-loud glade.

And I shall have some peace there, for peace comes dropping slow,
Dropping from the veils of the morning to where the cricket sings;
There midnight's all a glimmer, and noon a purple glow,
And evening full of the linnet's wings.

I will arise and go now, for always night and day
I hear lake water lapping with low sounds by the shore;
While I stand on the roadway, or on the pavements grey,
I hear it in the deep heart's core.

THE SORROW OF LOVE

The brawling of a sparrow in the eaves,
The brilliant moon and all the milky sky,
And all that famous harmony of leaves,
Had blotted out man's image and his cry.

A girl arose that had red mournful lips
And seemed the greatness of the world in tears,
Doomed like Odysseus and the labouring ships
And proud as Priam murdered with his peers;

Arose, and on the instant clamorous eaves,
A climbing moon upon an empty sky,
And all that lamentation of the leaves,
Could but compose man's image and his cry.

WHEN YOU ARE OLD

When you are old and grey and full of sleep,
And nodding by the fire, take down this book,
And slowly read, and dream of the soft look
Your eyes had once, and of their shadows deep;

How many loved your moments of glad grace,
And loved your beauty with love false or true,
But one man loved the pilgrim soul in you,
And loved the sorrows of your changing face;

And bending down beside the glowing bars,
Murmur, a little sadly, how Love fled
And paced upon the mountains overhead
And hid his face amid a crowd of stars.

ADAM'S CURSE

We sat together at one summer's end,
That beautiful mild woman, your close friend,
And you and I, and talked of poetry.
I said: "A line will take us hours maybe;
Yet if it does not seem a moment's thought,
Our stitching and unstitching has been naught.
Better go down upon your marrow-bones
And scrub a kitchen pavement, or break stones
Like an old pauper, in all kinds of weather;
For to articulate sweet sounds together
Is to work harder than all these, and yet
Be thought an idler by the noisy set
Of bankers, schoolmasters, and clergymen
The martyrs call the world."

                And thereupon
That beautiful mild woman for whose sake
There's many a one shall find out all heartache
On finding that her voice is sweet and low
Replied: "To be born woman is to know—

Although they do not talk of it at school—
That we must labour to be beautiful."

I said: "It's certain there is no fine thing
Since Adam's fall but needs much labouring.
There have been lovers who thought love should be
So much compounded of high courtesy
That they would sigh and quote with learned looks
Precedents out of beautiful old books;
Yet now it seems an idle trade enough."

We sat grown quiet at the name of love;
We saw the last embers of daylight die,
And in the trembling blue-green of the sky
A moon, worn as if it had been a shell
Washed by time's waters as they rose and fell
About the stars and broke in days and years.

I had a thought for no one's but your ears:
That you were beautiful, and that I strove
To love you in the old high way of love;
That it had all seemed happy, and yet we'd grown
As weary-hearted as that hollow moon.

THE COLD HEAVEN

Suddenly I saw the cold and rook-delighting heaven
That seemed as though ice burned and was but the more ice,
And thereupon imagination and heart were driven
So wild that every casual thought of that and this
Vanished, and left but memories, that should be out of season
With the hot blood of youth, of love crossed long ago;
And I took all the blame out of all sense and reason,
Until I cried and trembled and rocked to and fro,
Riddled with light. Ah! when the ghost begins to quicken,
Confusion of the death-bed over, is it sent
Out naked on the roads, as the books say, and stricken
By the injustice of the skies for punishment?

THE WILD SWANS AT COOLE

The trees are in their autumn beauty,
The woodland paths are dry,
Under the October twilight the water
Mirrors a still sky;
Upon the brimming water among the stones
Are nine-and-fifty swans.

The nineteenth autumn has come upon me
Since I first made my count;
I saw, before I had well finished,
All suddenly mount
And scatter wheeling in great broken rings
Upon their clamorous wings.

I have looked upon those brilliant creatures,
And now my heart is sore.
All's changed since I, hearing at twilight,
The first time on this shore,
The bell-beat of their wings above my head,
Trod with a lighter tread.

Unwearied still, lover by lover,
They paddle in the cold
Companionable streams or climb the air;
Their hearts have not grown old;
Passion or conquest, wander where they will,
Attend upon them still.

But now they drift on the still water,
Mysterious, beautiful;
Among what rushes will they build,
By what lake's edge or pool
Delight men's eyes when I awake some day
To find they have flown away?

THE SECOND COMING

Turning and turning in the widening gyre
The falcon cannot hear the falconer;
Things fall apart; the centre cannot hold;
Mere anarchy is loosed upon the world,
The blood-dimmed tide is loosed, and everywhere
The ceremony of innocence is drowned;
The best lack all conviction, while the worst
Are full of passionate intensity.

Surely some revelation is at hand;
Surely the Second Coming is at hand.
The Second Coming! Hardly are those words out
When a vast image out of *Spiritus Mundi*
Troubles my sight: somewhere in sands of the desert
A shape with lion body and the head of a man,
A gaze blank and pitiless as the sun,
Is moving its slow thighs, while all about it
Reel shadows of the indignant desert birds.
The darkness drops again; but now I know
That twenty centuries of stony sleep
Were vexed to nightmare by a rocking cradle,
And what rough beast, its hour come round at last,
Slouches towards Bethlehem to be born?

A PRAYER FOR MY DAUGHTER

Once more the storm is howling, and half hid
Under this cradle-hood and coverlid
My child sleeps on. There is no obstacle
But Gregory's wood and one bare hill
Whereby the haystack- and roof-levelling wind,
Bred on the Atlantic, can be stayed;
And for an hour I have walked and prayed
Because of the great gloom that is in my mind.

668

I have walked and prayed for this young child an hour
And heard the sea-wind scream upon the tower,
And under the arches of the bridge, and scream
In the elms above the flooded stream;
Imagining in excited reverie
That the future years had come,
Dancing to a frenzied drum,
Out of the murderous innocence of the sea.

May she be granted beauty and yet not
Beauty to make a stranger's eye distraught,
Or hers before a looking-glass, for such,
Being made beautiful overmuch,
Consider beauty a sufficient end,
Lose natural kindness and maybe
The heart-revealing intimacy
That chooses right, and never find a friend.

Helen being chosen found life flat and dull
And later had much trouble from a fool,
While that great Queen, that rose out of the spray,
Being fatherless could have her way
Yet chose a bandy-leggèd smith for man.
It's certain that fine women eat
A crazy salad with their meat
Whereby the Horn of Plenty is undone.

In courtesy I'd have her chiefly learned;
Hearts are not had as a gift but hearts are earned
By those that are not entirely beautiful;
Yet many, that have played the fool
For beauty's very self, has charm made wise,
And many a poor man that has roved,
Loved and thought himself beloved,
From a glad kindness cannot take his eyes.

May she become a flourishing hidden tree
That all her thoughts may like the linnet be,
And have no business but dispensing round
Their magnanimities of sound,
Nor but in merriment begin a chase,
Nor but in merriment a quarrel.

O may she live like some green laurel
Rooted in one dear perpetual place.

My mind, because the minds that I have loved,
The sort of beauty that I have approved,
Prosper but little, has dried up of late,
Yet knows that to be choked with hate
May well be of all evil chances chief.
If there's no hatred in a mind
Assault and battery of the wind
Can never tear the linnet from the leaf.

An intellectual hatred is the worst,
So let her think opinions are accursed.
Have I not seen the loveliest woman born
Out of the mouth of Plenty's horn,
Because of her opinionated mind
Barter that horn and every good
By quiet natures understood
For an old bellows full of angry wind?

Considering that, all hatred driven hence,
The soul recovers radical innocence
And learns at last that it is self-delighting,
Self-appeasing, self-affrighting,
And that its own sweet will is Heaven's will;
She can, though every face should scowl
And every windy quarter howl
Or every bellows burst, be happy still.

And may her bridegroom bring her to a house
Where all's accustomed, ceremonious;
For arrogance and hatred are the wares
Peddled in the thoroughfares.
How but in custom and in ceremony
Are innocence and beauty born?
Ceremony's a name for the rich horn,
And custom for the spreading laurel tree.

LEDA AND THE SWAN

A sudden blow: the great wings beating still
Above the staggering girl, her thighs caressed
By the dark webs, her nape caught in his bill,
He holds her helpless breast upon his breast.

How can those terrified vague fingers push
The feathered glory from her loosening thighs?
And how can body, laid in that white rush,
But feel the strange heart beating where it lies?

A shudder in the loins engenders there
The broken wall, the burning roof and tower
And Agamemnon dead.
                Being so caught up,
So mastered by the brute blood of the air,
Did she put on his knowledge with his power
Before the indifferent beak could let her drop?

SAILING TO BYZANTIUM

I

That is no country for old men. The young
In one another's arms, birds in the trees
—Those dying generations—at their song,
The salmon-falls, the mackerel-crowded seas,
Fish, flesh, or fowl, commend all summer long
Whatever is begotten, born, and dies.
Caught in that sensual music all neglect
Monuments of unageing intellect.

II

An aged man is but a paltry thing,
A tattered coat upon a stick, unless
Soul clap its hands and sing, and louder sing
For every tatter in its mortal dress,

Nor is there singing school but studying
Monuments of its own magnificence;
And therefore I have sailed the seas and come
To the holy city of Byzantium.

III

O sages standing in God's holy fire
As in the gold mosaic of a wall,
Come from the holy fire, perne in a gyre,
And be the singing-masters of my soul.
Consume my heart away; sick with desire
And fastened to a dying animal
It knows not what it is; and gather me
Into the artifice of eternity.

IV

Once out of nature I shall never take
My bodily form from any natural thing,
But such a form as Grecian goldsmiths make
Of hammered gold and gold enamelling
To keep a drowsy Emperor awake;
Or set upon a golden bough to sing
To lords and ladies of Byzantium
Of what is past, or passing, or to come.

BYZANTIUM

The unpurged images of day recede;
The Emperor's drunken soldiery are abed;
Night resonance recedes, night-walkers' song
After great cathedral gong;
A starlit or a moonlit dome disdains
All that man is,
All mere complexities,
The fury and the mire of human veins.

Before me floats an image, man or shade,
Shade more than man, more image than a shade;

For Hades' bobbin bound in mummy-cloth
May unwind the winding path;
A mouth that has no moisture and no breath
Breathless mouths may summon;
I hail the superhuman;
I call it death-in-life and life-in-death.

Miracle, bird or golden handiwork,
More miracle than bird or handiwork,
Planted on the star-lit golden bough,
Can like the cocks of Hades crow,
Or, by the moon embittered, scorn aloud
In glory of changeless metal
Common bird or petal
And all complexities of mire or blood.

At midnight on the Emperor's pavement flit
Flames that no faggot feeds, nor steel has lit,
Nor storm disturbs, flames begotten of flame,
Where blood-begotten spirits come
And all complexities of fury leave,
Dying into a dance,
An agony of trance,
An agony of flame that cannot singe a sleeve.

Astraddle on the dolphin's mire and blood,
Spirit after spirit! The smithies break the flood,
The golden smithies of the Emperor!
Marbles of the dancing floor
Break bitter furies of complexity,
Those images that yet
Fresh images beget,
That dolphin-torn, that gong-tormented sea.

LAPIS LAZULI

(For Harry Clifton)

I have heard that hysterical women say
They are sick of the palette and fiddle-bow,
Of poets that are always gay,
For everybody knows or else should know
That if nothing drastic is done
Aeroplane and Zeppelin will come out,
Pitch like King Billy bomb-balls in
Until the town lie beaten flat.

All perform their tragic play,
There struts Hamlet, there is Lear,
That's Ophelia, that Cordelia;
Yet they, should the last scene be there,
The great stage curtain about to drop,
If worthy their prominent part in the play,
Do not break up their lines to weep.
They know that Hamlet and Lear are gay;
Gaiety transfiguring all that dread.
All men have aimed at, found and lost;
Black out; Heaven blazing into the head:
Tragedy wrought to its uttermost.
Though Hamlet rambles and Lear rages,
And all the drop-scenes drop at once
Upon a hundred thousand stages,
It cannot grow by an inch or an ounce.

On their own feet they came, or on shipboard,
Camel-back, horse-back, ass-back, mule-back,
Old civilisations put to the sword.
Then they and their wisdom went to rack:
No handiwork of Callimachus,
Who handled marble as if it were bronze,
Made draperies that seemed to rise
When sea-wind swept the corner, stands;
His long lamp-chimney shaped like the stem
Of a slender palm, stood but a day;
All things fall and are built again,
And those that build them again are gay.

Two Chinamen, behind them a third,
Are carved in lapis lazuli,
Over them flies a long-legged bird,
A symbol of longevity;
The third, doubtless a serving-man,
Carries a musical instrument.

Every discoloration of the stone,
Every accidental crack or dent,
Seems a water-course or an avalanche,
Or lofty slope where it still snows
Though doubtless plum or cherry-branch
Sweetens the little half-way house
Those Chinamen climb towards, and I
Delight to imagine them seated there;
There, on the mountain and the sky,
On all the tragic scene they stare.
One asks for mournful melodies;
Accomplished fingers begin to play.
Their eyes mid many wrinkles, their eyes,
Their ancient, glittering eyes, are gay.

LONG-LEGGED FLY

That civilisation may not sink,
Its great battle lost,
Quiet the dog, tether the pony
To a distant post;
Our master Caesar is in the tent
Where the maps are spread,
His eyes fixed upon nothing,
A hand under his head.
Like a long-legged fly upon the stream
His mind moves upon silence.

That the topless towers be burnt
And men recall that face,
Move most gently if move you must
In this lonely place.

She thinks, part woman, three parts a child,
That nobody looks; her feet
Practise a tinker shuffle
Picked up on a street.
Like a long-legged fly upon the stream
Her mind moves upon silence.

That girls at puberty may find
The first Adam in their thought,
Shut the door of the Pope's chapel,
Keep those children out.
There on that scaffolding reclines
Michael Angelo.
With no more sound than the mice make
His hand moves to and fro.
Like a long-legged fly upon the stream
His mind moves upon silence.

THE CIRCUS ANIMALS' DESERTION

I

I sought a theme and sought for it in vain,
I sought it daily for six weeks or so.
Maybe at last, being but a broken man,
I must be satisfied with my heart, although
Winter and summer till old age began
My circus animals were all on show,
Those stilted boys, that burnished chariot,
Lion and woman and the Lord knows what.

II

What can I but enumerate old themes?
First that sea-rider Oisin led by the nose
Through three enchanted islands, allegorical dreams,
Vain gaiety, vain battle, vain repose,
Themes of the embittered heart, or so it seems,
That might adorn old songs or courtly shows;

But what cared I that set him on to ride,
I, starved for the bosom of his faery bride?

And then a counter-truth filled out its play,
The Countess Cathleen was the name I gave it;
She, pity-crazed, had given her soul away,
But masterful Heaven had intervened to save it.
I thought my dear must her own soul destroy,
So did fanaticism and hate enslave it,
And this brought forth a dream and soon enough
This dream itself had all my thought and love.

And when the Fool and Blind Man stole the bread
Cuchulain fought the ungovernable sea;
Heart-mysteries there, and yet when all is said
It was the dream itself enchanted me:
Character isolated by a deed
To engross the present and dominate memory.
Players and painted stage took all my love,
And not those things that they were emblems of.

III

Those masterful images because complete
Grew in pure mind, but out of what began?
A mound of refuse or the sweepings of a street,
Old kettles, old bottles, and a broken can,
Old iron, old bones, old rags, that raving slut
Who keeps the till. Now that my ladder's gone,
I must lie down where all the ladders start,
In the foul rag-and-bone shop of the heart.

JOHN MASEFIELD
(1878–1967)

CARGOES

Quinquireme of Nineveh from distant Ophir,
Rowing home to haven in sunny Palestine,
With a cargo of ivory,
And apes and peacocks,
Sandalwood, cedarwood, and sweet white wine.

Stately Spanish galleon coming from the Isthmus,
Dipping through the Tropics by the palm-green shores,
With a cargo of diamonds,
Emeralds, amethysts,
Topazes, and cinnamon, and gold moidores.

Dirty British coaster with a salt-caked smoke stack,
Butting through the Channel in the mad March days,
With a cargo of Tyne coal,
Road-rails, pig-lead,
Firewood, iron-ware, and cheap tin trays.

D. H. LAWRENCE
(1885–1930)

THE ELEPHANT IS SLOW TO MATE

The elephant, the huge old beast,
   is slow to mate;
he finds a female, they show no haste,
   they wait

for the sympathy in their vast shy hearts
   slowly, slowly to rouse
as they loiter along the river-beds
   and drink and browse

and dash in panic through the brake
   of forest with the herd,
and sleep in massive silence, and wake
   together, without a word.

So slowly the great hot elephant hearts
   grow full of desire,
and the great beasts mate in secret at last,
   hiding their fire.

Oldest they are and the wisest of beasts
   so they know at last
how to wait for the loneliest of feasts,
   for the full repast.

They do not snatch, they do not tear;
   their massive blood
moves as the moon-tides, near, more near,
   till they touch in flood.

RUPERT BROOKE
(1887–1915)

THE SOLDIER

If I should die, think only this of me:
    That there's some corner of a foreign field
That is for ever England. There shall be
    In that rich earth a richer dust concealed;
A dust whom England bore, shaped, made aware,
    Gave, once, her flowers to love, her ways to roam,
A body of England's, breathing English air,
    Washed by the rivers, blest by suns of home.

And think, this heart, all evil shed away,
    A pulse in the eternal mind, no less
        Gives somewhere back the thoughts by England given;
Her sights and sounds; dreams happy as her day;
    And laughter, learnt of friends; and gentleness,
        In hearts at peace, under an English heaven.

EDWIN MUIR
(1887–1959)

THE HORSES

Barely a twelvemonth after
The seven days war that put the world to sleep,
Late in the evening the strange horses came.
By then we had made our covenant with silence,
But in the first few days it was so still
We listened to our breathing and were afraid.
On the second day
The radios failed; we turned the knobs; no answer.
On the third day a warship passed us, heading north,
Dead bodies piled on the deck. On the sixth day
A plane plunged over us into the sea. Thereafter
Nothing. The radios dumb;
And still they stand in corners of our kitchens,
And stand, perhaps, turned on, in a million rooms
All over the world. But now if they should speak,
If on a sudden they should speak again,
If on the stroke of noon a voice should speak,
We would not listen, we would not let it bring
That old bad world that swallowed its children quick
At one great gulp. We would not have it again.
Sometimes we think of the nations lying asleep,
Curled blindly in impenetrable sorrow,
And then the thought confounds us with its strangeness.
The tractors lie about our fields; at evening
They look like dank sea-monsters couched and waiting.
We leave them where they are and let them rust:
"They'll moulder away and be like other loam."
We make our oxen drag our rusty ploughs,
Long laid aside. We have gone back
Far past our fathers' land.
                    And then, that evening
Late in the summer the strange horses came.

681

We heard a distant tapping on the road,
A deepening drumming; it stopped, went on again
And at the corner changed to hollow thunder.
We saw the heads
Like a wild wave charging and were afraid.
We had sold our horses in our fathers' time
To buy new tractors. Now they were strange to us
As fabulous steeds set on an ancient shield
Or illustrations in a book of knights.
We did not dare go near them. Yet they waited,
Stubborn and shy, as if they had been sent
By an old command to find our whereabouts
And that long-lost archaic companionship.
In the first moment we had never a thought
That they were creatures to be owned and used.
Among them were some half-a-dozen colts
Dropped in some wilderness of the broken world,
Yet new as if they had come from their own Eden.
Since then they have pulled our ploughs and borne our loads,
But that free servitude still can pierce our hearts.
Our life is changed; their coming our beginning.

EDITH SITWELL
(1887–1964)

STILL FALLS THE RAIN

The Raids, 1940. Night and Dawn

Still falls the Rain—
Dark as the world of man, black as our loss—
Blind as the nineteen hundred and forty nails
Upon the Cross.

Still falls the Rain
With a sound like the pulse of the heart that is changed to the
      hammer-beat
In the Potter's Field, and the sound of the impious feet

On the Tomb:
                Still falls the Rain
In the Field of Blood where the small hopes breed and the human brain
Nurtures its greed, that worm with the brow of Cain.

Still falls the Rain
At the feet of the Starved Man hung upon the Cross.
Christ that each day, each night, nails there, have mercy on us—
On Dives and on Lazarus.
Under the Rain the sore and the gold are as one.

Still falls the Rain—
Still falls the Blood from the Starved Man's wounded Side:
He bears in His Heart all wounds—those of the light that died,
The last faint spark
In the self-murdered heart, the wounds of the sad uncomprehending dark,
The wounds of the baited bear—
The blind and weeping bear whom the keepers beat
On his helpless flesh . . . the tears of the hunted hare.

Still falls the Rain—
Then—O Ile leape up to my God: who pulles me doune—
See, see where Christ's blood streames in the firmament:
It flows from the Brow we nailed upon the tree
Deep to the dying, to the thirsting heart
That holds the fires of the world—dark-smirched with pain
As Caesar's laurel crown.

Then sounds the voice of One who like the heart of man
Was once a child who among beasts has lain—
"Still do I love, still shed my innocent light, my Blood, for thee."

ROBERT GRAVES
(1895–   )

DOWN, WANTON, DOWN!

Down, wanton, down! Have you no shame
That at the whisper of Love's name,
Or Beauty's, presto! up you raise
Your angry head and stand at gaze?

Poor bombard-captain, sworn to reach
The ravelin and effect a breach—
Indifferent what you storm or why,
So be that in the breach you die!

Love may be blind, but Love at least
Knows what is man and what mere beast;
Or Beauty wayward, but requires
More delicacy from her squires.

Tell me, my witless, whose one boast
Could be your staunchness at the post,
When were you made a man of parts
To think fine and profess the arts?

Will many-gifted Beauty come
Bowing to your bald rule of thumb,
Or Love swear loyalty to your crown?
Be gone, have done! Down, wanton, down!

TURN OF THE MOON

Never forget who brings the rain
In swarthy goatskin bags from a far sea:

It is the Moon as she turns, repairing
Damages of long drought and sunstroke.

Never count upon rain, never foretell it,
For no power can bring rain
Except the Moon as she turns; and who can rule her?

She is prone to delay the necessary floods,
Lest such a gift might become obligation,
A month, or two, or three; then suddenly
Not relenting but by way of whim
Will perhaps conjure from the cloudless west
A single rain-drop to surprise with hope
Each haggard, upturned face.

Were the Moon a Sun, we would count upon her
To bring rain seasonably as she turned;
Yet no one thinks to thank the regular Sun
For shining fierce in summer, mild in winter—
Why should the Moon so drudge?

But if one night she brings us, as she turns,
Soft, steady, even, copious rain
That harms no leaf nor flower, but gently falls
Hour after hour, sinking to the tap roots,
And the sodden earth exhales at dawn
A long sigh scented with pure gratitude,
Such rain—the first rain of our lives, it seems,
Neither foretold, cajoled, nor counted on—
Is woman giving as she loves.

THE PRIMROSE BED

The eunuch and the unicorn
   Walked by the primrose bed;
The month was May, the time was morn,
   Their hearts were dull as lead.

686

"Ah, unicorn", the eunuch cried,
  "How tragic is our Spring,
With stir of love on every side,
  And loud the sweet birds sing."

Then, arm and foreleg intertwined,
  Both mourned their cruel fate—
The one was single of his kind,
  The other could not mate.

CONFESS, MARPESSA

Confess, Marpessa, who is your new lover?
Could he be, perhaps, that skilful rough-sea diver
Plunging deep in the waves, curving far under
Yet surfacing at last with controlled breath?

Confess, Marpessa, who is your new lover?
Is he some ghoul, with naked greed of plunder
Urging his steed across the gulf of death,
A brood of dragons tangled close beneath?

Or could he be the fabulous Salamander,
Courting you with soft flame and gentle ember?
Confess, Marpessa, who is your new lover?

STEVIE SMITH
(1902–71)

WHO KILLED LAWLESS LEAN?

The parrot
Is eating a carrot
In his cage in the garret

Why is the parrot's
Cage in the garret?
He is not a sage
Parrot: his words enrage.

Downstairs
In his bed
Lies the head
Of the family
He is dead.

And the brothers gather
Mutter utter would rather
Forget
The words the parrot
Said.

When high in his cage swinging
From the lofty ceiling
Sat the pet screaming:
"Who killed Lawless Lean?"
It was not at all fitting.

So they put the parrot
In his cage in the garret
And gave him a carrot
To keep him quiet.
He should be glad they did not wring his neck.

THE MURDERER

My true love breathed her latest breath
And I have closed her eyes in death.
It was a cold and windy day
In March, when my love went away.
She was not like other girls—rather diffident,
And that is how we had an accident.

NOT WAVING BUT DROWNING

Nobody heard him, the dead man,
But still he lay moaning:
I was much further out than you thought
And not waving but drowning.

Poor chap, he always loved larking
And now he's dead
It must have been too cold for him his heart gave way,
They said.

Oh, no no no, it was too cold always
(Still the dead one lay moaning)
I was much too far out all my life
And not waving but drowning.

PRETTY

Why is the word pretty so underrated?
In November the leaf is pretty when it falls
The stream grows deep in the woods after rain
And in the pretty pool the pike stalks

689

He stalks his prey, and this is pretty too,
The prey escapes with an underwater flash
But not for long, the great fish has him now
The pike is a fish who always has his prey

And this is pretty. The water rat is pretty
His paws are not webbed, he cannot shut his nostrils
As the otter can and the beaver, he is torn between
The land and water. Not 'torn', he does not mind.

The owl hunts in the evening and it is pretty
The lake water below him rustles with ice
There is frost coming from the ground, in the air mist
All this is pretty, it could not be prettier.

Yes, it could always be prettier, the eye abashes
It is becoming an eye that cannot see enough,
Out of the wood the eye climbs. This is prettier
A field in the evening, tilting up.

The field tilts to the sky. Though it is late
The sky is lighter than the hill field
All this looks easy but really it is extraordinary
Well, it is extraordinary to be so pretty.

And it is careless, and that is always pretty
This field, this owl, this pike, this pool are careless,
As Nature is always careless and indifferent
Who sees, who steps, means nothing, and this is pretty.

So a person can come along like a thief—pretty!—
Stealing a look, pinching the sound and feel,
Lick the icicle broken from the bank
And still say nothing at all, only cry pretty.

Cry pretty, pretty, pretty and you'll be able
Very soon not even to cry pretty
And so be delivered entirely from humanity
This is prettiest of all, it is very pretty.

THE SMALL LADY

In front of the mighty washing machine
The small lady stood in a beautiful dream,
"That these clothes so clean (oh what a relief)
  Must still be ironed, is my only grief."

But then came a great witch passing on the air
Who said, "What is it you still wish for, my pretty dear?
Would you like to be a duck on a northern lake,
A milky white duck with a yellow beak?"
"Aroint thee, false witch!" cried the lady with a brave face,
"Human inventions help properly, magic is a disgrace."
The witch flew off cackling for the harm was done,
"I smell water," cried the lady and followed her into the setting sun.
And now in a false shape, on the wind-driven black pelt
Of that far northern lake, she is without help:
Crying, Away, away,
Come, ray of the setting sun,
Over the lake
Spread thy red streak,
Light my kingdom.

Heart of my heart, it is a mournful song,
Never will this poor lady come home.

JOHN BETJEMAN
(1906-   )

THE CITY

Business men with awkward hips
And dirty jokes upon their lips,
And large behinds and jingling chains,
And riddled teeth and riddling brains,
And plump white fingers made to curl
Round some anaemic city girl,
And so lend colour to the lives
And old suspicions of their wives.

Young men who wear on office stools
The ties of minor public schools,
Each learning how to be a sinner
And tell "a good one" after dinner,
And so discover it is rather
Fun to go one more than father.
But father, son and clerk join up
To talk about the Football Cup.

VERNON WATKINS
(1906–67)

GRAVESTONES

Look down. The dead have life.
Their dreadful night accompanies our Springs.
Touch the next leaf:
Such darkness lives there, where a last grief sings.

Light blinds the whirling graves.
Lost under rainwet earth the letters run.
A finger grieves,
Touching worn names, bearing daughter and son.

Here the quick life was borne,
A fountain quenched, fountains with sufferings crowned.
Creeds of the bone
Summoned from darkness what no Sibyl found.

Truly the meek are blest
Past proud men's trumpets, for they stilled their fame
Till this late blast
Gave them their muted, and their truest name.

Sunk are the stones, green-dewed,
Blunted with age, touched by cool, listening grass.
Vainly these died,
Did not miraculous silence come to pass.

Yet they have lovers' ends,
Lose to hold fast, as violets root in frost.
With stronger hands
I see them rise through all that they have lost.

I take a sunflower down,
With light's first faith persuaded and entwined.
Break, buried dawn,
For the dead live, and I am of their kind.

W. H. AUDEN
(1907–73)

THE SOLDIER LOVES HIS RIFLE

The soldier loves his rifle,
   The scholar loves his books,
The farmer loves his horses,
   The film star loves her looks.
There's love the whole world over
   Wherever you may be;
Some lose their rest for gay Mae West,
   But you're my cup of tea.

Some talk of Alexander
   And some of Fred Astaire,
Some like their heroes hairy
   Some like them debonair,
Some prefer a curate
   And some an A.D.C.,
Some like a tough to treat 'em rough,
   But you're my cup of tea.

Some are mad on Airedales
   And some on Pekinese,
On tabby cats or parrots
   Or guinea pigs or geese.
There are patients in asylums
   Who think that they're a tree;
I had an aunt who loved a plant,
   But you're my cup of tea.

Some have sagging waistlines
   And some a bulbous nose
And some a floating kidney
   And some have hammer toes,
Some have tennis elbow

And some have housemaid's knee,
And some I know have got B.O.,
   But you're my cup of tea.

The blackbird loves the earthworm,
   The adder loves the sun,
The polar bear an iceberg,
   The elephant a bun,
The trout enjoys the river,
   The whale enjoys the sea,
And dogs love most an old lamp-post,
   But you're my cup of tea.

*

Lay your sleeping head, my love,
Human on my faithless arm;
Time and fevers burn away
Individual beauty from
Thoughtful children, and the grave
Proves the child ephemeral:
But in my arms till break of day
Let the living creature lie,
Mortal, guilty, but to me
The entirely beautiful.

Soul and body have no bounds:
To lovers as they lie upon
Her tolerant enchanted slope
In their ordinary swoon,
Grave the vision Venus sends
Of supernatural sympathy,
Universal love and hope;
While an abstract insight wakes
Among the glaciers and the rocks
The hermit's sensual ecstasy.

Certainty, fidelity
On the stroke of midnight pass
Like vibrations of a bell,
And fashionable madmen raise

Their pedantic boring cry:
Every farthing of the cost,
All the dreaded cards foretell,
Shall be paid, but from this night
Not a whisper, not a thought,
Not a kiss nor look be lost.

Beauty, midnight, vision dies:
Let the winds of dawn that blow
Softly round your dreaming head
Such a day of sweetness show
Eye and knocking heart may bless,
Find the mortal world enough;
Noons of dryness see you fed
By the involuntary powers,
Nights of insult let you pass
Watched by every human love.

MUSÉE DES BEAUX ARTS

About suffering they were never wrong,
The Old Masters: how well they understood
Its human position; how it takes place
While someone else is eating or opening a window or just walking
        dully along;
How, when the aged are reverently, passionately waiting
For the miraculous birth, there always must be
Children who did not specially want it to happen, skating
On a pond at the edge of the wood:
They never forgot
That even the dreadful martyrdom must run its course
Anyhow in a corner, some untidy spot
Where the dogs go on with their doggy life and the torturer's horse
Scratches its innocent behind on a tree.

In Brueghel's *Icarus*, for instance: how everything turns away
Quite leisurely from the disaster; the ploughman may
Have heard the splash, the forsaken cry,
But for him it was not an important failure; the sun shone

As it had to on the white legs disappearing into the green
Water; and the expensive delicate ship that must have seen
Something amazing, a boy falling out of the sky,
Had somewhere to get to and sailed calmly on.

LOUIS MACNEICE
(1907–63)

CONVERSATION

Ordinary people are peculiar too:
Watch the vagrant in their eyes
Who sneaks away while they are talking with you
Into some black wood behind the skull,
Following un-, or other, realities,
Fishing for shadows in a pool.

But sometimes the vagrant comes the other way
Out of their eyes and into yours
Having mistaken you perhaps for yesterday
Or for to-morrow night, a wood in which
He may pick up among the pine-needles and burrs
The lost purse, the dropped stitch.

Vagrancy however is forbidden; ordinary men
Soon come back to normal, look you straight
In the eyes as if to say "It will not happen again",
Put up a barrage of common sense to baulk
Intimacy but by mistake interpolate
Swear-words like roses in their talk.

NORMAN MACCAIG
(1910–   )

SPACE FICTION

I said the word "spatial", and in it
a micro-universe created itself, whirling
and fizzing and letting off
inaudible explosions.

I said "akimbo" and in it a crowd of
Chinamen doubled over with laughing in
every direction.

I said "seven" and there was a perspective
of gibbets, each with a little 7
hung from a rope's end.

I said "semantic space"—and a macro-universe
was filled, was a plenum of identical
images of you.

I risked it, I said "you", and the word
burst. I watched its expanding universe,
its continuous creation, dangling akimbo
amongst inaudible explosions.

ROY FULLER
(1912–   )

THE FAMILY CAT

This cat was bought upon the day
That marked the Japanese defeat;
He was anonymous and gay,
But timorous and not discreet.

Although three years have gone, he shows
Fresh sides of his uneven mind:
To us—fond, lenient—he grows
Still more eccentric and defined.

He is a grey, white-chested cat,
And barred with black along the grey;
Not large, and the reverse of fat,
His profile good from either way.

The poet buys especial fish,
Which is made ready by his wife;
The poet's son holds out the dish:
They thus maintain the creature's life.

It's not his anniversary
Alone that's his significance:
In any case mortality
May not be thought of in his presence.

For brief as are our lives, more brief
Exist. Our stroking hides the bones,
Which none the less cry out in grief
Beneath the mocking, loving tones.

LAST SHEET

. . . Suddenly it's autumn, I think, as I look in the garden—
A gloomy dripping world, tree-tops lost in cloud.
Is it possible that anyone so silly can
Write anything good? I don't hear, like poor Virginia,
The birds outside the window talking Greek. I see
My blackbird visitor and wonder where he sleeps,
As sleep he must. And catch my face in the pane,
Becoming ancestral, a cartoon of the mask
To which I've always been indulgent. And turn
To put a disc of Debussy on the machine:
This is what I'd have written had I had genius.
A pity to have got so far along the road
And then never arrived. Give my regards to the Minister
And tell him I've drafted a comprehensive instrument
For the administration of suburbia.

This is the time the robin starts to sing at dusk,
Like a cog catching on cardboard, but the human throat
Is not subject to seasons except those of the withering heart.
They're trying to cure me of my maladjusted glands—
Amusing; rather like trying to change the art of Sickert:
"I've always been a literary painter,
Thank goodness, like all decent painters," he said.
One can joke, but nevertheless the situation is tragic—
A human lifetime's limited store of eggs, and then
Their very last descent into the longing womb.
It's certainly on the cards that I shall never write
Another letter. This will have to stand, as usual,
For the prodigies I was about to tell you of,
For the connections I never quite saw, the melodies
Played gently while the beauteous statue reconciled
The jarred generations, and Sicily and Bohemia.

DYLAN THOMAS
(1914–53)

THE FORCE THAT THROUGH THE GREEN FUSE
DRIVES THE FLOWER

The force that through the green fuse drives the flower
Drives my green age; that blasts the roots of trees
Is my destroyer.
And I am dumb to tell the crooked rose
My youth is bent by the same wintry fever.

The force that drives the water through the rocks
Drives my red blood; that dries the mouthing streams
Turns mine to wax.
And I am dumb to mouth unto my veins
How at the mountain spring the same mouth sucks.

The hand that whirls the water in the pool
Stirs the quicksand; that ropes the blowing wind
Hauls my shroud sail.
And I am dumb to tell the hanging man
How of my clay is made the hangman's lime.

The lips of time leech to the fountain head;
Love drips and gathers, but the fallen blood
Shall calm her sores.
And I am dumb to tell a weather's wind
How time has ticked a heaven round the stars.

And I am dumb to tell the lover's tomb
How at my sheet goes the same crooked worm.

A REFUSAL TO MOURN THE DEATH, BY FIRE, OF A CHILD IN LONDON

Never until the mankind making
Bird beast and flower
Fathering and all humbling darkness
Tells with silence the last light breaking
And the still hour
Is come of the sea tumbling in harness

And I must enter again the round
Zion of the water bead
And the synagogue of the ear of corn
Shall I let pray the shadow of a sound
Or sow my salt seed
In the least valley of sackcloth to mourn

The majesty and burning of the child's death.
I shall not murder
The mankind of her going with a grave truth
Nor blaspheme down the stations of the breath
With any further
Elegy of innocence and youth.

Deep with the first dead lies London's daughter,
Robed in the long friends,
The grains beyond age, the dark veins of her mother,
Secret by the unmourning water
Of the riding Thames.
After the first death, there is no other.

DO NOT GO GENTLE INTO THAT GOOD NIGHT

Do not go gentle into that good night,
Old age should burn and rave at close of day;
Rage, rage against the dying of the light.

Though wise men at their end know dark is right,
Because their words had forked no lightning they
Do not go gentle into that good night.

Good men, the last wave by, crying how bright
Their frail deeds might have danced in a green bay,
Rage, rage against the dying of the light.

Wild men who caught and sang the sun in flight,
And learn, too late, they grieved it on its way,
Do not go gentle into that good night.

Grave men, near death, who see with blinding sight
Blind eyes could blaze like meteors and be gay,
Rage, rage against the dying of the light.

And you, my father, there on the sad height,
Curse, bless, me now with your fierce tears, I pray.
Do not go gentle into that good night.
Rage, rage against the dying of the light.

ROBERT CONQUEST
(1917–   )

SEMANTIC

Dawn: a good wind blows from the sea;
Noon: the shadow falls like lead;
Evening: an amplitude of dying clouds.
The day takes form inside the poet's head.

Or he goes further: "Dawn—the day's salt"; fact
Seems to dissolve into those tides of dream.
But (as, when concepts like *electron* seem
So sharp and are by that much inexact,

Strict wave-mechanics ripple to a blurred
Unfrozen matrix of activity)
He shows abstractions as not things but skills
And forms the stricter fields of subtlety
Around that simple particle, the word.

And reads dawn lifting from the shadowy hills.

JOHN HEATH-STUBBS
(1918–   )

NOT BEING OEDIPUS

Not being Oedipus he did not question the Sphinx
Nor allow it to question him. He thought it expedient
To make friends and try to influence it.
In this he entirely succeeded,

And continued his journey to Thebes. The abominable thing
Now tame as a kitten (though he was not unaware
That its destructive claws were merely sheathed)
Lolloped along beside him—

To the consternation of the Reception Committee.
It posed a nice problem: he had certainly overcome
But not destroyed the creature—was he or was he not
Entitled to the hand of the Princess

Dowager Jocasta? Not being Oedipus
He saw it as a problem too. For frankly he was not
By natural instinct at all attracted to her.
The question was soon solved—

Solved itself, you might say; for while they argued
The hungry Sphinx, which had not been fed all day,
Sneaked off unobserved, penetrated the royal apartments,
And softly consumed the lady.

So he ascended the important throne of Cadmus,
Beginning a distinguished and uneventful reign.
Celibate, he had nothing to fear from ambitious sons;
Although he was lonely at nights,

With only the Sphinx, curled up upon his eiderdown.
Its body exuded a sort of unearthly warmth

(Though in fact cold-blooded) but its capacity
For affection was strictly limited.

Granted, after his death it was inconsolable,
And froze into its own stone effigy
Upon his tomb. But this was self-love, really—
It felt it had failed in its mission.

While Thebes, by common consent of the people, adopted
His extremely liberal and reasonable constitution,
Which should have enshrined his name—but not being Oedipus,
It vanished from history, as from legend.

DONALD DAVIE
(1922–   )

ORPHEUS

named them
and they danced,
they danced: the rocks, stones, trees.

What had possessed them,
or him? How did it help?

What had got into those stones,
throwing up puffs
of yellow dust as they bounced, and could he
hear them, an irregular percussion
there in the blinding sunlight
like a discotheque at a distance?

No, I'm afraid not; weightless.
For them to dance
they had to be light as air,
as the puff of air that named them.

Thistledown rocks! Who needs them?

Well but, they danced for joy,
his holy joy
in stones, in there being stones
there, that stones should be,
and boulders too, and trees . . .

Is that how it was? One hopes so.

DANNIE ABSE
(1923–   )

POEM AND MESSAGE

Out on the tormented, midnight sea
your sails are blown in jeopardy.
Gales of grief and terrors force
you from the spirit's chartered course.

But, in the storm, lighthouses mark
rocks of dangers in the dark;
so from this shore of cold I write
tiny flashes in the night.

Words of safety, words of love,
a beacon in the dark to save
you from the catastrophic sea,
and navigate you home to me.

Dear, vague as a distant star, I,
in the huge night's amorphous lie,
find one small and luminous truth
of which our usual love was proof.

And I call your name as loud I can
and give you all the light I am.

WATCHING A CLOUD

A lacy mobile changing lazily
its animals, unstable faces, till

I imagine an angel, his vapours sailing
asleep at different speeds. My failing:

to see similes, cloud as something other.
Is all inspiration correspondences?
Machinery of cloud and angel both are silent,
both insubstantial. Neither violent.

And, truly, if one shining angel existed
what safer than the camouflage of a cloud?
There's deranged wind up there. God its power!
Let me believe in angels for an hour.

Let sunlight fade on walls and a huge blind
be drawn faster than a horse across this field.
I want to be theological, stare through
raw white angel-fabric at holy bits of blue.

Let long theatrical beams slant down
to stage-strike that hill into religion. Me too!
An angel drifts to the East, its edges burning;
sunny sunlight on stony stone returning.

MOLLY HOLDEN
(1927–   )

HARE

He lives on edge throughout his days,
home-fixated, short of sight,
dark heart beating as to burst his breast,
given to sudden panic fright
that sends him hurtling unpredictably
through crops, round quarries, over stones.
And has great eyes, all veined with blood,
and beautifully-articulated bones.

Superstition gives him an unchancy name,
any power that you might mention;
certainly he haunts the corner of the eye,
the edge of the attention
on open downs where movement is surprising,
caught and gone again with every glance,
or jack-knifing quietly through adjacent hedges
beyond the golden stubble-fires' dance.

But he is no more than flesh and blood,
living all his speedy life with fear,
only oblivious of constant danger
at his balletic time of year
when spring skies, winds, the greening furrows
overcome hunger, nervousness, poor sight,
fill him with urgent, huge heroics,
make him stand up and fight.

TED HUGHES
(1930–   )

CROW BLACKER THAN EVER

When God, disgusted with man,
Turned towards heaven,
And man, disgusted with God,
Turned towards Eve,
Things looked like falling apart.

But Crow   Crow
Crow nailed them together,
Nailing heaven and earth together—

So man cried, but with God's voice.
And God bled, but with man's blood.

Then heaven and earth creaked at the joint
Which became gangrenous and stank—
A horror beyond redemption.

The agony did not diminish.

Man could not be man nor God God.

The agony

Grew.

Crow

Grinned

Crying: "This is my Creation,"

Flying the black flag of himself.

JOHN HORDER
(1936–   )

THE SICK IMAGE OF MY FATHER FADES

The sick image of my father fades.
When I was three he used to take me
Tied up in a sack to the cliff's edge
And threaten to throw me over. The wind
Was ghastly, and his hands shook with terror.
I whimpered like a fretful dog. Fear
Stole over me, and I shrieked and screamed.

My father said, shall I break your legs
Before throwing you over? You should then land
On the sand without the sudden crunch crunch
Of breaking bones. I looked up at him, pleading.
Then he would laugh out loud like a normal man,
And let me clamber back onto his back, so that I forgot
The sheer drop from the cliff's edge, just for a moment.

SEAMUS HEANEY
(1939–   )

THE TOLLUND MAN

I

Some day I will go to Aarhus
To see his peat-brown head,
The mild pods of his eye-lids,
His pointed skin cap.

In the flat country nearby
Where they dug him out,
His last gruel of winter seeds
Caked in his stomach,

Naked except for
The cap, noose and girdle,
I will stand a long time.
Bridegroom to the goddess,

She tightened her torc on him
And opened her fen,
Those dark juices working
Him to a saint's kept body,

Trove of the turfcutters'
Honeycombed workings.
Now his stained face
Reposes at Aarhus.

II

I could risk blasphemy,
Consecrate the cauldron bog
Our holy ground and pray
Him to make germinate

The scattered, ambushed
Flesh of labourers,
Stockinged corpses
Laid out in the farmyards,

Tell-tale skin and teeth
Flecking the sleepers
Of four young brothers, trailed
For miles along the lines.

III

Something of his sad freedom
As he rode the tumbril
Should come to me, driving,
Saying the names

Tollund, Grabaulle, Nebelgard,
Watching the pointing hands
Of country people,
Not knowing their tongue.

Out there in Jutland
In the old man-killing parishes
I will feel lost,
Unhappy and at home.

AUTHOR INDEX

INDEX OF TITLES

(Asterisk denotes excerpt from poem)

INDEX OF FIRST LINES

(Asterisk denotes excerpt from poem)

724

Out upon it, I have loved, 180
Over two shadowless waters, adrift as a pinnace in peril, 617
O wild West Wind, thou breath of autumn's being, 449
O world! O life! O time!, 461

Piping down the valleys wild, 327
Plague take all your pedants, say I!, 524
Poor mortals that are clogged with earth below, 198
'Poor wanderer,' said the leaden sky, 627
Portion of this yew, 634
Proud Maisie is in the wood, 373

Quinquireme of Nineveh from distant Ophir, 678

Rarely, rarely, comest thou, 459
Red Rose, proud Rose, sad Rose of all my days!, 663
Rhyme, the rack of finest wits, 113
Ring out your bells, let mourning shows be spread, 48
Rough wind, that moanest loud, 462

Saint Peter sat by the celestial gate, 416
Say not the struggle nought availeth, 557
Scots, wha hae wi' Wallace bled, 342
Season of mists and mellow fruitfulness, 477
See how the orient dew, 187
See, Winter comes, to rule the varied year, 268
Set me whereas the sun doth parch the green, 27
Shall I compare thee to a summer's day?, 71
She came among us from the south, 591
She dwelt among the untrodden ways, 350
Should auld acquaintance be forgot, 345
Since there's no help, come let us kiss and part, 59
Sitting by a river side, 52
Small, busy flames play through the fresh-laid coals, 465
Some day I will go to Aarhus, 715
Some time ago there was a rich old codger, 8
St. Agnes' Eve—ah, bitter chill it was!, 479
Stand still, and I will read to thee, 98
Still falls the Rain—, 683
Still to be neat, still to be dressed, 111
Strange fits of passion have I known, 349
Suddenly I saw the cold and rook-delighting heaven, 666
. . . Suddenly it's autumn, I think, as I look in the garden, 702
Summer is icumen in, 6
Sunset and evening star, 518

Surprised by joy—impatient as the wind, 348
Sweet Auburn! Loveliest village of the plain, 298
Sweet day, so cool, so calm, so bright, 140
Sweetest love, I do not go, 96
Sweet peace, where dost thou dwell? I humbly crave, 141
Swiftly walk o'er the western wave, 460

Tears, idle tears, I know not what they mean, 515
Tell me, tell me, smiling child, 554
That civilisation may not sink, 675
That is no country for old men. The young, 671
That's my last duchess painted on the wall, 522
That time of year thou mayst in me behold, 74
The blessed damozel leaned out, 584
The brawling of a sparrow in the eaves, 664
The curfew tolls the knell of parting day, 228
The curtains were half drawn, the floor was swept, 589
The Daughters of the Seraphim led round their sunny flocks—, 335
The elephant, the huge old beast, 679
The eunuch and the unicorn, 686
The everlasting universe of things, 444
The expense of spirit in a waste of shame, 77
The faery beam upon you, 112
The force that through the green fuse drives the flower, 703
The night was winter in his roughest mood, 313
The parrot, 688
The rain set early in tonight, 519
There is a smile of love, 339
There was an old man in a tree, who was horribly bored by a bee, 552
There was an old man who said, "Hush! I perceive a young bird in this bush!",
  552
There was an old man with a beard, who said, "It is just as I feared!, 552
There was a roaring in the wind all night, 360
There was a time when meadow, grove, and stream, 355
There was a young person of Smyrna, whose grandmother threatened to burn
  her, 552
The sea is calm tonight, 573
The sick image of my father fades, 714
The soldier loves his rifle, 695
The sun is warm, the sky is clear, 457
The sun was shining on the sea, 594
The time you won your town the race, 658
The trees are in their autumn beauty, 667
The unpurged images of day recede, 672
The wild winds weep, 326

731

The woods decay, the woods decay and fall, 513
The world is charged with the grandeur of God, 639
The world is too much with us; late and soon, 347
The world's great age begins anew, 456
The year's at the spring, 548
They flee from me, that sometime did me seek, 25
They sing their dearest songs, 635
They that have power to hurt, and will do none, 75
They went to sea in a sieve, they did, 550
This cat was bought upon the day, 701
This is my play's last scene; here heavens appoint, 107
Those hours that with gentle work did frame, 69
Thou art not, Penshurst, built to envious show, 120
Thou fair-haired angel of the evening, 325
Though I am young and cannot tell, 112
Thou grief and fondness in my breast rebel, 270
Thou hast made me; and shall thy work decay?, 105
Thou hermit haunter of the lonely glen, 464
Thou large-brained woman and large-hearted man, 486
Thou mastering me, 643
Thou still unravished bride of quietness, 475
Through Alpine meadows soft-suffused, 567
Tiger, tiger, burning bright, 333
'Tis not that I am weary grown, 209
'Tis the witching hour of night, 471
'Tis the year's midnight, and it is the day's, 100
To and fro in the city I go, 637
To drift with every passion till my soul, 654
To Mercy, Pity, Peace and Love, 328
True genius, but true woman! dost deny, 496
Turning and turning in the widening gyre, 668
'Twas brillig, and the slithy toves, 593
'Twas on a Holy Thursday, their innocent faces clean, 330
'Twas on a lofty vase's side, 292

Vanity, saith the preacher, vanity!, 527
Virgins are like the fair flower in its lustre, 233

Wake, friend, from forth thy lethargy! The drum, 114
Was it the proud full sail of his great verse, 75
We are as clouds that veil the midnight moon, 444
Wee, sleekit, cow'rin, tim'rous beastie, 341
Weland, that dauntless man, well learned to bear, 4
Well-meaning readers, you that come as friends, 182
We sat together at one summer's end, 665

Western wind, when wilt thou blow?, 6
We stood by a pond that winter day, 625
We were apart; yet, day by day, 558
"What are the bugles blowin' for?" said Files-on-Parade, 661
What beckoning ghost, along the moonlight shade, 264
What dire offence from amorous causes springs, 235
What if this present were the world's last night?, 108
What means at this unusual hour the light, 493
Whenas in silks my Julia goes, 127
When as the rye reach to the chin, 57
When daisies pied and violets blue, 79
When forty winters shall besiege thy brow, 69
When God at first made man, 144
When God, disgusted with man, 713
When icicles hang by the wall, 79
When I consider every thing that grows, 71
When I consider how my light is spent, 158
When I do count the clock that tells the time, 70
When I have fears that I may cease to be, 467
When I look forth at dawning, pool, 626
When in April the sweet showers fall, 7
When in disgrace with fortune and men's eyes, 72
When in the chronicle of wasted time, 76
When love with unconfined wings, 185
When my love swears that she is made of truth, 78
When my mother died I was very young, 329
When raging love with extreme pain, 28
When some proud son of man returns to earth, 408
When the hounds of spring are on winter's traces, 610
When the lamp is shattered, 461
When to the sessions of sweet silent thought, 72
When winter snows upon thy sable hairs, 54
When you are old and grey and full of sleep, 665
Where, like a pillow on a bed, 93
Who has not heard of the Vale of Cashmere, 405
"Who is it that this dark night, 47
Who says that fictions only and false hair, 138
Who says that Giles and Joan at discord be?, 123
Why did I laugh tonight? No voice will tell, 468
Why is the word pretty so underrated?, 689
Why so pale and wan, fond lover?, 180
"Why weep ye by the tide, lady?, 372
With blackest moss the flower-plots, 504
With fingers weary and worn, 490
With how sad steps, O Moon, thou climbest the skies!, 46
Worlds on worlds are rolling ever, 455

ШA